THE LAST REVOLUTIONARIES

THE
LAST
REVOLUTIONARIES

German Communists and Their Century

CATHERINE EPSTEIN

HARVARD UNIVERSITY PRESS
CAMBRIDGE, MASSACHUSETTS, AND LONDON, ENGLAND
2003

Library of Congress Cataloging-in-Publication Data

Epstein, Catherine.
The last revolutionaries : German communists
and their century / Catherine Epstein.
p. cm
Includes bibliographical references and index.
ISBN 0-674-01045-0
1. Communists—Germany—Biography.
2. Communism—Germany—History— 20th century.
I. Title.

HX274.5 .E68 2003
320.53'2'0943—dc21   2002032926

Designed by Gwen Nefsky Frankfeldt

FOR MY MOTHER

CONTENTS

ILLUSTRATIONS

ABBREVIATIONS

CIA	Central Intelligence Agency
CPSU	Communist Party of the Soviet Union
DBD	Democratic Peasants' Party of Germany
DEFA	German Film Studio
DFD	Democratic Women's Federation of Germany
DM	German mark
DWK	German Economic Commission
EKO	Eisenhütten Industrial Complex-East
FBI	Federal Bureau of Investigation
FDGB	Free German Federation of Unions
FDJ	Free German Youth
FRG	Federal Republic of Germany
GDR	German Democratic Republic
HUAC	House Un-American Activities Committee
IML	Institute for Marxism-Leninism
KJVD	Communist Youth Organization of Germany
KPD	Communist Party of Germany
LPG	Agricultural Production Cooperative
NDPD	National Democratic Party of Germany
NES	New Economic System
NKFD	National Committee for Free Germany
NKVD	People's Commissariat of Internal Affairs
NSDAP	National Socialist Workers' Party of Germany
OSS	Office of Stategic Services
PDS	Party of Democratic Socialism
RFB	Red Front Fighters League
RFMB	Red Women and Girls League
SBZ	Soviet zone of occupation
SED	Socialist Unity Party of Germany
SMAD	Soviet Military Administration in Germany
SPD	Social Democratic Party of Germany
SS	Elite of Nazi Storm Troopers (*Schutzstaffel*)
Stasi	Ministry of State Security
USPD	Independent Social Democratic Party of Germany
VVN	Association of Those Persecuted by the Nazi Regime
ZPKK	Central Party Control Commission

THE LAST REVOLUTIONARIES

INTRODUCTION

IN DECEMBER 1994, I MET WITH KARL SCHIRDEWAN, A SHORT, ROUND-
headed, elderly gentleman who had joined the German communist
movement in 1923. In the mid-1950s, Schirdewan had been second only
to Walter Ulbricht in the Socialist Unity Party (SED), East Germany's ruling communist party. Schirdewan now lived in a small house in the outskirts of Potsdam, once part of East Germany and now a leafy suburb of
united Berlin. During the interview, Schirdewan recounted his life in
the Weimar Republic, in Nazi Germany, and in the German Democratic
Republic (GDR). Toward the end of our conversation, he discussed his
view of political developments since 1989, when a popular revolution
toppled the SED regime. He claimed that West Germans were acting as
"conquerors" and "colonizers" of the former GDR.[1] These remarks reminded me that Schirdewan's political life had come almost full circle.
Just as in the Weimar Republic, Schirdewan now belonged to a scorned
political movement; he was a member of the embattled Party of Democratic Socialism (PDS), the successor to the discredited SED. These book-
ends of a life in communism enclosed a remarkable political biography.
In the intervening decades, Schirdewan had participated in illegal resistance to the Nazis, had spent some eleven years in Nazi prisons and concentration camps, had helped found and rule the GDR, had suffered
through a communist purge, and had seen his socialist state collapse.
Karl Schirdewan had lived the twentieth-century communist experience.

This book is the story of how veteran German communists like
Schirdewan weathered the storms of the twentieth century: the dangers
they faced, the risks they took, the sacrifices they made, the rewards
they reaped, and the losses they endured. The communists who people
the following pages had all joined the German Communist Party (KPD)
before Hitler came to power on January 30, 1933. They were, and were

considered, exceptional in the German communist movement. To guard against infiltration by the Gestapo, the Nazi secret state police, the KPD admitted very few new members during the Nazi era. Pre-1933 KPD cadres were thus the only German communists who participated in the communist resistance to Nazi rule. After World War II, some twelve years of dangerous, conspiratorial revolutionary activity separated these party cadres from all other communists who joined the KPD / SED in 1945 and thereafter.

Even by the dramatic standards of their times, pre-1933 German communists followed extraordinary life trajectories. They joined the KPD in Weimar-era Germany, when becoming a communist entailed personal risk and material deprivation. Once Hitler came to power, they were, after Jews, the most persecuted individuals. In Nazi Germany, KPD cadres engaged in life-threatening but futile antifascist resistance; their reward was Gestapo imprisonment and concentration-camp incarceration. To escape Nazi persecution, some German communists fled to Soviet exile where, in turn, they were sucked into the whirlwind of Stalin's Great Purges. Others left for Western exile, where they continued to wage the antifascist struggle through propaganda efforts, all the while impoverished and constantly harassed by official agencies. Finally, some German communists fought the antifascist fight in the ranks of the International Brigades during the Spanish Civil War. These Nazi-era experiences left veteran communists steeled in struggle, hardened in their political beliefs, and convinced of their own moral righteousness.

In the wake of Soviet triumph in 1945, veteran German communists believed themselves the victors of History. They now selflessly dedicated themselves to the building of a socialist society in Eastern Germany. As survivors of the communist resistance movement against Hitler, they enjoyed tremendous authority and prestige; they embodied the moral imperative of the new East German order. Celebrated as "old" or "veteran" communists, longtime party members became the GDR's most prominent politicians and the voice of the regime's official memory. In East Germany, Old Communists seemed to have reaped the harvest of their pre-1945 revolutionary sacrifices. Yet for all their seeming triumphs, many individual veteran communists suffered ignominious fates in the GDR. The SED subjected numerous longtime communists to a disciplinary regime that was, by any standard, cruel. These veteran revolutionaries nonetheless refused to abandon the communist movement. For them, the 1989 revolution against SED rule was a disheartening surprise. As millions of East Germans poured through the breached Berlin Wall, veteran communists could only watch the sorry denouement of their socialist experiment. In the ensuing reunification of Germany, they saw their political achievements all but lost.

Pre-1933 KPD cadres have been captured in a variety of terms. They most often referred to themselves as "old comrades" *(alte Genossen);* they occasionally used the term "Old Communists" *(alte Kommunisten).* Others have called them "the great old ones" *(die großen Alten),* "the old guard" *(die alte Garde),* "old functionaries" *(Altfunktionäre),* "communists of the old sort" *(Kommunisten alter Prägung),* "old Stalinists" *(Altstalinisten),* and "old fighters" *(alte Kämpfer*—a term with Nazi overtones, as longtime NSDAP members were also known as "old fighters"). In generational terminology, veteran communists have been known as the "founding generation" *(Gründergeneration),* "the founding fathers" *(Gründerväter),* and "the first generation" *(die erste Generation).* A rather idiosyncratic yet vivid appellation for longtime communists is "the unimprovables."[2] In this work, the term "veteran communists" is most frequently used: pre-1933 KPD cadres were veterans of both a political movement and a militant antifascist struggle. All of these expressions, however, evoke the archetypal veteran-communist life trajectory—the unique, inimitable experiences of a group of communists who survived the unprecedented political upheaval of the past century.

ALTHOUGH LONGTIME German communists led fascinating lives, their collective importance ranges well beyond the intriguing particulars of their individual stories. Most importantly, the collective biography of veteran communists is paradigmatic of the twentieth-century communist experience. Pre-1933 KPD cadres lived the entire sweep of communist history. Even their Soviet counterparts, Old Bolsheviks, did not experience all the vicissitudes of the communist movement. Old Bolsheviks made the Russian Revolution of 1917, forged a new Soviet state in the 1920s, and were murdered in the Great Purges of the 1930s. But they did not know the experience of legal political opposition, they did not endure sadistic persecution by a fascist regime, and they did not see their state swept away by the tidal wave of History. Veteran German communists did. They experienced legal (and briefly illegal) political opposition in the Weimar Republic, savage torture under the Nazi regime, a long period in power in East Germany (that included the founding of a new state and a series of terrifying purges), and the collapse of their socialist regime. The biography of pre-1933 KPD cadres is thus the biography of twentieth-century communism.

Veteran German communists practiced a fervent loyalty to the party and its cause; this was, perhaps, the defining attribute of followers of twentieth-century communism. They remained true to communism even though they witnessed—and often participated in—all the many debacles of their movement. Ironically, many of the sufferings endured by longtime German communists were inflicted not by fascist enemies, but by fellow comrades. In the early years of Hitler's regime, pre-1933 communist cadres followed their party's strategy of mass illegal resistance that landed many of them behind Nazi bars. They remained loyal to their cause even though many of their fellow comrades were murdered in the Great Purges in Soviet exile in the late 1930s. They vigorously defended the Nazi-Soviet Non-Aggression Pact of August 1939 even though they had just spent years battling the Nazi regime. Only one ranking KPD functionary broke with Soviet-style communism during the war years: Herbert Wehner, who later became a leading figure in the West German Social Democratic Party (SPD).[3] In the postwar era, veteran communists remained loyal to communism even though the SED unleashed a series of purges against them in the 1950s. And they maintained their communist faith even though in subsequent decades they saw the modalities of "really existing socialism"—that is, socialism as implemented in Soviet-style regimes. Only a handful of longtime communists fled the GDR.[4]

Pre-1933 KPD cadres not only followed the paradigmatic communist life trajectory; they ruled a country, East Germany, for some forty-five years. Various studies have noted the importance of veteran communists in the GDR. Three scholars of East German elites, for example, have written of the "long hegemony of the power elite of Old Communists."[5] Lutz Niethammer, one of the most influential historians of East Germany, has argued that "Old Communists stood at the pinnacle of the ruling bureaucracy."[6] Likewise, the German historian Dorothee Wierling has stated that "forty years after its foundation, the GDR was essentially still ruled by . . . those born before and around the First World War and formed by the prewar communist movement."[7] Walter Ulbricht and Erich Honecker, the two powerful SED leaders who led the GDR from 1945 until 1989, were veteran communists. With few exceptions, the most influential members of the Politburo, the SED's most powerful body, had joined the KPD before 1933. Veteran communists also led East Germany's vast party and state bureaucracies; for example, longtime communist Erich Mielke headed the notorious Ministry of State Security (better known as the Stasi). But the influence of Old Communists was hardly limited to a circle of high-ranking party functionaries. Many of the GDR's most prominent cultural figures—such as the novelists Anna Seghers and Johannes R. Becher—were veteran communists. Finally, many longtime communists served as diplomats, newspaper editors, factory managers, and directors of academic and other institutions in the GDR.

The influence that veteran communists had in the GDR was not unusual in Soviet-style regimes. In all of the Eastern European communist parties, prewar communists made up a tiny minority but exercised inordinate influence in party affairs.[8] Until the 1980s, every leader of these parties had been involved in communist politics before 1945; in most cases, these leaders had joined a communist party well before 1933. But veteran communists in East Germany nonetheless occupied a somewhat different position. In the interwar period, the KPD had been a legal party and the second largest communist party in Europe—second only to the Communist Party of the Soviet Union (CPSU). This lent veteran German communists a particularly keen sense of being the avant-garde—not only to younger German communists but also to communists of other nationalities.[9] At the same time, although the KPD's leadership and rank and file had been decimated by Hitler's Gestapo and Stalin's secret police (the NKVD), the number of prewar communists was greater in East Germany than in any other satellite Soviet state. In the GDR, veteran communists—who numbered some sixty thousand in the first years of the regime—could more fully penetrate society than their East Central European counterparts. Strewn throughout the middle and upper levels of the GDR's party and state bureaucracies, factory administrations, and academic and cultural institutions, veteran communists were able to transmit their hard-core revolutionary mores to a wide strata of East German workers, functionaries, and other professionals.

The symbolic value of Old Communists in the GDR ranged beyond that of most longtime revolutionaries in East Central Europe. Although the SED leadership made an elusive attempt to foster a German "socialist nation," the presence of the West German state made all appeals to the "nation" extremely problematic. From the 1970s onward, when the bright future of communism seemed dimmed by political apathy and poor economic performance, the SED leadership increasingly drew on veteran communists' revolutionary heroics in an attempt to sustain communist legitimacy. This symbolic exploitation of Old Communists found a parallel only in multinational Yugoslavia, where the communist leadership was also unable to appeal to the "nation" for legitimacy. There the "Partisan Generation"—whose members had fought with Tito during World War II—served as the functional equivalent of longtime communists in the GDR. In both Yugoslavia and East Germany, revolutionary tradition came to serve as a substitute for national traditions. But in both cases it proved a weak substitute. The failure of revolutionary tradition to inspire the populations of these socialist states is illustrative of the more general failure of communist systems to preserve their legitimacy.

MANY STUDIES of German communism explore communist ideology, organization, and political tactics.[10] This work, however, examines the communist experience—how German communists lived their political views.[11] And live their political views they did. When individuals joined the KPD during the Weimar Republic, they made more than a political decision. They chose a whole new way of life. Party members structured their lives around their movement. They read the communist press, sent their children to party youth groups, endured unemployment for their political beliefs, and spent their days and evenings engaged in KPD activities (attending party meetings, marching in demonstrations, peddling communist literature, and recruiting new members). After 1933, communists lived their beliefs clandestinely. Many were forced underground, while others aided those in hiding. Most KPD cadres engaged in some form of antifascist resistance activity—from leafleting to the sabotage of German industry. Many communists experienced brutal persecution by the Nazis; others withstood the challenges of Soviet and Western emigration. These experiences ultimately forged a tough, uncompromising mentality that veteran communists brought to their rule of East Germany.

Unlike most works on German communism, this study bridges the all-important 1945 divide and is thus able to address the relationships among the different eras of German communism.[12] It explores, for example, the consequences of the pre-1945 communist experience on the postwar politics of veteran KPD cadres. It also examines the many continuities between the Weimar-era KPD and the postwar SED. Because the Soviet Union always played a central role in the German communist movement, many continuities between the KPD and the SED were reinforced by Moscow's hegemonic practices in East Central Europe after 1945. This helps to explain why many developments in the GDR were indistinguishable from those in the other East Central European countries—even though the SED regime could draw on a significantly stronger communist tradition. At the same time, though, East Germany was among the most rigid and inflexible of the Soviet satellite states. And this, at least in part, may be attributed to the presence and influence of so many veteran communists in the GDR.

Although literally thousands of studies on the GDR have appeared since 1989, none address the role of longtime communists in East Germany. This is a major gap in the literature on the GDR. As we shall see,

pre-1933 KPD cadres forged what was essentially an Old Communist regime. They set the political agenda for East Germany. Their concerns—
such as antifascist struggle, the danger of enemy infiltration, and the provision of basic goods—became the regime's concerns. Veteran communists also brought their political mores to bear on East German politics.
The sanctity of party discipline, the fear of factions, the purging of real or
suspected opponents, and the authoritarian hierarchy that characterized
East German politics all stemmed from veteran communists' experiences
in the pre-1945 period. In contrast to other works on German communism, this study offers both a broad examination of the sweep of German
communism and a new interpretation of East German history—one that
focuses on veteran communists and their influence in the SED regime.

Since the various East German archives opened in the wake of the
1989 revolution, many scholars have focused on researching conflict in
the GDR. Important studies have depicted a surprising degree of conflict
within the highest leadership bodies, within the SED rank and file, and at
the grassroots of East German society.[13] But while the emphasis on conflict is an important corrective to earlier monolithic views of the GDR, it
has also come to obscure one of the regime's most notable features: its remarkable stability. Between 1945 and 1989, East Germany saw only one
popular uprising—on June 17, 1953. And although some open conflict
occurred within the SED during the first decade or so of its rule, all inner-
party opposition ceased after 1958. In part, this stability was achieved by
outright coercion or the threat of repression—from wide-ranging Stasi
activities to the intimidating presence of Soviet tanks on East German
soil. In addition, the SED was able to export discontent. Many disaffected
East Germans "voted with their feet" before the Berlin Wall was built in
1961. Thereafter, the SED regime selectively expelled some malcontents
to West Germany.

But other factors also played a significant role in maintaining the stability of the East German regime. For one, veteran communists held
firmly to a particular set of political goals and values and were able to
transmit their political mores to a somewhat younger generation of SED
functionaries—the so-called Hitler Youth generation—that provided the
mainstay of the vast East German party and state bureaucracies. For
reasons connected with members' own life experiences, the Hitler Youth
generation deeply respected veteran communists. It was thus willing
both to embrace Old Communists as leaders of the SED and to practice
veteran communists' political values. As a result, the East German elite
was relatively uniform. In contrast to much recent scholarship, this
study analyzes some of the forces that kept the GDR together for so long,

rather than on those that tore it apart in 1989. In fact, however, these two developments were inextricably linked. Precisely because veteran communists were able to cling to power for such a long time, they were able to prevent reforms or other changes that might have altered the course of the SED regime—and thus the events of 1989.

This collective biography challenges some received truths on veteran German communists. There is, for example, a series of unexamined assumptions about the effect of Nazi-era experiences on veteran communists. Longtime communists who emigrated to the Soviet Union are thought to have returned to (East) Germany as disciplined, terror-stricken cadres who unquestioningly implemented their party's line. In fact, however, it was precisely these veteran communists who put up some of the most spirited challenges to Ulbricht's rule. Surviving the Great Purges seems to have bolstered the confidence of KPD cadres; at a time when Soviet authorities were vetting German communists, these party members had passed muster. There is also a common argument that veteran communists who survived Nazi captivity advocated a more tolerant or humane form of socialism. But this, too, proves false. The experience of surviving Nazi captivity actually heightened many long-time KPD cadres' Stalinist proclivities; it was precisely party networks and adherence to party discipline that allowed communist cadres to survive Nazi brutality. Finally, it is often said that KPD members who found exile in Western countries were exposed to many political viewpoints and enjoyed the benefits of Western-style democracy. As a result, it is argued, they also came to advocate a more tolerant or democratic socialism. But once again, this is generally not true. KPD members in Western countries suffered constant harassment from government authorities—ranging from work or residency restrictions to internment or even imprisonment. These experiences, in turn, only heightened their disdain for capitalist democracies. This work demonstrates that virtually all veteran communists shared profoundly Stalinist political views—views that were generally not lessened, but rather reinforced by the various communist experiences of the Nazi era.

Numerous scholars of East Germany argue that a number of veteran communists became "reformers" or otherwise "opposed" SED rule. Any such discussion, of course, hinges on the definition of "reform" and "opposition." In this work, both terms are held to a rather strict standard: the term "reformer" is applied to those who wished to alter the communist system by loosening party control over society, or at least over some particular area of society (such as the economy). Similarly, "opposition" is used in the sense of opposition to the communist system, not opposition to the personal rule of an individual communist leader. As the British historian Peter Grieder has amply documented, a number of leading veteran communists opposed both Ulbricht's personal rule and certain aspects of his policies.[14] But this does not mean that these individuals were reformers in the sense just described. Virtually all veteran communists shared a firm belief that communist power once attained should not be attenuated, much less relinquished. Individuals such as Karl Schirdewan or Fred Oelßner, both of whom were purged in 1958, were not failed reformers. They opposed the personal rule of Walter Ulbricht and some of the SED leader's more draconian policies, but had they actually ousted Ulbricht, they would not have fundamentally altered the character of the SED regime. This was outside the ken of their political imaginations. After their experiences in Weimar and Nazi Germany, these veteran communists, at the height of their powers, were intent on upholding Soviet-style socialism. It was only much later—often after years on the margins of SED politics—that some purged communists came to reconsider their political beliefs.

In the GDR, longtime communists enjoyed great prestige and influence simply by dint of having participated in the past antifascist struggle. As members of the pre-1933 KPD, they were the very embodiment of revolutionary virtue and personal authenticity. Even their bodies spoke to the sacrifices they had made in the name of communism; decades into the East German regime, some Old Communists still bore the scars of the physical abuse they had endured during the Nazi era. In some ways, however, it is surprising that the GDR, a self-professed Marxist-Leninist regime, attached such great importance to its veteran communists. Communist ideology, after all, emphasizes the role of impersonal forces in History writ large. It is also aggressively future-oriented, seeking legitimacy through future promise rather than past performance. And it presupposes the scientific administration of society. The influence of veteran communists in East Germany belied all of these Marxist-Leninist notions. Veteran communists exercised enormous personal authority in the GDR; they and their past antifascist exploits were used to bolster SED legitimacy; and, even though by education and inclination they were singularly unprepared to manage a complex industrial society, they remained at the pinnacle of SED power right up until 1989.

In the course of this project, a fascinating theme emerged: the politics of biography.[15] The very biographies of veteran communists, it turned out, were subject to a number of political uses. During the Weimar and Nazi eras, past biographical exploits and foibles contributed to the political stature of communist cadres. After the war, party authorities willfully distorted the biographical facts contained in personnel or other files so as to raise suspicions about certain groups of veteran communists. Those pre-1933 KPD cadres who had spent the Nazi years in Western countries were especially vulnerable to such distortions, but those who had been in concentration camps and even those who had fought with the International Brigades in the Spanish Civil War saw their personal biographies subject to negative revisions. In many cases, this resulted in political demotions or unemployment, but in some cases it led to arrest, imprisonment, and even party-sanctioned murder. Veteran communists, however, also saw their biographies used to legitimate SED rule. The party exploited their biographies to create an official memory of antifascist struggle and heroism. But for veteran communists, this process proved a double-edged sword. Although heroized in official SED hagiography, Old Communists saw, and at times contributed to, the trivialization of their own biographies. This was because the SED propaganda mill created a relentlessly stereotypical image of the antifascist revolutionary; veteran communists became mere walking symbols of the collective archetype of the antifascist hero. Finally, after 1989, the biographies of veteran communists were subject to another political use: they were now scrutinized so as to discredit the former SED regime in the new, united Germany. The politics of biography proved an enduring feature of twentieth-century communism.

THE ARGUMENTS of this study are based on research on hundreds of Old Communists.[16] The narrative of this book, however, is woven around the lives of eight veteran communists: Franz Dahlem, Gerhart Eisler, Erich Honecker, Emmy Koenen, Fred Oelßner, Karl Schirdewan, Fritz Selbmann, and Walter Ulbricht. How representative of the German communist experience are the lives of these eight communists? These individuals were, on the whole, more prominent than their peers: at one time or another, five belonged to the Politburo, and all eight belonged to the Central Committee or its predecessor, the Party Executive, in East Germany. Otherwise, however, these longtime KPD cadres experienced the typical vicissitudes of participation in the communist movement. At the same time, the lives of each of those featured are typical of particular groups of veteran communists. The lives of Emmy Koenen and Gerhart Eisler, for example, are suggestive of all longtime communists who emigrated to Western countries during the Nazi era. Emmy Koenen was a KPD women's functionary and, in postwar East Germany, briefly headed the mass political organization for women, the DFD. Her life also illustrates the marginal position that women veteran communists occupied in their movement.

Gerhart Eisler was a charismatic communist who led a colorful revolutionary life. A bourgeois intellectual of Jewish descent, Eisler joined the factional battles of the Weimar-era KPD. On the losing side, he was banished as a Comintern agent to China, the United States, and Western Europe. In 1946, Eisler, who lived in American exile during World War II, became one of the first victims of the anticommunist hysteria that swept the United States at the onset of the Cold War. Back in (East) Germany after a dramatic escape from the United States, Eisler endured a new series of setbacks in his socialist regime. Eisler's life illustrates a number of facets of the German communist experience: the latent anti-Semitism of the KPD / SED, the moral compromises that communist intellectuals made, the effect of Western exile on the political views of KPD apparatchiks, and the cruel fate that awaited former Western émigrés on their return to (East) Germany.

The lives of Karl Schirdewan, Fritz Selbmann, and Franz Dahlem show that the experience of concentration-camp survival reinforced Stalinist political mores among veteran communists. Karl Schirdewan engaged in illegal resistance to the Nazis, spent eleven years in Hitler's prisons and concentration camps, and in the postwar years, made his way up the SED party hierarchy. In the mid-1950s, he was one of the most powerful men in the GDR. After 1956, however, Schirdewan came to oppose Walter Ulbricht. His example suggests the character of veteran communist opposition: although some longtime communists vociferously rejected Ulbricht's personal rule, they did not fundamentally oppose Soviet-style socialism in the GDR. Similarly, Fritz Selbmann, who headed the Saxon KPD in 1933, spent twelve years in Nazi prisons and concentration camps. In the GDR, he was a leading economics official until, along with Schirdewan, he was ousted from his political positions in 1958. Thereafter, Selbmann penned well-received novels and other writings. In the course of his long communist career, Selbmann, a rough-and-tumble sort, had numerous run-ins with his party. His life suggests the many hard knocks that strong individuals took from the communist movement.

Franz Dahlem was a longtime rival to Walter Ulbricht. He joined the KPD Politburo in the last years of the Weimar Republic, emigrated to France in 1933, served in the Spanish Civil War, and was imprisoned in both French internment camps and Mauthausen concentration camp during World War II. After 1945, Dahlem held some of the most influential posts in the SED regime. In 1953, however, he suffered an ignominious downfall for alleged political mistakes that he had made in 1939. Dahlem was the quintessential victim of the SED's biography-based purges. In later decades, he waged an epic struggle for his public rehabilitation. His efforts were finally rewarded when he was able to publish his memoirs and, in the peculiar style of the GDR, achieve his own and many other purge victims' rehabilitation.

Fred Oelßner survived the Nazi era in Soviet exile and became the SED's chief ideologist. In the mid-1950s, Oelßner bitterly opposed Ulbricht's personal rule. Along with Schirdewan and Selbmann, Oelßner was purged from his political posts in 1958. His career suggests how former exiles to the Soviet Union were not, as they are often depicted, cowed cadres. Finally, Walter Ulbricht and then Erich Honecker led East Germany between 1945 and 1989. Ulbricht survived the Great Purges in Soviet exile to become the unquestioned leader of the GDR. But in 1971, his erstwhile mentor, Honecker, staged a successful coup against him. Thereafter, Honecker ruled East Germany according to a worldview that he had adopted in the Weimar-era KPD, honed during a decade in Nazi prisons, and frozen during a quarter century of participation in the highest echelons of SED politics. Although the biographies of Walter Ulbricht and Erich Honecker are well known, this study includes significant new discussion of these two leaders in the context of veteran communists and their influence in the GDR.[17]

This is the story of German communists who survived the trials of twentieth-century communism with not only their bodies, but also their communist souls intact. The following pages thus do not cover certain groups of individuals who lived some of the German communist experience. They do not include those who joined but then left the KPD before 1933, nor those—such as Arthur Koestler—who left the KPD during the Nazi era; these individuals did not participate in the full trajectory of German communism. In addition, this study does not cover those German communists who lived in West Germany after 1945. These communists did not have the experience of power; instead, as in the Weimar Republic and in post-1989 Germany, they remained on the fringes of the West German political spectrum.[18]

In the following pages, longtime German communists are treated as one relatively undifferentiated group. Longtime German communists shared a mentality that their biographical, professional, or other differences could not dissolve. First and foremost, all pre-1933 KPD cadres believed in the communist mantra "the party is always right." They all submitted to the dictates of party discipline. They all maintained a fervent loyalty to their party and the Marxism-Leninism that it espoused. They all joined the KPD by 1933 and stuck to the German communist movement through thick and thin. Decades of communist isolation, beginning in the Weimar era and stretching through the Cold War years, made these KPD cadres dependent on their party; indeed, for many the party came to provide the sustenance and nurturing of a family, in some cases even an ersatz for family lost to Nazi persecution or estranged due to political animosity. Veteran communists were also joined by an intense pride in East German achievements—particularly in the widely cast social welfare net and the GDR's relative industrial prowess. Finally, veteran communists shared a common past that they had come to cherish. Of all activities, they perhaps most enjoyed exchanging memories and recounting anecdotes of their actions during the Nazi years. Despite disparate biographical experiences, professional interests, and cultural proclivities, veteran communists shared a cohesive set of social, psychological, and ideological commonalities.

Veteran KPD cadres belonged to the small, tightly bound world of German communism. It is no coincidence that the longtime communists discussed here all knew each other and, indeed, knew each other for decades; the same—to one degree or another—would have been true for almost any other group of longtime German communists. Dahlem and Ulbricht, for example, worked together as functionaries in the KPD's Berlin headquarters in the early 1920s. Schirdewan and Honecker were both present at an important meeting of functionaries of the KJVD (the KPD's youth organization) in 1932. Emmy Koenen knew Franz Dahlem and his wife in the 1920s and took a KPD course taught by Fred Oelßner just as the Nazis were coming to power. Dahlem and Eisler worked together in Spain in 1937 and in Paris in 1938 and 1939. During World War II, Schirdewan and Selbmann were both imprisoned in Sachsenhausen and, later, Flossenbürg concentration camps. In the early postwar years, Ulbricht and Dahlem were two of the most influential communists and belonged to the same powerful party bodies, the Politburo and Secretariat. Schirdewan and Honecker had a series of run-ins that began in the late 1940s. Schirdewan, Oelßner, and Selbmann were all purged together in 1958. Ulbricht, who initially promoted Honecker, was ousted by his former protégé in 1971. Finally, Dahlem, while writing his memoirs in the 1960s and 1970s, corresponded with almost all of the others. These veteran German communists—along with their peers—shared a world of work, persecution, rivalry, friendship, and not least, memory.

MUCH OF the material used in this book comes from the SED party archives now housed in the branch of the Bundesarchiv, the German state archives, in Berlin. This work has benefited from the relatively liberal policies that govern access to personnel and other files of the former East German regime. Although party personnel files are not unproblematic, they contain a wealth of fascinating information about longtime communists. In addition, the SED regime systematically collected the archival papers of veteran communists—correspondence, reminiscences, personal documents, and much more. The present study is thus able to draw on an unparalleled range of sources to capture the remarkable interwar generation of East Central European communists—a group that historians and others have neglected because the sources were (and, to some extent, still are) inaccessible.[19]

I looked, of course, for material at the famous Stasi archives. But much to my surprise—and even more so to the surprise of the archivist working on my inquiry—the Stasi holds very little material on the veteran communists featured in these pages. It seems that the Stasi had relatively little interest in pre-1933 KPD cadres, who were among the most loyal communists in the GDR. Beyond the absence of Stasi documents (which have provided rich material for other studies on East Germany), numerous other problems with sources plague the study of veteran German communists. For the period before 1945, for example, there are relatively few contemporary documents. Many Weimar-era documents were lost in the upheaval of the subsequent Nazi years. During the Nazi era, it was often too dangerous to document communist activity or, once again, the documents were lost in the convulsions of the times. Much of the material on the pre-1945 period was thus written down in East Germany—in personnel files, autobiographical writings, or correspondence between veteran communists. All of these documents, however, were politically motivated and as such reflect the political agendas of their authors.

While there are enormous quantities of material on veteran communists in the GDR years, these documents, as is so often the case, remain silent on many of the most intriguing questions; they almost never, for example, speak to the regime's intentions vis-à-vis Old Communists. In addition, for political reasons, the SED rarely officially recognized the category "veteran communist": in postwar East Germany, former communists and social democrats were supposedly subsumed on an equal basis into the SED, the party formed by the merger of the KPD and SPD in Eastern Germany in 1946. In spite of its mania for statistics, the SED thus almost never compiled information specifically on its veteran communist members. Moreover, Old Communists, ever good communists, followed the rules of conspiracy long after the revolution was won. They had seldom kept diaries in the Weimar and Nazi eras, and also did not do so in the GDR years. The letters that veteran communists wrote in the postwar period usually did not reflect the full range of their East German experiences—often explicitly so. Despite dozens of hours of interviews, scores of autobiographies, and reams of official archival documents, the lives of veteran German communists remain tantalizingly elusive.

THESE DIFFICULTIES of documentation notwithstanding, the following chapters tell the story of veteran German communists and their century. This is a story fraught with paradox. Although veteran communists saw themselves as steeled revolutionaries, they cowered before their party. Although the KPD suffered terrible defeats in the 1930s, longtime communists clung tenaciously to their party. Although savagely persecuted in Nazi Germany, veteran communists founded a regime that practiced profound injustices in East Germany. Although collectively heroized in the GDR, they saw their individual antifascist pasts ruthlessly vilified by the SED. And finally, although self-styled revolutionaries, they adopted or applauded increasingly conservative policies as the East German decades wore on. But the story of veteran German communists is not only paradoxical. It is also tragic. This is the story of individuals consumed by political commitment. Veteran communists lived and fought for a set of political ideals that they believed would solve the ills of the world. They participated in the great twentieth-century conflicts among liberalism, fascism, and communism. Out of the cataclysmic clash of these political ideologies, they imagined, created, and ultimately lost a political regime. Theirs was the tragedy of expectations unmet, dreams unfulfilled, and utopias unrealized. Veteran communists followed a long, dramatic, and often cruel road through History.

1

OUTCASTS

Communists in the Weimar Republic

ALL GERMANS WHO JOINED THE KPD DURING THE WEIMAR REPUBLIC were born in Imperial Germany, at a time when the Kaiser ruled and Prussian militarism held sway. Imperial Germany, however, was not all banquets and bayonets. The vast majority of future communists were born into a vibrant working-class milieu that also characterized Imperial Germany. This milieu was the product of Germany's rapid economic development and the country's failure to adopt a political system suited to the industrial age. As children and adolescents, most future communists encountered the adverse effects of violent strikes, unemployment, blacklisting, and grinding poverty. These were exacerbated by the enormous upheaval that accompanied World War I and its aftermath: war, revolution, general strikes, attempted coups, hyperinflation, and ultimately, the Depression. For some 300,000 Germans, communism came to offer the most compelling answer to the great turmoil of the era.

THE OLDEST of the veteran communists featured in the following pages, Franz Dahlem, was born in Lorraine, then a part of the German empire, in 1892. Dahlem's family was solidly working class. His father worked as a railroader, and his mother, a pious Catholic, was a frugal homemaker who tried to stretch her husband's meager wages to cover the needs of a growing family. Since Dahlem's father was always employed, the family never knew the dire poverty that some communists suffered as children. In his memoirs, *Jugendjahre* (Years of youth), Dahlem nonetheless recounted how he and his two younger brothers augmented the family income by gardening, hunting sparrows, foraging for wild berries and mushrooms, and collecting apples and other fruits that had fallen to the ground. As an older boy, Dahlem earned a few pennies working for nearby farmers during the hops and wine-grape harvesting season.[1]

Although most future communists left school at the age of fourteen, Dahlem enjoyed several more years of formal education. In 1911, however, Dahlem's parents decided that their son should begin work. Dahlem found a two-year apprenticeship at the Arnold Becker export firm in Saarbrücken. Up to this point, Dahlem had had little exposure to socialist politics. At the firm, however, a foreman, Karl Leonhard, showered attention on the young apprentice; Leonhard, it turned out, was a member of the SPD. Hoping for a new recruit to his cause, Leonhard brought Dahlem to party meetings and other events. At his first SPD meeting, Dahlem later wrote, he was immediately taken with the political argumentation and the comradely atmosphere.[2] But he was no more specific as to why he was initially drawn to socialism. This lack of specificity is actually common to memoirs by longtime communists; perhaps these veteran communists thought the attractions of socialism so obvious that there was no need to detail what they had found so appealing.

When Dahlem first encountered the SPD, the party was enjoying enormous electoral successes; indeed, in the elections of 1912, the party became the largest faction in the Reichstag, Germany's parliament. The SPD nonetheless suffered several fundamental weaknesses. First, it was deeply divided. A revisionist wing followed Eduard Bernstein and his views that an evolutionary process of reform would inevitably bring socialism. A radical faction sided with Rosa Luxemburg and her belief that the imminent demise of capitalism demanded preparations for the seizure of revolutionary power. Finally, a centrist group, under Karl Kautsky, argued that regardless of the future of capitalism, the party should focus on forging a powerful organization that would push for workers' political and economic demands. In addition, the SPD was very isolated in Imperial Germany. In Guenther Roth's famous phrase, the SPD and the working classes it represented were "negatively integrated" into Wilhelmine society.[3] Although a dynamic working-class culture spanned everything from a powerful press to workers' choirs and burial societies, middle- and upper-class Germans were highly suspicious of the SPD and its milieu. Indeed, even though Bismarck's oppressive 1878 antisocialist laws had long since been rescinded, most Germans viewed the SPD as a body of dangerous outsiders. Once Dahlem's employer, Becker, learned of his foreman's political activities, he found an excuse to fire Leonhard. And when he learned that Dahlem shared Leonhard's politics, Becker sent Dahlem to another firm to finish his apprenticeship. Dahlem thus knew firsthand the hostility aroused by socialist politics in Imperial Germany.

When Dahlem had completed his apprenticeship, he followed

Leonhard to Cologne. He now officially joined the SPD and got involved with its youth club. The club's rooms offered young socialists meeting space and a well-stocked library. Club activities included reading circles, discussion groups, song evenings, and hiking trips. These young socialists also enforced strict moral attitudes: tobacco, nicotine, and physical relationships between club members were not tolerated. For young people attracted to socialism, the youth club provided a close-knit social life. Dahlem met his future wife, Käthe Weber, in the club's rooms. At the same time, the group engaged in hardcore politics: organizing political meetings, selling calendars and socialist literature, and distributing leaflets and newspapers. These young socialists tended toward the radical wing of the SPD and, as Dahlem recalled some sixty years later, they privileged party discipline: "We paid very close attention to maintaining discipline and rigorously attacked any violations thereof." As Dahlem explained: "That was an unavoidable and existential necessity for our movement; in 'black' Cologne our activities were very carefully watched by the reaction and every misstep was blown up and used as propaganda against social democracy as a whole."[4] Dahlem's experiences in the prewar SPD youth movement would also characterize German communism; there, too, an all-encompassing way of life would demand strict discipline from its adherents.

In August 1914, World War I began, and it brought the intense divisions within the SPD to the fore. Most SPD members supported their parliamentary faction's vote for "war credits," that is, for granting the government authority to issue bonds to pay for the war. But some radical party members were furious with the party leadership. Dahlem later remembered that he and other young socialists felt "let down" by the SPD's vote for war. The Cologne youth group was against fighting an "imperialist war" on behalf of their "exploiters and oppressors."[5] Despite his opposition to the war, Dahlem was drafted in October. He first saw combat in France, but was transferred to the Eastern Front in the spring of 1915. There he suffered a shoulder wound. Between hospital stays, training courses, a stationing in Mesopotamia, and bouts of malaria, Dahlem saw little active front duty.

As a soldier, Dahlem continued to avidly follow SPD politics. As early as December 1914, Karl Liebknecht defied the SPD leadership by voting against the second bill for war credits. Liebknecht and Rosa Luxemburg also distributed an illegal antiwar publication, the *Spartacus Letters,* and thus became known as Spartacists. More centrist SPD leaders, however, also came to doubt the wisdom of their party's continued and unconditional support for the war. In 1917 they founded a new socialist party— the Independent Social Democratic Party (USPD). The Spartacists, in turn, joined the USPD. The new party urged the German government to begin peace negotiations. In *Jugendjahre,* Dahlem wrote that during the spring of 1917 he "felt that he belonged" to the USPD.[6] And in September 1917, Dahlem made a conscious decision not to seek work in a business after the war. Instead, as he wrote a fellow comrade, "I can and want to serve the workers' cause." He later noted in his memoirs that "a clear proletarian class viewpoint on the events of the time" had led him to decide to "put all my strengths at the service of the party."[7]

Like so many World War I soldiers (and future communists) of the "Front" Generation, Dahlem was radicalized by his wartime experiences. For four long years, this generation lived fear and blood, death and destruction. Although the Front Generation was radicalized in different ways—its members were just as likely to adopt the ideas of the radical right as those of the radical left—those who belonged to it shared a belief that the old bourgeois European order was moribund. They were to seek a brave, bright new world that would give meaning to their wartime sacrifices.

After revolution swept Germany in November 1918, the SPD and USPD formed a provisional national government in Berlin. At this time, Dahlem was in an army barracks in the East Prussian town of Allenstein. He quickly joined in revolutionary activity. Dahlem became a member of the soldiers' council in Allenstein and helped to seize and then publish a local newspaper. According to his memoirs, Dahlem was disappointed that the Allenstein revolutionary council supported the SPD rather than more radical political groups. At the end of November, he was demobilized and went back to Cologne. There, Dahlem hoped to persuade the local USPD to adopt a more radical political line.

At this time, some socialists were taking an even more revolutionary tack. In Berlin on December 31, 1918, Rosa Luxemburg and Karl Liebknecht founded the KPD in opposition to both the SPD and the USPD. This new communist party opposed participation in Germany's emerging parliamentary democracy and hoped for a more thoroughgoing revolution—a Bolshevik revolution—for Germany. Although Dahlem later claimed that he supported the Spartacists at this time, he did not join the new party: "Then, though, I doubted whether the timing of a new split in the workers' movement was right."[8] It would take almost two years for Dahlem to find his way to the KPD—and to the many dramatic vicissitudes that were to mark his communist career.

WHILE FRANZ Dahlem was still engaged in USPD politics, a future rival, Walter Ulbricht, was already active in KPD politics in Leipzig, a traditional center of German working-class politics. Unlike the Catholic milieu in which Dahlem grew up, Ulbricht was born into the Leipzig social democratic movement in 1893. His father was a tailor and local SPD functionary, his mother a seamstress and SPD member; his parents had actually met through socialist work. As a child, young Walter listened to political conversations in the family kitchen; as a youth he participated in a workers' sports club; at fifteen, he joined the local educational club for young workers; and at seventeen, he became a member of the wood-workers' trade union. Between 1907 and 1911, Ulbricht learned the fur-niture-making trade. According to all of his biographies, Ulbricht was a passionate learner—whether of politics, nature, or high culture—during these and subsequent years. On the completion of his apprenticeship, Ulbricht undertook the time-honored journeyman's trip. For the better part of a year, he traveled through Germany, Austria, Italy, Switzerland, Belgium, and Holland. On his return to Leipzig in 1912, Ulbricht joined the SPD. Rather like Dahlem at this time, Ulbricht immersed himself in the activities of local social democratic institutions: the Leipzig workers' educational institute, its library, and the party school.

With the outbreak of hostilities in 1914, Ulbricht became a militant opponent of the war. In Leipzig, he helped to copy and distribute Karl Liebknecht's antiwar statements. Ulbricht thus earned the dislike of the Leipzig SPD leader, Richard Lipinski. According to one source, Lipinski tipped off German military authorities to Ulbricht's antiwar activities. As a result, Ulbricht was drafted and Lipinski rid himself of a querulous antiwar militant in his party organization.[9] Ulbricht spent much of the war working as a wheelwright in Macedonia and Serbia; he also caught malaria and spent many months in military hospitals. Like Dahlem, Ulbricht devoted much of his time as a soldier to political activities. He clandestinely circulated political literature, including Spartacist leaflets, sent him by his Leipzig comrades. Known to his commanders as a left-wing radical, Ulbricht was subject to various petty and demeaning mili-tary punishments and was left with a lasting disgust of, in his words, "the spirit of the Prussian military."[10] In 1918, Ulbricht deserted his troop train as it was passing near Leipzig. He was soon picked up, sentenced to two months of jail, and transferred to Belgium. There he was caught with revolutionary leaflets and once again imprisoned. With the onset of rev-olution in November, Ulbricht's guards helped him to escape. Ulbricht was soon back in Leipzig.

It was long believed that Walter Ulbricht was a founding member of the KPD in central Germany in January 1919. According to a recent biog-raphy, however, this was not actually the case; instead, the legend of an early KPD membership was circulated to lend additional revolutionary legitimacy to Ulbricht's biography. Like Dahlem, Ulbricht was a member of the USPD and only became a KPD member in December 1920. But un-like Dahlem, Ulbricht was already active in KPD politics at the beginning of 1919.[11] And the KPD desperately needed all the help it could get—whether from party members or others. The new party was plagued with a shortage of funds, poorly trained functionaries, and high membership turnover. Moreover, just weeks after its founding, the KPD lost the two leaders that had lent it revolutionary sparkle. In the second week of January, the so-called Spartacist Uprising, an armed uprising of about a thousand radicals who hoped to overthrow the national government, belatedly came under KPD control. The SPD government swiftly quelled the uprising and arrested Rosa Luxemburg and Karl Liebknecht. Soon thereafter, these two revolutionaries were murdered while in government custody; months later, Luxemburg's body was fished out of one of Berlin's many canals.

Among communists, these murders aroused sadness, outrage, and a desire to vindicate the murdered leaders' lives. As one longtime communist and influential KPD teacher, Hermann Duncker, wrote his wife in late 1919: "I always feel as though the death of Karl and Rosa left us orphaned. But we still want to do further work in their direction, to have them live on in us."[12] The murders of Luxemburg and Liebknecht marked the beginning of a long and mutual antipathy between the two main workers' parties of the Weimar Republic. Just months later, on May 1, 1919, the SPD government, in a bloody show of force, put down a communist uprising led by Eugen Leviné in Munich. The next day, Duncker wrote his wife: "Legal murder now rages down there on the Isar. That's the socialist government's May Day! It's not to be believed—and yet it's true."[13] Duncker, like so many longtime German communists, came to be haunted by fears of SPD governmental repression. In May 1921, he confided to his wife, "I dream almost every night of persecution and arrest."[14]

In the meantime, Ulbricht experienced the SPD government's harassment of communists and KPD sympathizers firsthand. In early 1919, he was forced underground after police issued a warrant for his arrest. He was charged with the illegal distribution of "communist-Spartacist" literature. Ulbricht was jailed in November but released for lack of evidence shortly thereafter. He then continued his work for the KPD. Once he became a party member in December 1920, he quickly climbed the KPD hierarchy. In no small measure, this was due to his assiduous organizing abilities. Indeed, although Ulbricht lacked the personal warmth and fiery rhetorical skills necessary for a popular politician, he more than compensated for these weaknesses with his remarkable talent for revolutionary grunt work. He tirelessly organized the distribution of fliers, the hanging of posters, the details of meetings, the editing of newspapers, the collection of funds, and even the procuring of illegal weapons. In June 1921, he was named party leader of Thuringia, where the KPD was both badly divided and poorly organized. In just two short years, Ulbricht was to create a strong regional party organization there. His first trip to Moscow, the center of world revolution, also took place in 1921. Ulbricht was chosen as a delegate to the Fourth World Congress of the Comintern, the Soviet institution that directed the activities of affiliated national communist parties. For the first and last time, Ulbricht met Lenin—an important point of pride for him, as well as for all communists of his generation who had the same privilege. By early 1923 Ulbricht had been elected to the KPD's twenty-one-person Central Committee and tapped to work in party headquarters in Berlin.

During the early years of the Weimar Republic, the KPD experienced a number of leadership changes; each was preceded by bitter debates and resulted in new party policies. Following the murders of Liebknecht and Luxemburg, Paul Levi led the KPD for some two years. Levi wished to end the KPD's putschist activity and to form a more disciplined, centralized party. He also opposed Comintern meddling in German communist politics. To some fellow comrades, Levi seemed insufficiently revolutionary. In early 1921, he was replaced by Heinrich Brandler. Brandler almost immediately led a reckless uprising in Saxony; this futile armed insurrection, known in communist lore as the "March Action," claimed some 150 lives.

In the next years, however, Brandler tempered his revolutionary zeal and even came to advocate communist participation in local state governments. This, in turn, led to another political fiasco. In the fall of 1923, communists joined coalition state governments in Saxony and Thuringia. In response, the national government sent an army into Saxony. The KPD then called for a general strike and an armed uprising, orders that Brandler rescinded at a last-minute meeting when he was unable to secure local SPD support. The revocation of the orders did not reach Hamburg, however, where several hundred communists fought a hopeless battle with police for three days. Governmental repression was as swift as it was harsh. The KPD was declared illegal, a situation that lasted about six months, and some 5,768 communists were arrested and imprisoned.[15] These events, greeted with dismay by party members, set off another vicious party debate. A voluntaristic "ultra-left" faction, led by Ruth Fischer and Arkadi Maslow, captured the KPD leadership in April 1924. These young party intellectuals believed that Brandler's timid leadership had thwarted a potentially successful German revolution.

When Ulbricht came to work in party headquarters in 1923, he worked with none other than Franz Dahlem. One author claims that Ulbricht "immediately developed the enduring antipathy of a bureaucrat to Dahlem and his obliging ways," but there is no evidence that the two men disliked each other at this early stage; this characterization was probably founded on incorrect stereotypes of both men—particularly Dahlem.[16] Ulbricht and Dahlem worked in the party's Organizational Department, the department that oversaw grassroots work among KPD members. Ulbricht was charged with the revitalization of the party's grassroots units. Following Comintern dictate, he was to "bolshevize" basic party cells—that is, to reorganize the party's grassroots units into factory, rather than neighborhood, cells. Ulbricht thus became known as "Comrade Cell."

During the Weimar Republic, KPD membership ebbed and flowed according to political events. In March 1920, the party had a membership of about fifty thousand. Later that year, however, the Comintern chose the KPD as its German member party; it also stipulated that all other German socialist parties that wished to enjoy Comintern membership would have to unite with the KPD. After a divisive battle in December 1920, the majority of the USPD went over to the communists; this was when Dahlem and Ulbricht joined the KPD. The united party now had a membership of some 359,000 members.[17] After the KPD's failed uprising in Saxony in March 1921, party membership dropped to 157,613. But in 1923, the year of the Great Inflation, it soared to 294,230. After the Republic began to enjoy a certain stability in the mid-1920s, KPD membership once again dwindled. From 1924 to the onset of the Great Depression in 1929, party membership hovered around 125,000.[18]

In 1924, Ruth Fischer and Arkadi Maslow purged alleged "right" supporters of Brandler. Although neither Dahlem nor Ulbricht were keen supporters of the former KPD leader, the new leadership disbanded the Organization Department because it was supposedly a bastion of Brandler influence. In the language of communist historiography, Dahlem later wrote of these events: "With the Cell Division as our base, we conducted a determined struggle against the fateful anti-factory line of the ultra-left majority group in the Party leadership. The group around Ruth Fischer put an end to this 'opposition' by liquidating both the Trade Union and Cell Divisions. Comrade Walter was packed off to work abroad, and I was sent to Thuringia as political director of the district."[19] For Ulbricht, "abroad" meant working for the Comintern in Moscow. Ulbricht initially learned Russian at the Lenin School, the Comintern's college for international revolutionaries. In the fall of 1924, he was sent to Vienna to organize strikes. There, however, he was jailed for some months for using a false passport. Ulbricht next did short stints of Comintern work in Prague and Moscow. All the while, though, he was itching to get back to Germany and KPD politics.

By October 1925, Stalin had become angered by the independence of the Fischer-Maslow leadership. He thus had the Comintern send an "open letter" to KPD members in which it rebuked the party leadership for sabotaging its instructions and for other alleged shortcomings. This set the stage for the final change in communist leadership that took place in the Weimar Republic. In a measure of the bitterness of KPD politics, by the early 1930s, no former KPD leader was still a party member and, of those who survived the Nazi era, none came to East Germany.

In Ernst Thälmann, a former Hamburg docks worker, the KPD had finally found its leader—a man who both slavishly followed Stalin's orders and who, by all accounts, was enormously popular among the communist faithful. With his gruff yet warm proletarian ways, "Teddy," as Thälmann was known, captured the hearts of the KPD rank and file. Ulbricht could now return to Germany. He would never again find himself on the "wrong side" of KPD politics; indeed, he would now play an important role in purging the party of "oppositionalists." In 1929, Ulbricht became a member of the Politburo and regional party leader of Berlin-Brandenburg.

GERHART EISLER was one individual whom Ulbricht would help purge. Eisler was actually Ruth Fischer's younger brother; Ruth Fischer was Elfriede Eisler's nom de guerre. The Eisler siblings, although born in Leipzig (Gerhart in 1897), grew up in Vienna, where their father wrote neo-Kantian philosophical books; Gerhart later wrote that because the family lived off of royalties from these works, there "were always great material difficulties at home."[20] A younger brother, Hanns Eisler, would achieve renown as a composer; although only briefly a KPD member in 1926, Hanns was a longtime communist supporter and would eventually compose the music for East Germany's national anthem (as well as for numerous Hollywood film scores). In the interwar KPD, Gerhart and his siblings were unusual in that their family belonged, in Gerhart's later words, to the "bourgeois intelligentsia."[21] All three siblings had some higher education; Ruth and Gerhart attended university, while Hanns studied at a music conservatory. By contrast, according to a party census in 1927, less than 1 percent of KPD members had any university training.[22] During the 1920s, anti-intellectualism became a feature of KPD political culture. Although intellectuals (including Ruth Fischer) had made up one-third of the KPD's most important body, the Politburo, in 1924, none were members in 1929.[23]

The Eislers were of Jewish origin, but the family was completely assimilated and never practiced Judaism. Interestingly, besides Ruth Fischer, a number of the KPD's early leaders were also of Jewish descent—Luxemburg, Levi, and Maslow. By the mid-1920s, however, relatively few individuals of Jewish origin remained in the leading bodies of the party; by the end of the Republic, there were virtually none. According to one historian, the KPD was well aware of omnipresent anti-Semitism in Weimar Germany and, for tactical reasons, tried to keep Jews out of prominent party positions. The party did not engage in propaganda campaigns against anti-Semitic feeling and, to strengthen its popularity, occasionally even deployed anti-Semitic rhetoric. But the KPD was not an anti-Semitic party. Rather, it had little reason to focus on Jewish issues. German Jewry was overwhelmingly bourgeois, and the party had little chance of attracting Jewish voters, much less Jewish party members. The exact percentage of KPD members with Jewish backgrounds is unavailable, but it is estimated that in 1927 0.7 percent of party members, or roughly one thousand individuals, were of Jewish descent.[24] At the same time, those like the Eisler siblings who did join the KPD had usually distanced themselves from their Jewish origins and thus had little interest in Jewish matters. They were, in their own minds, German communists—neither German Jews nor Jewish communists. Like all KPD members, they saw themselves as struggling for universal emancipation; they believed that the communist revolution would resolve all social and other problems (including, if they considered the issue at all, the "Jewish Question"). In postwar East Germany, approximately seventy longtime communists with Jewish backgrounds achieved some renown.[25]

Like Dahlem and Ulbricht, Eisler was radicalized by the war and returned from the Front a committed leftist revolutionary. As he wrote in a short biography for East German party authorities: "1918 returned from the battlefields to Vienna, became a member of the newly founded KPÖ [Communist Party of Austria]. Worked as an agitator and journalist. Was a member of the Red Guard and was elected to the Austrian Workers' and Soldiers' Council. Took part in the struggles of Austrian Communism. In 1919 was arrested in Styria, released after a short time. Together with Hungarian comrades (Revai, Bela Kun, etc.), I published and was secretary of the journal *Kommunismus*. At the end of 1920 or the beginning of 1921, I was called to Berlin and became secretary of the journal *Die Internationale*."[26] Once in Germany, Eisler worked closely with Ruth Fischer on the left fringe of Berlin politics. Eisler's wife at this time later recalled: "We were all very poor during these years. And we were all extremely happy. It was not only because we were young idealists; we were part of a growing movement, we belonged to a party which had gained recognition."[27] In the next years, however, Eisler moved away from the ultraleftist politics of his sister and the once close siblings became deeply estranged. Later on, and for reasons that will become clear, Charlie Chaplin would quip that "with the Eislers, family relations are like those in Shakespearean dramas."[28]

By 1923, Eisler belonged to the "middle group" of the KPD and had become a candidate member of the Central Committee. His group advocated cooperation with the SPD and the rejection of ill-prepared revolutionary adventures. When Ruth Fischer became party leader in 1924, there was little toleration of such moderate views. Fischer removed her brother from the Central Committee and relegated him to relatively unimportant party work. Eisler's sojourn in KPD obscurity ended, however, with his sister's political demise. Thereafter, Eisler was editor of the daily communist newspaper, *Rote Fahne* (Red flag), and a member of the Berlin regional party leadership. In 1927, even though in custody in Berlin's Moabit prison, Eisler was elected a candidate member of both the Politburo and the Central Committee. Soon thereafter, however, he once again ran afoul of his party's leadership. In early 1928, following Comintern instructions, Thälmann veered his party sharply to the left. The KPD now adopted a very intransigent position toward the SPD. Indeed, social democracy—branded by the KPD as "social fascism"—was declared the greatest enemy of communism. According to Thälmann, "social democracy . . . is the most dangerous pillar of the enemies of revolution. It is the main social pillar of the bourgeoisie, it is the most active factor of fascistization."[29] As has often been noted, the KPD's campaign against "social fascism" prevented the party from focusing on what would soon prove a far more dangerous enemy, Hitler's NSDAP. It also precluded the emergence of a united left against the Nazi threat. And finally, it showcased the KPD's dogmatism, intolerance, and political inflexibility.

To Gerhart Eisler and other more moderate KPD functionaries, open antagonism toward the SPD seemed a poor strategy for winning the German working classes over to communism. KPD leaders labeled Eisler and others like him "conciliators." But although the "conciliators" were moderate in the content of their political views, they were aggressive in the pursuit of their political goals. They now tried to depose Thälmann. In this, they were aided by the so-called Wittorf Affair. In September 1928, it became known that John Wittorf, Thälmann's brother-in-law and political aide, had embezzled party funds. Although Thälmann was never implicated in the crime, he attempted to cover up the matter. When Eisler and his political allies learned of the scandal, they used it to their political advantage: they convinced a majority of the Central

Committee to vote for Thälmann's ouster. At this point, however, Thälmann turned to Stalin, who insisted on the KPD leader's reinstatement. Many Central Committee members now reconsidered their initial votes. Ulbricht, for example, in Moscow at the time, immediately cabled to protest the Central Committee's decision. Shortly thereafter, Ulbricht, Dahlem, and numerous other Central Committee members signed a public declaration distancing themselves from their initial votes. Thälmann easily won back his position. The tables turned, and those who had opposed Thälmann found themselves politically ostracized. In 1929, for example, Ulbricht declared, "The Party Congress has decreed that the conciliators are not allowed to exercise any leading functions in the party . . . The unanimous statement of the Party Congress . . . against the rotten opportunism of the conciliators proves that the few conciliatory party members are completely isolated."[30] The aggressive rhetoric and the organizational measures taken against the conciliators illustrates what by the late 1920s had become a defining feature of KPD politics. As one historian has written, "KPD members . . . learned unceasing and vitriolic factionalism as a way of life in the party."[31] Those party members who advocated political views at odds with the KPD leadership were not only unwelcome—they were enemies.

This marked intolerance toward opposing views would characterize all twentieth-century orthodox communist parties. But observers of the Weimar-era KPD point to the domestic roots of the party's intense factionalism. In part, this brutal politics reflected the Front experience of party cadres; during World War I there were friends and enemies, but nothing in between. Since enemies were life-threatening, they had to be "liquidated." As Eisler's first wife recalled decades later: "'No mercy for the enemy,' was another one of the Gerhart proverbs."[32] The KPD's obsession with the enemy also reflected the more general German proletarian experience, in which, as workers' memoirs suggest, enemies were omnipresent as "exploitative bosses, feared policemen, and faceless bureaucrats."[33] And it was related to what one author has argued was the central dilemma of the interwar KPD—the fact that the party was a revolutionary party in nonrevolutionary times. In the absence of genuine enemies who could be defeated (the bourgeois state, the capitalist class), internal enemies had to be invented; this was the only available channel for the party's revolutionary impulses.[34]

Following the defeat of the conciliators, Eisler was sent to Moscow. According to his later wife, Hilde Eisler, Gerhart spent an entire night debating the KPD's "social-fascism" policies with Stalin; thereafter, "Gerhart was no longer allowed to work in the party, but instead was sent by the Comintern to China."[35] The Comintern and other Soviet institutions maintained extensive illegal operations throughout the world. Soviet agents directed the activities of national communist parties, organized strike movements and industrial sabotage, and "liquidated" alleged communist renegades. A number of longtime German communists spent decades in illicit work for various Soviet authorities. In East Germany, veteran communist Ruth Werner published a best-selling page-turner of an autobiography—later made into a film—that documented her dramatic twenty-year career as a Soviet agent.[36] Other German communists, such as the legendary Richard Sorge, a Soviet spy in the Far East, were not so lucky: Japanese authorities discovered Sorge's true identity and sent him to the gallows in 1944. The KPD, it should be noted, also maintained its own domestic and foreign espionage operations.[37] In addition, spying was considered a normal part of daily communist activity. German communists were expected to collect and pass on information to party authorities about their workplaces, their neighborhoods, and even their party cells. The extraordinary spying operations of the notorious East German Stasi had a precedent in interwar Soviet and KPD practices.

Gerhart Eisler went to China in 1929. What exactly he did there remains something of a mystery, but whatever it was, it was very dangerous. In 1927, Stalin had had a real debacle in China when the nationalist Kuomintang, officially allied with the Comintern, massacred Chinese communists in Shanghai. The Chinese Communist Party was now illegal and its party members, for good reasons, were highly suspicious of Soviet representatives. Disguised as a salt merchant, Eisler headed the Comintern's Shanghai political branch. Eisler and his branch communicated Comintern directives to the Chinese Communist Party, served as a conduit for messages between that party and Moscow, and submitted "reports concerning all social problems involved in the labor movement in China"—surely a euphemism for political and industrial espionage.[38] Some authors have suggested that Eisler engaged in more nefarious activities. It is said that he reimposed Stalinist orthodoxy on the Chinese Communist Party. According to one author, "Gerhart Eisler [was] sent specifically to China to root out the Trotskyism which had flowered wildly after the bloody defeat of the Chinese Stalinists."[39] Ruth Fischer, hardly an unbiased observer, later claimed that Eisler, to gain Stalin's goodwill, "went to China and murdered his closest friends."[40] In 1947, she testified before the House Un-American Activities Committee that "in these Chinese purges [Gerhart Eisler] behaved so cruelly and carried out the orders so well, that the report about him in Berlin said that he was really the hangman of the rebellious Chinese Communists."[41] Eisler's unflattering image as a sinister Comintern agent dates from this period. Arthur Koestler, who knew Eisler in the early 1930s, described him as "a smooth-faced, smooth-mannered careerist, [who] succeeded in maintaining his place in the Comintern hierarchy by intrigue and self-abasement."[42] In 1931, Eisler returned to Moscow a seasoned Comintern agent.

FRITZ SELBMANN was also radicalized by the Front experience. Selbmann described his experiences up to 1945 in an autobiography titled *Alternative—Bilanz—Credo* (Alternative—result—creed).[43] Born in 1899, Selbmann was the son of a coppersmith. After leaving school at age fourteen, Selbmann worked at a factory and then a sawmill. In 1917, Selbmann was drafted; he was not, it should be noted, an unwilling recruit. But soon after his arrival at the Western Front, Selbmann saw a column of German soldiers who had been blinded by a German gas attack intended for the enemy. Selbmann later claimed that "the horror of the war overwhelmed me."[44] He became staunchly antiwar and from then on refused to fire any weapons. Like so many other future communists, Selbmann heard political conversations and was inundated by political leaflets while in the trenches. By war's end, he had become a "determined agitator against the war"—still a far cry from a committed communist.[45]

In the next months and years, Selbmann lived the dramatic political upheaval of postwar Germany. In 1920, he joined the USPD after a year and a half of "continuous disappointments" with the "treacherous majority socialists."[46] Selbmann now studied socialist literature, including *Das Kapital* and the *Communist Manifesto,* and began to apply Marxist analysis to his own situation. In 1921, he organized a strike at a stone quarry where he was working. As a result, he lost his job and was unable to find work elsewhere. He spent the next months organizing strikes in the stone quarries of southwestern Germany. But after a political argument with his father, a convinced social democrat, Selbmann left home for the mines of the Ruhr. Here he encountered organized communism for the first time. One evening, a roommate, a night shift worker, left a copy of Lenin's *State and Revolution* in their room. Selbmann picked up the brochure and stayed up half the night reading it; later, many other veteran communists would also claim that *State and Revolution* played an important role in their conversion to communism. As Selbmann wrote in his autobiography: "It was an exciting night for me, one of the most exciting in my life . . . Just as Saul had become Paul through his vision of

Damascus, in this one night I became a communist."[47] Selbmann's use of religious imagery to convey his political conversion suggests that for him—as for many others—communism became religion.

Selbmann joined the KPD in 1922. For much of the 1920s, he was deeply involved in the party's revolutionary activities. He surely found the illicit and violent aspects of revolution titillating: hanging forbidden posters, collecting illegal arms, distributing banned literature, procuring false documents, and harboring communist fugitives. Selbmann's first "party orders" were "to prepare the armed insurrection."[48] He was soon designated the KPD's military leader for the subdistrict of Buer. There he formed, trained, and inspected units of the "Proletarian Hundreds," paramilitary units set up by the KPD at this time. To arm his men, Selbmann stole dynamite and piping and then built highly explosive hand grenades. Much to his disappointment, however, there was no armed insurrection in 1923. The Proletarian Hundreds were soon outlawed and Selbmann was forced underground and briefly jailed. In 1925 Selbmann joined the newly established Red Front Fighters League (RFB), another KPD paramilitary organization.

Even though most KPD veterans had disavowed the Great War, both the KPD and the RFB reflected the ethos of war. Flags, banners, uniforms, the clenched-fist salute, and disciplined marching formations all belonged to the street theater of Weimar-era communism.[49] Indeed, as one study notes, in the KPD's political style, "the political position was judged, forces were grouped, combat orders were given, and marches organized."[50] The RFB played no small role in projecting the party's combative nature. As Selbmann later wrote with obvious relish: "These years were filled with continuous brawls, street fights, demonstrations, and parades—and the RFB was always and everywhere present."[51] With its activities, the RFB transgressed the capitalist order. Weimar authorities actually banned the rowdy organization in 1929. For Selbmann and many of his comrades, however, these RFB infractions were the romance of revolution; this was a love affair at once absorbing, dangerous, and very exciting.

This is not to say that communists did not have real love affairs. They did. But KPD membership placed enormous burdens on personal relationships. Party members, for example, were frequently blacklisted; the threat of unemployment and family penury always loomed large. KPD members spent little time at home: most of their evenings and other free time were devoted to party activities. And imprisonment for political activity frequently parted communists from their families. Fritz Selbmann was jailed just as his girlfriend learned that she was pregnant.

Fritz Selbmann exhorts a May Day crowd, Leipzig, May 1, 1932. (Bundesarchiv, Koblenz, Bild 183/19260/7)

For Selbmann, his arrest was "not so terrible," but for his future bride, these months were "a journey if not through hell, then indeed through a piece of purgatory."[52] The KPD also sent its members on various missions that separated them from their families. Beginning in late 1928, Selbmann spent six months in Moscow at the Lenin School. Thereafter, as a full-time KPD functionary, he headed up the party organizations in Upper Silesia from 1930 to 1931, and in Saxony from 1932 to 1933. Each time he changed jobs, he moved his wife and small children, but even then, Selbmann spent most of his time on the road and only "came home once every few weeks for two days."[53] This marriage nonetheless lasted until Selbmann's wife died of a heart ailment in 1939.

The private lives of Dahlem, Ulbricht, and Eisler all reflected these men's political passions. When Dahlem returned to Cologne in 1918, he and Käthe Weber planned to marry. But as Dahlem later wrote, "Initially there was no time for that. We still hoped in the near future for a revolutionary upswing that would correct the mistakes and failings of November. All our attention was aimed at that; personal matters had to take second place."[54] When Dahlem finally did marry Käthe some months later, he did so, as he noted in his memoirs, "between two political meet-ings."[55] Despite an inauspicious beginning, this marriage was to endure some fifty-five years. By contrast, Walter Ulbricht was married in 1920; three weeks later, he was forced underground. Although the Ulbrichts had a daughter in 1921, the couple—often separated by Walter's political work—grew apart. Within a few years, Ulbricht had no contact with his wife and daughter. In 1919, Gerhart Eisler, just days after meeting the woman who would be his first wife, told her: "I love you; I want you to share my life. It is not going to be a soft and easy one. I am a revolution-ary. I have dedicated my life to a great idea, the greatest, in fact, the idea of socialism. When you understand more about it, you will know that there will be little time for anything but this one great cause!"[56] This mar-riage ended in 1923—but at the very least, Eisler had been open about his priorities. During these years, communism and private life were ill-suited to each other. Longtime communists left a trail of broken marriages and abandoned children. In the next decades, underground hiding, impris-onment, exile, and internment would also take their toll on intimate re-lationships. But communism was not always destructive of personal ties. When both partners had a passion for communism, the trials of the era created even stronger bonds of love and commitment. Along with the Dahlems, a number of other communist couples shared remarkable marriages.

BUT WHAT of women communists? Among the major parties in the Weimar Republic, the KPD held the dubious distinction of having the fewest female members and attracting the fewest female voters. Women ranged from 9.1 percent of party members in July 1920 to 16.5 percent of party members in 1929.[57] For many women, the KPD's combative poli-tics may have seemed too masculine and belligerent. The party presented itself as a body of young, male, muscle-rippled proletarian workers. The party's activities—armed uprisings, violent strikes, militant demonstra-tions, and uniformed marches—also reflected its masculine self-image. The KPD shunned any image of itself as soft or feminine. Indeed, in the communist literature of the period, these qualities characterized the enemy. Social democrats were depicted as old, fat, impotent, and fe-male, while communists were invariably virile, tough, and male.[58] In addition, the KPD conveyed ambiguous images of women. Although the party preached a rhetoric of women's emancipation, party propaganda frequently depicted women as "objects of sympathy and pathos."[59] But the communist press also circulated images of the "proletarian new woman." In many ways like her male counterpart, she was, as one historian has written, "youthful, healthy, slender, athletic, erotic."[60] Neither image may have appealed to the hard-pressed, hard-working proletarian woman of the 1920s. Finally, the KPD focused little attention on traditional women's issues. The party assumed that the problems that women faced, just like all other social problems, would be resolved by the coming revolution.

Those few women who did join the KPD played an important role in day-to-day communist activities. They did the necessary, yet often dull, grassroots political work: selling communist literature, collecting money for the party, soliciting door-to-door, and so on. They also peopled street marches and demonstrations, and for their militant husbands, provided a domestic safe haven from the cruel Weimar world. Despite these contributions, female comrades were often slighted by their male counterparts.[61] Moreover, since women did not participate in communist street-fighting bands and were rarely arrested by Weimar authorities, they did not share in those experiences that lent revolutionary prestige and forged tight bonds among male communists. Curiously, the KPD was unique among the Weimar-era parties in that two women—Rosa Luxemburg and Ruth Fischer—briefly led the party. But they were anomalies within the male-dominated KPD. In the mid-1920s, fewer than 7 percent of the 504 leading KPD functionaries were women.[62] And to the extent that they were tapped for KPD leadership positions at all, women were relegated to the departments that dealt specifically with women's issues. The interwar KPD bequeathed a decidedly masculine political culture on the postwar East German SED, a party in which women—even veteran women communists—would have little influence.

One woman who found her way into the Weimar-era KPD was Emmy Zaddach (later Damerius, then Koenen). Emmy's life was, in many ways, typical of German women communists. She was born in Berlin in 1903. Her father was a metalworker; her mother a cook, washerwoman, and seamstress. Emmy later wrote: "I left my parents when I was 19 and a half years old because my father beat me black and blue with his belt . . . my childhood was full of difficult experiences. My father was an alcoholic and since he had no stature elsewhere, he was a despot in the family." As a child, Emmy earned money washing dishes and going shopping for a restaurant; during the war, she took care of her younger brothers while her parents and sister worked. Emmy left school at age fourteen and then worked as a clerk for a printing firm. At age eighteen, she began "a search for the meaning of life." She joined a youth hiking group, but after Walter Rathenau, the German foreign minister, was assassinated in 1922, she told the group "hiking is not enough, one must concern oneself with questions of politics and the economy." Emmy then tried out various pacifist and anarchist groups.

In 1922, Emmy married Helmut Damerius, an actor who joined the KPD in 1923. In 1924, Emmy joined the party after KPD members studied Marxist-Leninist literature with her so that, after many weeks, she was "freed from the anarchist egg shells." Emmy's first political function was to sell party brochures and newspapers door-to-door in apartment buildings. As Emmy wrote: "I did that with my infant in my arms, while the stroller stood in the entranceway." She earned praise at a KPD meeting because of her unexpectedly good sales of literature. When asked how she did so well, she responded: "First I read all the material myself, otherwise I can't recommend anything." Her next function was utterly typical for female comrades: "women's work." Emmy was told to establish the Red Women and Girls League, or RFMB, in Steglitz, the part of Berlin in which she lived. The KPD founded the RFMB as the female version of the RFB; RFMB members also marched together in disciplined formation, but the organization, as Emmy herself later noted, never had much success with attracting proletarian women.

During her first year as a KPD member, Emmy continued to work at her job with the printing company. Like her male comrades, however, she soon learned that her political convictions were an economic liability. In 1925, she lost her job and, because the firm blacklisted her, found no regular employment for the next years. In 1928, she began to work for a company that published left-wing dailies. At the same time, she became ever more involved in party affairs. Emmy staffed the Women's Department of the Berlin-Brandenburg KPD regional leadership and later coordinated the work of all of the local women's departments in the region.[63] She also participated in the party's many street actions. At one demonstration that Emmy attended with Käthe Dahlem, a policeman struck her in the head with a rubber truncheon. According to Emmy, "Käthe Dahlem was able to hold me up so that I didn't collapse and wasn't trampled on by the surging crowd. Due to strong headaches, I was treated by doctors for months."[64] In November 1932 Emmy was sent to attend a three-month, full-time course at the KPD's Rosa Luxemburg School. In the midst of her course, the Nazis came to power and her classes were abruptly ended. Emmy would soon join her male comrades in underground communist work.

ONE OF Emmy's teachers at the Rosa Luxemburg School was Fred Oelßner. Although Oelßner was born the same year as Emmy, 1903, little else joined these two young communists until they met as teacher and student in a communist classroom. Oelßner grew up in a socialist family; his father, Alfred Oelßner, was also a longtime communist. In 1917 Fred Oelßner joined the USPD's youth group, the Socialist Proletarian Youth, and headed the organization in the Halle-Merseburg region from 1918 to 1920. He joined the KPD in 1920 and participated in the armed uprising in Saxony in March 1921. Fearing arrest, Oelßner fled the region and began work as a trainee and then editor at various local communist newspapers throughout Germany. In 1923, Weimar authorities sent Oelßner to jail for a year for preparing "treason." After completing his sentence, Oelßner, a talented writer, continued his work for party newspapers. In 1926, the KPD chose Oelßner to study at the Lenin School in Moscow.

For communists of Oelßner's generation, the Soviet Union was nothing short of mecca. Communists eagerly traveled to the heartland of the revolution to see the new society in the making. Oelßner was no exception. In various columns for the KPD newspaper in Aachen, the last city in Germany in which he had worked, Oelßner wrote glowing reports of what he saw in the first socialist country. Oelßner's initial column about the train ride he and his fellow students took to Moscow is a caricature of naive observation. In contrast to the crowded German trains and rude, corrupt German conductors and customs officials, the Russian trains "were simply brilliant." The seats were as wide as beds and, indeed, at night turned into soft beds for which the Russian conductor handed out "sparkling white" sheets. At the border, trains had to go through an immense archway to enter the Soviet Union. As Oelßner wrote: "This archway seemed to us to be the entrance to another world: outside, beyond the arch, was the old, ramshackle, slowly rotting Europe . . . Here, however, behind the arch, shone the young, germinating, and blossoming Russia." On the train, Oelßner and his comrades also enjoyed enormous meals that "give us the key to why people here all look so well fed. They don't know the undernourishment of the German worker."[65] Everywhere Oelßner went in the next months, he found evidence of the success of the Soviet experiment. Soviet peasants, for example, could visit the Central House of Peasants in Moscow, where they could seek agronomical advice from the professional staff. They could also enjoy a museum of agriculture, a movie hall, a library and reading room, and a games room. Peasants could spend the night and take their meals for a "laughably small" ten kopeks a day. In Oelßner's view, "The German peasants would feel much happier under this 'dictatorship' than under the Hindenburg-'democracy'."[66] Oelßner visited a shoe factory where "the factory rooms are big and bright, and equipped with good ventilation." Furthermore, the women received the same wages as men; in Oelßner's words, "There is no 'lesser value' attached to women's work." After examining wages and the cost of living, Oelßner confidently concluded "that the situation of the industrial proletariat is significantly better than in Germany."[67] For Oelßner, "Here in Russia pretty much everything is good, even the God of weather" (on one occasion, the "God of weather" had unexpectedly allowed him to carry through his travel plans).[68]

Many other longtime communists shared the rose-tinted glasses that Oelßner wore in the Soviet Union. They desperately wanted to believe in the new Soviet society; this was, after all, what they were devoting their lives to impose on Germany. And what they saw was, in many ways, attractive—particularly when compared with crisis-riddled Germany. In the Soviet Union, there was virtually no unemployment, workers were not persecuted, and there was tremendous excitement about building a new society. KPD members thus placed their trust in the Soviet Union and the correctness of its ways. In a measure of their fondness for the Soviet Union, many German communists came to view the first socialist state as their real home. Returning to Germany from Russia in 1929, Fritz Selbmann later recalled: "As our train crossed the border I did not have the feeling that I was coming home. It seemed instead that I was coming from home and entering a strange, hostile world."[69]

Indeed, in the next decades, numerous German communists would view the Soviet Union as their true home: they became members of the CPSU or Soviet citizens. Walter Ulbricht was allowed to join the CPSU in August 1928.[70] Fred Oelßner was a member of the CPSU during his stay in Moscow between 1926 and 1932 and, after fleeing Nazi Germany, became a Soviet citizen and CPSU member in 1940.[71] Franz Dahlem was given Soviet citizenship (and a valid Soviet passport) in May 1941.[72] Possession of Soviet citizenship or CPSU membership was a source of great pride for German communists; after all, it signified that these communists belonged to the very heart of the revolution. In postwar East Germany, however, this aspect of veteran communists' biographies was always kept secret. Party authorities feared that such information would only bolster popular views that leading SED officials were not true Germans, but rather Soviet imports who were willing to sacrifice the best interests of the German nation for their Soviet masters. In the early 1950s, for much the same reason, veteran communists who held CPSU membership or Soviet citizenship were forced to relinquish these formal ties to the Soviet Union.

Not all KPD members who visited the Soviet Union were impressed by socialist achievements. One party member who visited the Soviet Union in the early 1930s was positively dismayed by conditions there: Erich

Mielke, later the longtime head of the Ministry of State Security in East Germany. Mielke and a fellow KPD comrade fled to the Soviet Union in 1931 after they had shot and killed two Berlin policeman. Once in Moscow, Mielke complained to the head of his émigré hostel that he preferred "the Alex"—the police headquarters in Berlin where Mielke had been briefly imprisoned in 1930. "In Alex," Mielke declared, "all new prisoners are sent to bathe, they are locked in a clean room, and the food is edible and clean. Here one has no room, the food is dirty or there is nothing at all to eat." Mielke threatened to return to Germany, but the party did not want this. It thus made sure that he was able to receive from his mother—via KPD courier—soap, toothpaste, leather oil, shaving items, motorcycle shoes, and a sports cap. In the next months, Mielke was enrolled in the Lenin School where, presumably, conditions were somewhat better for career revolutionaries.[73]

Fred Oelßner remained in Moscow until 1932. After he had completed his course at the Lenin School in 1929, he attended the Institute of Red Professors, where professors for Soviet universities were trained. He also taught courses to foreign communists at the Lenin School. Although Oelßner was a member of the CPSU, he did not lose his ties to the KPD; indeed, he often served as Thälmann's translator when the German party leader was in Moscow. In late 1932, Oelßner went back to Germany to teach political economy to Emmy Damerius and other students at the Rosa Luxemburg School. Much later, Emmy recalled: "Comrade Fred Oelßner taught political economy—and in a very fascinating way. I remember that for me his lessons could have lasted hours longer. The classes with him were for me the most instructive because they enabled me to work through *Capital* on my own for a long time thereafter. [Oelßner] was also popular with all the students because he understood how to connect the serious and not easy themes with practice—and he did this with a sense of humor."[74] Even before the official end of this three-month course, Oelßner was on the run from the Nazis. And some years later, Oelßner would have a new and rather less sanguine set of experiences in the Soviet Union.

WHILE OELßNER was in Moscow, Karl Schirdewan became an important functionary of the KJVD, the KPD's youth organization. Born illegitimate in 1907, Schirdewan had a sad childhood. He never knew his father and, early on, was abandoned by his mother. Schirdewan spent his early childhood in a series of foster families and a Catholic children's home for orphans. In 1914, he was adopted by the Schirdewans, a kind working-class couple who shared custodial duties at the Botanical Institute in Breslau. In 1918, however, Schirdewan's adoptive mother died of consumption. His adoptive father remarried soon thereafter, but Schirdewan never cared much for his new mother. He left school at age sixteen to begin an apprenticeship at a grain company. After that company went bankrupt, Schirdewan was unable to find a new apprenticeship. Instead, he found jobs as an errand boy and office clerk. As Schirdewan later wrote in his memoirs, "I was thus very young when I entered a really tough working life."[75] Schirdewan, like many younger pre-1933 KPD cadres, did not belong to the Front Generation, but rather to what would be called the "Lost" Generation. The Lost Generation did not fight in World War I, but it lost its childhood to the war, its adolescence to postwar upheaval, and its opportunities for employment and much else to the Depression.[76]

Striving for a "life free from exploitation and fear of the next day," Schirdewan joined the communist youth group in 1923; it became known as the KJVD in 1925. In his memoirs, he wrote that he considered joining the SPD's youth group, but found it "insufficiently militant." By contrast, the communist youth group "was just right for me . . . first and foremost, the KPD strove to create a youth organization that was politically steeled and most effective in aggressive clashes." As even Schirdewan noted, the KJVD failed to attract many youth; in the last years of the Weimar Republic, its membership ranged from thirty-five thousand to fifty thousand.[77] But those young people who did join the KJVD—often the children of communist parents—were extremely devoted to the KPD and its cause. Unlike other political youth groups that engaged in cultural or sports activities, the KJVD was focused purely on politics. Indeed, KJVD members became the errand boys of the KPD. In the words of one historian, "They sold newspapers, painted slogans, glued posters, collected dues, engaged in agitation, and made up the voice choruses" at demonstrations and other events.[78] Through such tasks, Schirdewan worked his way up the KJVD hierarchy. By 1928 he was a member of the KJVD's Central Committee, and in 1929 he became chairman of the KJVD in Silesia. Through participation in the adult political activities of the KJVD, Schirdewan and others like him no doubt came to think of themselves as the young avant-garde of the coming revolution.

The KJVD also engaged in the factional politics of its parent party. In the spring of 1931, Schirdewan became director of the KJVD's Young Guard publishing house, but he soon lost his position due to factional politics. At this time, Heinz Neumann, a brilliant young KPD intellectual, called for more physical violence—even individual acts of violence—

against communist enemies, including the Nazis. His slogan, "Beat the fascists wherever you meet them," soon became famous. Thälmann initially supported Neumann, but soon became wary of the uncontrolled violence that Neumann espoused. A bitter rift within the KPD ensued, and it soon spread to the KJVD. In the youth organization, many young cadres found Neumann's impatient tactics appealing. Neumann's supporters thus gained the upper hand in the KJVD leadership. Schirdewan, who supported Thälmann, was soon sent off to head the KJVD in East Prussia, on the outskirts of the Republic. It would not be the last time that he would experience fluctuating fortunes within the communist movement.

In the early 1930s, Schirdewan joined the growing numbers of the unemployed. In Depression-era Germany, as many as one in three employable individuals was without work.[79] The communists (and even more so the Nazis) enjoyed a huge upsurge in votes and party membership. By the end of 1932, the KPD had 360,000 members, 252,000 of whom had paid their party dues.[80] The unemployment statistics for KPD members during the Depression years are truly astonishing. Among party members, the jobless numbered 21 percent in 1927, 60 percent in October 1930, 80 percent in 1931, and 85 percent in 1932.[81] Ironically, this meant that some longtime communists never worked in production; unable to find employment in the Weimar years and imprisoned or exiled during the Nazi years, these champions of the proletariat occupied full-time positions in the East German party and state bureaucracies after 1945. During the Depression years, however, mass unemployment left KPD and KJVD members with time on their hands. They could now devote much, if not all, of their time to communist activities. At the same time, party work often provided communists, including Schirdewan, a financial lifeline. Several authors have argued that functionaries' financial dependence on the movement assured their obedience to the party line.[82] As early as 1921, Wilhelm Koenen, later the husband of Emmy Damerius, justified his obeisant conduct in a factional battle by stating, "I certainly won't jeopardize my nice position in party headquarters."[83] A decade later, when the employment situation was considerably worse, many other KPD functionaries surely followed Koenen's example.

The Depression and its accompanying mass unemployment had a number of important consequences for KPD politics. Following both Soviet practice and a long German socialist tradition, communists looked to a strong, centralized state to intervene in social problems. The failure of the state to resolve the Depression-era economic and social problems only heightened KPD opposition to the Weimar Republic. It also reinforced the communist view that parliamentary politics was a mere bourgeois sham. At the same time, the experience of the Depression influenced how longtime communists ruled postwar East Germany. In the GDR, pre-1933 KPD cadres pursued full employment policies and provided generous state subsidies for the basic necessities of life. Although all Soviet satellite states followed similar policies, these state welfare measures had a special resonance for veteran German communists.

Mass unemployment also meant that KPD politics shifted from the factories into the streets—to parades, rallies, demonstrations, and even street battles.[84] In the last years of the Republic, in keeping with the "social-fascism" line, KPD and KJVD street politics were directed as much against the SPD (viewed by many communists as the party behind the hated Weimar Republic) as against the Nazis. In November 1932, Schirdewan attended a secret meeting of KJVD functionaries in Prieros. There, Thälmann reminded the young communist cadres that they were to battle both fascism and "social-fascism." Even in the face of mounting Nazi successes, hostility toward the SPD continued to preoccupy the communist movement. As Schirdewan later recalled of SPD-KPD relations, "I was always the witness of large, at times very polarized rallies and bloody clashes. We were not able to set aside our differences [and] to bring about the potential and necessary unity to defend Weimar."[85] Schirdewan correctly noted that the KPD's stance prevented the formation of a united left response to the Nazis. He failed to remember, however, that the militant, street-fighting KPD did not wish to preserve what it viewed as the corrupt, repressive Weimar system.

THE PRIEROS meeting of KJVD functionaries was also attended by another young communist, Erich Honecker, who would eventually play a major role in stripping Schirdewan of his political power. Much more importantly, though, Honecker would lead East Germany from 1971 to the regime's demise in 1989. Honecker was born in 1912. His father, a miner, belonged to the SPD before the war, joined the USPD during the war, and became a KPD member soon after the war. Much as Ulbricht grew up with socialism, Honecker grew up with communism. As a small child, he was allowed to listen while his father and his comrades discussed politics. As a ten-year-old, Honecker joined the communist children's group in Wiebelskirchen, the small town in the Saar where the Honeckers lived. This children's group, according to Honecker, "distributed leaflets of the party, sold its newspapers . . . collected pennies in solidarity with striking workers and Soviet Russia, and participated in political demonstrations." Honecker also wrote that he and other children were often placed at the

front of demonstration marches so as to break through police block-
ades; the hope was that the police would not fire at or otherwise harm
the children. As Honecker later stated, "At an early age we could already
feel ourselves as real comrades-in-struggle in the great proletarian movement."[86] As a youth, Honecker joined a workers' gymnastics and sports
club. Along with his brother and father, he also played in the RFB's
brass band in Wiebelskirchen. In 1926, he joined the KJVD; by 1928, he
headed that organization in his hometown. In 1929, Honecker joined
the KPD. For Honecker, communism was always a way of life; as he wrote
in his memoirs, his entry into the party was "a natural consequence of
my background, childhood, and adolescence."[87]

In the late 1920s, Honecker did an apprenticeship as a roofer but, like
so many others of the Lost Generation, he never found a job in his pro-
fession. In any event, by about 1930, Honecker was essentially a "career
revolutionary." During that year, the KPD chose him, barely eighteen
years old, to attend a one-year course at the Lenin School in Moscow.
Honecker was wildly enthusiastic about the first socialist state: "For me,
too, Lenin's country was my fatherland, his party my party, his youth
organization my youth organization. In the Red Army soldiers who
jumped onto the steps of the train, I saw my brothers and comrades—although I did not know them personally."[88] Honecker apparently had a
very successful year at the Lenin School. At the end of his course, his
teachers wrote of him: "A very talented and diligent comrade. Distinguished himself through his active participation in conferences and con-
sultations. Thoroughly acquired the course material. Understands very
well how to relate theory to the class struggle in Germany."[89] Armed
with the latest revolutionary knowledge, Honecker returned to Germany
where, in late 1931, he became KJVD leader of the Saarland. Like
Schirdewan, Honecker participated in the street politics of the waning
days of the Weimar Republic. And he, too, went to various KJVD functionary meetings, including the conference in Prieros. This was the only
time that he ever met Thälmann. As Honecker later wrote: "I did not
imagine then that I would never see Thälmann again. And he could not
have imagined the details of what the next months would bring."[90] In
late January 1933, the Nazis seized power. For communists, the end of
the Weimar Republic was as unexpected as it would be disastrous.

DURING THE Weimar Republic, German communists had formed, in
Benedict Anderson's famous phrase, "an imagined community." As Anderson writes, "an imagined community" is made up of those who "will
never know most of their fellow-members, meet them, or even hear of

them, yet in the minds of each lives the image of their communion."[91] Although Anderson's work describes a nation, it is appropriate for the interpretation of the German communist experience. Much like a nation, the communist movement was all-encompassing. It offered a vibrant club culture, a large and varied press, and a system of schools for political education. It also provided many of the trappings of a nation. German communists had a ritual calendar including May Day and the annual LLL parades in January (Luxemburg, Liebknecht, and Lenin had all died in that month); a cult of martyrs who had fallen in the socialist cause (akin to the cult of the fallen soldier); and even formal documents (party membership booklets as well as forged identity cards and passports for conspiratorial use). Like all nations, German communists had a clear-cut sense of the other; they knew who did and did not belong to their movement. Moreover, communists felt themselves to be outcasts of the German nation. And the rest of the German population saw them as such— as nefarious outsiders who wished to submit Germany to the tutelage of an alien power, Soviet Russia. Finally, like all too many nations, communists had a messianic, teleological vision of history. They had no doubt that the proletariat was destined to win the ongoing class struggles.

The vast majority of German workers never joined the KPD. And many who did stayed in the party for brief periods of time. Party officials often lamented the high membership turnover.[92] But for some tens of thousands of fiercely loyal cadres, the party was the end all and be all.[93] These German communists viewed themselves as embattled underdogs in a tough fight for survival. They were willing, indeed eager, to sacrifice their time, energy, work, and relationships for the communist cause. But what was their cause? This was and would continue to be very much an "anti" movement: against the status quo, against capitalism and parliamentary democracy in Germany. It was also a movement concerned with means, not ends; it was bent on destroying the given order, not creating a new order. It was thus consumed by revolutionary tactics, the organization of illegal activity. The values that the movement espoused—from a determined militancy to a Manichean mentality—all reflected an "anti" attitude. By contrast, KPD members do not seem to have been particularly moved by an egalitarian or humanitarian vision of the world. Beyond pointing to the Soviet model, they did not articulate a vision of the future communist world. And they certainly shunned the values of compassion, conciliation, and compromise—all necessary for the consolidation of enduring political orders.

By any number of measures, the interwar KPD was a failure. Although the party cultivated a militant image, it did not succeed in overthrowing the Weimar government. Although the KPD presented itself as the voice of the industrial proletariat, it did not succeed in winning over most working-class Germans to communism. And although the KPD later prided itself on its antifascism, it kept the German working classes from banding together against the Nazi threat. In later decades, however, the SED would stylize the KPD's Weimar-era struggles into legendary endeavors. Heroism, it seems, was born of futility. The KPD's various insurrections—from the Spartacist Uprising of 1919 to the Hamburg revolt of 1923—were recast as glamorous revolutionary actions against the "Weimar system." The marches, strikes, and demonstrations orchestrated by the KPD, along with the arrests and imprisonments inflicted on party members, became the stuff of glorious communist biography. Longtime communists would come to lovingly recall these political exploits, for the biographical fact of participation in the Weimar-era KPD marked their true loyalty to communism. These communists had, after all, joined the movement when the rewards were few and the risks many—risks that over the next years would prove far greater than many comrades could have imagined.

2

PERSECUTED

At Home and Abroad after 1933

ONCE HITLER CAME TO POWER IN JANUARY 1933, KPD MEMBERS
found themselves imperiled. In the new Nazi Germany, they were no
longer scorned outcasts. They were hunted prey. And they would now
face untold persecution—both at home and abroad. Inside Nazi Germany, communists immediately began to resist the new regime. Due to
the KPD's disastrous strategy of mass illegal resistance, however, many
party cadres soon found themselves behind Gestapo bars. By 1935, Fritz
Selbmann, Karl Schirdewan, and Erich Honecker had all been arrested
and sentenced to long prison terms. At the same time, in the mid-1930s,
a few thousand German communists, including Emmy Damerius and
Fred Oelßner, emigrated to the Soviet Union. These KPD members soon
faced the nightmare of the Great Purges. Finally, several thousand communists managed to escape to Western European and other countries.
From there, KPD cadres, including Walter Ulbricht, Franz Dahlem, and
Gerhart Eisler, helped to organize resistance to the Nazi regime. They also
participated in the Spanish Civil War on the side of the Spanish republican government.

In East Germany, the antifascist struggle of KPD cadres during the Nazi
period would become the stuff of communist legend. According to the
SED, the KPD had led a unified and successful antifascist struggle against
Nazi oppression. Countless films, novels, memoirs, museum exhibitions,
and political rites and rituals would commemorate an allegedly glorious
communist past. The SED was to heroize the illegal resistance against the
Nazis, mythologize concentration-camp incarceration, idealize emigration to the Soviet Union, embellish KPD propaganda achievements in
Western exile, and romanticize fighting in the Spanish Civil War.

But the experiences of KPD cadres during the Nazi era were very different from what the SED later claimed. During these years, the KPD and its

cadres saw numerous communist disasters. Although many individual communists acted with great integrity in inhumane situations, the KPD's collective role involved little heroism and much suffering. The KPD never led a unified antifascist resistance between 1933 and 1945—there was no united movement against the Nazis. Although illegal communist activity never posed a serious threat to Hitler's regime, tens of thousands of KPD members nonetheless landed behind Nazi prison bars; most communists thus spent much of the Nazi era not as active resistors, but as impotent prison or camp inmates. In addition, thousands of party members were murdered in the Great Purges in the Soviet Union. KPD propaganda efforts in Western exile also proved futile. The Spanish Civil War was lost to Franco's forces. And the 1939 conclusion of the Nazi-Soviet Pact flew in the face of the party's professed antifascism. Despite these debacles, many party cadres remained committed to communism; indeed, their experiences during the Nazi years heightened their attachment to the KPD.

ALTHOUGH THE KPD had always prided itself on its conspiratorial prowess, the Nazi seizure of power actually caught the party unprepared. Emmy Damerius later recalled that immediately after Hitler was named chancellor, police raided the Rosa Luxemburg School.[1] The KPD Central Committee then decided to divide the course and had its various groups meet at different Berlin workers' pubs. A day or two later, Fred Oelßner, who was already living underground, was teaching one of these groups political economy in the back room of a pub. All of a sudden, as he remembered, "Police vans drove up and stormed into the restaurant." Fearing certain arrest, Oelßner slipped out of a back door, down a corridor, and through a courtyard, exiting through an unguarded entrance way. He then joined a growing crowd watching the police action. Oelßner saw his students packed into police vans and driven away. He later found out that they were brought to police headquarters at Alexanderplatz, registered, and then released.[2] A day or so later, the Central Committee abruptly ended the course. Emmy Damerius and the other students were instructed not to go home to their own apartments since the police, they were told, considered them "agents of Moscow." As Emmy later wrote, that meant to "go underground."[3]

All over Germany, communist functionaries haphazardly plunged into illegality. On February 7, the Central Committee met for one last time. With the utmost secrecy, some forty Central Committee members—including Walter Ulbricht, Franz Dahlem, and Fritz Selbmann—were transported to and from the Ziegenhals sports club on the outskirts of Berlin.

Warned that the police were closing in, Ulbricht broke up the meeting in the midst of Thälmann's speech—the KPD chairman's last to his devoted functionaries. Thälmann was arrested on March 3; he would spend the next eleven years in Nazi captivity, only to be murdered in Buchenwald concentration camp in 1944. All other leading KPD officials now also found themselves hunted by Nazi authorities. Initially, Politburo members stayed in Germany to coordinate communist resistance. But by May 1933, the party leadership had decided to establish foreign headquarters. And by the end of October, all but one Politburo member had left Germany for safer destinations abroad. For a short time, Politburo member John Schehr directed KPD activities within Germany, but he was arrested in late 1933 and shot to death while allegedly trying to escape prison in February 1934. Nazi Germany had very quickly become a most dangerous place for leading KPD functionaries.

Official communist doctrine insisted that the Nazi regime marked the last gasp of German capitalism. Mass resistance, the KPD believed, would hasten an imminent revolutionary crisis and spell the end of the hated capitalist order. This resistance strategy, however, was ill-fated. The open nature of mass resistance—the fact that it involved the production of large numbers of illegal leaflets, posters, and other materials—made it relatively easy for the Gestapo to track down and arrest those involved in such resistance work. German communists nonetheless followed their party's orders. They leafleted, hung posters, and published underground newsletters. They also gathered information on the German economy, rearmament policies, and the mood of the German population. Finally, they rebuilt communist networks after successive waves of Gestapo arrests. Participation in these resistance activities, however, left party members ever more dependent on the KPD. It was, after all, trusted comrades who provided false papers, safe meeting places, underground housing, and the other accoutrements of conspiratorial activity. The party also provided meager funds to support its illegal cadres. Resistance activity strengthened the sense of isolation and "otherness" that communists had already felt in the Weimar Republic; communists were now truly cut off from the mainstream of German life. Although communist resistance did little to undermine the Nazi regime, it did much to solidify German communist culture.

THE EXPERIENCES of Fritz Selbmann, Karl Schirdewan, and Erich Honecker illustrate the lives of communists involved in resistance activities inside Nazi Germany between 1933 and 1935. Selbmann, the regional party leader in Saxony, initially organized a semilegal campaign for the March 5 national elections in which he and eighty other communists won Reichstag seats. The following week, however, the KPD was banned and all its Reichstag seats nullified. Thereafter Selbmann, like so many other communists, went completely underground. He lived in a room in a busy area of Leipzig. During the day, he engaged "in the minimum of office work that is necessary even for the leadership of an illegal organization: reports, information, analyzing newspapers, developing fliers and the like." Evenings, however, Selbmann always went to "a conference or rendezvous at an illegal meeting-place." Since he was well known to police, he adopted a disguise: "I grew a beard, combed my hair down to my brow, wore a suit that no one knew me in, and went without glasses." This illegal existence lasted all of four weeks. On April 11, he met his secretary in the woods. She was accompanied by another comrade, a man who had worked for the party for years, but who had not known Selbmann's illegal whereabouts. According to Selbmann, "This man was my Judas. He betrayed me that same afternoon to the police, and that evening I was arrested."[4] That Selbmann believed he had been turned in by a party member is significant. The interwar KPD had always harbored suspicions of agent provocateurs in its midst. With good reason, the Nazi seizure of power turned this suspicion into an obsession. KPD members became even more vigilant about their fellow comrades. The party all but closed its ranks so as to halt the influx of potential agents. It also reorganized its cells so that they were made up of just five or sometimes as few as three communists; individuals often knew only their cell leader. The Gestapo nonetheless infiltrated many communist networks. In 1933 alone, it is believed that some 100,000 communists were arrested.[5]

In 1933 and 1934, Karl Schirdewan headed the illegal activities of the KJVD in Saxony and then in northern Germany; he eventually belonged to the three-man leadership of the KJVD for all of Germany. Much of Schirdewan's work focused on maintaining contacts with his KJVD subordinates. His life became a constant round of illegal meetings in which he gave instructions and passed on material to his fellow comrades. He also devoted considerable energy to the production and distribution of illegal leaflets. As he later wrote in his memoirs, since it was no longer possible to reach large numbers of people with the spoken word, "leaflets had to be produced. Typewriters and duplicating machines became important weapons in the illegal struggle."[6] To evade capture by the Gestapo, Schirdewan had to frequently change his living quarters. Moreover, Schirdewan, who was single at the time, could not risk sexual liaisons; these, he believed, could compromise his work. As Schirdewan later wryly commented: "Since we actually hadn't committed ourselves to celibacy, this was tough."[7] He also adopted various disguises—once that of an amateur ichthyologist, on another occasion that of a Nazi party member. All this, Schirdewan wrote, meant that "my personal life changed in a far-reaching way. I became restless, the victim of persecution. The physical burdens to which I and my comrades were exposed through illegality grew enormously. I was constantly out and about. On the same day I often had several tasks that had to be accomplished in places very far away from each other."[8] Schirdewan nonetheless carried off a number of significant exploits. He managed, for example, to gather the KJVD functionaries of northern Germany at a popular lake near Hamburg. As Schirdewan later wrote: "Understandably, we had to adapt the conference to the situation. We thus swam around a lot, engaged in our little jokes, and acted as harmless bathers no different from the other swimmers. During seemingly insignificant chats I explained the political situation, handed out current assignments, and distributed [illegal] materials—bit by bit, of course."[9] Schirdewan continued his illegal work until February 1934, when he met another member of the three-man KJVD leadership, Ewald Kaiser, in the Hamburg train station. Unbeknownst to Schirdewan, Kaiser had already been arrested. Schirdewan was immediately surrounded by five police officers and put under arrest.

Erich Honecker was also deeply involved in illegal KJVD resistance work. After the Nazi seizure of power, he initially worked in the relative safety of his home region, the Saar; at the time, this region was under international mandate. In late 1933, however, Honecker was sent to lead the KJVD in the Ruhr area of Germany. There he set up headquarters in various huts in remote garden colonies. He organized the smuggling and distribution of communist literature produced by KPD comrades in nearby Holland; this material was disguised as popular cookbooks or cheap paperbacks with innocuous-sounding titles. Honecker also developed his own leaflets to circulate current political news. His group maintained a typewriter, duplicating machine, and other illicit materials in the boiler room of a Catholic hospital. In his memoirs, Honecker described an exploit of which he was particularly proud: on a windy day, he and a fellow comrade managed to throw some 250 leaflets out of a department store window that overlooked one of the busiest intersections in Essen. Honecker's illegal work in the Ruhr was quite successful. The Gestapo was unable to infiltrate his organization and no members of his group were arrested during his tenure as KJVD leader.[10] Honecker, however, had several close calls. On one occasion, he was even briefly held by police—who failed to ascertain the true identity of their detainee. In the fall of 1934, the KPD leadership sent Honecker back to the Saar. According to Honecker, his year in the Ruhr had been "a year of strenuous illegal work, . . . a year of tense vigilance, a year of constant changing of living quarters, a year without sufficient funds, a year of hope and setbacks, a year of constant threats, but also [a year] of multi-faceted and good solidarity."[11]

Honecker next worked on the KPD's campaign to keep the Saar from rejoining Germany; in 1935, the Saar population was to vote on its region's future. This referendum proved a resounding defeat for the KPD: over 90 percent of voters chose to join Hitler's Reich.[12] Thereafter, Honecker was once again on the run. The KPD sent him on missions to Paris, Prague, and various parts of Germany. In the summer of 1935 he was named to the KJVD leadership of Greater Berlin—a thankless task, given that so many young comrades had already been arrested there. The same fate soon befell Honecker. In December 1935 he met a courier from Prague, Sarah Fodorová, who gave him a baggage-claim ticket to pick up a suitcase of contraband literature. When he went to claim the suitcase, Honecker became suspicious when the attendant briefly disappeared with the tag. Once he had the suitcase, Honecker hailed a taxi, rode in it for a bit, but then jumped out, leaving the suitcase behind. The very next day, he was arrested as he was leaving his apartment. Honecker's capture was part of one of the last big waves of communist arrests. By the end of 1935, the Gestapo had ferreted out all but small pockets of communist resistance. Until the war years, there was very little organized communist resistance inside Nazi Germany. In the early 1940s, however, some active communist resistance circles once again emerged. All, however, were broken up by the Nazis. Not a single leader of these circles survived the Third Reich.

Once arrested, KPD cadres suffered brutal treatment at the hands of Gestapo authorities. On the second day of his captivity, Fritz Selbmann was placed in solitary confinement. His cell "was a real police hole; cold, raw stone floor; the walls had been painted many years before with oil paint that was now peeling and dirty; the glass of the window high up in the cell was opaque and the cell was thus constantly semi-dark. The mattress on the wooden plank bed was bone hard; the sheet had not been changed for the new occupant. The blankets were without covers and smelled terribly of disinfectant." But Selbmann knew that he had "untold luck." Although his interrogators resorted to "the argument of rubber truncheons," he was spared the worst of physical tortures.[13]

Karl Schirdewan was not so fortunate. He experienced savage interrogations in which Gestapo authorities hoped to elicit information about

communist cadres still at large. As Schirdewan later wrote: "As soon as
the questions began, so did the torture: every day from 10:30 in the evening to 3 in the morning. Blind with rage they struck at me. They picked
me up and then threw me on a long table. Then they assaulted me with
rubber truncheons and bull whips and beat me from head to foot. At
first I shrieked terribly. I felt an indescribable pain . . . I didn't yield a single detail."[14] Schirdewan was soon moved to Berlin and taken to the Gestapo's notorious Columbia House. There he suffered further mistreatment: poor food, constant observation, demeaning teasing, and even
insufficient time to use the toilet.

Erich Honecker also experienced physical abuse. He later wrote that
"neither the physical and psychological torture of the Gestapo bureaucrats, nor the many hearings in front of the investigating judge during
the year and a half of detention pending trial could dissuade me from
my communist worldview."[15] In fact, however, what happened during
Honecker's interrogations remains a subject of controversy. According to
one author who based his account on Gestapo files, Honecker revealed
more than was absolutely necessary about his illegal work. He allegedly
named the identity of a certain "Fritz" as Bruno Baum, the head of the illegal KJVD in Berlin, and betrayed Sarah Fodorová to the Gestapo.[16]

In prison, Selbmann tried to continue his political activities. But there
was not much that he could do. According to a 1945 report for the KPD,
"while in custody awaiting trial I was always completely isolated. I nonetheless tried to exploit the few opportunities [that I had] to keep up ties
with party comrades, exchange opinions about political developments,
carry out discussions with prison officials and, through my visitors,
sometimes have my views reach comrades on the outside." Selbmann believed that his "decisive contribution to party work lay in my conduct in
the trial proceedings against me." According to Selbmann, not just he,
but the entire KPD was on trial. As a result, "my general line was: defense
of the policies of the party without consideration of my person, no implication of other comrades, and the deflection of informers' denunciations
against the party." In 1935, the Nazis sentenced Selbmann to seven years
in prison for "preparing treason." This long-suffering communist spent
the next four-and-a-half years in solitary confinement. Once again, he
could not engage in political activity: "The possibilities of illegal activity
were very slight. I nonetheless used every possible opportunity for discussion with comrades and sympathizers. It was possible to establish a
contact to Comrade [Ernst] Schneller and to organize a written exchange
of ideas."[17]

Selbmann tried to use his time in prison as a sort of school. He taught himself to read English and worked his way through the prison library. In his letters to the outside world, he included passages on his current readings—Nietzsche, Dickens, Schopenhauer, Cervantes, Ricarda Huch, Rahel von Varnhagen, Shakespeare, Lessing, and more. Selbmann's letters to the outside world generally conveyed the image of a relaxed prisoner: "You fear for my nerves? Don't be afraid! 'Til now I have not noticed them."[18] But these letters were intended to calm loved ones at home. In his later memoirs, Selbmann was rather more open about the difficulties of imprisonment. He had to contend, for example, with personal problems that he could not resolve in prison. Shortly after he was jailed, his wife was also arrested; his two children, six and eight years old, were to be placed in an orphanage or in the foster care of a Nazi. As Selbmann wrote in his memoirs: "I, however, sat in my cell and could do nothing . . . in these weeks I got to know one of the most abominable feelings for a man responsible for others, . . . the feeling of impotence and hopelessness. For twelve years, there was nothing for which I hated the Nazis more than that they had put me in this position."[19] At least in part, Selbmann's fury lay in the contradiction between his current powerlessness and his self-image as a strong, forceful communist cadre.

LIKE THEIR male counterparts, women communists also resisted the Nazis. True to KPD tradition, however, the focus of their resistance was women's work. In the first months of the Nazi regime, Emmy Damerius and her fellow KPD women functionaries in Berlin distributed leaflets at unemployment offices, subway stations, and department stores. They also released balloons with the message "the KPD lives" from the second story of the famed Tietz department store at Berlin's Alexanderplatz. At the end of May 1933, Emmy and others arranged a conference of all KPD women functionaries in Berlin. Approximately thirty women arrived in pairs at the Krumme Lanke subway station where, Emmy later reported, "two control guards directed the comrades just with body movements . . . if they turned their backs on those who had arrived it meant to wait, if they pulled a handkerchief out of a purse and brought it up to their noses, it meant 'open passage.'" The women gathered in a nearby café, where they acted as a "circle of housewives" drinking coffee and doing their knitting. Soon they moved out to a clearing in the woods. There, Emmy instructed her comrades about their immediate tasks. KPD women were to establish contacts with social democratic workers and win them over to their party's politics. They were to help women workers defend themselves against worsening labor conditions. They were to distribute handwritten or typed chain letters repeating foreign news items and reporting on workers and their anti-Nazi actions. Women comrades were also to start whispering campaigns and to circulate anti-Nazi jokes. Finally, KPD women were to help the families of those communist functionaries who had already been arrested. After Emmy concluded her speech, the meeting was broken off because the women felt that they were being watched. As Emmy later recalled, "We began to quietly sing schmaltzy songs . . . Some comrades acted as though they were still looking for particular plants . . . many small groups went through the woods singing and laughing so that no one could have thought that responsible women comrades had discussed their illegal work. Despite the early termination [of the meeting], all the participants went back to their neighborhoods full of courage and with a new strength." In August 1933, the KPD leadership nonetheless disbanded the illegal women's departments and integrated women cadres into general party work. As Emmy noted, due to arrests and persecutions that had compromised the KPD's resistance activities, "the party had to concentrate its strength and the illegal cadres had to fill some gaps."[20] Emmy now became a political instructor in one of the KPD's subdistricts in Berlin. Soon, however, she found herself on the Gestapo's search list. In June 1934 she was told by party officials to go to Prague to pick up a visa for the Soviet Union.[21]

Unlike Emmy Damerius, many KPD women had their own, rather specifically female communist experience in the first months and years of the Nazi regime: the arrest of their husbands. These KPD women now not only had to fend for themselves, but also needed to aid their spouses jailed in the labyrinthine Nazi prison system. In some cases, these women benefited from the solidarity of fellow party comrades—in the form of money, groceries, children's clothes, and advice on how to get permission to visit their husbands.[22] The experiences of women communists with arrested husbands is documented in a rare set of letters written by longtime communist Käte Duncker to her imprisoned husband Hermann in 1933. Hermann Duncker, a founding member of the KPD, had been arrested in February. On March 2, Käte instructed Hermann: "I am told that you can write. I already sent a pad of paper; today envelopes follow . . . I'm sending some laundry. Please change your clothes immediately and put the dirty laundry in the enclosed sack . . . I have not yet received permission to speak with you. The lawyer is working hard." On March 14, Käte wrote that the last letter she had received from her husband was dated March 6: "If on my visits to Spandau [where Hermann was imprisoned] I did not regularly meet comrades who had been released and who had seen you recently, I would be totally desperate. Why such a totally sadistic torture?" In August, Nazi authorities searched the

Dunckers' apartment for incriminating material. Käte was furious: "It is not only that every drawer was ransacked . . . and that some dear spiritual friends in the form of books were packed up and hauled away . . . what particularly bothers me is that every aspect of my life is observed by countless hidden eyes." Käte now felt hounded by snitching neighbors and zealous Nazi bureaucrats—"their fantasies 'schooled' by trashy novels and crime thrillers." Käte's letters suggest that her life was a constant round of worrying about Hermann, consulting his lawyer, visiting official agencies to inquire about his situation, and riding to and from Spandau to visit and drop off his laundry and other items. Last but not least, Käte tried to keep up her husband's flagging spirits. In October, after she learned that Hermann had been transferred to the Brandenburg Penitentiary, she wrote: "My dear, please, please, don't be depressed; in Brandenburg there is also a path to freedom and many have already been released from there."[23] And, indeed, Duncker was among the lucky ones. He was released in November 1933.

GERMAN COMMUNISTS who actively opposed the Nazis were enormously proud of their resistance endeavors. During these months—or occasionally years—KPD members lived the communist ideal: they practiced the tough rules of revolutionary activity, they depended on the brotherhood of their fellow comrades, and they felt themselves to be active agents in the unfolding drama of History. Their experiences confirmed their Leninist belief that they were the chosen avant-garde of History. Why else, KPD members reasoned, would Nazi authorities so mercilessly battle their movement? The brutal persecution that they endured led them to view the battle between fascism and communism as *the* central drama of the Nazi era. Nazi persecution also lent German communists a sense of moral superiority that would help them to survive the ordeals of the next years. In 1934, for example, Schirdewan wrote his stepmother about the "honorable reasons for my persecution and subsequent trial."[24] Selbmann, Schirdewan, and Honecker would all remain in Nazi captivity until the spring of 1945. In the meantime, their few comrades at large inside Nazi Germany and their many comrades abroad in Soviet and Western emigration would forge ahead with the party's struggle against fascism.

IN THE mid-1930s, several thousand German communists emigrated to the Soviet Union.[25] They were considered very privileged; relatively few Soviet visas were granted to German communists stranded in Hitler's Germany. Those communists who came to the Soviet Union were initially delighted to live in the very heart of the world revolution. But the thrill of revolutionary Moscow soon gave way to the fear of Stalin's Great Purges. After the murder of the Leningrad CPSU leader, Sergei Kirov, in December 1934, waves of arrests engulfed foreign communists. Among KPD members who emigrated to the Soviet Union, over 70 percent, or close to three thousand German communists, were arrested at some time in the 1930s; most of these communists subsequently lost their lives.[26] Even the KPD leadership was not spared. Stalin murdered more Politburo members than did Hitler. And those KPD leaders and members who survived Soviet exile were deeply implicated in the terror.[27]

The experience of the Great Terror broke down bonds of solidarity among communists exiled in the Soviet Union. In the beginning, most German communists probably believed the counterrevolutionary and other heinous charges heaped on their fellow comrades. After all, they reasoned, they themselves were innocent and had not been arrested. Years of warnings about enemy infiltration into the communist ranks no doubt gave the accusations a certain plausibility. As the numbers of arrests grew, however, many longtime communists must have wondered about the truth of the charges. KPD members nonetheless did next to nothing to help comrades under suspicion. Suspect comrades, along with their family members, were treated as pariahs; in the halls of the Hotel Lux (where many exiled German communists lived) or in chance encounters in the Moscow streets, they were no longer greeted by fellow communists whom they had known and worked with for years.

Emmy Damerius was one German communist who was allowed to emigrate to the revolutionary heartland. Like so many other communists, she was initially thrilled to find refuge in the Soviet Union. As Emmy later recalled in a piece intended for an East German audience: "I was giddy when I entered the territory of the first workers' and peasants' state of the world . . . I would have liked to have hugged everyone."[28] In this uncritical piece, however, Emmy revealed none of the difficulties that she had encountered in the Soviet Union in the mid-1930s. That was left to several other pieces written for the SED party archives. In one, she described the climate of vicious denunciations, mysterious arrests, and unexplained deaths. Emmy's experiences of the Great Purges began in 1935, when she attended a large party meeting of Comintern staff. There, the Comintern official Manuilsky denounced a Hungarian party member as an "enemy of the party." This man, in turn, defended himself. As Emmy noted: "This discussion was for me one of the most questionable that I ever experienced. Concrete examples of [the Hungarian's] failings were lacking—Manuilsky, with all his speaking talent and political knowledge, did not make these clear." Emmy continued: "This atmosphere upset me and I know that the same was true of many others. It contributed to the fact that German comrades no longer visited each other, for anyone could accidentally be mixed up in any affair."[29]

In the spring of 1936, the man with whom Emmy had been living for some years, Leo Scharko, a Polish member of the KPD, was arrested. After a few weeks, Scharko finally managed to get a hearing with prison authorities. According to Emmy, "He came home after a few weeks of imprisonment and was totally changed. His humor was gone. I didn't press him, but it was clear that he had taken on some assignment. That was clear to me through his regular appointments and how nervous he was every time he went to those meetings." The implication is that Scharko was to denounce others. When Emmy left Moscow for Paris in December 1936, Scharko was ostensibly still a free man. The two corresponded; for Emmy, this involved cover addresses and invisible ink. She learned that Scharko was accused of forging an academic degree because there was no record of this degree in his personnel file. Under an assumed name, Emmy wrote the German institution asking for a copy of the degree that Scharko had earned. She then sent the copy on to Scharko. "It made it to Scharko in Moscow. But that was his misfortune. He had thus proven that he had contacts to Nazi Germany." Emmy did not comment on the fact that her actions, at least superficially, had done her lover in. Emmy concluded this passage with the simple words, "Since 1937 there has been no trace of Leo Scharko."[30]

Like Emmy Damerius, Fred Oelßner survived Soviet exile. But he experienced career setbacks in Moscow in the late 1930s. After Hitler came to power, Oelßner staffed the Central Committee's illegal propaganda department. For a disguise, he took on the identity of a boat motor salesman—even though he knew precious little about boat motors.[31] In December 1933, he left Germany for Paris and Prague. He arrived in Moscow in 1935. He was then given a position of lecturer at the Lenin School. But as he wrote in a short curriculum vitae in 1950, "On October 1, 1936 [I was] fired 'for political reasons.' I never officially learned the reasons . . . Proceedings of the KPD determined a few wrong formulations in a manuscript that I had written but that I had already corrected myself. No party punishment. During this time translations and other writing activities. Through the regional committee of the CPSU (B), employment in the Bop paper processing plant in Moscow in September 1938."[32] The period between his firing from the Lenin School and his new employment at the paper factory must have been extremely trying. Oelßner surely wondered whether he, too, would be arrested. By 1940, however, Oelßner had become a Soviet citizen and by 1941 he was once again working for KPD authorities.

Many German communists faced arrest and torture at the hands of their fellow comrades. Bernhard Koenen, later the brother-in-law of Emmy Damerius, was arrested twice between 1937 and 1939; in Weimar Germany, Koenen had headed the KPD's regional organization in Halle-Merseburg. After his first arrest, Koenen informed the KPD leadership in Moscow that officials of the NKVD, the Soviet police institution charged with carrying out the purges, were using force, blackmail, and torture to elicit confessions. Koenen agreed to have his statement passed on to Stalin's office. This, in turn, resulted in his second arrest.[33] But Koenen was fortunate. He was released in 1939 and later held a number of important positions in East Germany. By contrast, Emmy's first husband, Helmut Damerius, suffered a much worse fate. Emmy and Helmut Damerius had divorced in 1927. In 1931, Helmut and his agitprop theater troupe, the famed "Kolonne Links," emigrated to the Soviet Union. Damerius settled in Moscow and became a Soviet citizen in 1935. In March 1938, he was arrested. He spent the next eighteen years in labor camps and provincial outposts of the Soviet empire. He recorded his experiences in his posthumous *Unter falscher Anschuldigung* (Under false accusation), published in 1990. Damerius's story is all too typical of the cruelty visited on longtime communists in the Soviet Union.

After his arrest, Damerius was locked away in a filthy, overcrowded group cell—so overcrowded that the men had to take turns sleeping on the piss pot. He was occasionally called to interrogations. There, among other inanities, he was told to confess that he was a Nazi agent attempting to recruit members for Hitler Youth, the official Nazi youth organization. When his interrogator let loose "a flood of curses, abuses, and threats," Damerius was tempted to fight back, but he knew that the interrogator would call in help. And then, Damerius later wrote, "I feared that they could kill the communist in me."[34] Damerius was sentenced to seven years in a work camp for "suspicion of spying." He soon found himself in the Taiga, chopping down the trees of the Polar North. His life became a grueling round of exhaustion, hunger, and cold. Damerius periodically ended up in the camp sick bay. On one such occasion, Damerius encountered a German nurse, also a longtime communist. The two exchanged memories of better days in the Weimar Republic: "We went into raptures about the great parades of the working youth, of the Youth Congress in Leipzig, of the Whitsun meeting of the Red Front Fighters League in Berlin."[35] In Stalin's gulag—as in Hitler's concentration camps—the canonization of communist exploits in the Weimar Republic had already begun.

But recalling Weimar days was a rare happy interlude for Damerius. At one point, Damerius was imprisoned in the work camp for alleged counterrevolutionary agitation. He was given daily only three hundred grams of soggy black bread and a ladle of thin soup. He was then transferred to a cell crawling with bugs; these bugs, Damerius later wrote, gave a person "no peace, did not leave him alone, and sucked up his blood." But Damerius refused to give up his communist convictions. When called to an interrogation, Damerius found "a human bug [who] did not want blood, but rather signatures from me that tried to suck out my communist worldview. I couldn't refuse the bugs my blood, they took it against my will. But I could still refuse my signatures under false statements that wanted to make me into a counterrevolutionary or a fascist."[36]

Damerius was unable to fathom the source of his troubles. "Despite all my personal unhappiness, my trust in Soviet power and in the party and in Stalin who embodied both could not be shaken." Indeed, in the course of his time in the work camp, Damerius wrote Stalin seventeen times; he never, of course, received a reply. Damerius, like so many other longtime communists, really believed that Stalin and the party knew nothing of the gulag. "I was so naive . . . apparently there is nothing more difficult or more horrible in life than to wake up from dreams that one imagined to be reality."[37] In 1945, Damerius completed his sentence. He nonetheless had to spend another year in the camp. And after he was released, he was banned to Kazakhstan and not allowed to move about freely in the Soviet Union. In 1948, he read a newspaper account about a delegation of East German women, headed by Emmy Damerius, that was visiting the Soviet Union. Damerius sent Emmy a telegram asking for help. Although Emmy sent him a reply, Damerius was unable to get permission to go to East Germany. He spent another eight years in the wilds of Kazakhstan—doing renovation and other construction work—until he was able to establish contact with his old friend and fellow actor Arthur Pieck, the son of the East German president. As Damerius wrote Arthur: "Unbroken in body and soul, I am 'despite everything' still the one you knew. Of course, all these many years were a 'tough nut.' But regardless of how it was, I was always in my spirit and strivings with all of you in Germany. That's how it was, that's how it is, and that's how it will stay."[38] Arthur Pieck set the bureaucratic cogs into motion that finally allowed Damerius to return to East Germany in 1956. Although Damerius had experienced the worst excesses of the Soviet system, he preferred a flawed communism to what he saw as an unbridled capitalism.

Some longtime communists in Soviet exile faced another kind of trauma: their children were arrested and then disappeared without a trace. Gustav Sobottka, for example, a KPD member since 1920 and an important party trade-union official, saw his twenty-year-old son, also named Gustav, arrested in February 1938. In a series of terribly sad petitions to leading CPSU and Comintern functionaries, Sobottka described what he and his wife endured after their son's arrest. For months, the Sobottkas were not told where their son was imprisoned. In November the NKVD telephoned late at night and said that their son sent greetings and that his mother should bring fresh laundry to the NKVD building. In June 1939, the Sobottkas learned that their son was in the Taganka Prison and that due to insufficient evidence, his trial could not take place. At this point, the Sobottkas hoped that their son would soon be released. But nothing happened. Meanwhile, Gustav Sobottka lost his job and the couple faced a nasty bureaucratic run-around concerning an extension of their permission to live in Moscow. This permission was finally granted in December 1939. At this time, however, Sobottka's wife told her husband: "What crime did we commit that we are treated in this way? Haven't we worked our whole life for the workers' movement, haven't we sacrificed all? You have worked for twenty years for the Soviet trade unions . . . you never had time for the family or vacation, only work for the party, and now there's no work for you. Your son has been arrested, you have been thrown out of work . . . No, one doesn't treat people who worked for the workers' movement for thirty years this way. This is how one treats criminals and if we are criminals than they should beat us dead, but not treat us in this way." Sobottka noted that this was the "desperate outburst of a lunatic."[39] In fact, the very next day, his wife had a complete nervous breakdown and Sobottka brought her to a psychiatric clinic.

Later that December, Sobottka was told that things looked good for his son. But there was still no release. At this point, Sobottka wrote Molotov questioning the methods of the Soviet legal system. As Sobottka ended his letter: "Should these 23 years of my life [since the Russian Revolution] have been a lie? I still can't believe that. I still believe that my life and my struggle and my striving for a communist society were and are a just cause."[40] In October 1940 Sobottka learned that his son had died in prison. In the spring of 1945, he would lead one of the three groups of KPD members that returned from Soviet exile to establish communist rule in Eastern Germany.

Although German communists in Soviet exile knew the reality of Soviet-style socialism—purges, famine, shortages, and bureaucratic indifference—their experiences in the first socialist state seldom led to a questioning of their political beliefs. Although a few purge victims turned their backs on communism, most German communists who survived this era in Soviet exile maintained their communist faith. For them, the Soviet Union symbolized both the possibility of radical change and the future hope of mankind. Emmy Damerius, for example, wrote that she left the Soviet Union in 1936 "with the powerful feeling [that I wished] to devote all of my strength . . . to establishing in Germany a workers' and peasants' state." She continued: "I was not bothered by the still existing backwardness in some areas of the Soviet Union, nor by the difficulties in supplying the population. I could explain all of this. The occurrences surrounding the first show trials also didn't bother me. In the beginning I believed in a wide-ranging conspiracy. But when absolutely trustworthy German comrades were also arrested, what was going on appeared mysterious to me and most of my friends." Emmy nonetheless explained: "But I still held to my view that the Soviet Union is no paradise and that we had to report in a more nuanced way about what was absolutely new in the world. I saw in the Soviet Union something in principle new. A workers' and peasants' power had been created that really ruled and had chased away the exploiting classes."[41] Like so many longtime German communists, Emmy was more than willing to overlook Soviet shortcomings; for her and other KPD cadres, the Soviet revolution could not be judged according to the same criteria as capitalist regimes.

But there were also other reasons why communists exiled in the Soviet Union retained their communist faith. Those who were never arrested probably felt quite secure after the Purges. After all, they had not been purged at a time when party members had been so closely vetted. At the same time, Soviet exile reinforced KPD members' dependence on, and thus attachment to, their party. It was the party leadership (or the Comintern) that determined KPD members' work, place of residence, and other existential needs. It was also the party that determined whether a cadre was considered reliable or renegade. In addition, communists were bound to their movement by a silent complicity; at the very least, they were all knowing bystanders of the Great Purges. Had they questioned their political convictions, they would also have had to confront their own past actions—the denunciation of fellow comrades, the mistrust of loyal party members, and the rejection of communists in need. Finally, the Soviet Union had offered these communists much-needed refuge and had proclaimed itself the beacon of the antifascist struggle. For communists who had fled Hitler, the struggle against Nazi Germany was of paramount importance.

AFTER 1933, thousands of communists left Nazi Germany for what later became known as the "Western emigration." From Paris, party leaders directed the exiled KPD's two most important tasks: the organization of illegal resistance inside Hitler's Reich and the explication of KPD policy to communists and noncommunists alike. Walter Ulbricht and Franz Dahlem were among the most influential party leaders now based in France. Dahlem had joined the KPD's Politburo in 1929 and had then run the party's trade union organization, the Revolutionary Trade Union Opposition. After Hitler came to power, he worked illegally in Berlin for a few months. Along with Wilhelm Pieck, Dahlem then established the party's headquarters in Paris in May 1933. In February 1934, however, Dahlem was sent back to Berlin as the last Politburo member to coordinate illegal activity inside Nazi Germany. Dahlem decentralized the party's organization in order to make it more secure from Gestapo infiltration. He thus oversaw the process by which the KPD was divided into larger autonomous territorial units that were linked to sectional party leaderships located in nearby foreign countries. In July 1934, his task accomplished, Dahlem returned to Paris. When Emmy Damerius reported to the KPD's Paris headquarters at the end of 1936, Dahlem integrated her into the party's extensive network to support the communist resistance inside Nazi Germany.

Emmy initially went to Zurich, where the KPD directed illegal resistance in southern Germany. After six months of helping to smuggle material to Germany from Switzerland, she was reassigned to Prague. Emmy organized materials that were to be smuggled to Berlin, Saxony, and Silesia. Although this resistance work took place outside of Nazi Germany, it still involved considerable risk. On one occasion, Emmy took anti-Nazi material in a suitcase with a false bottom on a flight from Paris to Prague. To her horror, she discovered that her flight was making a stopover in Nazi Germany. Emmy, who was traveling on false Austrian documents, had to go through passport control in Nuremberg. She waited anxiously until, to her relief, she was the last traveler on her flight to have her passport returned; luckily, her suitcase was not searched. As she later commented, though, "since this flight I nevertheless knew very exactly where my heart was located."[42] The dangers involved in resistance activities in exile—which were illegal in the host countries—also left KPD cadres very dependent on their fellow comrades. They, too, relied on each other to provide the materials and solidarity necessary for such illicit activities.

While rank-and-file communists engaged in dangerous antifascist resistance work, KPD leaders became embroiled in a bitter political battle over communist strategy. Since the late 1920s, the communist movement had spent much of its energy battling the noncommunist left.

Now, however, threatened by Nazi Germany, Stalin wished to gain allies in the West. Moreover, the head of the Comintern, Georgi Dimitrov, had concluded that the division of the German working class into social democratic and communist camps had paved the way for Hitler's seizure of power. Beginning in 1934, Stalin and Dimitrov initiated a dramatic new political course: communist parties were now to work together with bourgeois and other socialist parties to forge a broad "unity front" of all antifascist forces. While on a trip to Moscow in August and September 1934, Wilhelm Pieck and Walter Ulbricht were the first KPD leaders to learn that a new Comintern strategy was in the offing. Against considerable resistance from other Politburo members (who were unwilling to work with the much-hated SPD), these two leaders successfully pushed the KPD to adopt the new strategy. At its Seventh World Congress in October 1935, the Comintern publicly proclaimed its united-front policy. Shortly thereafter, the KPD officially adopted the new line at its so-called Brussels Conference (the conference actually took place outside of Moscow, but was given its name to thwart Nazi authorities).

The battle within the party leadership over the united-front strategy marked the moment at which Wilhelm Pieck and Walter Ulbricht came to dominate KPD politics. As the main advocates of the new line, Pieck and Ulbricht gained enormous political authority both within the exiled party leadership and, more importantly, among Soviet and Comintern officials. Although Thälmann remained official chairman, Pieck was now named acting party leader for the duration of the party chairman's imprisonment. Ulbricht, along with Franz Dahlem who had come over to the united-front line in a timely fashion, was charged with the "operational leadership" of the party. Based in Prague, this "operational leadership" was to run clandestine KPD resistance activities inside Nazi Germany as well as the party's various propaganda endeavors in Western Europe. In the next months and years, Pieck and Ulbricht used their newfound power to settle scores with past and present rivals. Two Politburo members (and rivals) who had opposed the Comintern's new strategy, Hermann Schubert and Fritz Schulte, soon lost their lives in the Great Purges; other opponents lost their political positions and influence. In addition, aided by the Comintern, Pieck and Ulbricht reorganized party leadership bodies to enhance their authority. In 1937, the Politburo was disbanded and replaced with a "Secretariat of the Central Committee of the KPD" based in Paris. Ulbricht was named its head. Although Pieck remained acting party chairman and the party's Comintern representative, Ulbricht had reached the pinnacle of KPD power.

The KPD leadership attempted to put the united-front strategy into practice. In November 1935, Ulbricht and Dahlem met with leaders of the exiled SPD in Prague. Years of hostility, however, had taken their toll. The two parties' leaders had very different notions concerning a united-front policy, and SPD leaders remained highly suspicious of KPD motives. This meeting ended without agreement. In Paris, the KPD leadership also tried to create a broad "People's Front" movement. It was headed by a committee that involved a number of prominent noncommunist intellectuals and politicians, including the novelist Heinrich Mann. Although the committee issued a number of antifascist appeals, the "People's Front" ultimately foundered on the KPD's attempts to dominate the movement. This was especially evident after Ulbricht was named KPD representative to the committee. Mann is reported to have said that he could not work with a man like Ulbricht who "suddenly claims that the table at which we are seated is not a table at all but a duck pond and expects me to agree with him."[43] The KPD thus never actually forged a united antifascist front. In all the various centers of KPD emigration, the party's desire to dominate united-front organizations drove potential allies away.

Although Ulbricht had so recently enjoyed political triumph, he now suffered a political setback. His uncooperative meddling in the "People's Front" greatly angered Willi Münzenberg, an influential party cadre who was genuinely interested in creating a united front beyond KPD control. Münzenberg, a longtime KPD member who had enjoyed a friendship with Lenin, was known as the "Red Millionaire"; he had run a KPD media empire in Weimar Germany and had successfully moved his operations to Paris after 1933. In late 1937, Münzenberg charged Ulbricht with "Trotskyism." Ulbricht was recalled to Moscow and subjected to a party investigation. As Ulbricht knew only too well, these were dangerous times for communists under suspicion. But he weathered the storm. Although under investigation, Ulbricht assiduously participated in the ongoing purges of fellow KPD comrades. He not only denounced various party cadres as agents, but also served on a party commission that investigated—and generally found guilty—members who had fallen under suspicion. At the same time, Münzenberg was investigated by Comintern authorities for his alleged independence and failure to follow KPD orders. He was expelled from the party in March 1939 and died under mysterious circumstances in 1940. Ulbricht, by contrast, was cleared by the Comintern in July 1939.[44] He then continued his KPD work in Moscow. He wrote articles for the party press, held political seminars, and most importantly, served as the KPD representative to the Comintern. But he enjoyed precious little real political power. The exiled KPD had failed to advance revolution in Germany, had little following inside Hitler's Reich, and was entirely dependent on the whim of Comintern officials. Ulbricht was a leader of a party that seemed destined for utter obscurity.

SHORTLY AFTER the Comintern established its new united-front strategy, the Spanish Civil War broke out. For leftists, the Spanish Civil War became the most important theater of the antifascist struggle; the effort to preserve the Spanish Republic was billed as a heroic battle of justice against oppression. Tens of thousands of foreign volunteers rushed to Spain to join the International Brigades, the international fighting force organized to defend republican Spain against Franco's fascist onslaught. The International Brigades included more than five thousand Germans, some 60 to 70 percent of whom were KPD members.[45] Many German communists who fought with the International Brigades or who otherwise participated in the Spanish Civil War later became prominent East German functionaries.[46]

The solidarity of the International Brigades became legendary; it captured the imagination of Brigade volunteers and several generations of European and American leftists. Walter Janka, a pre-1933 KPD member who would run afoul of East German political authorities in the 1950s, wrote of his initial experience in Spain: "Despite the whirl of languages there were no difficulties. The self-discipline was extraordinary. Although most of the foreigners did not know each other, they acted like old comrades. Despite different political views and party memberships, they stood fast together."[47] The reality of the Brigade experience, however, soon contrasted sharply with the legend. Not only were there innumerable tensions between the various national groupings, but Stalin's Great Terror also extended to this fighting force. Soviet security authorities, aided by Western European communists, arrested and / or murdered supposed "Trotskyists" and other "deviant" leftists behind republican battle lines.

In late December 1936, Franz Dahlem was sent to Spain to coordinate KPD cadre policy. His reports to the party leadership suggest that ferreting out politically suspicious individuals was among his chief concerns. In August 1937, for example, Dahlem wrote the KPD leadership in Paris that "we desperately need two absolutely reliable party cadres since we also need to do some purging here . . . Without fail . . . decide on measures that will secure that the people sent here are checked better. Too many unreliable and hostile elements are getting through."[48] Similarly, on a visit to Spain in late 1936 and early 1937, Ulbricht alerted Soviet officials about those communists who had, for whatever reason, fallen under suspicion.[49] A number of other German communists were also working for Soviet security in Spain, including Erich Mielke.[50] At the same time, Dahlem was very anxious to preserve the lives of loyal party members. As he told the Comintern in March 1938: "It is urgently necessary that some of the most valuable, experienced cadres of the KPD—the same is true for all the illegal parties—are secured for the future political and military work in their home countries." Dahlem suggested that many of the best KPD functionaries be withdrawn from active front duty and used for military training or political agitation.[51] This preoccupation with preserving cadres for the future revolution would also characterize communist conduct in Hitler's concentration camps.

While in Spain, Dahlem served as the Comintern's political commissar to the International Brigades. In this capacity, he was charged with organizing political schooling in the various Brigade battalions. One of Dahlem's close associates in Spain, Heinrich Rau, later the chairman of the East German State Planning Commission, wrote a series of letters to a friend in which he described his life in Spain. In November 1937 he wrote: "With us there is the old daily grind: learning, grumbling, still more learning, etc. Yesterday was a holiday: there were cigarettes! Otherwise—occasionally shots are even fired."[52] As Rau's remarks suggest, between intermittent periods of fighting, communist cadres spent much of their time in Spain studying Marxist-Leninist doctrine. This political schooling focused on instructing Brigade members on the correct communist analysis of contemporary events and denigrating the various interpretations offered by competing leftist groupings. As Dahlem later told the Comintern, due to the "actions of the Trotskyite POUM [actually an independent Socialist party], a concrete battle against Trotskyism was carried out. In the framework of political lessons, circles for [political] schooling, and through the newspapers, we appealed to the vigilance of every individual."[53] Dahlem also helped to set up a small KPD school in Bennocassim, on the Spanish Mediterranean coast.

Gerhart Eisler, back in Europe from a Comintern stint in the United States, was sent to work with Dahlem. He traveled to Spain with Dahlem's wife, Käthe, in October 1936. According to a 1953 report written for SED authorities, Eisler's main task was to head a radio station, the German "Freedom Station," broadcast on the 29,8 frequency and thus known as Freedom Station 29,8. The Spanish government allowed German communists regular use of a powerful radio transmitter located outside of Madrid. The station broadcast antifascist programming to much of Western Europe, including Nazi Germany. Eisler wrote the text for the radio station's first broadcast on January 10, 1937 and prepared numer-

Franz Dahlem (third from left) with the International Brigades during the Spanish Civil War. Dahlem joins in a fighting salute. Note the hostage on the right. Near Madrid, July 1937. (Bundesarchiv, SAPMO-BArch, Bild Y 10-31303)

ous other broadcasts. At the same time, Eisler was responsible for the publication of the Brigade newspaper in German and French and put together other propaganda materials for the Interbrigadists. To his and Dahlem's disappointment, however, the KPD leadership in Moscow recalled Eisler to Paris in the summer of 1937.[54]

Among communist cadres, participation in the Spanish Civil War both reinforced many of the values prized by the Weimar-era KPD and heightened cadres' attachment to the party. The discipline and hierarchy inherent in military service reinforced the party's Stalinist political culture. In Spain, communists were to defer to higher authorities, unconditionally follow orders, and subordinate their individuality to the collective mission. At the same time, fighting in the Spanish Civil War offered a rare combination of adventure, idealism, and camaraderie. In April 1937 Heinrich Rau was at the International Brigades training camp in Albacete. From there, he wrote a friend: "How am I? I have had to loosen my belt, am healthy and feel better than I have for years."[55] Rau's morale was no doubt so good because he was finally living the KPD ideal. Given the initial military successes of the International Brigades, he and others felt themselves to be strong, potent soldiers in the antifascist cause; they were fighting fascism not with the mere words of propaganda, but with the powerful force of arms. Just like German communists in Soviet exile, however, KPD members in Spain found themselves at their party's mercy. They had no official papers (most had long since been expatriated by Germany), and within Spain there was no institution (such as an embassy) that would represent their interests. The KPD was thus the only institution that would provide for them. In November 1937, Heinz Hoffmann, later East Germany's minister of defense, lay injured in a Madrid hospital. After Käthe Dahlem sent him food there, he wrote and thanked her: "The food was not only a material help but it also showed me again that I am not alone. [It showed me] that the party thinks of everyone and cares for everyone."[56] Like the other "antifascist" experiences that KPD members had during the 1930s, fighting in the Spanish Civil War reinforced communists' attachment to their chosen cause.

AT THE end of 1937, Dahlem was told to leave Spain and to report to Moscow. In East Germany, Dahlem would write a two-volume, nine-hundred-page memoir of the fateful twenty months between when he left Spain and when World War II began in September 1939.[57] In this memoir, however, Dahlem failed to mention that he had observed the show trial of the Old Bolsheviks Nikolai Bukharin and Genrikh Yagoda in March 1938. In a memoir fragment published only after the collapse of the GDR, Dahlem wrote, "These days [of observing the trial] left a deep impression on me, who from my own rich experience knew the harshness of class struggle, the insidiousness, slyness, and unscrupulousness of our class enemies." Precisely because of his past experiences, Dahlem argued, he found this trial convincing. He also gave a number of other reasons—ranging from his trust in the Soviet Union to various examples of meritorious German communists becoming renegades—for why he did not question the veracity of the trial's findings.[58] Written long after he himself was purged in 1953, this piece was intended to justify Dahlem's (in)actions in the more troubling chapters of communist history.

Dahlem spent five months in the Soviet capital. In May 1938, he replaced Ulbricht as the leader of the KPD's Secretariat in Paris. As head of the four-man Secretariat, Dahlem was now responsible for the operational, day-to-day leadership of the KPD and for the party's illegal resistance within Germany. As he later wrote in his memoirs, he accepted this position "in no way lightly, for I was very aware of the magnitude of the responsibility given me within the leadership of the party."[59] Dahlem was joined in the Paris Secretariat by Paul Merker and Paul Bertz, as well as by a leader of the Austrian Communist Party, Johann Koplenig. A number of ranking KPD officials in Paris also worked closely with this

Secretariat, including Alexander Abusch, Anton Ackermann, and Gerhart Eisler.

In Paris, Eisler continued his propaganda activities begun in Spain. He provided material to the Freedom Station 29,8, penned articles for various illegal KPD publications intended for Nazi Germany, and otherwise wrote material on the orders of the KPD Secretariat. He once went to a ski hut on the Czech-German border and, along with Wilhelm Koenen (now the partner of Emmy Damerius), met with and gave instructions to KPD comrades who had crossed over from Nazi Germany. On another occasion, he went to Denmark and Sweden to bring KPD cadres political instructions for their work in Germany.[60] In the summer of 1937, Eisler also met his future wife, Hilde, in the illegal Paris office of Freedom Station 29,8. As Hilde, another longtime German communist, later wrote, "One morning [Gerhart] appeared in this office with a large pack of newspapers under his arm. He rummaged around the scraps of papers and newspaper cuttings in the various pockets of his suit and began to dictate to me an appeal for the struggle against Hitler."[61] Hilde was clearly taken with Eisler's rumpled appearance and rhetorical brilliance. Among German communists, at least, Eisler exercised a personal magnetism. Dahlem later wrote that his wife "Käthe admired Gerhart and, for good reason, thought very highly of him. She always said that he could, as a rule, enchant the world around him."[62] And Grete Keilson, a pre-1933 KPD member who eventually married the atomic spy Klaus Fuchs, recalled of Eisler in Paris: "Then as later he was really a sparkling fireball. He was gallant and charming but was also known for his sharp tongue."[63]

On August 23, 1939, Hitler and Stalin stunned the world by announcing a German-Soviet Non-Aggression Pact. Although this pact turned communist policy on its head, the KPD issued a declaration about the pact just two days later. In this declaration, written by Gerhart Eisler and Anton Ackermann, the KPD praised the Soviet "act of peace."[64] Many communists did the necessary mental acrobatics to make sense of Stalin's surprising move. Heinrich Rau, for example, who was now living in Paris and organizing relief for German refugees, wrote his wife in Moscow: "Here there is great excitement because of the Non-Aggression Pact with Germany! Understandable! The card houses, so nicely constructed, have fallen apart . . . [The Western powers] based their military conception on the notion that in the case of war [they would] steer the offensive thrust of Hitler-Germany towards the East." Rau continued:

But now Hitler has to ask for a Non-Aggression Pact . . . The dream of a crusade against Bolshevism is ruined . . . The whole policy [of Hitler and the Western powers] up to now has lost its basis. Why? . . . Because the Soviet

Union is so strong, Hitler does not dare armed conflict! Because the German people are so very against an attack on the Soviet Union, that Hitler cannot dare a "crusade against the East." Because the masses in all the democratic countries stand so positively toward the Soviet Union and so negatively toward Hitler-Germany, that the reactionary forces cannot dare an intervention on the side of Hitler against the Soviet Union . . . The Soviet Union, the German people, [and] the masses of all countries have achieved a victory, a great victory![65]

Other communists did not share Rau's enthusiasm for the pact. Indeed, this new twist of Soviet policy sowed confusion and disarray among the communist faithful. Hermann Duncker, who was in Paris but not party to the Secretariat's deliberations, wrote his wife on August 24: "The Treaty in Moscow weighs very heavily on my soul. But the play surely has *several* acts."[66] One month later, however, as Hitler and Stalin divided Poland between them, Duncker wrote his wife: "I am horrified about the new negotiations between Hitler-Stalin! I would *never* have thought *this* possible. That one had to live to see *this!* Won't anything wash away this mischief?!—An about-face of *all* values! *I* can't go along anymore with *this* dialectic!—One can never build socialism on the basis of *Hitlerism!* Oh, the devil!—I would never have thought *such* a turn of events possible. This is beyond *me!*"[67] Although many communists must have shared Duncker's disgust with the new Nazi-Soviet cooperation, few dared to express their feelings openly. Indeed, defending the Nazi-Soviet Non-Aggression Pact soon became a benchmark of communist loyalty; "waffling" on the pact, a sign of communist disloyalty. For all that communists defended the pact, however, they could not erase the fact that Stalin had joined hands with a communist archenemy, Hitler. The internationally acclaimed antifascism of the communist movement had been exposed as hollow rhetoric.

In just a few short years, German communists had been forced to change their most basic political viewpoints several times; moreover, each new Comintern line directly contradicted previous policy. In the early 1930s, the Comintern adhered to a "social fascism" doctrine; communists were told to revile social democrats and other leftists as the main pillars of bourgeois reaction. In 1935, however, the Comintern engaged in an abrupt turnabout. In the new united-front strategy, communists were to cooperate with the SPD and other bourgeois and leftist groups to battle the fascist menace threatening Europe. But in 1939, communists were once again expected to follow another about-face. They were now to cooperate with Nazi Germany against the so-called imperialist powers—the United States, France, and Great Britain. This last policy was particularly galling to many communists; after all, KPD members knew all too well the miserable fate of communists inside Nazi Germany. For German communists, the twists and turns of Comintern doctrine could not have been easy to follow with conviction, much less to defend with vigor. But follow and defend they did.

In the beginning of September 1939, just after the outbreak of World War II, Dahlem and his fellow Secretariat members made a decision that would have far-reaching consequences for their political careers. In the summer of 1939, the French government had stipulated that all male foreign refugees were to register with French authorities; failure to register was to result in deportation. The KPD Secretariat now had to decide whether male party members in France should comply with the law. The Secretariat knew that once German communists registered with the police, French authorities would know their whereabouts. Yet if German communists did not register, they would be living illegally in France—with all the drawbacks that that entailed. Within the Secretariat, Dahlem and Merker thought that KPD members should comply, while Bertz opposed the registration of KPD cadres. In any event, the Secretariat decided to urge KPD members to register. In his memoirs, Dahlem explained that it was unrealistic for the party to attempt to maintain itself illegally in France; moreover, he claimed that he had had the support of the French Communist Party in this decision.[68] In early September, almost all leading KPD officials in Paris appeared at the sports stadium at Columbes to register. Most, including Dahlem, were then held and later transferred to French internment camps. Gerhart Eisler, who was actually already under arrest—French authorities had picked him up just hours after he had written the KPD's commentary on the Nazi-Soviet Pact—soon joined his fellow KPD comrades in the French camps.

The Secretariat's decision, although perhaps well considered, ultimately proved disastrous for the party. Many of the KPD's leading officials in Western Europe were now locked away in isolated French internment camps. Anton Ackermann, who registered at Columbes but managed to avoid custody because of a medical condition, soon made his way to Moscow, where he reported on the actions of Dahlem's Secretariat. In August 1940, the members of the KPD Central Committee present in Moscow officially declared that "the foreign Secretariat made up of comrades Dahlem, Merker, and Bertz had liquidated itself." This declaration also pointed to other alleged political errors that Dahlem had made. Just before he had gone to register, for example, Dahlem had written the French premier, Edouard Daladier, asking that the KPD be allowed to continue its struggle against fascist Germany in France. This, the Central

Committee declared, "meant a support of the French government in its war against Germany" (at a time when the Soviet Union was cooperating with Nazi Germany).[69] Although this document was harshly critical of Dahlem, his Secretariat, and others who had worked with him, the Moscow KPD leadership did not take any measures against these party comrades. That would happen later—much later in East Germany.

THE YEAR 1939 marked the worst of times for German communists. Tens of thousands of KPD members were imprisoned in Hitler's jails and concentration camps. Inside Nazi Germany, there were only very small pockets of organized communist resistance. Among communists who had emigrated to the Soviet Union, most had fallen victim to the Great Purges. KPD leaders who survived the Purges were utterly dependent on the Comintern. The Spanish Republic, a beacon of hope for all antifascists, had fallen. The Spanish Civil War was lost. The KPD leadership in Paris had essentially walked freely into French internment camps. And all communists had to answer for the Nazi-Soviet Non-Aggression Pact. Some KPD cadres now jumped the communist ship and abandoned their political faith. But many others remained true to communism. Indeed, for many German communists, participation in the party's struggles during these years—whether inside Nazi Germany, in the Spanish Civil War, or in the Soviet Union or other countries—actually redoubled their commitment to the party and its cause. In the next years, German communists would face yet another set of trials in Hitler's concentration camps and in the far-flung centers of KPD emigration. And here, too, many would persevere in their loyalty to the party and its communist doctrine.

3

SURVIVORS

Communists during World War II

DURING WORLD WAR II, GERMAN COMMUNISTS FACED BOTH OLD and new challenges in their continuing antifascist struggle. Many KPD cadres who had served out their prison sentences in Nazi Germany were now transferred to the horrific world of Hitler's concentration camps. Karl Schirdewan and Fritz Selbmann suffered and survived the war years together in Sachsenhausen and then Flossenbürg concentration camps. Franz Dahlem, who was deported to Germany in 1942, endured several years in Mauthausen concentration camp. Erich Honecker, whose prison sentence was to end in 1945, spent the war years in Brandenburg Penitentiary. These KPD cadres were lucky to even survive; it is estimated that the Nazis murdered some twenty thousand German communists.[1] Other KPD members who had already escaped Nazi Germany spent the war years in Soviet or Western exile. In the Soviet Union, Walter Ulbricht and Fred Oelßner engaged in propaganda efforts to "reeducate" German prisoners of war who had been captured by Soviet forces. They also prepared for the communist takeover of Germany. Finally, in Britain and the United States, Emmy Koenen and Gerhart Eisler faced numerous challenges, including wartime internment and official anticommunist harassment.

By and large, the experiences of concentration-camp incarceration and Western emigration heightened the Stalinist proclivities of KPD cadres. This was not necessarily to have been expected. Indeed, Karl Schirdewan and some other communist concentration-camp survivors claimed later—after they had run afoul of the SED—that their camp experiences had set them apart from their more Stalinist comrades who had returned from Soviet exile.[2] They suggested that their camp experiences had made them more tolerant of other political views and more respectful of basic human rights. There is little evidence, however, that this was generally the case. At the same time, many scholars have argued that Western emigration tempered the Stalinist views of KPD cadres and made these party members more appreciative of bourgeois civil rights and parliamentary democracy.[3] But once again, this was often not the case. Nazi captivity and Western exile actually reinforced the Stalinist tendencies of German communists.

THE HISTORY of German communists in Hitler's concentration camps is a paradoxical tale of courage and complicity, solidarity and sordidness. In the camps, German communists endured all the privations of concentration-camp life: cold, hunger, sickness, exhaustion, beatings, torture, and the other dehumanizing techniques employed by their guards. They nonetheless organized many brave acts of resistance to the Nazi regime. They also practiced a model solidarity: comrades provided each other with extra food rations, easier work assignments, longer stays in camp sick bays, and spiritual support. German communists, however, engaged in a number of morally questionable practices to ensure their survival in the camps. They successfully vied with so-called Green prisoners (inmates imprisoned for criminal rather than political activities) for *Kapo* positions—positions of authority in camp administrative hierarchies. KPD cadres also upheld their Weimar-era party culture—sometimes with deathly consequences for party members alleged to have committed political infractions. The experiences of Schirdewan, Selbmann, and Dahlem in various concentration camps illustrate the choices and compromises that German communists made in their efforts to survive the Nazi regime.

Karl Schirdewan came to Sachsenhausen in 1939. There, according to his memoirs, he immediately felt the effects of communist solidarity. The man in charge of his barracks (the *Blockälteste*), a communist, warned him that he would soon be assigned to a hard-labor work company. But he reassured Schirdewan: "We will do everything so that you can get through these first difficult weeks reasonably well . . . We will do everything so as to get you out of this situation as soon as possible. We will try to get you assigned to another work company." And he continued: "As you have perhaps already noticed, there is great solidarity among us here." This solidarity, Schirdewan noted, "was not limited to words. Evenings when I came back to my barracks totally exhausted, comrades helped to bathe, apply ointment, and tie up my sore hands and feet. Especially in the first days, this help proved decisive." Fellow communists also supplemented Schirdewan's meager rations. And, as Schirdewan later remembered, "The concrete help for survival was only one side of the matter. Just as important was that feeling that our cooperative conduct radiated a considerable strength. I soon felt that this was the most important motivation [to persevere in the camps]."[4] When Fritz Selbmann arrived in Sachsenhausen in 1940 after years of solitary confinement, he too found "what had lived for seven years only in my thoughts, the party as a living community of like-minded individuals and their brotherly solidarity."[5] For Schirdewan and Selbmann, as for so many other communists, the material, political, and spiritual support offered by comrades made an intolerable situation somewhat bearable.

Although communist political activity was extremely dangerous, KPD members in Sachsenhausen continued to resist the Nazi regime. Any hint of clandestine activity reaching camp authorities could (and sometimes did) lead to punishment or even execution. Party cadres thus strictly followed the rules of communist conspiracy. They did not name an official party leadership in Sachsenhausen (although some respected party members—including Selbmann and Schirdewan—essentially occupied leadership roles). They masked their meetings as birthday celebrations. They carefully hid their communications and other equipment. And perhaps most importantly, they carefully scrutinized every individual party cadre who entered the camp. According to Schirdewan, "We informed each other of every individual, his conduct during hearings, in his trial, and in jail, in so far as such information was already available. Under conditions in which every word spoken in a wrong place could mean an agonizing death, such scrutiny was simply a duty."[6] Even in Hitler's camps, the ruthless investigation of party cadres' past biographies— a central feature of communist political culture—was practiced.

In Sachsenhausen, party members engaged in ongoing KPD controversies and, in the process, continued their factional politics of the Weimar era. There was, for example, a heated debate about the Nazi-Soviet Non-Aggression Pact of 1939. According to an autobiographical novel written by Fritz Selbmann in 1961, *Die lange Nacht* (The long night), a new communist arrival to the camp found party members deeply divided on the issue: "Arguing is no longer the word for it. Many of them have really become enemies."[7] Selbmann soon became a leading advocate of the position that the Non-Aggression Pact was simply a Soviet tactical maneuver. By contrast, other KPD members took the Nazi-Soviet Pact at face value. They insisted that British imperialism represented the greatest threat to the communist movement and that the Soviet Union would benefit from a war between the "imperialist" powers. Selbmann tirelessly badgered party members to adopt his views.[8] Schirdewan, who actually agreed with Selbmann, later castigated the tactics that Selbmann used in these inner-party conflicts. Schirdewan noted Selbmann's "violation of the respect and comradely solidarity with the simple comrades. His impatience toward those comrades who were honestly trying to find the right way and whom he repelled through his domineering, obstinate conduct. Not helping but dominating. This is how one could best characterize his personal conduct in the struggle for individual comrades."[9] Selbmann, however, later defended his actions: "It was impossible to think of positive [communist] work before such opportunism and reconciliationism had been overcome in the party. The altercations were pursued with the permissible sharpness given the conspiratorial conditions."[10] Selbmann and his political allies were convinced that only a correct political line—and the eradication of all other communist views—could maintain KPD cadres' morale and thus ensure communist survival in the camp.[11]

The KPD leadership in Sachsenhausen, just like the party leadership in other camps, was very eager to have communists placed in Kapo positions.[12] Although the SS camp hierarchy initially favored Greens, so-called Reds (leftist political prisoners) soon also came to hold these coveted positions. These functions, as Schirdewan noted, gave "real chances for the rescue of countless prisoners and for the creation of somewhat more bearable living conditions in the camp. We thus consistently used them in this manner." For the Kapos themselves, these supervisory positions generally involved privileges such as special access to food or other supplies. They also involved less difficult manual labor or even desk jobs in camp offices. In addition, Kapos were in a position to ameliorate the plight of others. They decided on individual camp work assignments and, on any given day, could excuse individuals from work. They were also involved in more immediate life-or-death decisions: they could strike individual names from transport or medical-experimentation lists. Communist Kapos thus often made the difficult decision to have a non-communist rather than a communist killed. Kapo positions could also be used to foment resistance activities within the camp. Schirdewan himself ran the camp library, a position that allowed him to mask various political writings as harmless volumes. Moreover, according to Schirdewan, the camp library "became a center of active resistance, where the exchange of information and the organization of conspiratorial and solidarity actions" took place.[13] Although Fritz Selbmann did not have a Kapo position in Sachsenhausen, he was saved by the decision of "friends" to have him work in the truck repair shop of the brickmaking commando; this was, as Selbmann noted, "not hard or especially dangerous work."[14]

The morality of occupying Kapo positions was hotly debated by communists and other inmates in the camps. Camp prisoners questioned whether taking on such functions helped to preserve the camp's brutal regime. Since the SS was heavily dependent on prisoner help in running the camps, Kapos were essentially aiding the SS in its miserable task. Other KPD members argued that communist Kapos, unlike their corrupt Green counterparts, were able to improve the situation in the camps for all prisoners. In his memoirs, Schirdewan argued that "our will to preserve as much as possible humane living conditions had a positive effect on all the prisoners."[15] Regardless of the moral price of taking on Kapo positions, KPD networks were tremendously successful in preserving the lives of party members: German communists had significantly higher survival rates than other camp prisoners.[16]

In October 1942, Schirdewan, Selbmann, and sixteen other communists in Sachsenhausen were taken to the camp prison, the "Bunker." They were placed in solitary confinement, in dark cells with no furniture save for piss pots. Schirdewan and Selbmann were cell neighbors and, according to Schirdewan, the two men communicated by knocking on the walls (Selbmann never mentioned Schirdewan in his memoirs since Schirdewan was persona non grata in East Germany when they were published).[17] Although they could barely see out of their respective windows, both men had cells that looked out onto the area where the SS flogged prisoners; agonizing screams of pain thus accompanied their sleepless nights. Eight weeks later, Schirdewan and Selbmann, along with the others, were awakened at night and given clothing. All assumed the worst—that this would be their last night. Instead, however, the men soon found themselves riding on a prison train across Germany, locked two-by-two into cells. Schirdewan and Selbmann shared one of these cells and had long and interesting discussions. Schirdewan later wrote that Selbmann was "versed in many areas and [was] also artistically talented." The two men discussed at length a three-act theater piece about Judas Iscariot that Selbmann had thought out; the play must have addressed the theme—and communist obsession—of betrayal. According to Schirdewan, "These conversations might seem under the given circumstances a bit absurd, but for us they were both an intellectual training and an effort to maintain dignity and an identity."[18]

Selbmann, Schirdewan, and the other men were brought to Flossenbürg concentration camp. SS leader Heinrich Himmler had ordered these Sachsenhausen communists to be moved to Flossenbürg as punishment "for building communist cells in the camp, organizing revolutionary work, and privileging political prisoners."[19] The eighteen men were distinguished by blue jar caps that they were forced to sew on to various parts of their camp clothing; they thus were named "Blue Points" *(Blaupunkte)*. Flossenbürg was known both for its harsh conditions (inmates quarried stone) and its Green dominance. But according to both Schirdewan and Selbmann, Green Kapos and prisoners saved the lives of the Blue Points. Schirdewan later wrote that "only the coincidence that we were known to a number of the 'Greens' as comrades who were absolutely reliable and ready to help all prisoners saved our lives. They had decided to protect us since we had saved many of their lives in Sachsenhausen in 1936 / 37."[20] The Greens provided the Blue Points with extra food rations and otherwise tried to improve their situation.

The Blue Points still faced tough times. According to Selbmann, initially he and the others "were imprisoned in dark bunker cells [they spent their nights in the camp prison], worked during the day in the most dangerous parts of the quarries, received only half of the regular rations, were given no socks or underwear even though the winters of the Upper Palatinate were tough, had to sleep on our plank-beds with wet clothes on rainy days, and had to go to work in these same wet clothes the following morning."[21] Selbmann was also forced by a sadist foreman to do all his work in the quarry at a running tempo. Schirdewan broke his foot when he and others inadvertently dropped a huge piece of stone. Eventually, however, their situation improved. Both Selbmann and Schirdewan came to work in the Messerschmidt airplane factory in the camp. There, Selbmann even became a Kapo supervisor, but his actions as a Kapo were controversial and, in the summer of 1945, would be the subject of a party investigation. Between Green help and their own solidarity, sixteen of eighteen Blue Points were able to survive Flossenbürg concentration camp.

LIKE SELBMANN and Schirdewan, Franz Dahlem faced a set of difficult choices and compromises in his odyssey through Nazi captivity. In June 1945, just weeks after his concentration-camp liberation, Dahlem wrote a thirty-five-page summary of his recent political activities for the KPD leadership; this document is quite remarkable for what it says about communist conduct in Hitler's concentration camps. After Germany invaded Poland in September 1939, Dahlem was interned by French authorities. He spent the next three years in the Vernet internment camp and in the Castres prison in southern France. In August 1942, the Gestapo demanded that Dahlem be sent to occupied France. From there, he was brought to Gestapo headquarters in Berlin. During the next seven months, Dahlem was questioned about his past political activities. He later wrote that although "there were often moments when the bureaucrats lost their patience and threatened to use other methods against me, in general I was treated properly and no physical force was used against me." He nonetheless began to suffer physically: "My health deteriorated rapidly in the damp cellar where we had no daylight. I was constantly hungry; the food was not bad, but there was too little of it and without the support of fortuitous friends [KPD networks also existed in Nazi prisons], I would have already gone under in the [Gestapo headquarters on] Prince Albrecht Street."[22] This Gestapo investigation ended without a trial and Dahlem, weighing just 105 metric pounds, was transferred to Mauthausen concentration camp in the spring of 1943.

In Mauthausen, Dahlem was immediately aided by his KPD comrades. On the day of his arrival, "In the evening, after the [work] commandos came back, Heiner [Heinrich] Rau, Jakob Boulanger, and other German comrades came and—thanks to their immediate help with medicine, with bread, and with margarine—I recovered my health and survived this difficult physical crisis." In the next weeks, Dahlem was given help by Green Kapos in the quarantine station. According to Dahlem, after the Germans lost Stalingrad, the Greens treated communists better since they feared that communists might rule in the postwar world: "As a former member of the Reichstag, and impressed by the many friends who visited me, I was now treated well. I was given secretarial work that meant that I could sleep at work and I received an additional portion of food." Dahlem added, "I immediately used this special treatment to help other comrades." Furthermore, he claimed that one of the Green Kapos, fearing for his future, "chummed up to me. I told him that so-and-so and so-and-so were my friends. He took these individuals out of their misery and they got an easier situation. For a long time, this bargaining with influential criminals was a tactical necessity for the rescue of our cadres." Dahlem thus made no secret of the fact that he had used his influence to rescue communist, but not other, inmates. After his period of quarantine, he was aided by Czech comrades who placed him in the technical department of the camp's construction bureau. He spent his remaining time in Mauthausen there and "since there was little guarding of the construction bureau, I mostly spent my time learning languages: French, Spanish, English, and later Russian."[23]

In Mauthausen, Dahlem helped to organize communist resistance. Since the camp was under Green dominance in 1943, communist political activity was no easy matter. As Dahlem wrote, "political work initially took place in the form of loose discussions on walks about events in the camp, military reports, and newspaper articles." Illegal communist activity also focused on solidarity work toward the sick, the weak, and the newly arrived. But Reds vied for Kapo positions and, as a result, came to occupy a number of positions in the camp secretarial office, in the office that determined work assignments, in the camp food warehouse, and in the depot where valuables were stored. According to Dahlem, conditions for the "preservation and rescue of our cadres got noticeably better. In a limited way, it became possible for us to help comrades with bread, with clothing, with shoes, with warmer blankets and so on; to have them assigned to better work commandos; to avoid having them sent away on 'suicide commandos' [jobs that entailed certain death]; to assign them to better barracks; to send comrades who were ill to the sick bay in barracks under our influence and to have them specially cared for there; and finally, to hide especially endangered comrades in the sick bay and to exchange their names with the names of the dead so that they could continue to live under a new number." In addition, Dahlem noted that "with the help of comrades who were secretaries or cleaners in the [camp's] political department or in the [camp] commander's office, it was possible to view files, to mislay papers or to have them disappear altogether . . . Thus it was possible—masked by the constant movement of tens of thousands of persons in and out of the camp—to obliterate traces [of individuals] and thus to accomplish the rescue of valuable cadres of different nations." Dahlem, however, made it very clear that such measures were extended only toward loyal communists: "Only the trustworthy comrades were included. The unreliable (Schwankende) or undisciplined [comrades] were dropped (abgehängt) and treated like other non-communist inmates."[24] As Dahlem's words suggest, party loyalty and discipline were prerequisites for physical survival.

Dahlem and other like-minded KPD leaders also began to introduce more conspiratorial, organized forms of communist activity. When Dahlem first got to Mauthausen, communists frequently stood around in little groups and exchanged information. According to Dahlem, this form of activity "was forbidden and a conspiratorial form of discussion among comrades about political questions was introduced." Party members were now divided into groups of three with one group leader. A camp leadership of three cadres, one of whom was designated secretary, was also formed; Dahlem generally spoke daily with the secretary. This form of political organization made it possible for KPD members to engage in more effective political work. At the same time, however, it placed communist cadres in a command-and-obey situation; there was little space for rank-and-file communists to pursue their own notions of communist activity. As Dahlem admitted, "The introduction of this form of organization did not take place without inner difficulties. There were comrades who wanted to know who made up the leadership, who understood their lack of knowledge [on this matter] as a sign of mistrust in them, and who spoke of inner-party democracy. But the argument that an undisciplined act by one individual was sufficient to bring a whole number of comrades to the gallows convinced even these comrades of the necessity of strict conspiracy." Nonetheless, as Dahlem noted, there were still comrades who were unwilling to go along with the new organization. The camp KPD organization thus took strict measures against them: "Comrades who did not maintain discipline or for whom this was inexplicable—there were some—were dropped and isolated."[25] Just as in other camps, KPD leaders and cadres in Mauthausen maintained their Stalinist political culture even in the face of Nazi inhumanity—a chilling reminder of the human propensity to answer persecution with persecution.

During the last months of the Nazi regime, communists in Mauthausen faced some new dilemmas. They feared that the SS would try to murder all of the camp's inmates—perhaps, according to Dahlem, by using poison gas at night. The various national communist leaderships thus formed an illegal military organization since, as Dahlem wrote, "we did not want to be killed like rats." Some foreign communists now pushed for an immediate armed uprising. But, as Dahlem noted, the illegal military organization did not even have weapons. The majority of the international communist leadership thus objected to an inmate uprising and none took place at this time. In the spring of 1945, Dahlem also faced a curious predicament. A member of the SS approached him and explained that he had lost favor with Himmler in 1943, had been deported to various concentration camps thereafter, and had ended up in Mauthausen. Early in 1945 he had been rehabilitated and was now working with the camp commander. This man believed that he might become head of the camp. He thus offered Dahlem a bargain. Dahlem and other communists would be given the opportunity to maintain order in the camp until the Americans or Soviets liberated it. In return, they were to guarantee that he, as an SS man, would not be beaten to death by camp prisoners. As Dahlem wrote, "I accepted, the party leadership agreed to this, and no other position was possible." In a sense, though, Dahlem had laid himself open to accusations of cooperation with the SS. In any event, the man never became camp commander.

Even as the Americans closed in on the area surrounding Mauthausen, camp authorities continued to shoot and gas thousands of prisoners. But relatively few communists were murdered at this time. This was because an Austrian communist, a cleaner in the camp's political department, had managed to remove a list containing the names of several hundred political inmates slated for execution. In early May 1945, as an American patrol unit neared the camp, the last of the Nazi guards left the camp. The illegal communist military organization now initiated an uprising.

Communists plundered the SS weapons depot and an international communist leadership ran the camp for some two days until the Americans arrived. Soon thereafter, Dahlem made his way to Moscow. As he wrote, "The international party leadership could go its ways with the proud consciousness that over 600 communists of various nations, including valuable cadres who, thanks to the systematic political educational work and the preservation of strict conspiracy [in the camp], could return to their countries as active, useful fighters."[26]

IN CONTRAST to Schirdewan, Selbmann, and Dahlem, Erich Honecker spent a decade in Nazi prisons, mostly in the Brandenburg-Görden Penitentiary. Although conditions in Nazi prisons were generally less extreme, jailed communists had many of the same experiences as their comrades in concentration camps. As soon as Honecker arrived in Brandenburg, for example, he felt the effects of communist solidarity: "[The illegal party organization] organized the decisive resistance, the solidarity, and the unity of the political inmates. In the beginning I was in strict solitary confinement, but soon after my arrival I noticed this solidarity. Secretly I was slipped a piece of bread, or I was whispered some information about the international situation, about the situation inside Germany, or about events that had occurred in the jail. That gave me strength and made it easier to endure solitary confinement. But I was especially strengthened by knowing that the party continued to live and fight behind jail walls." Given prison conditions, such solidarity was important for physical survival: "Not a few of the guards treated the political inmates with exceptional brutality. With regard to provisions, hygiene, and health there obtained, in part, catastrophic conditions. During all these years hunger was our constant companion. Many comrades died from tuberculosis and other sicknesses. But most terrible were the executions that took place in one of the jail's garages. Most of those who died there were our comrades, often good acquaintances or close friends."[27]

Just as in the camps, prison authorities depended on inmates to help run the jailhouse regime. A prisoner who took on a prison function was known as a *Kalfaktor.* Just like the camp Kapos, jailhouse Kalfaktors used their privileged positions to better their own and, if they wished, others' situations. Honecker held several Kalfaktor functions. Soon after arriving in Brandenburg, he became a Kalfaktor for the jail doctors. "For the illegal party organization," he noted in his memoirs, "our activity as Kalfaktors for the prison doctors cannot be underestimated. We could thus establish and maintain contacts between communists and other political inmates, convey news, and give help to those comrades who most needed it."[28] In particular, since he decided when prisoners received medical treatment, Honecker was able to arrange conspiratorial meetings in the doctors' waiting rooms. After some two years in this function, Honecker was assigned a new Kalfaktor position. He now delivered materials to prisoners who were to produce various items for German companies. As he made his rounds, Honecker was able to exchange information with fellow prisoners and to deliver items stowed in his delivery bags. In his memoirs, Honecker claimed that his activities as a Kalfaktor helped the communist resistance in the jail. According to some authors, however, Brandenburg prison inmates later recalled that Honecker was perceived as an isolated individual who did not use his Kalfaktor positions to help out his fellow communists: he did not show solidarity toward other imprisoned KPD members, he did not help to maintain communist prison networks, and he insisted that prisoners fulfill their work quotas exactly. These same authors, however, suggest that it is possible that Honecker, an important KJVD functionary, carefully masked his resistance activities so that other inmates would not be aware of his true role in the communist prison organization.[29]

From 1943 onward, Honecker, a trained roofer, was assigned to a work detail that repaired roofs and other structures after Allied bombings. Although such repair work was something of a suicidal mission, it did allow prisoners a degree of freedom. Indeed, in early March 1945 Honecker and a fellow communist were even able to escape their work detail. According to some sources, Honecker's flight caused consternation among communists still imprisoned in Brandenburg; as a result, in the summer of 1945, the KPD would investigate this escape. Strangely, after Honecker was unable to find permanent refuge in war-torn Berlin, he returned to his prison work commando in mid-April. And even more curiously, Honecker was not punished. Perhaps the Nazi authorities who now protected him hoped that he, in turn, would help them under a new Soviet regime.[30] In any event, when Soviet soldiers freed the Brandenburg Penitentiary in late April, Honecker was among those who walked out of the jail's gates. For Honecker, as for so many other German communists, the Soviet army was a true—and personal—liberator. As one perceptive observer has noted, the "trauma" of his incarceration did not make Honecker "skeptical of dictatorship, but instead deepened his loyalty to the Soviet Union, which had saved his life."[31]

THE POLITICAL mores fostered by communist cadres in Hitler's prisons and concentration camps reinforced the radical Stalinist values of German communists.[32] Communists practiced a model solidarity toward each other. But this solidarity extended only as far as the loyal communist collective. Just as in the factional squabbles of the Weimar-era KPD, communists deemed "renegade" were cast out of the communist collective. In the prisons and camps, however, being "dropped" by the party carried draconian consequences. Since physical survival often depended on the "extras" organized by solidarity networks, communist outcasts became candidates for death. Moreover, in the life-and-death situation that prevailed in the camps, KPD Kapos could and did "liquidate" wayward communists—those who broke with communism, those who challenged Soviet policy, and those who neglected the rules of communist conspiracy.[33] Furthermore, prison and camp conditions also precluded inner-party democracy; indeed, the rules of communist conspiracy demanded that discussion of communist tactics or doctrine be kept to a minimum. The prison and camp situation also reinforced the KPD's aggressive masculine ethos: only those who steeled themselves for survival persevered. Finally, the prison and camp experience allowed German communists to foster their sense of Leninist elitism. KPD members saw themselves as part of an avant-garde mission to rescue cadres for the coming world revolutionary struggle.

The brutal experience of Nazi persecution in Hitler's prisons and concentration camps also reinforced German communists' loyalty to the KPD and the international communist movement. There were many reasons for this. Hannah Arendt has argued that in the chaotic concentration-camp world, inmates adopted Nazi categories of identity. In the strict camp hierarchy, such categories "promised some last shred of predictable treatment." As a result, she asserted, "it is no wonder that a Communist of 1933 should have come out of the camps more Communistic than he went in."[34] Other authors have suggested that strong political convictions helped political prisoners to survive the camps. Jean Améry, a concentration-camp survivor, wrote that a prisoner's political belief was "an invaluable help" in confronting the camp ordeal. Those prisoners who subscribed to a political ideology "survived better or died more dignified deaths" than other, nonbelieving prisoners.[35] The psychologist Bruno Bettelheim, who was held in Dachau and Buchenwald in 1938–1939, argued that concentration-camp imprisonment raised political prisoners' self-esteem because "former members of radical leftist groups . . . found in the fact of their imprisonment a demonstration of how dangerous their former activities had been for the Nazis." Bettelheim also noted that "old prisoners," generally left-radical political prisoners, "would daydream of the coming world war and world revolution. They were convinced that out of this great upheaval they would emerge as the future leaders of Germany at least, if not of the world. This was the very least to which their sufferings entitled them . . . In their daydreams they were certain to emerge as the future secretaries of state."[36] KPD members were indeed sustained in the camps by their faith in the inevitable victory of communism. Moreover, from 1943 onward, Soviet military victories only intensified the seeming truth of their communist convictions.

Communist concentration-camp survivors did not emerge from their harrowing experiences with a deeper respect for political tolerance or parliamentary democracy. This was true even though they had been imprisoned by an antidemocratic regime and had encountered prisoners with a wide spectrum of political views. Pre-1933 KPD cadres had survived the camps not because they had practiced inner-party democracy, but precisely because they had not. Only a strict authoritarianism had allowed the party collective to survive the brutal concentration-camp world. Moreover, since pre-1933 KPD cadres had seen how ordinary Germans had tolerated the Nazi persecution of communists, they were profoundly suspicious of how the German population would use parliamentary democracy. As a result, as the historian Jeffrey Herf has argued, communists such as Franz Dahlem believed after 1945 that the "memory of past crimes implied justification for a second German dictatorship."[37]

WHILE MANY German communists fought to survive Hitler's prisons and concentration camps, other KPD members spent the war years in Soviet exile. Once Germany invaded the Soviet Union, these communists had to face the fact that the Nazi-Soviet Pact, which they had zealously defended, had proven shamefully hollow. Moreover, they were forced to recognize that despite their best efforts, communist resistance within Nazi Germany had failed to prevent Hitler from attacking the socialist heartland. KPD cadres now tried to make up for their party's past shortcomings by zealously aiding the Soviet war effort. Following Comintern orders, Wilhelm Pieck and Walter Ulbricht coordinated exiled party members' wartime work. German communists were deployed to analyze Wehrmacht troop information and to devise leaflets, radio programs, and a loudspeaker campaign to undermine the morale of the German forces. Ulbricht, for example, personally oversaw the German-language programs of Moscow Radio. He also visited many prisoner-of-war camps. There, in an effort to win over Wehrmacht officers and soldiers, he held political discussions and set up antifascist courses. During the battle of Stalingrad, Ulbricht and fellow comrades also drove trucks equipped with loudspeakers to the front and barked propaganda at the nearby German troops. This was dangerous work—Ulbricht and the others were within shooting range of the encircled Wehrmacht.

Initially, German communist propaganda efforts had little effect. German officers, soldiers, and prisoners of war remained loyal to Hitler and Nazi Germany and skeptical of, if not downright hostile to, the Soviet system.[38] As Wehrmacht losses mounted, however, German communists began to see modest successes in their reeducation efforts. In the summer of 1943, a National Committee for Free Germany (NKFD) was established. Spearheaded by KPD leaders, this committee included a small group of German officers who had agreed to cooperate with their communist captors. The committee's initial goal was to garner support among prisoners of war for the fall of the Nazi regime; eventually, the NKFD was to evolve into a communist-led umbrella organization encompassing the entire anti-Nazi political spectrum. To generate support among German prisoners of war, the committee employed patriotic slogans and, to the dismay of exiled German communists, appropriated the black, white, and red colors of Imperial Germany.[39] Many KPD cadres now worked on the committee's various programs. They also taught "anti-fa" reeducation courses to select prisoners of war who were enthusiastic about the antifascist cause. Some two to three thousand prisoners of war completed these courses annually; many of these individuals would come to occupy influential positions in East Germany.[40]

When the war began, Fred Oelßner was working for the German section of the Inoradio radio station in Moscow. In October 1941, he and many other KPD cadres were evacuated to Kuibyshev, a town on the Volga in the southeastern corner of the Soviet Russian Republic. There Oelßner, under the pseudonym "Larew," headed the German section of Inoradio and was party secretary of the German group at the radio station. This section broadcast propaganda aimed primarily at German prisoners of war. Once the war turned to the Soviet Union's advantage, Oelßner returned to Moscow. In February 1944, he was named to the KPD's twenty-person Working Commission that was to clarify "political problems in the struggle for the overthrow of Hitler and the creation of a new Germany."[41] This commission met eighteen times in 1944—regularly every Monday evening in Pieck's rooms in the Hotel Lux.

The Working Commission made extensive preparations for communist political activity in defeated Germany. It also formed the nucleus of KPD cadres who would initially administer Soviet-occupied Germany. For the commission, Ulbricht was responsible for the topic "The Political Leadership in New Germany."[42] Oelßner, along with Anton Ackermann, was charged with working on questions of "Economy (Deformations. Consequences)." True to form, Oelßner was among the most active participants in the commission's discussions.[43] In late 1944 and early 1945, the KPD leadership also organized a variety of schools and other meetings to prepare exiled German communists in Moscow for their return to Germany. As published party documents suggest, Pieck, Ulbricht, and the other German communists had every intention of using tactical cunning, ideological persuasion, and outright coercion to establish a communist dictatorship among an unwilling German population.[44]

Just like communists who had endured Nazi captivity, German communists in Soviet exile were reinforced in their Marxist-Leninist views by their wartime experiences. The imminent victory of Soviet armies convinced these communists of the truth of their political convictions. Walter Ulbricht even claimed that History had demonstrated that the KPD was the "only chosen" party "that could take over the leadership of present and future struggles" in Germany.[45] These German communists also came to believe that only a dictatorship—perhaps masked as a democracy—could ensure the end of Nazism. As their limited success among German soldiers and prisoners of war suggested, the German population was still hopelessly nazified; moreover, twelve years of merciless anti-Bolshevik propaganda had soured Germans on Soviet-style socialism. Finally, these KPD cadres believed that their experiences in Soviet exile had destined them to lead the revolution in Germany. They had just spent years at the fount of revolutionary wisdom and knew the latest developments in Marxism-Leninism. They were, they thought, the true Leninist avant-garde.

THOUSANDS OF KPD members spent the war years in Western exile: in France, Great Britain, Scandinavia, Switzerland, the United States, and Central and Latin America.[46] While scholars have long claimed that these German communists returned to postwar Germany less Stalinist than those communists returning from Soviet exile, closer examination suggests that such assertions merit reconsideration. German communists went to Western countries skeptical of bourgeois democracy and their experiences there often did little to alter their views. Even though these KPD cadres spent years working independently of Moscow's tutelage, they continued to adhere to Stalinist political methods. And although they often cooperated with noncommunist leftists or liberals, these interactions did not soften their political views. The actual experiences of German communists in Western emigration explain why Western exile rarely tempered KPD cadres' political views and mores. For communists,

Western emigration involved endless harassment from immigration authorities, a ceaseless struggle to find and hold legal employment, frequent observation by state surveillance agencies, and months or years of internment in enemy-alien or other camps.[47] In the United States, the anticommunist persecution of Gerhart Eisler even culminated in Eisler's imprisonment and forced appearance before the House Un-American Activities Committee (HUAC). Although much scholarly opinion argues otherwise, Western emigration often reinforced the Stalinist values of KPD cadres.[48]

The East German memoirs of Emmy Damerius suggest the ways in which German communists perceived, or at least chose to convey, their experiences in democratic countries. When Emmy arrived in Czechoslovakia in 1937, she joined a community of over three hundred active German communists. According to Emmy, although communist agitation was in and of itself legal, aiding the communist resistance inside Nazi Germany "had to be concealed from the Czech political police who were almost all hostile to communism."[49] Emmy, who decoded reports from KPD cadres inside Nazi Germany, worked under strict cover. But in February 1938 she was arrested by Czech police authorities who, it turned out, had long had her under surveillance. In her memoirs, she noted the prison conditions that she endured in "bourgeois-democratic Czechoslovakia": "The guard harassed us in the tone of an old Prussian penitentiary guard. I answered his furious screaming by asking just as loudly if we had come to a branch of a prison of the Hitler government. Two women had to sleep on one small plank bed in their coats. Hygiene in the cell was quite repulsive. Five women had to share one bowl, one can of water, and one bucket for the call of nature. The bugs did not allow us rest at night. Maggots swam in the soup."[50] Emmy's comments suggest that she saw distinct parallels between fascist Germany and democratic Czechoslovakia. She was, however, released after just five days of imprisonment.

Emmy did not solely focus on her political work in Prague. She also fell in love: "In the Fall of 1937, my life in Prague would fundamentally change. Since I did not know where my next party orders would lead me, my good sense told me not to tie myself to Wilhelm Koenen. But in the end, as a deep affection seized us both, my good sense dissolved into thin air. Our late, happy love accompanied our common struggle for the political goals of our party."[51] At the time, Wilhelm Koenen was the KPD Central Committee's representative in Czechoslovakia. Through her ties with him (they would eventually marry), Emmy joined the world of high-level KPD functionaries. After her short arrest, the party designated

Emmy Koenen. (Bundesarchiv, SAPMO-BArch, Bild Y 10-265/73)

Emmy as Koenen's secretary. Emmy and others now "reorganized Koenen's entire organizational-technical work in order to secure our activity from spies and the Czech secret police."[52] But neither she nor Wilhelm Koenen stayed in Prague much longer. Emmy left Czechoslovakia at the end of February 1939. She later learned that the Gestapo had come to arrest her at her last Prague quarters on March 16—the day after the Nazi takeover of Czechoslovakia.[53] Separately, both Emmy and Wilhelm Koenen managed to flee to England.

Once in England, Emmy and other German communists were subjected to endless British bureaucratic chicaneries. According to Emmy, "In daily practice, the various conditions that refugee status entailed was a burden for us. In the beginning, for example, I was not allowed to engage in any political activity, or to take up work. A condition for entry was that one would pursue ways of moving on to another country. That was also the reason why we were given permission to stay in Great Britain for only two to six months."[54] Emmy claimed that British officials undermined an ongoing operation to rescue hundreds of KPD comrades still in Czechoslovakia: "The anti-communist, pro-Nazi British government sabotaged the granting of entry visas in every way possible." Some 360 German communists nonetheless made their way to London by September 1939.[55] Emmy and other German communists were also placed under British government surveillance: "We were observed from morning until evening. Across from us two secret policemen moved into a sec-

ond floor [apartment] and pushed back the curtains. They openly photo-
graphed every one who went in or out of our house . . . Months later two
uniformed policemen appeared one evening and took away most of our
identity cards . . . Our experiences told us that this could only be a pre-
lude to more serious measures. In any event our activity was to be throt-
tled. Since we no longer had identity cards, we could not leave London."[56] Emmy and her fellow comrades were not imagining this surveillance; it is confirmed by other sources.[57] But the worst was still to come.

Just as in other Western countries, German communists were interned
in Great Britain beginning in May 1940; republican France, of course,
had interned KPD cadres in 1939 and Sweden and Switzerland would do
so in the early 1940s.[58] In her memoirs, Emmy described Wilhelm
Koenen's rude arrest: "Early in the morning on May 10 two men from the
political police stormily rang the door bell. We were forbidden to speak
with each other. The two officials' conduct was directly hostile. Both
watched as Koenen dressed himself. They didn't even let him go to the
toilet alone . . . Koenen was held by the arms and treated like a criminal
as he was led to a car."[59] Initially interned on the Isle of Man, Koenen was
soon transferred to a camp in Canada. At the end of May, Emmy was also
sent to an internment camp on the Isle of Man. She later complained
bitterly about this camp. She and fellow inmates, for example, wanted to
produce a camp newspaper. The camp commander first forbade any
such newspaper on the grounds that the camp's inmates were Nazis. The
women, however, argued that such newspapers were permitted in the
men's camps. They produced a draft version, and according to Emmy,
"the completed draft version was then rejected because the views of
those women who supported National Socialism had not been included.
After all, [the women were told] democracy prevails in Great Britain."
Similarly, women in the camp were permitted to give lectures to each
other, but not to hold follow-up discussions. As Emmy sarcastically
noted, "That too belonged to English democracy in the women's
camp."[60] Emmy's experiences in England heightened her skepticism of
British democracy; to her, bourgeois democracy symbolized the curtail-
ment of foreign communists' civil and other rights.

Emmy was released from internment camp at the end of February
1941. She was told that if she did not find work immediately she would
have to leave London. In four days, Emmy scoured seventeen factories in
search of work as a seamstress; she was finally hired by a factory that
made soldiers' uniforms. She now experienced the miserable work conditions that so many German-speaking refugees endured in Western exile.
Emmy was paid piece rates that "were not sufficient for me to eat my

fill." Moreover, she could only afford a mouse-infested attic room with a view of a bombed-out building.[61] After two months, however, her comrades found her new work. Emmy worked briefly at the National Council for Democratic Aid, an organization devoted to publicizing conditions in British internment camps. She had a personal stake in the matter since Wilhelm Koenen was still interned. For a time in 1941, Koenen tried to convince British authorities to allow him to leave Canada for Mexico. Emmy learned, however, that the British Interior Ministry refused Koenen permission for this. As she later commented: "That's how the much-lauded personal freedom of bourgeois democracy is in practice."[62] Koenen was finally released in England in the spring of 1942. Thereafter, Emmy and Wilhelm Koenen's lives improved immeasurably. Harry Pollitt, the general secretary of the British Communist Party, secured an administrative position for Emmy at Britain's largest left-wing publishing house, Central Books. Besides doing her regular job at the company, Emmy held political courses for company employees. Between 1940 and 1944, Central Books increased tenfold the number of works published. As Emmy later wrote, "I view my work in Central Books as my part of the party's struggle against Hitler's fascism."[63] While Emmy ended up having some very positive experiences in England, her memoirs suggest that she viewed her emigration to England through Stalinist blinders.

Wilhelm Koenen was a leading spokesman for the KPD in English exile. Along with other KPD cadres who would later enjoy prominence in East Germany—including Kurt Hager, Jürgen Kuczynski, Grete Wittkowski, and Siegbert Kahn—he helped found the Free German Movement in Great Britain in 1943. This movement was a British-based counterpart to the NKFD. Initially, these German communists were able to secure some SPD exile politicians' support for their cause. As it became clear, however, that the KPD would insist on promoting Soviet postwar aims, the Free German Movement collapsed. As in France in the mid-1930s, KPD cadres demonstrated that they would not tolerate views at odds with those of official Soviet policy in supraparty antifascist organizations. This, of course, severely limited their political appeal to other exiled German politicians and wider circles of British leftists.

Curiously, exiled German communists did occasionally deviate from Soviet orthodoxy—by accident rather than design. Cut off from Moscow, KPD leaders sometimes devised their own responses to ongoing political events, which sparked some rare, unsanctioned public communist debate. Wilhelm Koenen was a party to the most significant of these debates. He and Paul Merker, a high-level KPD functionary exiled in Mexico, exchanged public letters over the role of "progressive forces" in Germany at the end of the war. In this debate, Merker argued that although all Germans (even communists) bore responsibility *(Mitverantwortung)* for Nazi crimes, Germans should nonetheless be allowed to determine their own future. Koenen, on the other hand, thought that all Germans shared guilt *(Mitschuld)* for the Nazi terror. Since no effective resistance movement had emerged against Hitler, the German people did not have the right to shape the reconstruction of their nation.[64] In the next months, Merker's view turned out to more accurately reflect official Soviet policy. In any event, this display of political independence in Western exile did not translate into later political autonomy in East Germany; both Merker and Koenen toed the party line in the postwar period.

Paul Merker was the undisputed leader of the small KPD group in Mexico. A member of Franz Dahlem's Secretariat in Paris in 1938–1939, Merker had been interned in France in 1939 and had come to Mexico City in 1942. There he became secretary of the Latin American Committee for a Free Germany, the Mexican-based counterpart to the NKFD, and editor of a periodical entitled *Freies Deutschland* (Free Germany). Merker now repeatedly asserted his solidarity with the Jews and their plight; during the Nazi years, he was the only leading KPD official to do so.[65] But despite his unorthodox views on Jewish matters, he upheld the Stalinist culture of the KPD in exile. Merker kept a very tight rein on his fellow party cadres. He would not, for example, allow other party members to receive mail pertaining to their party activities. Instead, all letters went directly to Merker, who then decided which letters he would share with their addressees.[66] Similarly, Merker held the sole key to the post office box of the Free Germany Movement and refused others access to the box.[67] Merker also expelled party members whom he believed harbored renegade ideas. In the KPD group in Mexico, for example, a debate developed about whether communists should cooperate with German generals captured by Soviet forces—a moot issue for communists a continent away from the relevant events. Merker believed that communists should not cooperate with captured German generals, but Georg Stibi, another longtime German communist, thought that they should; Stibi's position was later adopted by the KPD leadership in Moscow. In the meantime, however, Merker had Stibi expelled from the party. He then set about isolating Stibi and his wife from other German communists. Steffie Spira, a well-known East German actress, later wrote: "For a long time [the novelist] Anna [Seghers] possessed a note that Paul Merker pushed under her apartment door after she had been at the Stibis. The note said roughly the following: 'Now I know where you go in defiance of party resolutions. I have observed you.' P. Merker."[68] Distance from the Soviet Union did not deter Merker from preserving the Stalinist party methods of the Weimar-era KPD.

GERHART EISLER'S experiences abroad perhaps best illustrate why Western exile did not alter German communists' political convictions. In 1939, along with many other German communists, Eisler was interned by French authorities. Eighteen months later, desperate to leave, Eisler took up the Mexican government's offer of asylum for those who had fought in the Spanish Civil War. Since there were no direct ships from Marseilles to Mexico, Eisler and his companion, Hilde, took a ship that was headed to Martinique; from there, they hoped to move on to Mexico. Along the way, however, their ship was torpedoed, and British authorities interned the couple and other antifascists in Trinidad. After some weeks, the two were allowed to continue on to New York where they were promptly confined to Ellis Island. Immigration authorities interrogated them to determine whether or not they should be granted transit visas. At this hearing, Eisler made a number of false statements. He claimed that he had never been in the United States (he had served as the Comintern's representative to the United States from 1933 to 1935), that he had never been married (he had already been married twice), that his only relative in the United States was his brother Hanns (his sister, Ruth Fischer, was also there), and that he had never been a member of any communist organization or sympathetic to the communist cause.[69]

At the end of the hearing, the couple was granted transit privileges, but the American government had issued an order forbidding Germans or Austrians transit or exit visas to Latin American countries. The couple was thus forced to stay on Ellis Island. After a three-month campaign by Eisler's American friends, the couple was granted permission to enter the United States. Although Eisler repeatedly requested permission to leave for Mexico, his applications were always denied and his permit to stay in the United States was regularly extended. In the next years, Eisler worked as a journalist in the New York City area. Under the pseudonym of Hans Berger, he wrote articles for left-wing periodicals; helped found the *German-American*, a newspaper devoted to fighting Nazi Germany; and in 1945, along with two other German communists, published a book, *The Lesson of Germany*, a history of modern Germany that ended with the German invasion of the Soviet Union.[70] Since his earnings were very meager, Eisler was given a monthly stipend of $150 from a communist front organization; the stipend was issued under a false name, Julius Eisman. While in the United States, Eisler married Hilde. It was Hilde who largely supported the couple by working in a factory and then in a kindergarten. Later on, she worked as an accountant.[71]

As soon as Nazi Germany was defeated, Eisler applied to return to Germany. The American government, however, refused him—along with a small group of other KPD cadres who had found refuge in the United States—permission to leave the country. Eisler and his comrades then turned to the Soviet Consulate in New York. Several months later, it was arranged that a Soviet ship would take these German communists back to Europe. Eisler and the others now received official exit permits. In mid-October 1946, Eisler was poised to leave the United States. He had even placed some of his luggage on the ship that was to take him back to Europe. A few days before the ship's scheduled departure, however, an ex-communist, Louis J. Budenz, accused Eisler of being a dangerous figure "who never shows his face. Communist leaders never see him, but they follow his orders or suggestions implicitly." Budenz soon added that Eisler was "the agent of the Kremlin who directs all Communist activities in the United States."[72]

Eisler's permission to leave the country was revoked and Eisler was put under FBI surveillance to ensure that he would not leave the country. He now gave a series of interviews in which he flatly denied Budenz's allegations. *Time* magazine reported that "in their [the Eislers'] almost bare $35-a-month New York City apartment, balding Gerhart Eisler spouted 'ridiculous . . . stupid . . . nonsense' at the idea that he was a super-secret agent of Kremlin policy."[73] Hilde Eisler was also drawn into the affair. As she wrote, "One morning I woke up and was suddenly the wife of a super dangerous 'Kremlin agent.' My name and picture was found in all the newspapers, with the whole ballyhoo that the American Press brings to such 'sensations.'" According to Hilde, "about six to eight FBI men are assigned to us, day and night . . . Two stand in the courtyard, two sit on the steps above our apartment . . . the others sit outside in two, sometimes three cars, ready at any time to put on their engines. When we leave the house, the employees of this great American educator J. Edgar Hoover come with us. When we go shopping, they stand right in front of the shop door and scare to death the owner, who likes to talk with us a bit. When we go to a restaurant, they sit down at the next table. When we go to the movies, they sit a row behind us. We recently decided that they should see something worthwhile for their money and so we went to the film 'Russia on Parade.'"[74] At the end of October, Eisler's well-known leftist lawyer, Carol King, wrote a letter to the FBI requesting that the surveillance be stopped. As King remarked, "It is a surveillance which I am sure you yourselves recognize is not in accordance with American democratic traditions of freedom and individual liberty. Secret shadowing would be objectionable and contrary to proper democratic practices. However, in the case of Mr. Eisler the interest of your Bureau is so obvious and notorious that even the casual bystander must be apprized of the situation. The result is to cut Mr. Eisler off from all normal human contacts as effectively as if he were under an armed guard." King personally guaranteed that Eisler would appear "before any agency of the government seeking his presence."[75] King's request must have had some effect. Overt FBI surveillance, if not the Bureau's harassment, ceased.

Convinced that Eisler was a serious threat to American security, the FBI was eager to see him behind bars. It thus fed the Justice Department various reports suggesting Eisler's illicit activities. Eisler was called to testify before the HUAC in February 1947. Just days before his scheduled testimony, a warrant for his arrest as an undesirable alien was issued. Consequently, Eisler was taken to Ellis Island and denied bail. On February 6, 1947 he appeared in front of the HUAC—as a federal prisoner. At this hearing, Eisler insisted that he read a short prepared statement before being sworn in. The committee forbade this. After some back and forth in which Eisler continued to refuse to be sworn in before reading his statement, a committee member made a motion that Eisler be cited for contempt. The motion carried and the chairman of the committee, J. Parnell Thomas, ordered Eisler to be taken out of the hearing. Eisler left. Thereafter, a number of individuals, including Budenz and Ruth Fischer, testified against Eisler. Budenz mostly testifed about Eisler's stint in the United States as Comintern representative in the mid-1930s. According to Budenz, Eisler essentially ran the American Communist Party. Budenz confirmed to a committee member that Eisler "was the power behind the scenes in that maneuver" that removed Earl Browder as head of the American Communist Party.[76] When a HUAC committee member intimated that the two Canadians believed to have tried to pass on atomic secrets to the Soviets may have conveyed this information to Eisler, Budenz readily agreed that this was possible.[77] Budenz thus not only accused Eisler of running the American Communist Party in the 1930s, but also implicated him in atom-bomb espionage for the Soviets in the 1940s.

Ruth Fischer's testimony against her brother was nothing short of shocking. Fischer claimed that Gerhart was a murderer and a terrorist. In the twenty years since she had broken with the KPD, Fischer had become violently anti-Stalinist. She thus abhorred her brother and his politics; indeed, the two had not exchanged a word since 1933. Fischer was even convinced that Eisler was somehow involved in the murder of her longtime partner, Arkadi Maslow, who had died under suspicious circumstances in Havana in November 1941. Fischer believed that after she had visited Hanns Eisler, their composer brother, Hanns had passed on to Gerhart information about Maslow's location; Gerhart, in turn, had tipped off Soviet security about Maslow's whereabouts and had thus made Maslow's murder possible. Eisler always denied any involvement with Maslow's death. Curiously, however, in a December 1946 radio interview in which he was asked about this death, Eisler lied about where he was in November 1941. He said that he was in a French concentration camp when, in fact, he had already been in the United States for six months.[78] While it is certainly plausible that Maslow was murdered by NKVD agents, no concrete evidence linking Eisler to this possible crime has yet surfaced. Fischer also believed that Eisler had played a role in the Auschwitz death of Paul Friedländer, her ex-husband and the father of her son. Fischer claimed that while interned together in France, Eisler had learned that Friedländer opposed the Nazi-Soviet Pact. Eisler then allegedly made sure that Friedländer was put on a special list that guaranteed his extradition to Nazi Germany. Eisler always claimed that he knew nothing about the circumstances of Friedländer's deportation to Nazi Germany.[79]

At the HUAC hearing, Fischer testified, "I consider Eisler the perfect terrorist type, most dangerous for the people of both America and Germany. The fact that this man is my brother has only given me a deeper insight in the technique of Stalin's NKVD and the terror system it imposes on the peoples of Europe. In a totalitarian party, all human relations are deteriorated; a man who serves Stalin is conditioned to hand over to the GPU [State Political Directorate] his child, his sister, his closest friend." She then continued: "Since I learned that Eisler was in this country I have been exposing him. He has used the sympathy of the American people for the suffering and tortured victims of nazism to mask his dirty work . . . In the inner circles of the Comintern, it is well known that Eisler has denounced to the GPU many Nazi refugees living in Moscow. He is particularly responsible for the death of the German Communist Hugo Eberlein, the leader of Eisler's own caucuses, and of Nikolai Bukharin, the great Russian theorist, his one-time friend and protector." As Fischer explained later in her testimony, "Eisler went in 1937 to Moscow, and he gave evidence against most of his friends, Eberlein and Bukharin. Not he alone, many others were taken there for the same purpose . . . But I regard Eisler as responsible not only for the death of these two outstanding men, but for many unknown little people who have been caught in the purge." Fischer also claimed that in January

1944 "I exposed [Eisler] as head of the Comintern activities in this country or, to put it better, as the head of a network of agents of the secret Russian state police." And she cautioned HUAC that "Eisler's presence in Germany will help to build up another Nazi system which will differ from the old one only by the fact that the Fuehrer's name will be Stalin."[80] None of Fischer's accusations against her brother have ever been proven. The two siblings never had contact again—although both lived into the 1960s.

The HUAC decided that the testimony on Eisler, which included several incriminating documents inserted into the official record, should be turned over to the Department of Justice. According to the committee, there was a clear prima facie case against Eisler for perjury, contempt of Congress, conspiracy to overthrow the government, income-tax evasion, and passport falsification. The committee requested that the Department of Justice take "immediate and positive steps . . . to prevent this dangerous alien from leaving the United States."[81] Eisler was accused of income-tax evasion for not paying income tax on his monthly $150 stipend in 1941 and 1942. The perjury charge related to Eisler's 1941 immigration hearing, as well as to the fact that in the 1930s he had used a fraudulent American passport that bore his photograph, but the name of Samuel Liptzen. Since the HUAC assumed that all communists were engaged in a conspiracy to overthrow the government, Eisler was charged on this count as well. On February 18, Richard Nixon, then a junior HUAC member and a freshman congressman from California, made his maiden speech in Congress—on none other than Gerhart Eisler. Nixon made the case for a contempt of Congress citation against Eisler, calling him "an arrogant, defiant enemy" and "principal character" in "a foreign-directed conspiracy whose aim and purpose was to undermine and destroy the government of the United States."[82] The citation passed the House 370–1.[83]

Eisler now became something of a cause célèbre for the American left. He was freed from jail after ten weeks on $20,000 bail.[84] But in the spring of 1947, he still faced two separate criminal proceedings. In June, Eisler stood trial on the contempt of Congress charge; he was sentenced to one year in prison. A month later, Eisler stood trial on charges of perjury; he was sentenced to a jail term of one to three years. Eisler appealed both decisions. In November 1948, the Supreme Court granted his petition for certiorari and agreed to hear his contempt case—an important test case of HUAC's power to force reluctant witnesses to talk about their political views. By then, Eisler had also been arrested by the Immigration and Naturalization Service in connection with deportation proceedings. He was once again held on Ellis Island for three months and won his release only by initiating a hunger strike. As the American historian Ellen Schrecker has noted, at this point "the government wanted him deported but would not let him go."[85] Or, as Eisler himself told a judge, "It is a crime for me to leave this country and a crime to stay here. It is difficult not to write a satire, a very bitter satire on all of this, your Honor."[86]

Eisler's difficulties only mounted. Eisler found himself increasingly isolated from American leftists who felt vulnerable in the face of the violent anticommunist paranoia sweeping the country. He had a hard time making ends meet, and to secure funds, he took to the lecture circuit. He often found, however, that meeting halls were denied him or that college administrators would not allow him on campus. The Eisler couple was also homeless; neighbors' harassment had forced them out of their most recent apartment. The couple was thus living out of suitcases as guests in other people's homes. Finally, according to FBI suspicions, Hilde was having an affair with her Russian teacher.[87] In February 1949, Eisler nonetheless tried to be nonchalant about his precarious situation. As he wrote his brother Hanns and his wife, "We are still forced to live with this craziness—luckily I have gotten used to it."[88]

Eisler was actually desperate to leave the United States for East Germany. As he wrote to Paul Merker, who was already there, "What most annoys me is not the dirty tricks of the scoundrels here—one is used to such things—but the fact that I can't be with all of you where I could be more useful than here."[89] The East German leadership, however, was able to do precious little for Eisler. In 1947, it had planned a "help campaign" for him: it intended to hire a lawyer to help Carol King, to seek aid for Eisler from the Berlin Jewish community, to publicize Eisler's plight to foreign journalists, and to publish articles in the East German press about Eisler's predicament.[90] The SED co-chairman, Wilhelm Pieck, had also written the Soviet political advisor in occupied East Germany, Vladimir Semenov, asking for advice and questioning whether diplomatic channels might be used to free Eisler.[91] In November 1948, however, a high-level SED official noted that the "campaign for Gerhart has, with the exception of a few press notices, again petered out."[92] At this time, Pieck, once again reminded of the case, wrote the head of the East German education administration to arrange for a lectureship for Eisler at the University of Leipzig.[93] He also wrote Eisler, reassuring him that "my wishes absolutely match yours—that as soon as possible you help us here in Germany with the enormous work that we must achieve for a political transformation."[94] Despite Pieck's actions, nothing happened.

Eisler finally decided to take matters into his own hands. As the Su-

Gerhart and Hilde Eisler on their triumphant arrival in
East Germany, Berlin, June 1949. (Bundesarchiv, SAPMO-
BA, Bild Y 10-181/00)

preme Court was deliberating his case in May 1949, Eisler disguised himself as a blind man and purchased a twenty-five-cent visitor's ticket to
board the *Batory,* a Polish ship headed for Europe. Eisler stayed aboard
as the ship sailed out of New York harbor. Once safely out of American
territorial waters, Eisler asked the captain to inform Polish authorities of
his presence aboard. Eisler's escape from the United States soon became
known and when the ship made its planned landing in England, he was
arrested. After four weeks' detention in England, he was nonetheless allowed to fly on to Czechoslovakia. From there, he went to East Germany;
he was greeted as a hero come home.

Was Eisler guilty of the charges leveled against him? Eisler's conduct
seemed incriminating. Over and over again, he proved himself an invet-
erate liar. Why were the lies necessary? Eisler was known to have assumed a number of aliases—"Julius Eisman," "Edwards," "Hans Berger,"
and "Samuel Liptzin." Why were they needed? Eisler's refusal to testify
before HUAC also did not help his case. If he was the innocent refugee

that he claimed to be, what did he have to hide from the committee? Yet although Eisler appeared to be a murky, suspicious figure, there is no reliable evidence that he was involved in Soviet espionage, Comintern work, or running American Communist Party activities in the 1940s. Although Eisler readily admitted to SED authorities that he had helped the American Communist Party to implement Comintern decrees in the 1930s, he mentioned no similar activities in the 1940s.[95] Indeed, for whatever reason, it seems that he had been cut off from his Soviet ties while exiled in the United States. The main charge against him in the 1940s—that he was the Kremlin's "Red Boss" in the United States—appears to be completely unfounded. Eisler was a relatively innocent victim of a virulent Cold War anticommunism.

Eisler's nightmarish stay in the United States did little to convince him of the benefits of "bourgeois democracy." Just like other KPD cadres in Western countries, Eisler saw that Western democratic systems did little to protect the civil rights of German communists. To a certain extent, wartime exigencies exacerbated this situation; many Western countries believed that to effectively prosecute the war, German nationals had to be interned or otherwise limited in their freedom of movement. At the same time, most Western governments, as well as Western citizens, believed that communists posed a genuine threat to their democratic orders. Communist harassment—whether by employers, government authorities, or individual hecklers—was thus widespread. Communists were also vilified in the media. In one article about Eisler, for example, the author wrote that as a "professional revolutionary, Moscow model," Eisler was "almost a separate species of mankind."[96] And a classic Cold War film, *I Was a Communist for the FBI,* featured an actor who portrayed Gerhart Eisler as a menacing foreigner who controls the American Communist Party.[97] Given the harassment and bad press that he and other KPD cadres faced, it is hardly surprising that Eisler told a *Time* reporter, "Ah, believe me, it is not a pleasure to be a Communist in this country."[98]

For German communists, Western emigration was surely less traumatic than imprisonment in Nazi Germany or emigration to the Soviet Union. But the experience of Western exile nonetheless hardened many German communists' political views. Isolated on foreign soil, far from their revered KPD and Soviet leaders, and perhaps feeling guilty that they were not sharing the extreme persecution of their fellow comrades inside Nazi Germany, exiled KPD cadres clung to their one certainty: the party and its doctrine. At the same time, Western exile did not incline German communists to look kindly at bourgeois democratic systems. Indeed, when these KPD exiles finally returned to East Germany, they were often the ones who made the most scathing remarks about "so-called bourgeois democracy." Western emigration also generally did not make German communists more open to alternative political views, the protection of civil rights, or even reform socialism. On the contrary. It exposed them to "the class enemy"—and communists did not like what they saw.

THE GERMAN communists who survived the Nazi era came to Eastern Germany with a deeply felt belief in the correctness of their communist practices and convictions—which, after all, had allowed them to survive the ordeal of the Nazi years. As Karl Schirdewan wrote much later, "Despite all the suffering and all the dangers that I had experienced, my worldview had been strengthened."[99] Regardless of whether they had been in Soviet or Western exile or in Hitler's prisons or concentration camps, KPD cadres espoused a hard-edged Stalinism. Their excruciating experiences had left them tough and inflexible. They had often even lost their sense of humor; Erich Gniffke, an SPD politician in Eastern Germany, later wrote that "during his long prison years, [Franz Dahlem] had forgotten how to laugh."[100] Pre-1933 KPD cadres emerged from the Nazi era with a deep sense of a world divided into fascists and antifascists, communists and anticommunists, persecutors and the persecuted. They believed that they were the revolutionary elect, the avant-garde uniquely able and deserving to govern a socialist Germany; after all, they had seen their political views borne out by History—triumphant Soviet armies had marched into Central Europe. At war's end, armed with Stalinist values, a Manichean view of politics, and a profound sense that communism represented the future, pre-1933 KPD cadres set out to rule Eastern Germany. During the next forty-five years, they would tenaciously cling to the values and political lessons that they had learned during the Weimar and Nazi eras. They would apply these views to their rule of East Germany and, in the process, fundamentally shape the character of GDR politics.

4

VICTORS

The Founding of East Germany

IN THE SPRING OF 1945, ALLIED ARMIES SWEPT INTO GERMANY. ALL over Hitler's Third Reich, pre-1933 KPD cadres—hungry, haggard, and often hovering near death—were liberated from Nazi prisons and camps. They were now desperately eager to begin political work. As Heinrich Rau, who had been imprisoned with Franz Dahlem in Mauthausen, wrote his wife in Moscow shortly after his liberation: "The Red Army has given us life and freedom, now we want to usefully manage this precious property in the interest of our ideals, the ideas of Marx, Lenin, and Stalin. Hopefully we will soon have the opportunity to do this."[1] More than a decade of Nazi imprisonment had not dampened communists' enthusiasm to promote their political cause. Indeed, long years of political inactivity had only heightened the desire of German communists to work for their political ideals.

The end of World War II ushered in a new and profoundly different era of German communism. Veteran communists no longer belonged to a fringe oppositional movement subject to brutal torment. Instead, in close concert with Soviet authorities, they came to rule a substantial proportion of the German population. Pre-1933 KPD cadres began their political work in a Germany that was defeated, occupied, and partitioned. Approximately one-third of the country, the northeastern third, came under Soviet occupation. This area became the Soviet zone of occupation (SBZ) and was run by a Soviet occupation authority (SMAD), headquartered in Karlshorst, outside of Berlin. In the next weeks and months, longtime communists worked alongside SMAD officials to create municipal order in war-torn Germany, to initiate land reform and the nationalization of industry, and to begin denazification proceedings in Eastern Germany.

The emergence of a socialist East Germany was only possible because World War II had given birth to a new European reality: the Soviet Union had become a dominant continental power. But this new Soviet role did not go uncontested. The Soviet Union and the Western powers now vied over Europe's future socioeconomic order. Despite, or because of, rising Cold War tensions, longtime KPD cadres pushed ahead to forge a socialist regime in Eastern Germany. The founding of East Germany was the final chapter of the heroic communist trajectory that stretched from 1919 into the early 1950s. For veteran communists, the *Aufbau* (reconstruction) period was a time of enormous enterprise, immense personal sacrifice, and heady political activity. In addition, it was an era of great social and political mobility; in just a few short years, veteran communists, reviled and persecuted in Nazi Germany, came to occupy the corridors of power in the new socialist Germany. Yet it was also a period when many longtime communists faced career and other setbacks, when veteran communists jockeyed for political position and engaged in bitter personal rivalries, and when—to the extent necessary—the KPD / SED reimposed communist orthodoxy on its longtime cadres. And finally, it was a time when many veteran communists learned that their party suspected them of political deviance or otherwise found them wanting.

EVEN BEFORE the end of hostilities, three groups of ten communists each had been flown into Western Poland from Soviet exile. These groups were to direct communist activity in the SBZ. At the end of April, Walter Ulbricht and his "Ulbricht Group" made their way to Berlin. At the beginning of May, Gustav Sobottka headed a group to Mecklenburg, while Anton Ackermann led a group to Saxony; Fred Oelßner belonged to the "Ackermann Group." In the next weeks and months, communists who had spent the war years in Nazi-occupied Europe made contact with these former Soviet exiles. Erich Honecker, freed from Brandenburg Penitentiary at the end of April, found the Ulbricht Group on May 10. Fritz Selbmann, after a death march from Flossenbürg to Dachau concentration camp and a two-week journey back to Leipzig, established contact with the Ackermann Group as soon as Leipzig was turned over to Soviet occupation authorities at the beginning of July. Franz Dahlem, who had made his way from Mauthausen to Moscow, flew back to Berlin with the KPD chairman, Wilhelm Pieck, on July 1.

Dahlem, now once again a top KPD functionary, was charged with overseeing the party's personnel department. As a result, many veteran communists, after finally reaching party headquarters in Berlin, first met with Dahlem to discuss their future work. Karl Schirdewan, who almost died from disease and exhaustion on a death march in April, came to Berlin in the summer of 1945. As he later recalled: "[Dahlem] took lots of time for a detailed exchange of ideas with me . . . Of course, my future work soon became the focus of our conversation. Franz asked me about what I had in mind, and then he said: 'Everything is open to you—the party apparatus, the economy, the press!' I said that I wanted to work in the area of direct party work . . . He then offered me a leading position in the Department for West [German] Affairs in the executive party bureaucracy."[2] For veteran communists, the new era seemed to offer boundless opportunities.

All too soon, however, pre-1933 communists realized that their possibilities were tempered by the reality of postwar Germany. Both former Soviet exiles and those who had survived Nazi captivity were shocked by the wasteland of destruction. As Willi Bredel, a novelist and former Soviet exile, wrote his companion back in Moscow in May 1945: "I live in the villa of a Nazi big-wig and am sitting in the sunshine of a German May, writing you. All around me it is dreadful. Ruins, pain, refugees in flight."[3] Dahlem later recalled the bird's-eye view that he had had as his airplane descended into Berlin: "We saw a ghost city with skeletons of burned-out houses and mountains of stone ruins, over which towered iron girders twisted by fire—the center of Berlin."[4] Veteran communists, however, were even more dismayed by the moral and ideological ruin that they found among the German population. When Karl Schirdewan told a man that he had been sentenced by the Nazis and had therefore just come from a concentration camp, the man responded: "I won't give communists anything!" In his memoirs, Schirdewan commented: "I had not thought it possible that there were still people who refused simple help to those against whom they bore so great a share of guilt."[5] Fred Oelßner also later recalled the prevalence of Nazi prejudice. In May 1945, Oelßner, working for SMAD, ordered a printer to come with him to another city so as to produce a newspaper. The printer's family became distraught, apparently convinced that the man was destined for Siberia. Although Oelßner told the family otherwise, "the Nazi poison was stronger than my arguments." Through such encounters, veteran communists were confirmed in their view that the German population was hopelessly nazified. Such episodes only reinforced their belief that they were outsiders among their fellow countrymen. As Oelßner wrote: "At this time our first and greatest ideological task was to bring people back to reasonable thinking so as to gradually entrust them with socialist ideology. This task occupied us for years."[6] The gulf that had separated communists from other Germans had widened considerably during the Nazi era.

ON JUNE 11, 1945, the KPD presented the German people with an "Action Program." This program appeared to mark a radical departure from

Weimar-era KPD politics. It contained no reference to the "dictatorship of the proletariat" or to "Soviet power for Germany." It made no reference to Marxism-Leninism, communism, or even socialism. Instead, the program upheld private industry and property and explicitly rejected a policy of "forcing the Soviet system on Germany." It also called for the "establishment of an anti-fascist, democratic regime, a parliamentary-democratic republic with all democratic rights and freedoms for the people."[7] This moderate program was intended to allay fears that the KPD planned to install a Soviet-style regime. At the same time, however, party cadres pursued policies that were intended to ensure eventual communist control. The Ulbricht Group, for example, named bourgeois or social democratic activists as mayors of Berlin's various precincts, but placed veteran communists in jobs that involved personnel, police, and education. As Ulbricht reportedly told another member of the group: "It's quite clear—it's got to look democratic, but we must have everything in our control."[8]

Even before they had returned from Moscow, KPD leaders were suspicious of communists who had remained inside Germany during the Nazi era. These party cadres, they thought, had to "overcome the political backwardness that had resulted from many years of isolation in concentration camps and jails and through the ideological autarky of fascism."[9] Once in Germany, KPD leaders found their suspicions confirmed—especially among veteran cadres who had not belonged to communist leadership circles in Nazi camps and prisons. These communists had not been able to follow the twists and turns of wartime KPD politics and, as a result, the Ulbricht Group reported, often held "sectarian" views: they failed to staff municipal offices with noncommunist antifascists, advocated revolutionary forms of workers' control, cast a more radical light on the KPD's Action Program than was warranted, and found it hard to accept that the party now supported the continuation of the capitalist order in Germany.[10]

KPD leaders insisted that the KPD and the SPD should be reestablished as separate parties. They claimed this was necessary for "ideological clarification" in both parties, but they were actually concerned that former social democrats might gain the upper hand in a hastily formed workers' party. Inside Nazi Germany, however, some veteran communists had cooperated with social democrats in resistance groups or captivity and, as a result, advocated the immediate formation of a single working-class party. Numerous longtime communists who had stayed in Nazi Germany were also dismayed by Soviet occupation measures, including widespread stealing and looting, the rampant rape of German women, and the dismantling of East German factories for transport to the Soviet Union. In the summer of 1945, "sectarian" and otherwise unacceptable views among longtime communists were prevalent throughout the SBZ.[11]

Despite this widespread "sectarianism," Ulbricht and other KPD leaders need not have been so concerned about the political reliability of "home" cadres. Once most veteran communists heard the new party line, they were eager to adopt and defend it. As Gustav Sobottka reported at the end of May 1945: "We still find groups of party comrades everywhere . . . Many of them were imprisoned in conc[entration] camps. As far as possible, we have tried to convince the comrades of the correctness and importance of our current line. The comrades were delighted and understood the political tasks. Only a few isolated individuals believed or rather still held sectarian views and believed that they had to begin where they left off in 1933."[12] This is hardly surprising. Veteran communists had long been accustomed to changing their political views according to party dictate. Moreover, they had just seen how Soviet armies had triumphed in the greatest war ever fought—proof of the superiority of Soviet-style Marxism-Leninism. Many also owed their lives to a timely liberation by Soviet forces. And finally, after years in the political wilderness, these communists were more than eager to participate in the forging of the new Germany. They were not going to quibble about the party's ideological program. As a result, as one recent historical study has argued, "by the late autumn of 1945 the KPD had regained something of the discipline and cohesion which it had possessed during the Weimar years."[13]

The KPD leadership was even more suspicious of communists who had emigrated to Western countries. Even though loyal communist cadres were desperately needed in the SBZ, many "West émigrés" waited on packed suitcases for months or even years before they returned to Eastern Germany.[14] These exiled communists always thought that it was their host governments that prevented their speedy return; they assumed that they were held in exile so as to deprive Eastern Germany of valuable cadres for the Aufbau project.[15] According to Emmy Koenen, who returned to the SBZ in December 1945, many other KPD cadres remained in England as late as 1948 due to the "sabotage" of the British government.[16] While this was sometimes true in the first postwar months, it was rarely so after 1945—except, of course, in the case of Gerhart Eisler. Instead, it was Soviet and East German communist authorities who prevented the return of communist cadres to the SBZ. In 1946, for example, Heinz Schmidt, a veteran communist who was organizing the return of KPD cadres from England, privately complained to Franz Dahlem that Soviet officials had revoked a collective entry permit for some three hundred exiled antifascists and their families (many of whom were veteran communists). Antifascists were now to apply individually, but as Schmidt noted, two months had passed "without even a single entry permit having arrived here." Schmidt then commented that "no meeting with English authorities now passes at which they do not respond to our repeated requests for [exit] permits with a mocking comment about the delay of Soviet permits."[17] Similarly, in 1947, Walter Janka, a former émigré in Mexico, wrote of meeting Grete Keilson, a veteran communist who dealt with party personnel matters, about individuals (including longtime communists) who were abroad and eager to return to the SBZ: "Today Keilson declared that she first needed to carefully check every individual case . . . To my objection that we had no reason to be petty in the granting of visas, Keilson declared: 'As a party we have no interest in fetching back all sorts of people, but rather we must check and answer for every case, otherwise we'll have a situation in which people will sit around and we won't know what to do with them.'"[18] Although Keilson's reported remarks suggest that the SED leadership would have happily left pre-1933 KPD cadres abroad, almost all veteran communists who wished to return to East Germany from Western exile had done so by 1950.

IN APRIL 1946, the KPD and SPD were merged together into one party, the Socialist Unity Party, or SED. SMAD authorities insisted on the merger of the two leftist parties in order to bolster the KPD's waning popularity; the joining of the two parties was to channel the SPD's growing popular support toward the communist cause. This merger, however, was only achieved through coercion and was much resented—particularly by the SPD rank and file.

The founding of the SED was another step of the Soviet project to establish communist dominance throughout East Central Europe after World War II. A series of events now heightened tensions between the Soviet Union and the Western powers. In 1947, the United States created the Marshall Plan to aid European economic recovery; the Soviet Union, however, forbade the participation of East Central European countries. In February 1948, a communist coup in Czechoslovakia further worsened East-West relations. That same year, the Soviet Union began the Berlin Blockade; it hoped to absorb West Berlin, cut off from its Western ties, into the SBZ. In response, Great Britain and the United States initiated the Berlin Airlift. In an eleven-month operation that symbolized Western resolve to halt the encroaching Sovietization of Central Europe, millions of tons of supplies were flown in to maintain the Western sectors of the beleaguered city. Seeing little prospect for a united, democratic Germany, the Western Allies decided to establish a provisional West German state in September 1949. Stalin soon followed suit, and the SBZ was transformed into the GDR on October 7, 1949. The founding of the two Germanys, however, did not end Cold War tensions. Quite the contrary. In 1950, the Cold War even became hot—in a proxy war fought in Korea.

In Eastern Germany, veteran communists dominated the political system. At the SED's founding, the roughly sixty thousand pre-1933 communists—also known as "Old" Communists—made up less than 5 percent of the party's 1,280,000 members.[19] Precisely because their numbers were so relatively small, pre-1933 communists enjoyed undue influence within the SED.[20] The forerunner to the Politburo, the Central Secretariat, included seven former KPD members, all of whom were veteran communists, and seven former SPD members.[21] In the next years, in keeping with developments throughout East Central Europe, the SED declared itself to be a "Party of a New Type," that is, an orthodox Marxist-Leninist party in which discussion, much less opposition, was no longer tolerated. Many former social democrats were hounded out of the party. As a result, by 1950, seven of nine full members of the Politburo were veteran communists, as were five of six candidate members.[22] This numerical dominance of pre-1933 KPD cadres in the Politburo continued into the 1960s. In 1954, for example, 7 of 9 Politburo members were Old Communists; in 1958, 10 of 13 were veteran communists; and in 1963, 11 of 14 were pre-1933 communists.[23] The same was true of the Central Committee: until the mid-1960s, veteran communists made up over half of all full Central Committee members.

The influence of pre-1933 KPD cadres spilled well beyond the SED's highest leadership bodies. In the emerging bureaucracies of the East German state, Old Communists held many of the most influential positions. In the Ministry of State Security, for example, among the top twenty-seven leadership positions, twenty-five were initially held by pre-1933 communists.[24] Similarly, in the Ministry of Foreign Affairs, high-ranking positions (with the exception of that of foreign minister) were at first held almost exclusively by veteran communists.[25] Pre-1933 communists also served as longtime chairmen of the East German puppet parties formed in the late 1940s. Lothar Bolz chaired the NDPD, a party set up to integrate former Nazi party members into the East German system, while Ernst Goldenbaum chaired the DBD, the peasants' party. An Old Communist, Kurt Krenz, headed the Domowina, an organization that represented East Germany's small Sorb minority. Veteran communists also held numerous leading positions in many other areas of society. They

Colleagues, rivals, protégés, enemies: the SED Politburo elected on July 25, 1950. From left to right: (sitting) Hans Jendretzky, Otto Grotewohl, Wilhelm Pieck, Walter Ulbricht, Franz Dahlem; (standing) Erich Honecker, Erich Mückenberger, Anton Ackermann, Heinrich Rau, Wilhelm Zaisser, Hermann Matern, Fred Oelßner, Rudolf Herrnstadt. All but Grotewohl and Mückenberger belonged to the pre-1933 KPD. Berlin, 1950. (Bundesarchiv, SAPMO-BArch, Bild Y 10-36483)

ran factories, set up radio stations, directed public transportation systems, organized health care services, started up theaters, headed publishing houses, managed museums and archives, presided over academic and other institutes, and served as editors in chief of numerous newspapers and periodicals.

ALTHOUGH LONGTIME communists exercised great power in East Germany, they never led extravagant lifestyles there. They did, however, enjoy some privileges. Virtually all veteran communists had the official status of "victims of fascism" or "persecuted by the Nazi regime"; these two terms were used synonymously, although the former gradually gave way to the latter.[26] As early as May 28, 1945, the Berlin magistrate's office decreed that recognized "victims of fascism" were to receive a one-time payment of 450 reichsmark, as well as the right to a Category 1 ration card for three months. In addition, they were to be helped with housing and medical care.[27] There was, of course, a certain restitutive legitimacy to providing much-needed help to the survivors of Nazi persecution. After all, on their release from camps or return from exile, many "victims of fascism" had virtually nothing of their own: they were without money, clothing, bedding, furniture, and housing. But this was also true of other categories of Germans who were not granted "victim of fascism" status— such as those who had been bombed out of their homes or those who had been expelled from their homelands at war's end.

The privileges associated with the status of "persecuted by the Nazi regime" rankled a population that itself felt victimized after 1945. Grete Wittkowski, an important East German economics functionary, later recalled an episode that suggests not only the resentment that many Germans bore toward "victims of fascism," but also the sense of moral superiority and entitlement among the "victims": "The victims of fascism, among whom I belonged, received special identification cards that gave them the right to go shopping without having to wait in line. A few days after I had returned to Berlin, I went to the baker, two houses away, in order to buy bread for me and my family. There was a long line and I went to the front and showed my identification card. The women began to grumble and stew: 'We are all victims of fascism and not just you!' At first, I tried to deal with the matter good-heartedly, but when that had no effect I then said to them forthright and coarsely: 'If you had only been half so loud-mouthed while this war was being fought until five minutes after 12, then none of us would have to stand here, neither you nor I.' And that ended the discussion on this morning and for all future mornings."[28] Wittkowski's attitude, although understandable, did little to win over a population resentful of the "antifascist" order in the SBZ.

In 1950, a law was decreed that amounted to a social welfare program for those with the official status of "persecuted by the Nazi regime." Such individuals were granted pensions if they had become invalids through Nazi persecution. They were given favored treatment in housing assignments and interest-free loans to pay for furniture and other necessary household items. In addition, they were entitled to preferential health-care benefits, including otherwise hard-to-come-by spaces in old-age homes and sanatoriums. Those "persecuted by the Nazi regime" also enjoyed three extra vacation days per year (total vacation days were not to exceed twenty-four a year) and early retirement—at the age of sixty for men, and fifty-five for women (other East Germans were eligible for retirement at sixty-five and sixty, respectively).[29] In the next years, the privileges of those officially recognized as "persecuted by the Nazi regime" would be gradually extended.

ALTHOUGH PRE-1933 KPD cadres enjoyed some material privileges, they nonetheless waged a constant struggle to secure the basic necessities of life. According to a well-known cliché of these years, the Aufbau period was "a hard but fine time." Food, in particular, was in very short supply. Heating fuel, household supplies, and furniture were also hard to come by. Clothing, too, was difficult to find; one veteran communist later remembered that she "wore leaky wooden shoes" during the winter of 1946–1947.[30] Longtime communists lived in cramped and otherwise inadequate quarters. Cars were a rare luxury. But the era's great material shortages were compensated for by the élan of the times. Despite the material and other difficulties that they faced, longtime German communists enthusiastically pushed ahead with the Aufbau project. Indeed, they later recalled this period as a glorious time of excitement and exuberance, initiative and improvisation. In many ways, this was their finest hour: out of the physical and ideological ruins of Nazi Germany, they created a new revolutionary order.

As Ulbricht repeatedly stated, veteran communists now had to abandon revolution for administration.[31] Most pre-1933 KPD cadres, however, had little, if any, expertise in the functional areas in which they were to work; unlike former social democrats, Old Communists had rarely worked in municipal government during the Weimar era. Moreover, the vast majority had only completed the first eight years of the German school system. Some had never held regular jobs; the Depression and then Nazi persecution delayed their entry into the workforce. Veteran communists thus often initially protested their job assignments because they felt that they did not have the necessary competence. These protestations, however, carried little weight. In the KPD's authoritarian style, longtime communists received "orders," or their "deployment" or "use" was quickly "decreed." Veteran communists thus set out to fulfill their party mission as best they could. Improvisation and initiative became the leitmotifs of the era.

Longtime communists learned their new professions "on the job," found office space where none was to be had, and located materials or personnel believed to be unavailable. Fred Oelßner, for example, was told to set up a Department of Agitation and Propaganda. He later recalled that his new department was but a living room in the house that served as headquarters for the KPD Central Committee. For office supplies, he had only one typewriter and a typist—"a young girl in long pants, which at the time struck me as very saucy."[32] Similarly, Fritz Selbmann was named president of the Saxon employment office in August 1945. As he later wrote, "I was to become president of the state employment office, but there was no state employment office, there was neither an office, nor a building, nor any bureaucrats or employees or colleagues, there was nothing . . . Understandably, I was initially in a real muddle, because in general I did not know how I was now to begin. But I had the orders to build up an employment administration for Saxony and I now had simply to busy myself with this task. In a relatively short time I was then successful in putting together a staff of colleagues and a building."[33] Such passages could be repeated ad infinitum. For Old Communists, the Aufbau period was nothing short of heroic. Through bold initiative, they raised Eastern Germany from the ruins of defeat to the rudiments of a smoothly functioning order.

During the Aufbau period, revolutionary engagement was all consuming. Veteran communists were frenetically busy. As Dahlem later noted: "The demands on party functionaries were unimaginably large. Barely arrived, we threw ourselves into the work that claimed all of our strength from day to day, from early morning until late at night."[34] In July 1945, the KPD Secretariat decreed that "for salaried employees doing political work [in the party bureaucracy], the work day is unlimited."[35] This did not have to be decreed. Old Communists were more than willing to devote all the hours of their day to the Aufbau project.

At the same time, veteran communists energetically mobilized support for the KPD, and after April 1946, for the newly founded SED. As Emmy Koenen, then a leading official for the DFD, the mass organization for women, wrote: "For me, 1947 was taken up with great activity. My calendar notes, for example, that I gave speeches in 24 towns in Saxony; in eight towns in other states of our zone; in SED, DFD, FDGB, and co-operative schools, and at the Peasants' Congress, in Stockholm, in Hamburg, etc.; not to speak of all the other obligations."[36] Given the general lack of cars, fuel, hotels, restaurants, and other travel amenities, attending such party meetings and other functions was no simple matter.

Veteran communists also sacrificed what little personal life they had for their revolutionary cause. In August 1945, Fritz Selbmann even forgot his wedding day. One morning, his bride-to-be reminded him that they were to be married at ten o'clock. Selbmann, however, had planned to attend a number of meetings in Dresden (at the time he lived in Leipzig): "I was thunderstruck. I could not give up my ride to Dresden and my various meetings there. My wife had no choice but to cancel and set a later date for the planned wedding. I thus drove to Dresden to my meetings, and the wedding festivities went on at the registrar's office eight days later. Now I was a newly responsible husband with a head full of worries and thoughts about planning—not about my new marital status, but about what needed to be done in Dresden."[37] For Selbmann, as for many other Old Communists, the revolution had top priority.

Old Communists' breathless engagement in the Aufbau project was a response to the demands of a chaotic time and the excitement of building a new, antifascist society. It also, however, reflected veteran communists' immediate past experiences. Most longtime communists had just spent a decade imprisoned or in exile, in situations in which they could exercise little control over their lives. Their political convictions had criminalized them in Germany and marginalized them in exile politics abroad. The Nazi defeat and Soviet occupation of East Germany suddenly changed all this: Old Communists were finally in a position to act, and they did so with a vengeance. In addition, many pre-1933 KPD cadres believed that the construction of socialism in Germany would vindicate the loss of comrades and other loved ones in the violence of the Nazi era. Intense involvement with Aufbau work also helped veteran communists to channel the pain of their personal losses. As Maria Rentmeister, an important functionary for women's work, later wrote of the immediate postwar period: "It was not common for us comrades to speak about personal past experience. All had gone through so much and were now immersed in the daily tasks at hand."[38] Finally, the zealous participation of veteran communists in the Aufbau project had roots in Stalinist ideology. Voluntarism, the notion that a socialist society could be created by force of party and individual will, was very much a part of the postwar Old Communist ethos. By dint of imagination, hard work, and a little help from Soviet "friends," anything, longtime communists thought, could be done.

VETERAN COMMUNISTS enjoyed great social and political mobility in the immediate postwar years. Walter Ulbricht, once a leading functionary of an ostracized party in Weimar Germany, now became the most powerful political figure in the SBZ and later, East Germany. Although subject to the whims of Stalin and his representatives in Germany, Ulbricht nonetheless enjoyed considerable political power. Franz Dahlem was also a powerful communist functionary. As soon as he arrived back in Germany, Dahlem was made a member of the KPD's four-man Secretariat, the body that directed party activity; Walter Ulbricht, Wilhelm Pieck, and Anton Ackermann were the other Secretariat members. Once the KPD merged with the SPD in April 1946, Dahlem became a member of the SED's Central Secretariat. At the same time, Dahlem oversaw the party's central personnel department until 1949 and the SED's "West Department," the department that organized communist activity in West Germany, until 1951.

Erich Honecker, little known to KPD leaders in 1945, established his political career in the early East German years. In May 1945, a member of the Ulbricht Group chanced upon him at a busy Berlin intersection and brought him to KPD headquarters. Ulbricht rather arbitrarily designated Honecker as the party's youth secretary. In 1946, Honecker cofounded and became head of the Free German Youth (FDJ), the East German youth organization. In 1950, he became a candidate member of the Politburo. His leadership of the FDJ, however, was not uncontroversial. In 1951, Honecker organized the World Festival of Youth in East Berlin. This proved a managerial disaster; not only was there a shortage of housing and food for participants, but Wilhelm Pieck was not allowed on the speaker's podium because he had not been given an entry ticket. In 1952, Honecker had similar problems with a new youth organization, Service for Germany, whose members were to aid the Aufbau project through construction and other work. These youth were housed in relatively primitive camps where they faced inadequate food, unsanitary conditions, and sexually transmitted disease. When wind of these matters reached the Politburo, a majority voted to initiate a party investigation against Honecker. Ulbricht, however, had been absent from the Politburo meeting that decreed the investigation. On his return, he simply reversed the decree.[39] Despite Honecker's failings, Ulbricht assiduously— and successfully—promoted and protected the FDJ leader during the late 1940s and 1950s.

Karl Schirdewan also climbed the party hierarchy during the Aufbau years. Initially, he worked in Berlin party headquarters organizing KPD activity in the Western zones of Germany. In January 1946, however, he had to stop working because of the tuberculosis that he had contracted in Nazi captivity. Schirdewan spent the next fourteen months in various sanatoriums recuperating from the disease. As he later wrote, this setback was very demoralizing: "After all the endlessly long years of imprisonment I was finally free, and wanted to live." Moreover, he deeply regretted missing important political developments: "I now could not participate in the direct preparation of the unification of the two workers' parties, and it made me sad that I had to follow this now undisputed historical event from a sickbed."[40] By the spring of 1947, however, Schirdewan was sufficiently recovered to take on a new job. He now headed the SED department devoted to the study of KPD and SPD resistance to the Nazis. In 1949, Schirdewan was named head of the SED's West Department, and during the next years, he became ever more influential. In March 1952, he was named first secretary of the SED in Saxony and, in October of that year, after the GDR abolished the traditional states of Eastern Germany, first secretary of the SED in Leipzig. In January of 1953, Schirdewan was called back to Berlin to head a department in the SED's central bureaucracy. By July of 1953 he was a member of the Politburo.

WHILE SOME Old Communists made heady careers during the Aufbau period, others had various difficulties with their party. Both Fritz Selbmann and Fred Oelßner combined impressive careers with political setbacks during these years. Selbmann first made his postwar career in the East German state of Saxony. After a brief stint as head of the Saxon employment office, he became vice president of the Saxon economic administration. Between 1946 and 1948 he was minister of economics and economic planning in Saxony. In May 1947, Selbmann wrote a long memorandum to SMAD authorities in which he described the negative effects on the Saxon economy of Soviet economic planning and reparations policy. Selbmann suggested some twenty-five prerequisites that the SMAD should fulfill in order to ensure the "implementation of well-ordered economic planning." These included the provision of raw materials to factories so that these could fulfill their production plans and reparations payments set by SMAD authorities, the timely delivery of production and distribution plans, a firm commitment that the dismantling of East German factories had ended, and the transfer of economic decision-making to German authorities.[41] Selbmann later claimed that the upshot of his memorandum was that he was summoned to SMAD headquarters for a discussion with the deputy chief of economic questions. In this conversation, Selbmann not only reiterated the shortcomings of SMAD economic policy, but also emphasized the need for a central planning institution for the entire SBZ.[42] Whether or not they did so as a result of Selbmann's proposal, SMAD authorities soon formed the German Economic Commission (DWK), the nucleus of the nascent East German state.

In 1948, Selbmann left Saxony to become vice president of the DWK and to head its main administrative department for industry. Once the GDR was founded in 1949, Selbmann became minister of industry. In 1950, he became minister of heavy industry, and in 1951 minister of metallurgy and mining. Selbmann was deeply involved with some of East Germany's largest industrial projects, including the creation of Eisenhüttenstadt (originally known as Stalinstadt). As Selbmann later wrote: "The country needed iron—with this thought I went to sleep at night and woke up in the morning."[43] Eisenhüttenstadt, a factory / city built in the midst of open fields near the Polish border, eventually became East Germany's principal supplier of pig iron and steel products. In his postwar memoirs, Selbmann cast the construction of the industrial complex known as Eisenhüttenkombinat Ost (EKO) in heroic terms. He also, however, acknowledged the difficulties in building EKO. His open description of these difficulties was one reason why his postwar memoirs were never published in East Germany. What Selbmann failed to relate, however, was that the party censured him for his EKO work in 1952.

This party censure was the upshot of a long series of alleged shortcomings on Selbmann's part. In the postwar years, he had a reputation as an arrogant but useful comrade. The KPD / SED collected negative information about him from 1945 onward, and in 1950, the newly founded Stasi reported on Selbmann's passion for hunting wild game. Selbmann allegedly "drove around in an American luxury car" and had "made himself very unliked among farmers" while hunting wild game in Saxony.[44] Later reports accused Selbmann of hunting conduct even worse than that of Martin Mutschmann, the notoriously corrupt Nazi *Gauleiter* (district leader) of Dresden. Selbmann had apparently hunted out of season. Moreover, some questioned "whether a minister has the time to drive from Berlin to [the Saxon town of] Lengefeld every week to hunt and whether in the framework of the 5-year plan it is right to use so much gasoline for luxury purposes."[45] Another report bluntly stated, "Comrade Selbmann suffers from arrogance. He is first and foremost minister and then only comrade." This report also described Selbmann's alleged behavior on a trip to Moscow: "In Moscow Comrade Selbmann expected all present to treat him as a minister and to be at his service at all times— whether the translator, shoppers, or baggage carriers."[46]

In 1951, Selbmann was called in for an interrogation with Hermann Matern, the head of the Central Party Control Commission (the SED's disciplinary body). Selbmann tried to address the ongoing criticism about his supposed arrogance—a major shortcoming in a movement that valued the subjugation of the individual to the collective. Selbmann was asked, for example, "Why do you think that you are not a member of the Central Committee?" (The Central Committee was an influential party body of some eighty members and candidates at this time; Selbmann's wife Käte was a candidate member). Selbmann responded by stating, "I have seriously examined myself. I have a number of shortcomings, that is true. One of these mistakes is that I'm a fairly self-willed fellow, whom one must rein in. Since 1945, my work has involved many independent decisions." Selbmann then went on to explain that because he received relatively little help from the Saxon party leadership, "there developed in me a certain arrogance and an over-estimation of my own work . . . As a result there developed a sort of alienation from the party, al-

Fritz Selbmann directs matters at EKO, August 18, 1952.
(Bundesarchiv, SAPMO-BArch, Bild Y 10-1468/82)

though between me and the party there could never come a real alienation." Selbmann was also asked, "Isn't the main question really that you
place yourself beside the party?" To this, he responded: "That can't be
right. Even though I also have individualistic traits, I cannot be without
the party. If I placed myself beside the party, then I am no Marxist-Leninist."[47] As Selbmann showed, he was well versed in the demeaning practice of communist self-criticism.

In January of 1952, there were several explosions in the newly constructed blast furnace at EKO. As Selbmann wrote in his memoirs, these
explosions were due to the faulty design and rapid construction of the
furnace.[48] According to a 1952 Politburo decree, however, an investigation had determined that "the main responsibility" for the mistakes at
EKO lay with Selbmann. In its search for a scapegoat to explain the EKO
failure, the Politburo landed on Selbmann and his alleged arrogance; as
always, rather than fault the socialist system, the SED leadership blamed
human error—and not just innocent human error, but rather malicious
or otherwise antisocialist human error. Selbmann had thus allegedly not
followed "valuable guidelines" established by the party for the "rational
administration of the people's own industry." As the decree stated:

Because he believes that he can reach his goal faster with "directives" issued
by his administration, his recent conduct shows that he ignores the creative
initiative of the masses, without whose conscious and active cooperation
the reconstruction of our democratic peace economy in the planned speedy

tempo is impossible. Because Comrade Fritz Selbmann is also arrogant in his administration, ignores serious tips and warnings of his co-workers, does not deliberate with them collectively, and does not draw them into work that carries a sense of duty, prevents open criticism and self-criticism, and has long since not followed a serious personnel policy, he has only unsatisfactorily fulfilled the tasks given him by the party and government.

The Politburo decreed a "censure" for Selbmann.[49] Selbmann did not lose his position as minister. But the censure was nonetheless a significant disciplinary measure; it meant that Selbmann no longer had a clean party record and it thus deeply rankled this veteran communist.[50] In the next years, however, Selbmann would have even greater troubles with the SED party leadership.

Fred Oelßner also had some political difficulties in the early 1950s. Oelßner directed the KPD's Propaganda Department in 1945, headed the SED's central department of political schooling in 1946, and became a member of the SED Secretariat in 1949 and the Politburo in 1950. When Politburo delegations went to Moscow during these years, Oelßner often served as translator. In 1950, he was also named the SED's secretary of propaganda—essentially, the party's chief ideologist. In this capacity, he was editor in chief of *Einheit* (Unity), the SED's premier journal for ideology. Beginning in 1951, however, Oelßner's ideological work was harshly criticized. In that year, Ulbricht wrote a sharp memorandum to the *Einheit* editorial board in which he castigated two articles that the journal had published on "Ernst Thälmann's struggle to overcome the right opportunists in the KPD." According to Ulbricht, "I view this presentation as incorrect because the KPD was to appropriate Marxist-Leninist doctrine and deploy it in the struggle against right opportunism and left opportunism." Ulbricht thus claimed that the one-sided nature of the articles had led to an "undialectical position and is historically wrong."[51] Criticism of Oelßner's work soon escalated. In July 1952 he and his work were publicly criticized. This prompted Oelßner to write a self-critical statement.

In this statement, Oelßner claimed that the "harsh criticism" leveled against him for an unsuccessful draft resolution was unjust. He nonetheless stated, "My work must be criticized so as to lead to its improvement." He then detailed the "main shortcomings" of his work: insufficient direction of the Propaganda Department, of the journal *Einheit*, and of the various institutes under his control—the Marx Engels Lenin Institute, the Karl Marx Party College, and the Institute for Social Sciences. According to Oelßner, the problems with his work were due to ideological shortcomings. He had not followed the new Soviet or East

Fred Oelßner at the founding of the Worker-Peasant Faculty in Jena. Oelßner proudly holds a volume titled "We want to master knowledge." (Bundesarchiv, SAPMO-BArch, Bild Y 10-180/00)

German social scientific literature and he was not up to date on the new literature by the "enemy." Oelßner went on to state that the "consequence of these ideological shortcomings is a certain superficiality and abstraction of my whole theoretical work." He claimed that he saw no way out of his situation and was therefore asking the Politburo for help. As Oelßner wrote: "At the moment it is so that I must regularly attend three meetings per week (two Secretariat, one Politburo) that last almost a whole day (sometimes 12–13 hours). In addition, I sometimes have meetings of the *Einheit* editorial board and the Stalin Commission that also take a great deal of time. The remaining 2–3 days a week are not sufficient to somewhat prepare for the meetings and to have necessary discussions. With these burdens it is not even possible to consider serious academic work." Oelßner then suggested that he give up the editorship of *Einheit* and that he only take part in Secretariat meetings when ideological questions were discussed.[52]

Oelßner's statement suggests that he, like Selbmann, was well versed in the communist practice of self-criticism. It also conveys the enormous demands put on leading functionaries during the Aufbau years. The vicious Cold War competition that pitted the systemic performance of socialism against that of communism placed great pressure on SED cadres to perform their jobs well. In the event, the only upshot of Oelßner's statement was that the Politburo "took notice" of it.[53] Oelßner continued in all of his positions. But the fact that he was criticized so harshly and felt that he had to write such a statement suggests that his situation in the SED leadership was quite tenuous.

EVEN MORE than Fritz Selbmann and Fred Oelßner, Emmy Koenen faced professional setbacks in Aufbau East Germany. After the Koenens came to the SBZ, they were briefly sent to Halle. There, Emmy was an editor at the local newspaper, the *Mitteldeutsche Zeitung*. In the spring of 1946, however, Wilhelm Koenen was named co-chairman of the SED in Saxony—a powerful position in the SBZ. The couple moved to Dresden, and Emmy became an editor at the provincial *Sächsische Zeitung*. Like so many women veteran communists, she was also very involved in women's work. She helped various local women's committees to set up counseling centers, sewing centers, old-age homes, communal kitchens, kindergartens, and other municipal services. In March 1947, Emmy also participated in the founding of the DFD. The next two years marked the zenith of her career in East Germany. Initially, Emmy was deputy chairman of the DFD, but in May 1948 she became chairman of the organization. As head of the DFD, Emmy led a women's delegation to the Soviet Union in September 1948. There she heard from her former husband, Helmut Damerius; Damerius had spent years in the gulag and was desperately trying to return to the SBZ. Emmy sent him a euphoric letter about her marriage to Wilhelm Koenen, the ongoing changes in the SBZ, and her own ascendant career. As she wrote, "As you can see, not only have I remained intact, but I'm also the first chairman of the Democratic Women's Federation of Germany, the largest and most politically active supra-party women's organization."[54] Emmy also told Damerius that both she and her husband were members of the Party Executive, the forerunner to the Central Committee. Ulbricht, Dahlem, Oelßner, and Honecker all belonged to the Party Executive at this time; Emmy Koenen thus found herself in influential company.

Much to her distress, Emmy Koenen was abruptly removed from her DFD chairmanship in April 1949. At the beginning of April, she was told that she was to temporarily resign her position while she did a two-month "cure" in Hungary. Shortly thereafter, the SED Politburo decreed that she was to resign her position altogether. Elli Schmidt, a veteran communist who headed the Women's Secretariat in the SED's Central Committee bureaucracy, was now to become DFD chairman. Distraught, Emmy met with Franz Dahlem. According to Dahlem, Emmy "wanted to know why she was to give up her position, which policies of the federation's board had been politically wrong. She was never brought in to discuss this question and no one ever talked to her about the matter." As far as Emmy was concerned, she had been given no indication that her work was unsatisfactory. Dahlem then wrote: "All of this was spoken with great bitterness about the way in which an old party functionary was treated and it was clear that she is inwardly dissatisfied with the proposed solution of the matter." The next day, Dahlem wrote a brief memo in which he stated that Emmy could not leave for Hungary until she had resigned her position. Emmy, in turn, was so upset that she suffered a mild heart attack. She thus wrote a letter to the Politburo stating, "I do not momentarily feel myself in a situation to pursue this altercation to its end." Instead, she stated, she would not send a letter of resignation until she had been told both the actual wording of the decree and the reasons for her removal.

Otto Grotewohl, a former SPD politician who was now co-chairman of the SED, immediately replied, "It is not a matter of principal differences in political views. Rather, after all the deliberations the Politburo had come to the view that without the planned personnel changes, that are not limited only to you, a harmonious cooperation between the DFD and the Women's Secretariat of the party cannot be achieved. As far as this decree concerns you, it is not a personal setback; it by no means excludes that you will be used in a responsible position after your health has been restored. This is even intended."[55] Emmy, however, believed that she was removed because of her political differences with Elli Schmidt. Much later she wrote, "In the middle of 1949 I dropped out of the DFD work. The reason was not only my very poor health situation. There were differences of opinion between Comrade E[lli] Sch[midt] and myself that came to a head after she said: 'How much longer do you want to show consideration for the sh[itty] bourgeois women?' But there had not been a single case in which such a taking of consideration had been politically wrong. I just believed in persuasion and more persuasion and not simply for winking at these women . . . I also resisted a certain commanding tone. It is true that I dropped out of this work in keeping with the decrees of my party, but the work was dear to me and I did so very reluctantly."[56]

Why was Emmy removed from her DFD chairmanship? According to one source, she was forced out because she was an ineffective chairman.[57] In addition, she was apparently unable to get along with Elli Schmidt and took too conciliatory a political approach to noncommunist women. At the same time, however, the careers of some veteran women communists were clearly linked to their husbands' political fortunes. Emmy's removal was probably related to the fact that Wilhelm Koenen was losing political influence. By mid-1949, Koenen was no longer Saxon party chief. Although he was still a member of the SED's influential Central Secretariat, he—like so many other former West émigrés—now had a somewhat precarious hold on power. He was obviously unable to protect his wife and, in any event, lost his Central Secretariat position in 1950. At that time, as Emmy wrote Franz Dahlem many years later, "Wilhelm K[oenen's] office was simply taken away without any discussion. Yes, that's how one used to treat old comrades . . . one did not even have a discussion with Wilhelm K. Only I know how Wilhelm suffered from this."[58] Despite Grotewohl's assurances, Emmy never again held influential positions. Between 1950 and 1958, she worked at an East German publishing house, Die Wirtschaft (The economy), as an editor, department head, and deputy editor in chief. In 1958 she stopped her professional work altogether so that she could take care of Wilhelm, who was now almost blind. For his part, Wilhelm Koenen remained a Central Committee member, but otherwise held relatively uninfluential leadership positions in the East German parliament, or Volkskammer. Although her loyalty to the party remained intact, Emmy never lost her bitterness about the setbacks that she and her husband had endured in 1949–1950.

Emmy Koenen's career in East Germany was not unusual for women veteran communists. In the masculine party culture of the SED, women cadres had little chance of reaching the highest tiers of power. Only one woman veteran communist, Elli Schmidt, ever belonged to the Politburo—and she was only a candidate member between 1950 and 1953. Schmidt was married to Anton Ackermann, but the couple separated during these years. After 1953, Schmidt was the director of a fashion institute—a marginal position in a society that privileged heavy industry over consumer goods. Like Emmy Koenen and Elli Schmidt, many Old Communist women who had been very active in women's work during the first years of the regime had receded into the political background by the mid-1950s.

Several factors explain these women's waning influence. Initially, great importance was attached to mobilizing women for the SED's goals; since many men were still in prisoner-of-war camps or otherwise disabled from the war, women made up a majority of the active East German population. But as the demographics changed, political work among women became less important. In addition, some veteran communist women took on more traditional roles as their husbands became ever more ensconced in power; under the prevailing conditions of scarcity, it was always something of a full-time job to run an East German household. More importantly, though, women Old Communists were simply not valued as professionals by the SED leadership.

A few women veteran communists did attain influential positions in the GDR. Hilde Benjamin, the sister-in-law of the cultural critic Walter Benjamin, was the GDR's tough minister of justice from 1953 to 1967. Grete Wittkowski was an important economics functionary and president of the State Bank from 1967 until her death in 1974. Hanna Wolf headed the Karl Marx Party College from 1950 to 1983. All three of these women were longtime Central Committee members. They were, however, very much the exception. All three were single and did not have to care for husbands or children; Benjamin had lost her husband and Wittkowski her fiancé in the antifascist struggle. But although there were many other single women veteran communists, few had successful careers in the GDR. In some cases, such women were even eager to "marry" their political cause—that is, to devote all their energies to their professional work. But they were not promoted within the party or state bureaucracies. In the SED, the KPD's masculine culture triumphed.

In the first postwar years, many male veteran communists began traditional family lives; women veteran communists seldom had this opportunity. Longtime male communists benefited from the demographic situation in Eastern Germany: there were many more eligible women than men, and in many ways, male veteran communists were a "good catch" for women in the SBZ. In the charged atmosphere that accompanied the founding of the new political order, communist cadres who had participated in resistance activities enjoyed not only privileges and influence, but also personal charisma that doubtlessly translated into sexual appeal. Selbmann remarried in the summer of 1945. Karl Schirdewan married his girlfriend Gisela after he had recovered from his tuberculosis. And in 1949, Erich Honecker married Edith Baumann, a longtime SPD functionary—a marriage that symbolized the SED's unity of longtime communists and social democrats. In behavior typical of survivors of child-bearing age, many veteran communists also began families. The Schirdewans had three young children by 1953. Edith Baumann and Erich Honecker had a daughter. This marriage, however, soon ended because Honecker met a younger woman, Margot Feist, whom he married in 1953 and with whom he eventually had two daughters. In the Aufbau period, Old Communists not only helped found a new political order; they also helped found new generations of socialist men and women.

For most longtime communists this "settling down" allowed them, af-

ter decades of personal upheaval, to lead stable personal lives. This order-
ing of their personal situations was partly a reflection of German communist politics. Veteran communists shared the old social-democratic
preoccupation with the imitation of bourgeois lifestyles among the
working classes. It is thus no coincidence that Ulbricht sorted out his private life in the GDR; after divorcing his first wife, he married Lotte Kühn,
his companion of some eighteen years, in 1953.[59] Veteran communists
also generally accepted their movement's insistence that its cadres lead
personal lives beyond reproach. If communists led conventional lives,
they could not be politically compromised by sexual indiscretions,
whether heterosexual affairs or homosexual liaisons. At the same time,
the veteran communist desire for personal stability—after the trials and
separations of long years of exile and imprisonment—helps to explain
the striking conformity that longtime communists displayed vis-à-vis
the politics of the new SED regime.

WITH THE future of Eastern Germany at stake, veteran communist leaders faced enormous popular opposition. Soviet occupation policies,
publicly defended by KPD / SED leaders, were very unpopular. SMAD authorities initially insisted on dismantling much of the SBZ's economic
infrastructure for export to the Soviet Union. Later on, they demanded
huge reparations payments in materials and goods manufactured in the
SBZ. Random, unwarranted arrests by both Soviet and SED authorities
also alienated the population from the new order. In addition, many East
Germans opposed the suppression of unofficial political groups and ideas
as well as the SED's increasingly inflexible Marxism-Leninism. Ordinary
East Germans were also angered that so many Wehrmacht soldiers remained in Soviet prisoner-of-war camps. And many East German peasants were disappointed with the initial land reform and, in the early
1950s, with the forced collectivization of agriculture. Finally, the difficult
regimen of everyday life—long working hours, low pay, insufficient
goods, and poor living conditions—made for considerable discontent
among the East German population. Although many SBZ / GDR inhabitants "voted with their feet" and fled to West Germany, millions of other
disgruntled East Germans remained under SED domination.

Despite widespread popular opposition, veteran communists appear to
have generally accepted the transformation of East Germany into a Soviet-style regime. There was no organized opposition among longtime
KPD cadres to the new SED political order.[60] Among individual veteran
communists, oppositional views have proven difficult to document. This
is particularly true of those pre-1933 KPD cadres who held influential po-

sitions. Longtime communists in the lower party ranks who were known to be critical of their regime (and there were surely many) were simply not promoted within the party hierarchy. At the same time, many veteran communists who harbored critical views were doubtlessly reluctant to openly express or otherwise document their disapproval. Communist party discipline, along with the notion that dissent represented the enemy within, kept some longtime communists from voicing doubts or opposition to the politics of the KPD / SED. Living and working among a population resentful of SED rule may also have led to a solidaristic closing of Old Communist ranks. And there was political terror, in the form of public and secret investigations into their past lives, that left many longtime communists reluctant to express political doubts in the later 1940s and early 1950s.

Many observers have assumed that Old Communists who were former West émigrés or concentration-camp survivors opposed the policies of former Soviet exiles and advocated a more democratic, or less repressive, socialism.[61] There is, however, little suggestion that former West émigrés held Western democratic practices in any higher esteem than did former Soviet émigrés. Shortly after his return to the SBZ in 1949, for example, Gerhart Eisler made very clear his views about free elections. At a meeting of the Party Executive called to discuss the founding of the GDR, Eisler declared: "If we found a government, we will never again give it up—neither through elections nor other methods."[62] On other occasions, when asked to comment on the absence of free elections in the GDR, he is said to have retorted: "Free elections? So that the Germans could again elect Hitler?"[63] These comments may have been motivated by Eisler's mistrust of the German population that had voted Hitler to power. But Eisler's experiences in the United States also gave this veteran communist good grounds to question the nature of parliamentary democracy. Similarly, Wieland Herzfelde, a pre-1933 communist and radical publisher in the 1920s who was exiled in the United States, had little use for Western ways. In 1949, the famed diarist Victor Klemperer heard Herzfelde give a talk and noted that he had been "terribly sharply satirical about the USA."[64]

There is also little suggestion that Old Communists who survived Hitler's concentration camps advocated a more "humanistic socialism" or a greater concern with human rights. Fritz Selbmann's views on the death penalty are a case in point. In his postwar memoirs, Selbmann wrote, "I was personally opposed to the death penalty, chiefly as a result of the experiences that I had in fascist concentration camps." In 1947, however, Selbmann actually defended the death penalty. In that year, the SED in

Saxony decided to introduce a death penalty for those individuals engaged in black-market and "sabotage" activities. As the SED's spokesman
in the Saxon state parliament, Selbmann argued that the death penalty
was appropriate for economic sabotage since it was keeping "thousands
of little children from not getting what was necessary in order to keep
them healthy." Selbmann continued: "Don't think that I have approached the question of the death penalty irresponsibly . . . In the
course of many years in concentration camps . . . I had to observe many,
many executions . . . I know what the death penalty means and precisely
because I do, I consider it necessary that the state threaten the current
greatest enemies of the people with the sharpest penalty."[65]

On at least one occasion, however, Selbmann did question the brutal
methods of the Stasi. In a letter to Stasi minister and veteran communist
Wilhelm Zaisser, Selbmann noted that four men had been arrested in
connection with a gas explosion that had occurred in December 1950 at
a factory in Brandenburg. Selbmann wrote that one of these individuals, "a master smelter and very reliable progressive worker" had been arrested and "locked into a cold cellar without blankets." When the man
was released some twenty-four hours later, he needed immediate medical attention. Selbmann commented: "I do not want to question whether
it was necessary to arrest the four men. One could also have held a hearing in the factory. But I am convinced that when an arrest is necessary,
one cannot deal so negligently with the health and working strength of
a good worker who has not even yet been found guilty."[66] Whether
Selbmann ever again drew attention to the brutal excesses of Stasi methods, the fact that he did so once was very unusual for an Old Communist.
Were such concerns widespread and deeply held among veteran communist concentration-camp survivors, however, there would be many such
letters in the East German party or Stasi archives. This is not the case. Old
Communists—regardless of their biographical pasts—rarely intervened
in the miscarriages of justice that regularly occurred in the SBZ / GDR.

A few veteran communists engaged in crusty, proletarian "plain-speak-
ing." Fritz Selbmann harshly criticized Soviet economic policy in a secret
memorandum to SMAD officials in 1947. But while Selbmann was clearly
dissatisfied with various economic policies in the SBZ / GDR, he never
proposed nor was associated with significant economic reform.[67] Similarly, another veteran communist and concentration-camp survivor,
Fritz Große, wrote a scathing report to SMAD authorities in which he
mentioned, among other regime shortcomings, the conduct of Soviet occupation personnel and the lack of trade-union influence in the SBZ.[68]
Secret, forthright criticism, however, does not translate into opposi-

tion—the willingness to defend and uphold a coherent alternative to KPD / SED orthodoxy in party or public tribunals.

This is not to say that there was not political conflict among longtime communists. There was. This conflict was not, however, based on fundamental policy differences, but rather on rivalries between different groups of veteran communists or between individual Old Communists. Former Soviet émigrés were heavily overrepresented in influential party bodies and positions. Of the seven veteran communists who sat on the 1946 Central Secretariat, five were former exiles to the Soviet Union; in addition, Dahlem and Paul Merker, who had spent the war years in Mexico, belonged to this body. Similarly, in 1950, five of the seven longtime communists who were full members of the Politburo had spent the war years in the Soviet Union, while two, Dahlem and Heinrich Rau, were survivors of Mauthausen concentration camp. Many veteran communists who had not spent the war years in the Soviet Union resented the privileged status of former Soviet émigrés. In 1946, Fritz Große barely concealed his bitterness toward Moscow émigrés when he wrote: "A very high-ranking comrade said in a private conversation that there is really only a very small group of very reliable people, namely those who had come from Moscow . . . [Having been in] Moscow emigration is just as little a guarantee as [having been in] a c[oncentration] c[amp] that one will work faultlessly . . . With some of the [Moscow] émigrés there are present certain tendencies towards political cronyism and tendencies to apply certain phenomena schematically to Germany."[69] Große clearly resented the notion that only the Moscow émigrés were truly reliable; in his own hierarchy of political pasts, the Moscow émigrés occupied a rather low rung. Hans Lauter, a concentration-camp survivor who was purged in 1953, noted in a 1995 interview that tensions between "home" and Soviet-émigré communists "had nothing to do with [political] differences" but rather with personal antipathies. He personally had been "put off" by "the considerable arrogance" of the Soviet émigrés who had the attitude that "we are the ones who can do everything." Lauter also suggested that "home" communists had been envious of former Soviet exiles, for while "we did time in prison," those KPD cadres had been able to escape Nazi Germany and to participate in the ongoing discussions of communist doctrine.[70] At the time, of course, "home" communists had little inkling of the Great Purges' effect on the KPD emigration in Moscow.

There were also individual rivalries between former Soviet exiles and those with other biographical pasts. Walter Ulbricht and Franz Dahlem, for example, were intense rivals.[71] Ulbricht was known to call Dahlem a "senile fool."[72] But Dahlem had the stature and personal following within the KPD / SED to challenge or even replace Ulbricht. Some scholars have tried to discern political differences between the two men, yet this has proven largely elusive. One author has suggested that Dahlem disagreed with Ulbricht over certain personnel decisions and over whether the KPD / SED should have the character of a mass or cadre party; Dahlem allegedly wanted to emphasize the mass, rather than the cadre, aspects of the KPD / SED.[73] Another has argued that Dahlem thought "much more soberly and realistically" about the potential for communist success in West Germany.[74] Karl Schirdewan claims that Dahlem proposed talks with some liberal politicians in West Germany in 1953; this would suggest that Dahlem was more open to pursuing a conciliatory approach toward the division of Germany. According to Schirdewan, Ulbricht responded to the proposal "churlishly and scolded Dahlem like a schoolboy. There was a vehement verbal confrontation. Dahlem then packed his papers and left."[75] In several pages of close discussion on Dahlem's positions during the Aufbau years, the British historian Peter Grieder suggests these and other supposed differences between the two men. None of this evidence, however, points to very far-reaching differences between Dahlem and Ulbricht. As Grieder himself notes, "Dahlem was an accomplice rather than an opponent of Stalinization."[76] Dahlem was one of the most influential party functionaries during these years and, along with Ulbricht, helped to initiate policies that turned the GDR into a repressive socialist regime. Although he surely resented Ulbricht's personal power, Dahlem did not fundamentally oppose Ulbricht's policies.

The East German historian Wolfgang Kießling has suggested that Paul Merker, a former West émigré, "brought notions of democracy with him that did not fit into any Soviet mode." As a result, Kießling claims, Ulbricht saw Paul Merker as "his greatest rival." The latter claim is certainly exaggerated; Merker had neither the party stature nor the organizational base to rival Ulbricht. But what of Kießling's argument that Merker had brought home other notions of democracy? Kießling does not give any concrete evidence from Merker's time as a high-level SED functionary to support his claim.[77] Moreover, some of Merker's speeches at the time clearly undermine Kießling's argument. In May 1949, for example, Merker sharply attacked those who wanted more wide-ranging discussion within the SED: "There are members of our party who demand that a so-called objective discussion take place about the question of Trotskyism. But comrades, what does it mean to make such a demand? The party members who have been carried away by this do not have any consciousness of the role of the party and of discipline in the party; they lack respect for our great teacher, the Communist Party of the Soviet

Union (Bolsheviks)."[78] Yet Grieder has suggested that "although Merker went along with Stalinization, he does seem to have harbored misgivings." Grieder's evidence for this assertion rests on some statements that Merker made as state secretary in the Ministry of Agriculture in the late 1940s. Whereas Ulbricht was pursuing a hard line toward farmers, Merker "called for methods of persuasion rather than compulsion." But as Grieder himself notes, Merker's views after 1946 are "difficult to document."[79] Merker, however, did advocate one set of policies that differed markedly from the party line: he encouraged improved relations with German and world Jewry. He thus supported the state of Israel and financial restitution to the Jews for the Holocaust.[80] But his wish to compensate the Jews faced numerous obstacles in postwar East Germany: a prevalent communist anti-Semitism, fiscal constraints on the impoverished SED regime, and Soviet occupation laws on sequestered properties. Given the political realities of Aufbau East Germany, Merker, as he himself realized, could not hope to prevail in his views.[81]

It was, in fact, a former Soviet émigré, Anton Ackermann, who most openly opposed some of the policies of his fellow Old Communist leaders during the Aufbau period. In February 1946, Ackermann published an influential article in *Einheit* titled "Is There a Special German Road to Socialism?" Ackermann argued that Germans did not have to imitate the Soviet model of revolutionary violence to achieve socialism in Germany. Instead, prevailing special conditions—the fact that "bourgeois" democracy was in the hands of antifascists, rather than reactionaries—made it possible for Germany to avoid civil war and to thus take a peaceful road to socialism.[82] This theory was intended to make the KPD / SPD merger more palatable to the SPD and to rally a broad antifascist front for a unified, socialist Germany. Although Ackermann's views were initially those of the KPD / SED leadership (indeed, he had written the article on party orders), he was soon personally identified with the theory of a "special German road to socialism." He advocated this position with more conviction, and certainly longer, than the rest of the SED leadership.

Ackermann's attachment to the notion of German unity even led him to oppose a Party Executive resolution that he believed would further the division of Germany. In February 1947, Ackermann was against the formation of a public "association" between the SED and the West German KPD (that was, in any event, a puppet party of the SED), while the rest of the SED leadership thought it opportune to dissolve the KPD and to form the SED in West Germany. To Ackermann, a Western SED would have limited appeal and this, in turn, would hinder the building of a broad antifascist movement that would serve as a unifying force in Germany. As the next speaker, Pieck could not refrain from stating "that everything that he [Ackermann] said was totally wrong and confuses the issue."[83] Ackermann actually voted against the Party Executive's resolution to form the public association. This was one of the very rare instances in which a Party Executive and later, a Central Committee, vote was not unanimous. Ackermann's rather public opposition belies the notion that communist exiles from the Soviet Union were more Stalinist or disciplined party cadres than other veteran communists. In the official SED minutes of the meeting there was initially a sentence to the effect that Ackermann disagreed with the press communiqué of the meeting. A notation by Grotewohl, however, suggested that this sentence "was stricken" from the record "after personal consultation with Com[rade] Ackermann."[84] Although Ackermann bitterly disagreed with his party on this matter, he did not wish his opposition formally recorded; it was, after all, a serious breach of party discipline.

In 1948, Tito, Yugoslavia's communist leader and Partisan hero, insisted on maintaining his political independence from Moscow. Stalin, angered, broke with Tito. Thereafter, increasing pressure was placed on the other East Central European states to conform to Stalinist orthodoxy. In this situation, the notion of a "special German road to socialism" became untenable. In September 1948, Ackermann was forced to recant: "The theory of a special German road to socialism has proven to be false and dangerous. We must wage a bitter struggle to overcome it." In this speech to the Party Executive, at once exculpatory and self-critical, Ackermann argued that he initially had had orders from the Secretariat to write the article, that the theory had "become part of the ideology of our party," and that not a single comrade had attacked his views throughout 1946 and 1947. Ackermann nonetheless declared the theory "false, rotten, and dangerous" because, among other things, it had been "a concession to anti-Soviet opinion, to anti-Soviet rabble-rousing propaganda."[85]

Ackermann was willing to go only so far in his independent stance: once his theory was brought into political disrepute, he dropped it without further ado. Although Ackermann renounced the theory, he still became the scapegoat by which the SED leadership distanced itself from ideas once official, but now anathema. His political career never recovered from this debacle. In 1949, Ackermann became only a candidate member of the Politburo; in 1953, he was removed from the SED leadership.

THE AUFBAU years culminated in Ulbricht's declaration at the Second Party Conference in July 1952 that it was now time for "the planned con-

struction of the bases for socialism in the GDR." Since longtime communists had been working to create an antifascist order rather than an outright socialist one, this newly proclaimed goal was cause for great joy and
excitement. As Schirdewan, who attended the conference, noted, "Like
all the other delegates [to the conference], . . . I was naturally in raptures
about this prospect."[86] The year 1952, however, marked the apogee of naive socialist enthusiasm in the GDR. Behind the scenes, disturbing party
investigations into the past lives of many Old Communists had been ongoing for some time; these would reach a crescendo in the winter of
1952–1953. At the same time, the simmering discontents of East German
workers would soon boil over into the Uprising of June 1953. The exuberance of the summer of 1952 would give way to the sobriety of socialism
in practice. Although the heroic Aufbau era had come to an end, the lives
of Old Communists in East Germany had only just begun.

5

PURGED

Veteran Communists and Stalinist Terror

IN THE LATE 1940S AND EARLY 1950S, A BIZARRE SET OF PURGES OF
East German veteran communists took place. In a seeming perverse twist
of fate, Old Communists such as Fritz Selbmann, Gerhart Eisler, and
Franz Dahlem saw their past biographies questioned, manipulated, and
shorn of revolutionary valor. SED investigators, poring over information
in longtime communists' personnel files, attributed malicious intent to
harmless biographical details. Veteran communists who had participated
in wartime propaganda efforts in Western countries were accused of having been recruited by foreign intelligence agencies; those who had withstood torture under Gestapo interrogation were charged with the betrayal of comrades; those who had survived the ordeal of concentration
camps were accused of collaboration with Nazi authorities; and those
who had fought in the Spanish Civil War saw their military exploits ig-
nored. This experience of biographical manipulation was as wrenching
as it was inexplicable: longtime communists lost not only their revolutionary laurels, but also their positions and sometimes, their personal lib-
erty. As Paul Baender, a veteran communist who was arrested and interrogated by SED authorities in 1952, later recalled: "I was gradually given a
totally different biography. It was presented as reality again and again."
He added: "I came into an indescribable state. I was on the verge of com-
mitting suicide."[1]

The Cold War made these biography-based purges possible. In an era
of intense conflict between East and West, Soviet (and later SED) officials
became convinced that capitalist spies were undermining socialism
throughout East Central Europe—just as Senator Joseph McCarthy was
sure that Soviet agents were ruining the fabric of American life in the
United States. Stalin and his security chief, Lavrenti Beria, manipulated
these Cold War paranoias to initiate a wave of purges throughout East

Central Europe. In the GDR, in turn, Walter Ulbricht exploited the spy mania to augment his power and authority. Curiously, though, the purges of Old Communists in East Germany took place just as the SED was instituting a cult of the party's antifascist resistance struggle against Hitler. These were the years in which the party established memorials, rituals, and other commemorative practices designed to heroize the past exploits of its longtime cadres. But the budding cult of the antifascist resistance drew on the past lives of the very individuals who were or would soon be subject to biography-based purges. What, then, were these purges all about? And what was the relationship between these purges and SED attempts to draw legitimacy from the past antifascist struggle?

FROM 1945 until 1989, veteran communists in East Germany claimed political legitimacy through "antifascism." Even before the war had ended, communists in Soviet exile had pointed to the KPD's struggle against Hitler as an important historical achievement that legitimized communist claims to help shape a new Germany.[2] Shortly after his liberation from Mauthausen concentration camp, Franz Dahlem declared: "So we communists, confident and unflustered by all difficulties, bring forth from the concentration camps general trust and confidence in our own strength, capital that qualifies and entitles us, together with the proven antifascist fighters inside the country, to set to work: to attain the set goal of the creation of a new 'other Germany.'"[3] As Dahlem's speech suggests, longtime KPD cadres believed that their past experiences lent them moral capital and political authority. Fritz Selbmann also claimed the right of "victims of fascism" to help forge the new Germany. As he stated: "The victims of fascism, those who went to the scaffold, [those] who went to prison or concentration camp are the best of our German people . . . we want to participate in the helping and shaping of the new reconstruction of our life . . . to our ideals that [we brought] from the penitentiaries and concentration camps belongs the notion that those who proved themselves the best of our people are to work in decisive positions to shape our life."[4]

For veteran communists, antifascism had a very specific meaning: opposition to fascism as the highest stage of monopoly capitalism. Longtime communists had resisted the Nazi regime not because it was a vile racist dictatorship, but because it was a form of monopoly capitalism. The East German regime claimed that a communist class struggle against fascism was *the* drama of the Nazi era. It thus always downplayed the centrality of race and the Holocaust in Nazi policy and ideology. The SED's antifascism, however, was not restricted to drawing political legitimacy from the party's past struggle against the Nazi regime. It was also used to justify the party's postwar politics. According to the SED, East Germany was an antifascist order because it had swept away the material preconditions of fascism (by dispossessing the old Junkers and industrial elites through land reform and the nationalization of industry). By contrast, West Germany was something of a continuation of the Nazi regime. The SED thus always claimed that the GDR was engaged in an "antifascist" struggle against West Germany and, indeed, the entire capitalist world order.

In the SBZ, the celebration and commemoration of the antifascist resistance began immediately after World War II. In the summer of 1945, for example, the KPD's *Deutsche Volkszeitung* (German people's newspaper) carried a number of articles on antifascist resistance activities in Nazi prisons and concentration camps.[5] The second Sunday in September was designated as a day of official commemoration for antifascists murdered by the Nazis. This day of remembrance would become part of the East German revolutionary calendar—and a day on which survivors of Nazi prisons and camps were traditionally honored. In 1946, Alexander Abusch, a former West émigré, published a widely read book, *Der Irrweg der Nation* (The wrong path of the nation), in which he heroized the resistance fighters inside Germany. In a passage that would become stereotypical, Abusch emphasized the proletarian qualities of Ernst Thälmann, the KPD leader who had been murdered in Buchenwald in 1944, and others like him: "Not some superhuman qualities, but rather a morality born of real solidarity with their own people and deeply rooted insight creates such heroes." In the GDR, antifascist resisters would be portrayed as humble, courageous, all-sacrificing participants in a deadly collective struggle for a future utopia. As Abusch noted, "The true importance of the fighters of the German underground is that even though they were not able to rescue the honor of Germany, they embodied the hope of the future."[6]

The commemoration of the antifascist struggle was always highly politicized. In 1947, the SED sanctioned the founding of the Vereinigung der Verfolgten des Naziregimes (VVN)—the Association of Those Persecuted by the Nazi Regime. One of the VVN's most important tasks was to keep the memory of the antifascist resistance at the forefront of SBZ politics. The VVN sponsored several important exhibitions; put out a number of widely circulated books and brochures; aided the creation of many simple memorials at mass grave sites or other scenes of Nazi atrocities; and organized countless rallies, parades, wreath-layings, and other events to commemorate the antifascist resistance. According to one SED memorandum, the portrayal of the antifascist resistance was to show—

Franz Dahlem, Karl Schirdewan, and others lead an antifascist march commemorating the start of the Spanish Civil War. Front row, left: Karl Schirdewan; fourth from left: Franz Dahlem. Dresden, July 20, 1952. (Bundesarchiv, SAPMO-BArch, Bild Y 10-1288/79)

"as opposed to the claims of our enemy"—that the "main burden of the resistance to fascism rested on the shoulders of the working class and its progressive allies." Moreover, projects that illustrated the past antifascist struggle were to showcase the "exhortatory example" of the "old comrades": "The teachings and experiences of our old comrades in their illegal work should allow them, as especially trustworthy cadres of our party, to have an effect on the whole [party] organization. Their ties and loyalty to the party, proven by the past, should be an exhortatory example for the forging of new cadres in the future."[7] The popularization of the past antifascist struggle of party cadres thus had multiple political uses: it was to legitimate the left-wing resistance (and thus the new SED regime), to serve as a propaganda weapon in the incipient Cold War, and, not least, to provide role models for new party members.

THE PARTY'S interest in the past antifascist struggle also served a rather more sinister political purpose: the control of party cadres. As early as the summer of 1945, the KPD began to gather information on the past

conduct of its longtime cadres. The collection of biographical information on party cadres was long-established communist practice. Following
the Comintern's example, the KPD had gathered material on its cadres
and kept such information in meticulous personnel files since the early
days of the Weimar Republic. The work of Michel Foucault is suggestive
for how KPD (and later SED) authorities used personnel files to discipline
longtime cadres (although Foucault aimed to show how disciplinary
practices were rooted in everyday uses of personal records and not in
state or official party practices of record-keeping). In *Discipline and Punish,* Foucault argued that as ordinary individuals came to be the subjects of written medical and prison records in the seventeenth century, a
disciplinary regime developed that used biographical records as a "means
of control and a method of domination." In contrast to biographical
texts that idealized great men, the "turning of real lives into writing . . .
functions as a procedure of objectification and subjection." According to
Foucault, biographical record-keeping "belongs . . . to a certain political
function of writing" embedded in a "technique of power" based on individual differences. Written documents that record "the measurements,
the gaps, [and] the 'marks'" that differentiate one individual from another are thus powerful disciplinary instruments.[8]

The KPD / SED's extensive personnel files constituted a virtual panop-
ticon on every facet of veteran communists' lives. Again and again, longtime communists were asked to fill out biographical questionnaires in
which they stated their socioeconomic background, education, work experience, party functions, illegal activity, imprisonment during the
Weimar and Nazi years, dates and countries of emigration, activity during emigration, and much more. Old Communists could not hide or alter
biographical information contained in these files for, according to guidelines on party punishments, the stating of false biographical information
was to be "particularly harshly judged."[9] Indeed, altering facts from one
curriculum vitae to the next was a punishable offense.[10] But even though
biographical facts were fixed and ever-present in the party's personnel
files, they could, at any moment, be scrutinized anew. In Foucault's language, personnel files thus provided the party with the means for an
"ideal point of penalty," an indefinite discipline: "an interrogation without end, an investigation that would be extended without limit to a meticulous and ever more analytical observation, a judgement that would at
the same time be the constitution of a file that was never closed."[11] Similarly, the Austrian sociologist Klaus-Georg Riegel has noted that the significance of biographical facts could "change according to the political
situation, the position of the cadre in the apparat, the degree of power

of his faction," and so on. Such personnel files, then, presented untold potential evidence for "denunciations, investigations, repressions, censures, warnings, and disciplinings."[12] Information found in files was often deemed suspicious only years after entry. Communists could thus never be sure that their pasts would endure in a positive manner. As a well-known witticism in Eastern Europe in the 1950s went, "It's not the future that's in doubt. It's the past."

THE CASE of Fritz Selbmann illustrates how the KPD initially dealt with information about party cadres' conduct during the Nazi era. After receiving denunciatory reports about Selbmann's conduct in Flossenbürg concentration camp, on July 8, 1945 the KPD Secretariat ordered an investigation into Selbmann and his past activities.[13] Selbmann's actions as a Kapo had apparently angered a number of longtime communists. According to one of his accusers, Selbmann "did not conduct himself faultlessly toward the foreign prisoners. I often heard that he beat these prisoners. Once I saw myself how he beat a Polish prisoner in the paint workshop. His whole conduct was provocative. Apparently he felt himself not as a prisoner but rather as a guard." This accuser also insinuated that Selbmann, like all Kapos, engaged in homosexual activity with a lackey who was always in his presence. Finally, this accuser claimed that Selbmann wore the uniform of the camp police and that he carried a rifle.[14] According to another accuser, Selbmann often boxed foreign prisoners' ears or hit them in the ribs; Selbmann also allegedly made derogatory remarks about prisoners of other nationalities. This accuser further claimed that "already when these events happened, we were of the opinion that Selbmann would later have to answer to the party for this period of his concentration-camp imprisonment."[15] Another communist recalled that Selbmann was isolated from other comrades in Flossenbürg because of "beatings, non-comradely conduct, but also political differences."[16] Asked to comment on Selbmann's conduct, Karl Schirdewan reported that he had warned Selbmann not to take on the Kapo position. As Schirdewan noted, "The course of developments showed how correct these warnings were . . . [Selbmann] also allowed himself to get carried away and a few times beat other inmates in nervous irritation. For example, his only pair of shoes was stolen and he had to go about barefoot in the camp in winter. When he caught the evil-doer, he beat him." After this occurred, Schirdewan and another comrade demanded that Selbmann give up his function and not beat camp inmates. Although Selbmann did not give up his position, Schirdewan claimed that thereafter "a significant improvement took place."[17]

Selbmann rigorously defended himself against all such accusations. He admitted that he had boxed the ears of the two inmates who stole his shoes. But he argued that this had been a mistake on his part, and one that he had already acknowledged in the camp. Otherwise, he insisted, "I had always fought a sharp, principled battle against the methods of terrorizing prisoners by other prisoners. These are the facts of the case. Whatever else is said about the matter is nonsense." Selbmann flatly denied the homosexuality charges: to a "swine [his accuser] everything is swine." And Selbmann defended in no uncertain terms his general conduct in handling political disagreements in Sachsenhausen and Flossenbürg: "I directly assert that it was I, along with a number of other comrades, who defended the general line and the ideological heritage of the party against deviations and falsifications."[18] Selbmann also explained the matter of having joined the camp police. When the SS decided that a camp police force was to be made up of German camp inmates in the spring of 1945, KPD members in the camp decided to join the force if ordered to do so. They justified this decision by arguing that communists should exploit this opportunity, particularly since the force might be equipped with weapons. Many communists thus became members of the camp police force, were outfitted with uniforms, and in some cases were even given rifles (without ammunition, however).[19] This camp police force was ordered to guard the "death march" of Flossenbürg inmates to Dachau in April 1945. Selbmann argued that he and other communists on the police force made it possible for many prisoners to desert the march columns.[20] In the summer of 1945, even one of Selbmann's accusers agreed that the decision to join the camp police force had been correct.[21] Selbmann appears to have convinced party authorities that the accusations against him were groundless. In any event, the investigation did not hinder his career during the early Aufbau years: Selbmann became an important East German economics functionary.

Between 1945 and 1947 the KPD / SED launched numerous other investigations into the past conduct of veteran communists in Nazi prisons and camps.[22] Erich Honecker was subject to a party investigation in 1945. This investigation focused on the fact that Honecker had escaped from jail without permission from his fellow communists in the Brandenburg Penitentiary. Some of these KPD cadres had apparently feared that this flight might endanger party ties to the outside world or even the liberation of the jail. In the summer of 1945, however, the KPD determined that the escape had not jeopardized other prisoners. Honecker was nonetheless given a party censure "because of his undisciplined conduct."[23] As with Selbmann, this investigation into Honecker's past apparently had no consequences: Honecker was soon the party's most influential youth functionary.

During the early postwar years, the KPD / SED viewed allegations of past communist misconduct with considerable leniency. Party authorities did not want to draw attention to anything that might undermine the image of communist cadres. Indeed, party authorities expressly warned against prosecuting communists (and social democrats) for crimes that they may have committed in prisons or camps; this, they believed, would merely provide ammunition to the anticommunist cause. As one functionary wrote: "Given the political situation in Berlin, we believe that it is not advisable to initiate legal proceedings . . . against antifascists who did time in prisons or camps during the twelve years and who were members of one of the two workers' parties. With such proceedings we provide material—especially to the Americans—about how members of the workers' parties made themselves the fascists' henchmen in the camps."[24]

IN 1947, the SED began a systematic, official reconstruction of the illegal activities of party members during the Nazi era. Karl Schirdewan headed the department charged with this task. In his memoirs, Schirdewan stated that this work was to ensure that "really nothing and no one, none of our fighters, our male and female comrades, nothing of their deeds, nothing of the torture suffered, and also none of their tormenters were to be forgotten."[25] He also insisted that in his department's work "the examination of the conduct of comrades was by no means at stake."[26] But his department sent out an appeal to party members "to record in writing their activities and to send it to us," along with descriptions of "contrasting opinions and statements" and "discussions" that had occurred in prison and emigration.[27] This appeal for summaries of past political controversies among veteran communists suggests that the SED was, in fact, looking for potentially incriminating information on its longtime cadres.

Already in 1948, the SED adopted a much harsher stance in the evaluation of the past lives of veteran communists. This development reflected heightened Cold War tensions and the concomitant Stalinization of the SED. The SED created the Central Party Control Commission (ZPKK). This institution became the central site of Stalinist terror for party members; punishments, brutal interrogations, arrests, and curious disappearances took place within its purview. Hermann Matern, an Old Communist who had spent the war years in Soviet exile, headed the ZPKK from 1948 until his death in 1971. Matern and his colleagues were soon very busy. In 1949, in a measure illustrating the Cold War paranoia of these years, SMAD officials stipulated that individuals who had emigrated to Western countries during the Nazi years or who had been in Western or Yugoslavian prisoner-of-war camps were no longer to be trusted with important functions. The Soviets claimed that these individuals presented a potential security risk because they might have been recruited by foreign intelligence agencies while abroad.[28] Echoing Soviet officials, SED authorities claimed that "experiences teach that Anglo-American imperialism leaves no means untried to infiltrate the party of the working class in order to subvert and deflect it from its path." The SED thus decreed a screening of all such officials. The "first task" of the screening was to be "the thorough study of the available personnel files. When lacunae are ascertained, written additions are to be requested. Where contradictions and uncertainties are revealed, oral clarification and the taking of minutes [is to be] carried out." Investigators were also to determine whether there was an "undue" concentration of comrades from the same emigration or prisoner-of-war camp in any given office or department.[29]

Until 1950, the SED's official interpretation of the West emigration was similar to that of other "antifascist" experiences: émigrés in Western countries had heroically fought the antifascist fight, albeit in the arena of propaganda and public opinion. According to a new narrative scripted in Moscow, however, many former West émigrés were now cast in the role of foreign intelligence operatives recruited by an alleged American master spy, Noel H. Field. Field, an enigmatic communist sympathizer, had worked for the Boston-based Unitarian Service Committee in France and Switzerland during World War II. He channeled humanitarian aid to expatriate communist functionaries in France and Switzerland and occasionally served as a courier between various communist groups in neutral and occupied Europe. Field also facilitated contacts between German communists and Americans working for the Office of Strategic Services (OSS) under Alan Dulles. After the war, Field attempted to secure a university or other position in Eastern Europe. At this time he contacted several highly placed East German communists, including Paul Merker and Franz Dahlem. In May 1949 Field was lured to Prague, arrested by Czech authorities, and handed over to Hungarian security. In Budapest, he was accused of espionage activity. Although Field remains a murky figure, there is no evidence that he directed American spy operations.

In September 1949, the head of Soviet security in Berlin, Ivan Serov, indicated that the ZPKK should investigate all contacts between Field and German communists during the war.[30] The ZPKK's investigation culminated in a sensational August 1950 "Statement of the Central Committee" that rewrote innocent communist contacts with Field into a wide-ranging conspiracy to undermine communism. In a fantastic overestimation of KPD cadres' potential influence, the statement claimed that this conspiracy had supposedly delayed the opening of a Second Front (thus hindering Soviet war efforts), weakened resistance activity near the Franco-German border, and ultimately aided the division of Germany.[31] The statement named ten veteran communists, three of whom were already under arrest. Of these, Willy Kreikemeyer soon died under mysterious circumstances in prison; Bruno Goldhammer was sentenced to ten years in GDR jails; and Leo Bauer, who was tried before a Soviet military tribunal and condemned to death, was deported to the Soviet gulag in 1952. In addition, three others named in the statement were expelled from the party, including Paul Merker, who until recently had been a member of the Politburo.[32]

In a related affair, the ZPKK reinterpreted the past activities of veteran communists who had cooperated with the OSS in the last period of the war. Even though the ZPKK knew that most of these communist-OSS connections had been sanctioned by Soviet authorities (the United States and the Soviet Union were wartime allies), it now insisted that these communists had worked—and thus might still be working—for an American intelligence agency. Between the Field and OSS affairs, dozens of veteran communists who had found exile in Western countries were expelled from the party and / or demoted to less influential positions in the GDR.[33] Moreover, at least two veteran communists committed suicide once they learned that they were under investigation. As one, Rudolf Feistmann, wrote in a suicide note, "It is unbearable that the party mistrusts me. That is the worst. It means that life is no longer worth living."[34]

THE SED embedded a campaign against functionaries of Jewish origin into its biography-based purges—a reflection of the anti-Semitism that swept through the Soviet Union and East Central Europe during Stalin's last years. Although only a very small minority of veteran communists were of Jewish origin, these longtime communists were overrepresented in Western exile during the Nazi years. According to Franz Dahlem, the KPD kept these cadres, who were so endangered in Nazi Germany, abroad in the 1930s.[35] At the same time, their socioeconomic background—many came from middle-class backgrounds and were relatively well-educated—explains why these KPD functionaries were able to leave Nazi Germany at all. Now, however, their past emigration to Western countries became suspect. This was especially true once a Czech show trial in late 1952 found Rudolf Slansky and thirteen other longtime communists, eleven of whom were of Jewish background, guilty of conspiring to restore capitalism in Czechoslovakia.

In the GDR, the SED Central Committee published a resolution on "The Lessons of the Trial of the Conspiracy Center around Slansky." This resolution focused on Paul Merker and his supposed nefarious activities on behalf of Zionist agencies; Merker, it should be noted, was not of Jewish descent. Merker had already been purged in 1950 in connection with the Noel Field Affair. At that time, his past views on Jewish matters had played no role in either public or secret accusations against him. Now, however, he became the central figure in the GDR's anticosmopolitan campaign.[36]

Merker's championing of Jewish interests made him a seemingly ideal target. The SED's resolution on the Slansky case pointed to the "hostile role of the agent Paul Merker in the German emigration group in Mexico from 1942 to 1946," and claimed that "there is no doubt that Merker is a subject of the U.S. finance oligarchy. He calls for the compensation of Jewish property in order to facilitate the penetration of U.S. finance capital in Germany." Merker was now arrested. Several other veteran communists who were of Jewish origin—and who had been with Merker in Mexican exile—were also mentioned as Zionist agents: Alexander Abusch, Erich Jungmann, and Leo Zuckermann.[37] This resolution set the stage for a zealous campaign against both practicing Jews and those of Jewish background in East Germany.

Although Gerhart Eisler was not named in this Central Committee resolution, he had actually fallen under suspicion of agent activity just months after his return to East Germany. In December 1949, Vladimir Semenov, the Soviet ambassador to East Germany, questioned "whether or not [there are] agents in [the] bureaucracy near Eisler."[38] Despite Semenov's suspicions, Eisler continued to head the Office of Information. He was not, however, reelected to the Central Committee in 1950. Moreover, according to both Franz Dahlem and Eisler's wife, Hilde, Wilhelm Pieck had wanted Eisler to join the Politburo. As Dahlem wrote Hilde in 1978: "I only know that at a certain point Wilhelm Pieck proposed that he [Gerhart] become a member of the Politburo. That's how highly the 'old one' regarded him. I did too. [Gerhart] had the qualities [to be a Politburo member]." Dahlem then mysteriously added, "In this letter I cannot get into the reasons for why this fell through."[39] In July 1951, Eisler was curtly interrogated by the ZPKK about his past and present activities.[40] The tone of this interrogation was such that Eisler may well have worried about what was in store for him. But nothing happened until late 1952. At that time, Semenov intimated to ZPKK authorities that it was time to collect incriminating material against Eisler.[41] At the same time, Czech radio, broadcasting the proceedings of the Slansky trial, claimed that Eisler had links to Slansky's "imperialist conspiracy center." The fact that Eisler was mentioned in connection with the Slansky trial underscores the link between the suspicions against him and his Jewish origin. In December, Eisler lost his position and the Office of Information was disbanded. In February 1953, the Politburo decreed an investigation into Eisler's return from the United States and his ties to the West.[42] Eisler was a likely defendant in an East German show trial that was to parallel the Rajk and Slansky show trials in Hungary and Czechoslovakia. The various elements of Eisler's biography, including his Jewish background, seemingly "predestined Eisler" to be such a defendant.[43] Stalin's death in March 1953, however, halted ongoing show-trial preparations.

Eisler was told by party authorities that he was under suspicion, but he was not told why. Some two years later, the case remained unresolved. Seething with frustration, Eisler wrote SED party leaders: "As an Old Communist I understand perfectly well that when a comrade is brought under suspicion an investigation against the comrade must be initiated. But after more than two-and-a-half years of investigation against me, I now demand that . . . [it] . . . finally be concluded . . . I am sick and tired of allowing myself to be treated as a second-class comrade . . . The patience and discipline of an Old Communist cannot consist in being abominably treated without hope of end for many years."[44] In 1960, Eisler noted in a short biography that "from 1953 until 1955—without being told the reasons—I was forbidden to hold a party function and I worked during this time as a journalist, political writer, and agitator. In 1955 the investigation against me was stopped because the accusations proved utterly unfounded. Without a doubt, these two years belong to the most bitter of my life."[45] Much later, Hilde Eisler stated: "Only once did I see . . . Gerhart full of despair and desperately unhappy. That was in 1953 when he was . . . declared a non-person and totally debarred from influence. Then the man was broken, temporarily only . . . but really broken. The accusation against him was even more demeaning—namely, that he had produced this whole campaign in the United States against himself, in order to be installed here as an American agent. That's what he was told later, after he was rehabilitated . . . There were three years between 1953 and 1956 . . . Those were bitter years, very bitter."[46] There was indeed a bitter irony to the SED's interpretation of Eisler's past biography: actions that Eisler had taken while under suspicion as a Soviet spy were construed to suggest that he was an American spy. Once again, Gerhart Eisler found himself in an impossible situation. But this time the situation was brought on by the very party to which he had devoted the better part of his life. This loyal communist endured a decade of mistaken identities with potentially hair-raising consequences—all at the crossroads of Cold War politics.

Although Eisler did not suffer imprisonment or worse, a number of veteran communists of Jewish origin did. Indeed, it is notable that SED and Soviet authorities subjected longtime communists with Jewish backgrounds to some of the worst mistreatment meted out during these years. Although very few veteran communists were actually imprisoned at this time, a number of those of Jewish origin were.[47] One of these, Hans Schrecker, later wrote a letter to party officials in which he described the conditions that he endured in East German prisons. Schrecker, a journalist who had emigrated to England, was arrested in 1952 and accused of past contacts to Czech intelligence operations. In his first exchange with his interrogators, Schrecker wrote, "A torrent of invective was showered upon me . . . 'You criminal, you international spy, you filthy Jew have betrayed the party, you Trotskyite bandit, you wanted to create havoc, but our speedy intervention prevented you from any success.'" Between interrogations, Schrecker suffered miserable prison conditions: "I was transferred to a small dark cell. There were no windows, only electric light day and night. According to prison regulations, I had to hold my hands stretched out from my body, and my eyes were not allowed to be covered. It was a cold winter. The cell was unheated and cold air was blown in from an opening in the ceiling." Schrecker continued: "There was tight surveillance; approximately every one-and-a-half minutes, someone looked through a peephole in order to see whether I was sleeping and to prevent every possibility of sleep. Through this long period of sleeplessness I ended up in a state that I can now no longer judge. I went to sleep standing and fell apart." Interrogations nonetheless continued. Schrecker thought himself "buried alive and lost."

Schrecker's letter goes on for pages detailing both his poor treatment and the manipulation of various elements in his biography. In 1945, for example, Schrecker had given a report about the activities of the Free German Movement in France to a Czech journalist, Harry Richter. Shortly thereafter, Schrecker used this report as the basis not only for a public lecture, but also for a brochure published with the approval of the KPD leadership in England. Now, however, Schrecker was accused of passing sensitive material to Richter, who in turn was alleged to be a Czech intelligence operative. Schrecker ultimately signed various incriminating statements that were then used as evidence against him in a

Franz Dahlem, 1952. (Bundesarchiv, SAPMO-BArch, Bild Y
10-140/83)

secret trial; he was sentenced to eight years in jail. Summarizing his bitterness about what had happened to him, Schrecker wrote: "I fully understood that the party must intervene when serious accusations of criminal actions are raised against a comrade who during thirty years of party
membership has often held high functions. I did not understand why
the party did not feel it necessary to speak with me even once. The feeling of being abandoned by all comrades, except for my wife, crushed
me and is the key for why I found my life worthless and was ready to
throw it away. Everything that was the meaning and content of my life
seemed to me destroyed."[48] Although non-Jewish victims of the SED's
biography-based purges have also left descriptions of their miserable jail
experiences, Schrecker's testimony is among the most chilling testa-
ments found in the SED party archives. It is troubling indeed that such
anti-Semitic tendencies were tolerated in East Germany just seven years
after the Holocaust.

FRANZ DAHLEM also saw his past biography viciously reinterpreted at
this time. Dahlem's position had steadily eroded since 1949. In that year,

the resolution that called for the screening of all SED functionaries who had spent time in Western exile did not bode well for Dahlem; he belonged to this circle. Ulbricht was now able to strip Dahlem of his responsibility for SED personnel policy; two years later, he also took over Dahlem's supervision of communist politics in West Germany. Dahlem's troubles, however, only became patently obvious once the Central Committee passed its resolution on the Slansky trial. This resolution not only discussed supposed Zionist activities among veteran communists, but also starkly denounced the actions of the KPD's Secretariat in Paris in 1939. Although Dahlem was not actually named in this resolution, he had headed the Paris Secretariat at this time and was thus clearly responsible for its actions. According to the resolution, the KPD leadership's decision that all German émigrés should register with police authorities (as French regulations stipulated) had led to the "voluntary internment" of communists that "encouraged the interests of the imperialist West powers." As the resolution alleged, "The liquidation of German party groups weakened the resistance struggle in occupied France and prevented most of all the development of an effective agitation among the German occupation troops."[49]

In March 1953, the Politburo instructed the ZPKK to begin a "necessary investigation" into Dahlem's past.[50] In May, Matern reported the ZPKK's preliminary findings to the Central Committee. According to the ZPKK, "The voluntary internment was a capitulation for which Comrade Dahlem had full responsibility and that resulted from a totally false attitude towards the government of [French premier] Daladier and its reactionary and Soviet-hostile role." In addition, in August 1939 Dahlem had been recalled to Moscow but had not gone to the Soviet capital. Matern darkly ruminated: "It is our view that Comrade Dahlem has not yet said the true motives for why he did not go to Moscow, liquidated the party leadership, and voluntarily went into internment." The ZPKK chief also claimed that Dahlem had had more contact with Noel Field and those connected with him than he had admitted. In addition, Dahlem had supposedly had various contacts with other alleged imperialist spies and should have suspected their nefarious activities. Finally, Matern stated that the ZPKK was investigating Dahlem's conduct in Nazi captivity.[51] At this time, Dahlem was rumored to have conducted himself poorly during Gestapo interrogations and, in Mauthausen concentration camp, to have stalled an armed uprising by camp inmates in 1945.

Anton Ackermann, who had been party to the Secretariat's deliberations in Paris in 1939, now repeated charges concerning Dahlem's "liquidation measures" that he had made after escaping to Moscow in the spring of 1940. Ackermann charged that after the conclusion of the Nazi-Soviet Pact in August 1939, Paul Merker had made a "vile, incredibly crass anti-Soviet attack" at a Secretariat meeting. In response, Dahlem had "said nothing" and thus "remained on Merker's tow-rope." Ackermann claimed that there was a connection between Dahlem's "indifference" to Merker's anti-Soviet attack and "Dahlem's capitulatory conduct at the beginning of the war." "Dahlem," Ackermann insinuated, "made his disastrous mistake under the influence of the disguised Soviet enemy Paul Merker." Ackermann also castigated Dahlem's current conduct. The problem with Dahlem, Ackermann alleged, was not so much that he had made "serious mistakes" in the past, but that he now refused to acknowledge those errors: "He does not openly admit his mistakes . . . but instead repeatedly tries to scale down and to hush up his mistakes. He does not try to uncover the causes of his mistakes, but makes others responsible for his mistakes. He has done this since 1939 with a stubbornness that borders virtually on obsession." This, according to Ackermann, "had led Dahlem to other mistakes and had prevented him from drawing the correct consequences in a timely fashion, particularly in the area of cadre policy after 1945."[52]

The Central Committee now adopted a resolution that explicitly addressed Dahlem's past political blunders. Dahlem had allegedly engaged in "liquidation policies" by allowing German émigrés "to voluntarily enter the concentration camps of the Soviet-hostile Daladier government." Dahlem had also supposedly demonstrated "insufficient trust in the Soviet Union" because he had encouraged communist registration with the police even though France was "Soviet-hostile." The resolution further charged that Dahlem had offered the French government assistance against Nazi Germany at a time when the Soviet Union was allied with Hitler; Dahlem had sent Daladier a letter in which he offered communist cooperation with the French government in its conflict with Nazi Germany. Finally, the resolution accused Dahlem of demonstrating "total blindness towards attempts by imperialist agents to infiltrate the party," a reference to his brief postwar contact with Noel Field.[53]

Dahlem lost his Politburo, Secretariat, and Central Committee seats. This veteran communist, however, did not go down without a battle. At a Central Committee meeting in July 1953, Otto Grotewohl read passages of a letter that Dahlem had recently sent him. In this letter, Dahlem complained bitterly about his unjust treatment and issued a number of demands. He should be allowed to give the Central Committee a response to Matern's report. He wanted the Central Committee to know that he wished to have a special commission investigate his matter and that the

Central Committee should vote on this issue. Dahlem also insisted that "to be fair, the judgment of the Central Committee [i.e., the resolution] must be corrected before the party and the general public." And finally, Dahlem demanded that "the investigation be begun again, using correct investigating methods that are in accordance with a communist party, and that objective and morally irreproachable comrades be named as the leading comrades of the investigation."[54] With these remarks, Dahlem was suggesting that those who had investigated his case had been neither objective nor morally irreproachable—serious (and dangerous) charges for a communist cadre to make against top party leaders. None of Dahlem's demands were fulfilled. Dahlem was left to idle inactivity in Biesdorf, a suburb of Berlin. Apparently, though, he feared worse. In a December 1953 interrogation of Dahlem's son-in-law, Karl Mewis, Matern claimed that "[Dahlem] reckoned that he would be arrested."[55] In addition, it appears that Dahlem was being set up as a major—if not the major—defendant in an East German show trial.[56] Just as with Gerhart Eisler, however, Stalin's death and the more moderate political course charted by the new Soviet leadership halted any such trial preparations.

In 1974, Dahlem wrote a few pages in which he tried to make sense of what had happened to him in 1953. Although he had hoped to publish these passages in East Germany, Dahlem was never allowed to do so, and they were published only after 1989. In these pages, Dahlem claimed that he had fully understood the nature of communist purges only "when in our own party such monstrous accusations were raised directly against me. On the basis of charges raised by the criminal Beria and his henchmen, I was accused of cooperation with the American secret service through the supposed main agent of the CIA, Noel Field, as well as of ties with the French secret service and even the Gestapo. Now my eyes were opened!" But as Dahlem learned, even though the charges were fabricated, he could not make this known to party circles. As he explained: "As a member of the Politburo I now experienced myself how suddenly these false accusations were raised against me and even partly published without my being able . . . to refute the fabricated charges. Yes, in the ZPKK's 'investigation' my demands that I be allowed to face head-on the supposed witnesses for the prosecution and that I be allowed to see the supposed documentary evidence on hand against me were refused." In addition, Dahlem wrote, "I had to experience how the members of the Central Committee on the basis of these monstrous charges . . . were misled and so in more or less good conscience agreed to my condemnation." Although Dahlem could barely contain his outrage about what had occurred to him, he was also somewhat rueful about his own past participation in similar purges: "At the same time I could not and cannot spare myself the bitter accusation that I had acted in the past in a similar manner as now—in 1953—the members of the Central Committee acted against me." But Dahlem would not elaborate on why such purges had taken place. He only suggested that "the time is not right to explain the reasons for this and the events of those years [1950 and before], for this must happen in connection with the treatment of this period and in this process the concrete-historical background cannot be disregarded."[57]

FORMER WEST émigrés were not the only veteran communists who saw their past biographies maliciously reinterpreted in the early 1950s. As the case against Franz Dahlem suggests, communist conduct in Nazi prisons and concentration camps was now also open to suspicion. Indeed, Max Sens, a longtime communist who was a member of the ZPKK, warned his colleagues that concentration-camp inmates and prisoners in Nazi jails may also have been recruited as foreign spies: "There is developing a detrimental tendency to look only at the emigration and to completely overlook that other people also could have entered into hostile ties . . . Some comrades have forgotten that the imperialist influence was effective not only in Western states, but also in fascist Germany. Of course, this influence wasn't as strong in the jails and concentration camps of Germany, but it was also present, for as long as there is capitalism somewhere on earth, attempts to recruit agents in the revolutionary workers' movement will not cease."[58] It seems, however, that the ZPKK never actually found veteran communists who had entered into "hostile ties" with foreign espionage agencies while in Nazi captivity. But it did find countless other forms of communist betrayal among longtime KPD cadres who had been arrested and imprisoned by Nazi authorities.

In the early 1950s, the ZPKK recast many innocent actions by veteran communists in Nazi captivity into treasonous acts against the communist movement. Numerous veteran communists, for example, were alleged to have betrayed other communists during Gestapo interrogations. In fact, such communists had often only named communists whom they knew to be abroad or already under arrest; party authorities, however, did not take this context into account in their judgments. ZPKK investigators also manipulated the fact that many political prisoners who had served out their sentences in Nazi jails or camps were required, before discharge, to sign statements pledging to inform the Gestapo of illegal KPD activity. Although such individuals never reported illicit KPD actions to the Gestapo, the ZPKK nonetheless claimed that they had become Gestapo agents.[59] In some cases, ZPKK officials took Old Communists' past attempts to deceive the Gestapo as evidence of cooperation *with* the Gestapo. Gerhart Ziller, for example, an important economics functionary in the SED, had come up with a plan that he hoped would secure his release from Sachsenhausen concentration camp: he reported a fictional patent for a fan wheel that would ventilate Wehrmacht tanks. Ziller reasoned that when Nazi authorities learned of this patent, they would release him to work on military projects; this, he thought, would allow him to participate in further illegal activity. Although Ziller was never released from Nazi captivity, the fact that he had supposedly aided the Nazi military machine simmered in the SED's cauldrons. Every year or two, the SED launched a new investigation into the matter.[60] Ziller lived for years knowing that party authorities had found an aspect of his biography that could ruin his political reputation at any time.

In another kind of biographical manipulation, the ZPKK stripped some veteran communists of their masculinity. The ideal Old Communist was male, and he was a "hardened" revolutionary, "steeled" in struggle. When the ZPKK discovered faults in a veteran communist's past, it sometimes framed his character in terms countering this ideal. In 1950, Horst Sindermann, later a Politburo member from 1967 to 1989, was accused of "falling apart" and "becoming soft" during Nazi captivity. Although Sindermann had held the positions of first secretary of the SED in Chemnitz and Leipzig, he was now demoted to editor in chief of the newspaper *Freiheit* (Freedom) in Halle. In a long letter to the ZPKK, Sindermann refuted the charges that went to the heart of his masculine self-image and antifascist identity. He admitted that in Nazi prison he had one night "half insane, lost his nerves and screamed." This happened, he explained, after he had been chained to his bed for seven weeks while a bright electric bulb shone in his face and he was constantly forced to hear the grating sound of a toilet-flush system. Sindermann nonetheless insisted that his conduct in Nazi custody contradicted the ZPKK's evaluation of his past behavior. He had, he asserted, withstood solitary confinement; chosen to go to a concentration camp rather than commit himself to the Gestapo; and had falsified camp account books in Sachsenhausen where, for three years, he had successfully stolen food from the SS camp food storeroom for his fellow prisoners.[61]

SED and Soviet authorities also revisited investigations of communist conduct in Nazi concentration camps. In the first years after the war, party authorities had not viewed communist morality in the camps especially harshly. In 1950, however, communist survivors of Buchenwald concentration camp who had held Kapo functions were suddenly held accountable for their past actions. Soviet authorities even arrested two veteran communists who had been Kapos, Ernst Busse and Erich Reschke. Busse, who had been the Kapo in charge of the camp sick bay, was now accused, among other atrocities, of compiling lists of prisoners for medical experiments and, in the process, of saving the lives of German communists at the expense of other prisoners' lives—perhaps even of those of Soviet prisoners of war. When asked to justify these and other actions, Busse invoked what he may have thought was a communist line of defense: "We accomplished the preservation of our lives and the lives of the members of our organization . . . Known members of our illegal organization in the camp could live relatively peacefully and did not have to fear repression from the SS. SS measures resulting in the mass extermination of prisoners did not touch us. Furthermore, our functions in the camp administration allowed us to avoid hunger and want." Soviet authorities, apparently dismayed by such brazen answers, deported both men to the gulag. While other Buchenwald communists were not arrested, many were demoted to lesser positions in East Germany.[62]

In 1952, the SED once again investigated Selbmann's actions in Nazi captivity. On this occasion, allegations surfaced about his conduct when he was arrested in 1933 and while he was in Sachsenhausen concentration camp in the early 1940s. A Stasi report noted that when Selbmann was arrested in 1933, "He immediately admitted his correct name so that he would not be subject to torture . . . even though he supposedly had good [illegal] papers [involving another identity]." In Sachsenhausen, the Stasi reported, Selbmann allegedly "rejected a serious political work among the inmates of the camp since he had to preserve himself for the tasks after the destruction of fascism."[63] These accusations suggested that Selbmann was cowardly and arrogant—both significant communist shortcomings: cowardice could lead to blackmail, whereas arrogance could result in independent actions. In any event, Selbmann's conduct in Nazi captivity did not directly lead to a party punishment. Instead, the SED leadership censured Selbmann for his work at EKO in 1952; he was used as a scapegoat to explain some of the GDR's economic shortcomings. But Selbmann no doubt viewed the incriminating material on his biographical past as something of a sword of Damocles. He could never be sure that his past would not be used as a weapon against him. Moreover, Selbmann always remained intent on preserving his revolutionary reputation; he later wrote extensive memoirs of his time in Nazi captivity.

In the early 1950s, Spanish Civil War veterans were also dishonored; this happened not only in the GDR, but throughout East Central Europe.

Communist authorities questioned these military veterans' exploits in the International Brigades as well as their political engagement after the Spanish Civil War ended. In 1951, for example, the ZPKK found that during a military campaign in Spain one longtime communist had engaged in conduct that "was objectively harmful to the party, showed streaks of demoralization and therefore had a subversive effect on the troops."[64] In Czechoslovakia, meanwhile, communist president Klement Gottwald cast suspicion on these war veterans' conduct in French internment camps following the end of Spanish hostilities. According to the Czech leader, Interbrigadists "lived under very difficult conditions" in the French camps and were thus "the object of pressure and black-mail at first by the French and American secret services and afterwards by the German. Taking advantage of the difficult physical and moral state of the International-Brigade men, these espionage services succeeded in recruiting some of them as agents."[65] East German veterans of the Spanish Civil War soon felt the effects of these suspicions. Ludwig Renn, a well-known Old Communist novelist and Spanish Civil War veteran, wrote in private correspondence in 1952: "I hear it rumored that at the moment speaking about Spain is unwanted, and that everything connected with it is cancelled. Supposedly this is happening because there were too many traitors in Spain. I don't understand such points of view."[66] The suspicions surrounding Spanish Civil War veterans were accompanied by ominous party silence rather than the usual behind-the-scenes investigations.

TO A certain extent, survivors of Nazi captivity and former West émigrés colluded in the negative revision of their collective pasts. After 1945, veteran communists who had been in Nazi prisons or concentration camps often wrote denunciatory letters about the past conduct of their fellow comrades. Similarly, once the Noel Field resolution was published, Old Communists who had been in Western emigration inundated the ZPKK with letters and reports that included supplementary information on the supposed suspicious activities of those already implicated, and denounced yet others as possible agents of "imperialist powers." Although the ZPKK charges were patently absurd, former West émigrés nonetheless joined the hunt for alleged spies. Indeed, they racked their memories for past signs of suspicious activity among their cohort. They sometimes even rewrote their own emigration experiences of political slights and differences according to the various narratives now suggested by the ZPKK.

Wilhelm and Emmy Koenen interpreted past political differences in English emigration with Jürgen Kuczynski, a prominent East German intellectual and Old Communist of Jewish origin, to Kuczynski's alleged "class-hostile" attributes. In a letter to Matern, Emmy claimed that while Wilhelm Koenen was interned, Kuczynski attempted to undermine Koenen's political positions. As a result, Emmy had serious political differences with Kucyznski that went "so far in 1941 that he defamed my husband and pressed me to divorce him." Emmy claimed that Kuczynski's "political pursuit" of Wilhelm Koenen continued well after Koenen's return to London. According to Emmy, Kuczynski's actions "were unheard-of discussion methods in the KPD that I have belonged to since 1924 and could only be deployed by class-hostile elements." She concluded that "Jürgen Kuczynski is a hostile element and does not belong in our party."[67] Ironically, whether Emmy knew it or not, Wilhelm Koenen was apparently also under suspicion for agent activity. Hans Schrecker later stated that his interrogators had insisted that "comrades such as Wilhelm Koenen, Heinz Schmidt, Grete Wittkowski, Siegbert Kahn, Jürgen Kuczynski, . . . [and Walter] Janka had engaged in espionage activity along with me."[68] In any event, by rewriting the past into the ZPKK's current script, former West émigrés like Emmy Koenen signaled their willingness to believe the ZPKK's charges; they thus lent credence to ZPKK suspicions that the various communist emigrations in the West had been hotbeds of imperialist spies and scoundrels.

At the same time, those veteran communists who were purged did not turn their backs on the communist movement; in a sense, they too colluded in these purges. After Khrushchev exposed Stalin's crimes in his famous Secret Speech to the CPSU's Twentieth Party Congress in February 1956, the SED set up a "Commission of the Central Committee for the Examination of Matters of Party Members." Old Communists now wrote lengthy letters to party leaders in which they detailed the abuses they had endured in past years. In these letters, however, they also strove to convey their deep loyalty to the SED. Hans Schrecker, for example, claimed that he had incurred the hatred of his fellow prisoners "because of my incessant defense of the party and the state."[69] Paul Merker described cruel interrogations, a travesty of a trial, and years of solitary confinement. But he still wrote, "There is nothing that could dissuade me from my communist conviction and from my solidarity with the party and the socialist world." Merker also refused to believe that SED leaders were behind his persecution. Instead, he blamed Lavrenti Beria and his "proxies" in Germany. Ever a loyal communist, Merker thought to put the interests of his party above those of his person. As he wrote Wilhelm Pieck, he had done without a defense attorney and had acted with reserve during his trial proceedings, "so that the enemies of the GDR could not exploit my [court] appearance."[70] Franz Dahlem also remained stead-fastly loyal to the East German regime. In his unpublished 1974 mem-oirs, for example, he insisted: "But even the difficulties that the party heaped on me in 1953 could and has not shaken my loyalty to and love for the Leninist party and its powerful, blossoming country [the So-viet Union]; just as little could it [shake my loyalty and love] for my own party, whose unity and tenacity—especially then in the face of the class enemy's raging attacks against it—was always of the uppermost im-portance."[71]

For veteran communist purge victims, renunciation, or even open crit-icism, of the SED regime was almost inconceivable. Longtime commu-nists had spent a lifetime of suffering in the struggle for a socialist society. As one historian has written, they (and other veterans of the working-class movement) "felt a tremendous emotional attachment to the move-ment into which they had been born, and for the sake of which they had striven so long and suffered so much . . . the labor movement had given these veterans an almost spiritual sense of purpose to their lives . . . To break with the regime would mean acknowledging that all their struggles and sufferings had achieved nothing."[72] Leo Bauer, one of two purge vic-tims who actually forsook the GDR, later stated: "It is not easy to re-nounce a belief for which one was a combatant and for which one suf-fered."[73] Similarly, Alfred Kantorowicz, another veteran communist who fled the GDR (although he was not a purge victim), later wrote about why it was so difficult for Old Communists to criticize the SED. The Cold War, he argued, forced veteran communists to choose between East and West; they could not situate themselves between these two stark choices. If longtime communists criticized Soviet-style communism, it would be too readily viewed as the abandonment of their socialist principles: "Old Communists . . . wanted . . . to be damned to eternal silence and ruin rather than to take upon themselves the odium of apparent betrayal of their convictions."[74] By the early 1950s, veteran communists may also have felt that it was too daunting a task to reinvent themselves in middle or old age—especially given the energy they had devoted, and the sacri-fices they had made, to maintain their communist identities during the Nazi era.

SCHOLARS HAVE advanced a number of interpretations to explain these purges. Some have argued that Walter Ulbricht used them to remove real or potential rivals to his personal rule. This certainly rings true for the purges of such high-ranking Old Communists as Franz Dahlem or Paul Merker, but it does not explain why the past activities of so many lower-ranking veteran communists were also investigated. It is possible that Ulbricht or other top SED leaders assumed that these lower-ranking long-time communists were somehow supporters of Dahlem or Merker. There is, however, no evidence to suggest that the SED leadership thought this to be the case. Other historians have argued that former West émigrés and concentration-camp survivors were purged because they harbored ideas of communist rule at odds with the Stalinist views of former Soviet émigrés.[75] Former West émigrés or concentration-camp inmates, however, generally did not disagree with the KPD / SED leadership after 1945. It is, of course, possible that former Soviet émigrés *thought* that they did and thus—in something of a preventive strike—removed these individuals from influential positions. Although this was certainly true right after the war, there is, in fact, little evidence to suggest that this was the case in the later 1940s and early 1950s.

In many ways, these purges were arbitrary and irrational—essential features of Stalinist purges. They were arbitrary in that there was no reason why one particular individual and not another was caught up in the maelstrom of terror. There was also nothing that an individual could do to avoid being purged; no amount of groveling to party authorities, for example, could prevent an individual's purge. Moreover, although groups of communists with particular biographical backgrounds were targeted, not all members of any given group were purged. Some veteran communists who might have seemed likely purge victims never suffered career setbacks during these years. Kurt Hager, for example, who had spent the war years in England, climbed up the party hierarchy in the early 1950s. The SED also had plenty of potentially incriminating evidence on Erich Honecker, but nothing happened to him during these years. At the same time, these purges were irrational in that they were not based on rational criteria such as policy differences among veteran communists. Veteran communists who harbored mildly critical views of the SED do not appear to have been any more or less likely to become purge victims. Yet many longtime communists who never wavered from their party's Marxist-Leninist orthodoxy were targeted.

These purges nonetheless served a rational purpose: to sow terror in the party's ranks. For veteran communists, these purges were truly terrifying. Purge victims could not fathom why they, innocent communists, were now denounced as traitors to their cause. The arbitrariness of the purges also heightened mistrust and suspicion among Old Communists and helped to break down solidarities forged during long years of shared experiences. At the same time, the fact that veteran communists were purged by the manipulation of their biographies was particularly cruel.

Most longtime communists had few professional skills, but they did have one valuable asset: the charisma associated with their past participation in the antifascist struggle. Investigations into their past lives, however, sullied this most valued treasure. These investigations forcibly reminded Old Communists that the party, the arbiter of revolutionary reputations, held sway over all that was most meaningful to them. Veteran communists were now forced to acknowledge their party's fickle and incontestable power—and, in response, to measure their political conduct accordingly.

Although all of these purges disciplined longtime communists, the motives underlying the purges of former West émigrés differed from those underlying the purges of survivors of Nazi captivity. Soviet security concerns seem to have been a major factor in the purges against former West émigrés. Soviet authorities appear to have had a genuine paranoia about an international conspiracy of longtime communists who had spent the war years in Western exile. The East German purges were thus the counterpart to the bloodier purges and dramatic show trials that—for the same reasons—swept through East Central Europe during Stalin's last years. As the previous pages and evidence from other East Central European countries suggest, Soviet authorities were intimately involved in these purges. They suggested that whole groups of Old Communists (and others) be investigated; they insisted on incriminating evidence against particular veteran communists; and, either on their own or in conjunction with SED authorities, they arrested, interrogated, and sentenced some longtime communists to grueling punishments.

Scholars have argued that Soviet authorities initiated purges in the SED and other Eastern European communist parties in order to subordinate these satellite parties to Soviet power.[76] To a certain extent, this seems true of the East German case; through these purges, Soviet authorities effectively meddled in SED personnel politics. But Soviet officials cannot be entirely blamed for these purges. Although Soviet authorities initiated these purges, SED officials not only cooperated with their Soviet counterparts, but also pursued their own lines of investigation. Moreover, Walter Ulbricht and other members of the SED leadership benefited from these investigations: they removed uncomfortable rivals, they subjected influential veteran communists to party discipline, and they were able to explain GDR economic and other shortcomings by pointing to a vast conspiracy bent on undermining East German socialism.

Soviet authorities also occasionally instigated investigations against veteran communists who had survived Nazi captivity. In these proceedings, however, Soviet officials seemed somewhat less concerned with security matters and rather more with communist morality in the camps. At the same time, the purges against survivors of Nazi captivity served a different purpose: they ensured that no individual veteran communist would have an independent biographical charisma that could challenge the political authority of Ulbricht and other veteran communists who had spent the war years in the Soviet Union. For former Soviet émigrés, Old Communists who had survived Nazi prisons and concentration camps posed a particular threat. Not only did these veteran communists personally embody the SED's myth of antifascist resistance, but their biographies of heroic survival also easily lent themselves to a legendary pathos. There was to be no German Gomułka—the underground communist leader who became Poland's chief in 1956.

Investigations into the biographies of communist survivors of Nazi captivity were shrouded in secrecy. This is significant. The SED, eager to promote its myth of antifascist resistance, could not let the public know that the very communists on whom this myth was being built were actually under investigation for alleged misconduct. As a result, veteran communists who survived Nazi captivity were secret traitors, but public heroes. As public heroes, however, they were stripped of all individuality; the sufferings they endured, their acts of resistance, and their courage and solidarity were all cast in very stereotypical terms. This served the SED leadership's goals: uniquely individual heroes would detract from the legendary *collective* achievements of the party. To uphold the revolutionary stature of the party collective, SED authorities thus propagated an idealized image of the Old Communist resistance fighter while assiduously undermining the antifascist credentials of individual, real veteran communists.

THE VILIFICATION of Old Communists' past lives took place just as the SED stepped up its campaign to celebrate communist sacrifice and heroics in the "antifascist" struggle against Nazi Germany. In 1948, for example, the FDJ began a systematic propagation of the antifascist myth. It began a campaign to award "assault banners" with the names of antifascist martyrs to the winners of various competitions—generally youth work brigades that had accomplished various socialist successes. The FDJ newspaper *Junge Welt* (Young world) also began to carry weekly newspaper articles that celebrated fallen heroes of the antifascist struggle. Such articles were intended to introduce young East Germans to a legendary communist past. In October 1949, the FDJ issued formal guidelines on how its local groups could adopt the name of a fallen resistance fighter. The adoption of such a name was intended as a great honor.[77] In the late 1940s and early 1950s, the SED also began a sustained cult of Ernst Thälmann. In 1952, the youth organization for East German schoolchildren from the first through seventh grades, the Pioneers, was named for Ernst Thälmann. Virtually all East German children were thus exposed to many talks, books, films, and exhibitions on the martyred communist leader. These measures were intended to ensure that the myth of antifascist resistance would not be lost on East German youth—the SED's great hope for a future generation of socialist men and women untainted by Nazi ideology.

In the early 1950s, the SED also began to plan memorials at the various concentration camps on East German territory. In late 1951, the SED formed a "Planning Commission for Memorials" to turn the former concentration camps of Buchenwald, Ravensbrück, Sachsenhausen, and Lichtenburg, along with the Brandenburg Penitentiary, into commemorative sites. At Buchenwald, a museum and small ceremonial grounds were readied. In December 1953, the SED then decreed the construction of a major memorial at Buchenwald.[78] This memorial would feature a tower and a famous statue of triumphant resistance fighters by the Old Communist sculptor Fritz Cremer. With its opening in 1958, the Buchenwald Memorial became the premier site for the East German commemoration of antifascist resistance. Although all of these memorials commemorated the martyrdom of communist antifascists, they also helped to create a heroic aura around living survivors. It was survivors who often staffed the various planning commissions, who organized and ran tours at the various commemorative sites, and who gave the major speeches at memorial ceremonies recalling the past antifascist struggle.

These years marked the transformation of participants in the antifascist effort from "victims" or the "persecuted" of the Nazi regime to "antifascist resistance fighters." In practice, this narrowed the circle of those participants who would be honored in the GDR—essentially only long-time communists and a few other veterans of the German working-class movement. This new departure was symbolized by the founding of the "Committee of Antifascist Resistance Fighters in the GDR" in February 1953. This committee succeeded the VVN that had been disbanded some weeks earlier; for the SED leadership, the VVN represented the interests of too broad an array of vocal Nazi victims, including Jewish survivors of the Holocaust. The very title of the new committee suggested the importance of semantics to the developing antifascist myth: communists had not been merely victimized—they had also actively fought the Nazi regime. This emphasis on fighting not only underscored the SED's quest for political legitimacy through a combative antifascism, but also reiterated the gendered militancy of the SED's past and present antifascist struggle.

THERE WAS an intimate relationship between the glorified public image of the communist resister and the secret investigations into the past biographies of veteran communists. These investigations played into a Foucauldian strategy of discipline par excellence. These purges were the epitome of biography as discipline. The public revolutionary ideal set an impossibly high standard against which Old Communists were to measure their past conduct. Longtime communists came to understand that their shortcomings, failures, and compromises in the struggle against Hitler demonstrated that they had not been good enough communists when tested in the crucible of antifascist resistance. Veteran communists thus internalized the chasm between their own, often compromised biographies and that of the increasingly popularized revolutionary ideal. To make up for their past failures, longtime communists strove to be more perfect communists—that is, communists who would, in every possible way, uphold their SED regime. Just as these purges and other events of the Aufbau years had taxed veteran communists' loyalty to their regime, so too would East German developments in the next years and decades. But as in the past, longtime communists would maintain a stubborn allegiance to their revolutionary movement—not least because they had undergone the experience of biography-based purges.

6

RULERS

East German Politics during the Ulbricht Era

FROM 1945 UNTIL 1971, WALTER ULBRICHT DOMINATED GDR POLITICS. This was formalized in 1950, when Ulbricht was named general secretary of the SED. Ulbricht's position was strengthened by the advancing age and ill health of Wilhelm Pieck, the SED co-chairman and GDR president until his death in 1960. Although Ulbricht enjoyed both Soviet support and great influence among many ranking SED functionaries, he nonetheless faced challenges to his rule in the 1950s: Karl Schirdewan, Fred Oelßner, and a number of other pre-1933 KPD cadres came to oppose Ulbricht.

Historians now debate the character of this opposition—whether these veteran communists wished to introduce systemic reforms or merely to remove the SED leader. Ulbricht, however, brilliantly exploited long-standing Soviet and traditional KPD mores to preserve his position of power. He preyed on veteran communists' self-abnegation, devotion to party discipline, and fidelity to the Soviet Union and its socialist model. By 1958, he had purged all of his opponents. In the 1960s, Ulbricht then underwent something of a change of persona: he introduced a program to modernize East German socialism. But in a role reversal, Ulbricht saw his program thwarted by Erich Honecker and other longtime communists anxious to uphold Soviet-style socialism in the GDR. In 1971, Honecker, deploying Soviet political tactics that he had first learned in Weimar days, even ousted Ulbricht, his erstwhile mentor.

ULBRICHT'S TROUBLES began in the spring of 1953. The policy of the "rapid" or "forced" construction of socialism—proclaimed by Ulbricht in July 1952—had sowed widespread discontent among the GDR population. Among other repressive features, this program involved higher work norms for laborers and increased pressure on farmers to join collective farms. In response, hundreds of thousands of East Germans fled the GDR for West Germany. By May 1953, the post-Stalin Soviet leadership had become alarmed by these developments. Lavrenti Beria, Stalin's longtime security chief, led the way in demanding that the SED adopt a "New Course."[1] When the SED Politburo met to discuss this Soviet demand, several veteran communists spoke out against Ulbricht. Ulbricht's most forthright opponents included Rudolf Herrnstadt, Wilhelm Zaisser, Anton Ackermann, and Fred Oelßner. Herrnstadt was a former Soviet exile of Jewish descent who was editor of *Neues Deutschland* (New Germany), the SED's official newspaper. Zaisser, the GDR's minister of state security, had also spent the war years in the Soviet Union. Indeed, it is notable that all of these veteran communists had emigrated to the Soviet Union during the Nazi era. This suggests that former Soviet exiles—perhaps precisely because they had survived Soviet emigration—felt sufficiently secure within the SED to voice criticism of Ulbricht. It certainly belies the notion that former Soviet exiles were cowed cadres, broken by the experience of the Great Purges.

These veteran communists were angered both by Ulbricht's policies and by his personal rule. In contrast to Ulbricht, Herrnstadt apparently wished to better the treatment of the other GDR political parties, to improve the plight of workers, to implement less repressive measures toward the intelligentsia and the middle classes, and to end the dictatorial practices of party functionaries.[2] In addition, he appears to have opposed Ulbricht's willingness to sacrifice German unification for a separate East German state.[3] Oelßner also roundly criticized Ulbricht. He argued that it was necessary to subject the SED's "entire politics to a general review" and that the East German masses had to be won over "not by theories, but by measures." Oelßner further called for "freedom of associations. Relaxation of the state of the press." And he stated, "It is necessary to loosen the dictatorship. The policy toward the bloc parties [(official East German puppet parties) should be] honest (abandonment of tutelage). Class struggle [is] not [to be] incited, not [to be] screamed."[4] Ackermann and Zaisser also engaged in vociferous criticism of the SED's general secretary.

After much rancorous discussion, the Politburo issued a communiqué proclaiming the "New Course:" greater investments would be channeled toward consumer goods and the construction of heavy industry would be slowed. These new policies, however, failed to win the support of the GDR population. In mid-June 1953, construction workers in Berlin, angered by high work norms, put down their tools. In the following days, strikes and demonstrations against the regime spread to hundreds of cities, towns, and villages throughout East Germany. The demonstrations reached a high point on June 17, when the Soviet commander, Marshal Sokolovskii, ended the unrest by declaring martial law and deploying Soviet tanks in and around East Berlin. Although the uprising was quickly quelled, Ulbricht and other veteran communists never quite recovered from the trauma of workers rebelling against "their" socialist state. Years later, Ernst Wollweber, the minister of state security between 1953 and 1957, wrote that whenever he spoke with Ulbricht about state security, he noticed that "the fright of June 17, 1953 still haunted him."[5] And in August 1989, when faced with the GDR population's dissatisfaction with the SED regime, Erich Mielke, then the minister of state security, questioned whether another June 17 was in the offing.[6]

In mid-June, Ulbricht faced opposition on many fronts. The Soviet leadership was none too happy with him. Indeed, in the spring of 1953, Beria had even declared of Ulbricht: "In my whole life I have never seen such an idiot."[7] Ulbricht faced outright opposition from most Politburo members (Elli Schmidt and Hans Jendretzky, the first secretary of the Berlin SED, were also harshly critical of him). And among the East German population, disapproval of the general secretary and his policies was widespread. In the next months, however, Ulbricht was able to secure—and even bolster—his position of power. A consummate tactician, Ulbricht exploited the crisis situation that enveloped the SED leadership in the wake of the June Uprising. He alleged a Herrnstadt / Zaisser "faction," managed to split the Politburo opposition against him, and was able to convince Fred Oelßner, Karl Schirdewan, and some other veteran communists to side with him in his political battles.[8]

Following the Uprising, Fred Oelßner apparently reconsidered his views. At a Central Committee meeting that took place on the night of June 21–22, Oelßner declared that now was not the time for comrades "to unroll all of the problems" that "weighed on their hearts." As Oelßner stated: "But we are in the midst of a struggle, in a struggle that is not yet over. The quiet that reigns today may be gone by tomorrow. It is therefore necessary that the whole party go over to the offensive, that we penetrate the factories in order to show the masses what has actually occurred." Oelßner noted that many workers did not believe "that this was really an organized fascist provocation [the SED's official interpretation of the Uprising] . . . But we have clear-cut evidence that it was indeed an organized provocation." Oelßner then argued that "trials against provocateurs must begin. There must be open trials, and the press must report about them."[9] Despite his earlier concerns about the harshness of the SED dictatorship, Oelßner now adopted a hard-line attitude.

In the weeks following the June Uprising, various officially sanctioned meetings of Politburo members took place. In these meetings, Herrnstadt and Zaisser made proposals and statements that were soon used against them. In addition, the Politburo charged Herrnstadt with writing a document that was to explain the shortcomings of the party's policies and to elaborate measures to improve the political and economic situation in the GDR. This document was later labeled the platform of the Herrnstadt / Zaisser "faction." In this document, Herrnstadt offered a searing reckoning with the policy of the "rapid construction of socialism"; called for a "united, democratic, progressive Germany"; and castigated the work of party functionaries who all too often showed their "disregard of the working people" and administered the GDR by "personality cult instead of collective work."[10]

In early July, Ulbricht enjoyed precious little backing in the Politburo (only Hermann Matern and Erich Honecker clearly favored keeping him as general secretary of the SED). But he now regained the support of Soviet officials. Ulbricht was lucky in that the CPSU leadership had turned on and arrested Beria in early July; since the NKVD chief had opposed Ulbricht's rule of East Germany, Ulbricht could only benefit from Beria's fall. In addition, the Soviet leadership did not wish to further destabilize East Germany with a change of party leadership. Ulbricht now went on the offensive. At a Central Committee meeting in late July 1953, he alleged that "the group Herrnstadt and Zaisser . . . had led an inner-party group struggle in the party leadership." The SED dictator claimed that the two men had "developed a platform and attempted to force it upon the Politburo." According to Ulbricht, this platform argued that "the policies of the party were in the main incorrect" and that a "renewal of the party," including "a decisive change in the party leadership," was necessary.[11]

Fred Oelßner added additional "evidence" to the case against Herrnstadt and Zaisser. He railed against Herrnstadt's "arrogance." After quoting some of the most critical sections of Herrnstadt's document, Oelßner claimed that the Herrnstadt / Zaisser line "was a complete capitulation in a difficult situation for the party. Regardless of whether it was intended or not, the result was a Menshevist, party-hostile position directed at the head of the party and thus objectively directed toward supporting the enemy."[12] Oelßner not only made false accusations, but he also deployed the well-worn veteran communist tactic of linking political to personal failings. His motives for attacking Herrnstadt and Zaisser remain unclear. Perhaps he felt threatened by one or both of them (Zaisser had suggested that he might one day call for Oelßner's removal from the Politburo).[13] He may also have been intimidated by Ulbricht. Or he might have had a genuine belief that Herrnstadt and Zaisser were jeopardizing the SED. In any event, Oelßner now adopted the very same political methods for which he had so recently criticized Ulbricht.

Herrnstadt believed that if he mounted an effective defense, he would undermine the strength and unity of the SED. He therefore could not describe Ulbricht's "arbitrary acts" or how the suspicions concerning the alleged Herrnstadt / Zaisser "platform" had come about. Were he to do so, he thought, the "enemy" would learn of divisions within the Politburo, and a real division, as opposed to that fantasized by Ulbricht, would exist in the SED leadership. The only defense that he could employ, Herrnstadt thought, was to state that he "had struggled for the principle of collectivity."[14] At the Central Committee meeting, Herrnstadt and Zaisser thus initially allowed that they had erred in their political judgments, but that the allegations of factional and / or oppositional activity were simply unfounded. In the course of this Central Committee meeting, however, both came to practice self-criticism and to admit that they had, in effect, engaged in factional activity. As Zaisser stated: "I never had the intention, never the feeling or the will, to build a faction. The way things turned out, however, the comrades who speak here are correct when they speak of a Zaisser-Herrnstadt group or faction. Practically that is what occurred."[15] Similarly, Herrnstadt allowed that he had "objectively" engaged in a factional struggle against the top party leadership. While he, Zaisser, and others had wanted "to secure a collective work in the Politburo," their actions had had other effects. Speaking to Ulbricht, Herrnstadt declared: "We did not struggle against you, but rather for you. That is subjectively absolutely true. I am just beginning to be convinced that it was also objectively something else."[16] Both men believed that party loyalty demanded that they confess to the charges. They were thus caught on the horns of a tricky dilemma: proving their party loyalty meant admitting that they had "objectively" aided the enemy.

To what extent was Herrnstadt a reformer in 1953? Although his document was written in a stridently critical tone, it nonetheless shows the limits of this veteran communist's reformism. Herrnstadt saw the shortcomings of the party in the failings of party functionaries, not in the system of one-party rule. He thus thought that new personnel, with a new work ethic, could resolve the SED's dilemmas. The editor in chief of *Neues Deutschland* did not advocate freedom of the press, specific ways to increase work-place democracy, or free parliamentary elections. In addition, he did not advocate measures—such as secret, binding elections to party posts—that might have made the SED a more democratic party. All of Herrnstadt's proposals were well within accepted SED discourse. For years, the party had railed against bureaucratization and other "administrative" ills that plagued the party apparatus. The appeal to establish a unified Germany was official Soviet policy in 1953. Had Herrnstadt gained greater influence in 1953, he may well have modified some of Ulbricht's hard-line approaches. But although some historians have characterized Herrnstadt as a "reformer" or suggested that his downfall meant that a "historic chance was lost in 1953," it is very unlikely that Herrnstadt would have countenanced a fundamental weakening of SED rule.[17]

Herrnstadt and Zaisser now lost their Politburo and Central Committee seats and were subject to an increasingly rabid public campaign. The most serious charges came from Karl Schirdewan. As Herrnstadt bitterly noted, he knew Schirdewan "very well" and "despite the caution that marked his every step," Schirdewan "went further than any other comrades." In an article published in *Neues Deutschland,* Schirdewan was the first to castigate Herrnstadt and Zaisser as "enemies of the German people" and even as "Trotskyites." Herrnstadt also claimed that "at least one member of the party leadership, Schirdewan, was clearly aiming at [their] physical annihilation."[18] Schirdewan, however, has denied that this was his intention.[19] Although Herrnstadt and Zaisser were neither imprisoned nor executed, they remained "non-persons" until their deaths. Zaisser died in 1958. Herrnstadt was sent to do research in the state archives in Merseburg; he died in 1965.

Although it initially seemed to threaten Ulbricht's personal rule, the June Uprising ultimately allowed him to preserve his position of power. Ulbricht suffered a minor setback in that his title was changed from that of general secretary (as Stalin had been called) to first secretary of the SED. After the Uprising, though, he was able to dispose of a number of his Politburo critics; besides Herrnstadt and Zaisser, Ackermann, Schmidt, and Jendretzky were implicated in the alleged "conspiracy" and lost their leadership positions. Karl Schirdewan, at this time an Ulbricht supporter, was brought into the Politburo and the Secretariat. In a few short years, however, Schirdewan and Oelßner would be purged by the very man whose political career they had helped save; moreover, the tactics that were to be used against them were those that they had deployed against Ulbricht's critics in 1953.

AFTER THE June 1953 Uprising, veteran communist intellectuals by and large rallied to the SED; indeed, Johannes R. Becher, one of East Germany's most prominent novelists, even declared that "party discipline is our highest feeling of freedom."[20] But in February 1956, Nikita Khrushchev, the Soviet leader, gave a "Secret Speech" in which he described the crimes that Stalin had committed during his long decades of rule. In the next months, dissent swept through much of East Central Europe. Hungary even saw an open revolution—soon put down by Soviet tanks. In the heady months between Khrushchev's speech and the suppression of the Hungarian Revolution in November 1956, many veteran communist intellectuals in East Germany experienced pangs of ideological vacillation and political soul-searching. They criticized SED policy, advanced unorthodox viewpoints, and attempted to stretch the limits of acceptable intellectual discourse. The prolific economic historian Jürgen Kuczynski, for example, challenged received notions of Marxist-Leninist historiography.[21] Alfred Kantorowicz, an influential professor of German literature, castigated SED authors who simply touted the party line.[22] The physicist Robert Havemann, who would become the GDR's most prominent dissident, criticized the monopoly on truth granted to Marxist-Leninist philosophy.[23] Fritz Behrens, the director of the GDR's Office of Statistics, advocated factory self-management, decentralization of the economy, increased use of profitability criteria, and more worker participation in economic decision-making.[24] And Kurt Vieweg, director of the Institute of Agronomy, called for improvements in the system of collective farms (known as LPGs) and for the preservation of single-family farms; by the mid-1950s, upholding single-family farms was anathema to the orthodox SED leadership.[25]

For party authorities, the most dangerous intellectual was not an Old Communist at all, but rather a young, widely respected philosopher, Wolfgang Harich. In the summer and fall of 1956, Harich formulated a "Platform for a Special German Road to Socialism" that foresaw a host of political reforms, including personnel changes in the party leadership, a smaller state bureaucracy, the creation of workers' councils, the right to strike for trade unions, and the coexistence of LPGs with single-family farms. Harich's program nonetheless assumed the preservation of one-party rule and a socialist economic order. It also upheld Marxist-Leninist principles of party life such as "democratic centralism," "Leninist norms of party life," and "iron discipline" in carrying out party decrees.[26] Harich found like-minded colleagues at the Aufbau publishing house, including its Old Communist director, Walter Janka. Janka, a twenty-four-year veteran of the KPD / SED, could look back on a rich set of communist experiences: he had been imprisoned by the Nazis, had fought in the Spanish Civil War, had been exiled in Mexico, and had headed the DEFA film company and the Aufbau publishing house in East Germany. He had, however, become disillusioned with Ulbricht's regime. In his post-1989 memoirs, he wrote that he and others "spoke against the cult of personality, called for corrections in legal practice and condemned the abuse of power" in 1956. At the same time, however, as Janka later noted, "none of us thought of giving capitalism a chance in the GDR." Janka's primary goal, it seems, was "the socialist transformation of the GDR," that is, "to help make [the GDR] that which I had dreamed about for decades."[27] Janka apparently wanted a "true," although undefined, socialism in East Germany.

SED leaders viewed Harich and Janka with alarm. Both men were arrested in late 1956 and judged in separate show trials (along with a few co-defendants) in 1957. Janka was sentenced to five years of penitentiary for his role in the "state- and party-hostile grouping Harich-Janka." The "grouping's" ideological demands, investigating authorities alleged, demonstrated a "virtually organic uniformity of counterrevolutionary ideology" with "hostile groupings" in Hungary. This, they argued, suggested the "directing hand of the enemy, acting according to a single plan, the goal of which is to soften up the socialist order, to subvert and destroy it."[28] Party authorities also claimed that Janka and Harich had plotted to replace Walter Ulbricht with Paul Merker, the former Politburo member purged in connection with the Noel Field Affair.[29] In 1956, Janka had indeed brought Merker and Harich together. Although Janka had wished to promote Merker as an alternative to Ulbricht, there is no indication that Merker seriously considered challenging Ulbricht's rule; Merker was a broken man by 1956.[30] Harich apparently considered Franz Dahlem as a potential replacement for Ulbricht, but never actually established contact with Dahlem.[31]

Gerhart Eisler, now the deputy chairman of the State Radio Committee, also attracted the attention of party authorities. In the draft of an internal party document on "hostile activity," SED officials claimed that Harich discussed "aspects of his counterrevolutionary views" with a few individuals, including Gerhart Eisler. According to this document, Eisler had "not identified with [these views] but had rather opposed them, but the necessary firmness had apparently been lacking."[32] In short, Eisler had not shown sufficient vigilance when confronted with Harich's views. Interestingly, for unknown reasons, the paragraph mentioning Eisler was eventually dropped from the final document presented to the Central Committee in October 1957. Eisler's wife, Hilde, however, was implicated in the final document. Hilde Eisler was the editor in chief of a popular monthly magazine, *Das Magazin* (The magazine). Party authorities now claimed that one of her reporters, Trude Gröllmann, had ties to the editor in chief of *Constanze* (Constance), a similar periodical based in West Germany. According to the document, Hilde had allegedly "placed great value on herself having contacts to Huffzky [the editor in chief of *Constanze*] and told Gröllmann to organize such a meeting." Apparently, though, after the Harich trial, Hilde thought the better of such a meeting, and it never actually took place.[33] Once again, Gerhart Eisler found himself under suspicion by party authorities. This time, however, he appears to have emerged unscathed—as did Hilde.

Eisler's views in 1956 are actually not entirely clear. In a post-1989 interview, Hilde Eisler stated that Gerhart had been an "advocate of reforms" in 1956 and thereafter. She claimed that Gerhart was against the "doggedness" of SED cultural policy and had wanted "to avoid the stupid excesses"—such as books not being published—that the party carried out against artists and others.[34] Walter Janka, however, later recalled that Eisler was something of a hard-liner in 1956. In his memoirs, Janka related how Eisler fired an editor, Richard Wolf, at the State Radio because Wolf refused to edit a speech on the Hungarian Revolution by Harry Pollitt, the chairman of the British Communist Party, to Eisler's liking. Eisler allegedly told Wolf: "Either you write the commentary as the party expects, or you cannot be an editor." When Wolf refused, Eisler sent him walking.[35]

Like many other veteran communist intellectuals, Anna Seghers, president of the German Writers' Union, experienced a crisis of political conviction in 1956–1957. During Janka's trial, Seghers, who knew Janka both from Mexican exile and as her publisher at Aufbau, was seemingly torn between friendship and party loyalty, justice and party discipline. To Janka's bitter disappointment, however, Seghers refused to intervene on her publisher's behalf.[36] Instead, she reworked the Janka saga in a revealing short story, "The Just Judge." In this piece, Seghers wrote of how a young, successful judge, Jan, groomed by what is obviously the SED regime, comes to doubt the system in which he has enjoyed such career success. Jan's misgivings are triggered by the case of a Viktor Gasko, a veteran of the Spanish Civil War, who is suddenly arrested and accused of passing intelligence reports to contacts abroad. Jan, the investigating judge in the case, finds insufficient evidence of Gasko's guilt. But his superior, Kalam, who was imprisoned for over ten years in fascist prisons, tells him that there is no doubt as to Gasko's guilt. Jan continues his investigation. In one interrogation, Gasko, questioning socialism in practice, declares: "Our idea is the best that people have ever come up with. What are you making of this idea?" When Jan becomes uneasy about judging Gasko guilty, he is taken off the case and is himself arrested. Eventually, Gasko and Jan, imprisoned in the same work camp, run into each other. The longtime revolutionary pours his heart out to the younger man: "In Spain, when we were abandoned behind Franco's lines . . . I did not forget why life was worthwhile. And when our cause was lost, I also knew, and in the awful days of war, all the more. All the more. And then, then came, as it was called, the fulfillment of our dreams, and not just of ours, but of ancient people's dreams. And then happened what we experience, we were imprisoned with thieves and bandits. Who? Why?"[37] In her story, Seghers thus juxtaposed an orthodox veteran communist (Kalam) against a longtime communist (Gasko) who had come to question his socialist regime. As Seghers's piece suggested, some Old Communists brooded over the agonizing dilemmas that Soviet-style socialism posed: the corruption of socialist ideals in practice, the difficulties of defending the existing socialist order, and the question of whether present-day socialism justified the great sacrifices of the past. But while Seghers penned these doubts, she never publicly expressed them. The same is true of virtually all other veteran communists.[38] "The Just Judge" was published posthumously only in 1990.

All told, some twenty-nine veteran communist intellectuals were known or alleged to harbor critical tendencies in 1956 and 1957.[39] The backgrounds of these longtime party members are striking: almost half were of Jewish origin (14), many had grown up in middle-class households (17), and most had spent the Nazi years in Western exile (21). Indeed, the draft version of the document on "hostile activity" among the East German intelligentsia stated: "It is characteristic that those members of the intelligentsia predominantly involved [in 'ideological subversion'] lived for a longer time in capitalist foreign countries (England, France, USA . . . Prof. Kuczinski [sic], Kantorowicz, Vieweg, and others)."[40] Although the authors of this document seem to have initially explicitly targeted former West émigrés, this passage—for unknown reasons—was excised from the final draft of the document. On the whole, longtime communists who had emigrated to Western countries were not generally more likely than those with other backgrounds to criticize their regime. Among intellectuals, however, the combination of Western emigration, middle-class background, and Jewish descent does seem to have forged a more critical Old Communist mentality—or so party authorities thought.

Most quasi-critical veteran communists soon recovered their political orthodoxy. In late 1956, the SED leadership began a campaign against "revisionism," the communist code word for views and policies deemed too liberal. Most veteran communist intellectuals now engaged in ritual-istic self-criticism. In June 1957, the economist Fritz Behrens, for exam-ple, wrote a twelve-page self-critical memorandum that was distributed to Central Committee members. Behrens wrote, "One may not, as I in fact did, contrast state administration and the exploitation of economic levers in the management of the economy as irreconcilable opposites . . . my remarks in fact allowed false conclusions that by definition would have led to a weakening of our state power."[41] In 1958, Behrens pub-lished a statement in *Neues Deutschland* in which he claimed: "I admit that the views that I developed were objectively directed against the party line, that they were thus revisionist."[42] In 1960, the journal for party functionaries, *Neuer Weg* (New path) published a statement by Behrens on his "opportunistic conduct." Behrens declared: "Instead of supporting the party in the struggle for the leadership of the masses through socialist state power, . . . I devised a theory in which there was in fact no place for the leading role of the party . . . In this way, through my work, I . . . thus objectively supported forces that wanted the restoration of capitalism in the German Democratic Republic."[43] By 1960, Behrens had openly admitted that his views had been "revisionist," that he had tried to undermine state power and thus the dictatorship of the proletar-iat, that he had neglected the leading role of the party, and that he had supported those who wished to restore capitalism in the GDR. The fact that Behrens publicly confessed to these alleged failings underscores this Old Communist's desire to exercise continued influence. In the GDR, veteran communists who wished to maintain positions of authority had little choice but to engage in abject self-criticism or other forms of self-abnegation.

Party authorities greatly exaggerated the "party-hostile" character of the criticisms and proposed reforms voiced by veteran communist intel-lectuals in the mid-1950s. Only a few longtime communists suggested re-forms that, if implemented, might have altered the character of the re-gime. Most critical veteran communist intellectuals wanted more press freedoms and a spirit of open debate in academic settings. But they had neither the desire nor the intention to oust their Marxist-Leninist re-gime. Right or wrong, the SED was their party, communism their project. The events of 1956 left only a very few pre-1933 KPD members perma-nently disenchanted with communism; just two veteran communists, Kantorowicz and Karola Bloch, left the GDR at this time. Even Janka and Kurt Vieweg, who were both arrested and imprisoned, remained loyal to the East German regime. These intellectuals could not renounce the cause to which they had given the best years of their lives. They practiced self-criticism, rallied to the SED leadership, and hid whatever political doubts they may have entertained behind the facade of party unity.

VETERAN COMMUNIST intellectuals were not the only Old Communists touched by Khrushchev's revelations. In 1956, Karl Schirdewan was a member of the Politburo and the party's cadre chief. He was widely viewed as the second most powerful man in the SED. According to his post-1989 memoirs, Schirdewan came to question Ulbricht's rule after Khrushchev delivered his speech. Ulbricht, eager to deflect attention from Stalin's crimes, wrote an article in *Neues Deutschland* in which he declared merely that "one could not count Stalin as one of the classical theorists of Marxism."[44] By the summer of 1956, Schirdewan later claimed, "I decided to act openly against Walter Ulbricht's view that the cult of personality could be reduced to the realization that Stalin was not a classic theorist of Marxism-Leninism. I wanted to publicly set my opinion against his left-radical conservative attitude and obsession with power ... I wanted a change."[45] The character of this "change," however, remains in doubt. After 1989, Schirdewan claimed that the issues that most concerned him in the mid-1950s were the "establishment of inner-party democracy" and the "elimination of the rigid democratic central-ism."[46] He also stated that he had wanted to eliminate the "dictatorship of the proletariat," to allow independent political parties, and to abolish the "leading role" of the SED.[47]

In the mid-1950s, there is no doubt that Schirdewan was implaca-bly opposed to Ulbricht's personal rule. In a January 1958 statement writ-ten for the Politburo, he declared that "Comrade Ulbricht did not suf-ficiently heed proposals of Politburo members and acted without the prior approval of the Politburo." Schirdewan alleged that Ulbricht with-held information from Politburo members about "state-hostile" group-ings and that his conduct toward "leading comrades" was "false, impa-tient, and cold." He further accused Ulbricht of an "inability to objectively think through the opinion of another comrade and to view it as an expression of help and collegial advice in a party-like sense." Finally, he claimed that Ulbricht did not deal with "real or alleged differ-ences of opinion" in a "Leninist manner."[48] For Schirdewan, these were very bold assertions indeed; after all, veteran communists who had simi-larly criticized Ulbricht had all been removed from their positions in 1953.

But did Schirdewan oppose Ulbricht's policies? And if so, to what ex-tent? Ernst Wollweber later recalled that in late 1957 Schirdewan told him that he was concerned about the flight of so many East Germans from the GDR. According to Wollweber, Schirdewan stated that this "flight from the republic" raised the issue of whether "our policy was in all of its aspects correct."[49] The British historian Peter Grieder suggests that Schirdewan's questioning of SED policy went much further. Schirdewan allegedly urged the rehabilitation of former West émigrés, advocated milder policies toward East German youth and rebellious students, opposed the forced collectivization of agriculture, rejected the SED's hard-line positions toward the churches, and hoped to place the struggle for German reunification at the top of the SED's agenda. Schirdewan also apparently wished to invite Harich to discuss his views with the Politburo and, once Janka was arrested, to secure Janka's freedom. In addition, Schirdewan supposedly wanted to call an extraordinary party congress to elect a new Central Committee that would carry through a program of "controlled democratization." On the basis of these policy differences, Grieder contends, Schirdewan "advocated an alternative political course based on the conclusions of the twentieth party congress of the CPSU."[50]

Despite later claims, the historical evidence suggesting that Schirdewan was a radical reformer is actually very thin—largely memoirs by or interviews with Schirdewan himself. Even Grieder seems skeptical of some of Schirdewan's supposed positions.[51] In his 1958 statement for the Politburo, Schirdewan argued that his differences with Ulbricht did not add up to a general questioning of the party line: "I have never had any doubt about the correctness of the policies of our party, its general line."[52] In all likelihood, this was true. Schirdewan never spelled out the precise nature of his alternative policies, so it is difficult to determine whether these would have relaxed the East German communist dictatorship. He later claimed that it would have been much too dangerous to write out a platform or other document describing his views in the 1950s.[53] But he suggested that his oppositional stances could be read out of excerpts of speeches that he had given between 1953 and 1957 and that he included in his memoirs. These excerpts, however, express criticism that was virtually sanctioned by the SED regime. Schirdewan spoke out against the "cult of personality," on the need for collective leadership, on the importance of party officials maintaining links to the masses, for open "criticism and self-criticism," and against the "generals" in the party who simply engaged in "commanding."[54] Based on the available evidence, it does not seem that Schirdewan advocated systemic reforms in the mid-1950s. He probably developed such reform notions only after his political downfall.

Between 1956 and 1958, Fred Oelßner also vigorously opposed

Ulbricht's personal rule and some of his policies. Unlike Schirdewan, Oelßner had suffered a number of political setbacks after 1953. Ulbricht apparently "despised Oelßner's 'intellectualism'" and was known to "cut him off with remarks like 'Shut up!' or 'Stop talking, Fred!'"[55] In 1954, Oelßner had been relieved of responsibility for propaganda, and in 1955 he lost his position as Central Committee secretary of agitation. He was now deputy chairman of the Council of Ministers and chairman of its commission for "consumer production and provision of the population." In July 1956, Oelßner wrote a statement for the Politburo in which he declared, "We have not really yet begun the evaluation of the Twentieth Party Congress. That is why we haven't seen any fresh impetus in the party. In particular, we have shunned the question of the cult of personality . . . Is there a personality cult in the SED [?] Yes, it exists and in connection with it a personal regime that is primarily exercised by Comrade Ulbricht.—After the Twentieth Party Congress—due to the enemy's pressure—it has become even stronger. Every open criticism of Comrade Ulbricht is declared as inadmissible." Oelßner further stated that he was not in agreement with a number of measures taken by the party leadership after the Twentieth Party Congress, including Ulbricht's announcement that Stalin was not a classic Marxist theorist. According to Oelßner, "here again something is decreed, as is so often in ideological questions." Finally, Oelßner wrote that "many comrades in the party and Central Committee are dissatisfied with this regime, but they fear saying this openly. They are afraid that they will be marked as party enemies. This creates an unhealthy atmosphere in the party."[56] To Oelßner's dismay, the response to his statement was "icy silence. Not one comrade commented on the statement."[57]

In Politburo meetings, Oelßner continued his attacks on Ulbricht. In December 1956, Oelßner stated: "The discussion shows that the matter of collective leadership is not quite right . . . Much depends on the work of W. U. . . . we must *each and all* place *the party over the person!* . . . One must also sometimes tolerate criticism from other comrades—[One must] not consider oneself infallible . . . Walter loves com[rades] who don't have their own opinion. He tolerates *other* opinions only with *difficulty!* Revenge threatens!"[58] Some weeks later, Ulbricht responded: "Com[rade] Oe[lßner] has directed his whole fire against Ulbricht." He then charged Oelßner with "revisionism in agricultural policy." Ulbricht was referring to the fact that Oelßner had thought it appropriate to privatize agricultural equipment such as tractors. As Oelßner had once said, "Privately owned tractors do not have to be instruments of exploitation."[59] Oelßner had also suggested that the GDR government grant privileges given to LPGs to private farmers and halt enormous state subsidies to unprofitable LPGs.[60] Although Oelßner held comparatively liberal views on agriculture, this was not true of other areas of policy. In early 1957, for example, he had scathingly attacked Behrens and his reform proposals: "Is it not clear that Comrade Behrens is designing a travesty of socialism that looks devilishly like capitalism?"[61] Far from supporting critical intellectuals, Oelßner had played a leading role in suppressing their dissent.

During 1957, Oelßner's frustrations with Ulbricht's personal rule mounted. On January 5, 1958, Oelßner presented the Politburo with yet another statement. Here he declared: "I still believe that the personal regime resulting from the cult of personality that is primarily exercised by the first secretary of the Central Committee, Comrade Walter Ulbricht, is a danger for the party. This regime hinders the formation of a collective party leadership and often leads the party astray with rash and false decrees." Oelßner then gave a few examples: "The new Five-Year Plan had from its inception such disproportions that these could only give rise to a disorganizing factor in the economic process and great difficulties." In addition, preparations for a planned reorganization of the state apparatus had been "so little thought out and worked out" that its implementation will cause "great difficulties and bring about some damages." According to Oelßner, "The Politburo as the elected leadership collective was, in fact, left out of [the making of] all these important and many other decisions."[62] For Oelßner, collective leadership was the solution to the SED's ills. Oelßner's primary concern was not reforming Soviet-style state socialism, but rather moderating Walter Ulbricht's rule of East Germany.

In December 1957, a drunken celebration took place at the Wismut industrial complex. This celebration served as a pretext for Ulbricht to bring to a head his confrontation with Schirdewan and his other critics. At the Wismut gathering, Fritz Selbmann, now a deputy chairman of the Council of Ministers, and Gerhart Ziller, the Central Committee secretary of economics, made indiscreet remarks about internal party matters. Ziller allegedly stated that at the upcoming Thirty-fifth Central Committee Meeting there would be a great confrontation between Ulbricht and his opponents: "It's now a matter of by hook or by crook, everything is at stake. We will not allow ourselves to be eliminated one after the other. Either we will go to the dogs and will be labeled riffraff, or we will emerge as the winners."[63] A few days later, Ziller and Selbmann were called to account by the Politburo. That night, Ziller shot and killed himself. Soon thereafter, at a Politburo meeting in early January 1958, Erich Honecker claimed that the Wismut celebration had a "factional character."

Honecker would now play a leading role in the coming purge of Schirdewan, Oelßner, and others. Schirdewan and Honecker shared a long antipathy. Schirdewan disdained Honecker because of alleged short-comings in Honecker's antifascist past.[64] From his work of gathering biographical information on party cadres in the late 1940s, Schirdewan knew of questions surrounding Honecker's conduct in Gestapo interrogations and in Brandenburg Penitentiary. He probably also knew that because of these allegations, the CPSU had suggested that the FDJ leader not be "reelected" to the Central Committee in 1954 (Ulbricht, however, intervened and Honecker was able to retain his Central Committee membership).[65] In addition, in the early 1950s, Schirdewan had found Honecker's work as FDJ leader unimpressive.[66] Indeed, criticism of Honecker by Schirdewan and others had led Ulbricht to finally remove his protégé as FDJ leader and to send him to Moscow for a year of political schooling in 1955. On Honecker's return, Schirdewan tried to prevent the former FDJ leader from being named to the Central Committee Secretariat in 1956.[67] For his part, Honecker had complained of the "debating society" in Schirdewan's division as early as 1953–1954.[68] Honecker now linked Selbmann and Ziller, as well as Ernst Wollweber, to a "Schirdewan faction." He also criticized Oelßner. Other veteran communist Politburo members joined in the fray. Alfred Neumann claimed that the statements written by Schirdewan and Oelßner suggested that the two men were trying to place themselves above the collective—thus turning criticism of Ulbricht on its head. Heinrich Rau added that Schirdewan's statement had not dealt with party or political problems, but had only advanced "a line of subversion." And Hermann Matern claimed that Schirdewan was a liar who suffered from "pathological arrogance." The Politburo voted to form a delegation to go to Moscow to seek Soviet approval to remove Schirdewan and Oelßner from their functions.[69]

At the Thirty-fifth Central Committee Meeting that took place in February 1958, Ulbricht and his supporters publicly alleged a Schirdewan faction. Honecker led off the indictment. He claimed that through the Wismut Affair it had become clear to all Politburo members, with the exception of Schirdewan and Oelßner, that the "extraordinary serious course of events of this gathering point to a factional activity that must have gotten under way quite a while ago. Very soon it was proved that certain vacillations of Comrades Schirdewan, Wollweber, [and] Ziller in fundamental questions of the politics of our party and in some technical questions had come up in the fall of 1956 and thereafter led to group-like ties, at the head of which Comrade Schirdewan stood as the driving force." Honecker then made specific accusations. He alleged that in a speech to the Twenty-ninth Central Committee meeting, Schirdewan had spoken of democratization, but without emphasizing the "necessity of deploying security measures against the subversive work of the enemy." In addition, Schirdewan had allegedly disputed the existence of hostile groups and thought "that the intensification of vigilance was not consistent with the results of the Twentieth Party Congress." All of these differences, Honecker claimed, might have been resolved in the Politburo "had not Comrade Schirdewan heightened tensions with his petite-bourgeois megalomania, his unlimited conceit in his infallibility, and through his factional activity with Comrades Wollweber and Ziller."

Honecker also turned his fire on Oelßner: "Comrade Oelßner did not act in a party-like manner against the provocative attacks of Comrade Schirdewan. Instead of rejecting the provocations of Comrade Schirdewan together with the comrades of the Politburo, he for his part opened an attack against Comrade Ulbricht." In addition, Honecker claimed, Oelßner had wanted to dissolve weak LPGs and to preserve "overcentralization" in state management. Honecker argued that "these were and are questions that one could and can discuss objectively. But what did Comrade Oelßner make of this? A controversy of principle, come hell or high water." According to Honecker, "The fact that the majority of the Politburo rejected his point of view led him [Oelßner] to the completely unjustified declaration that there is no collectivity in the Politburo . . . After the adoption of decrees that did not find the approval of Comrade Oelßner, Comrade Oelßner often declared that the adopted decrees would lead to difficulties, rather than concentrating his whole strength on their implementation. Comrade Oelßner did not belong to the Schirdewan, Wollweber, Ziller group, but he lent it support in every way."

Fritz Selbmann also came under attack. According to Honecker, Selbmann had suggested that the successes of the Wismut operations were due to his person, rather than to the party. Furthermore,

[Selbmann] tried to tear open a rift between those comrades who were in penitentiaries and concentration camps during the barbaric Hitler-fascism era and those comrades who for a time, on party orders, directed and organized the work in Germany from abroad, especially from the Soviet Union, and [who] actively participated in the Great Patriotic War or other resistance movements against the Hitler bandits. "I was not in emigration," [Selbmann] said, "I was imprisoned, but did political work with Comrade

Schirdewan and Comrade Girnus under the most difficult conditions in the concentration camp . . . Under mortal danger we did political work here. Others, in safety, spoke over the radio to soldiers in the trenches."[70]

Honecker's repetition of Selbmann's alleged statement suggests that tensions between veteran communists with differing biographical pasts persisted well into the 1950s.

The charges against Selbmann soon grew more serious. Matern claimed that Ziller had told Selbmann for days on end in 1953 that "Comrade Ulbricht must be removed! That is the only rescue!" Selbmann had not reported this to party authorities, and so Ziller, although he held such dangerous views, was able to become a Central Committee secretary.[71] Albert Norden, a veteran communist and Oelßner's successor as Central Committee secretary of agitation, suggested that Selbmann's remarks contrasting former émigrés with concentration-camp survivors was a condemnation of Lenin, "who, as is well known, was in emigration before . . . and during the First World War." Norden also described Selbmann as often "haughty, arrogant, personally hurtful, and uncomradely." Furthermore, according to Norden, Selbmann had orchestrated his own "cult of personality" in a GDR and foreign media blitz. The goal of this press attention, Norden suggested, was to impress on ordinary comrades that "that is actually the man who can do everything! He should indeed hold much higher functions. He should not be a mere deputy minister-president!"[72] Kurt Hager spoke of Selbmann "yielding to petite-bourgeois views" and of his "bourgeois individualism."[73] Ulbricht accused Selbmann of having "a not correct relationship to the role of the party and to the party-like responsibility of a leading state functionary."[74]

Franz Dahlem, who had rejoined the Central Committee in 1957, repeated the charges against Schirdewan and other veteran communists. This is surprising on a number of counts. First, Dahlem had himself been unfairly purged in 1953. Moreover, according to a 1958 Stasi report, "[Dahlem] especially respected Comrades Schirdewan and Selbmann; he greatly valued their opinions—and not just in his direct work."[75] Dahlem now, however, claimed, "It is clear from the ongoing discussion that the conception of Comrades Schirdewan and Wollweber were and are based on a wrong evaluation of the political situation: . . . [on] an underestimation of the imperialist danger, a tendency to an evolutionary development that in practice leads to a retardation of the tempo of socialist development that would have destroyed us. The factional, unprincipled conduct of Comrade Schirdewan is politically clear." Dahlem attributed Schirdewan's conduct to "personal ambition" through which Schirdewan "had lost his right mind, placed his person over the party." Dahlem thus concluded, "I believe that Comrade Schirdewan's factional, unprincipled conduct must be understood and condemned by every party member, by every class-conscious worker, and by every thoughtful person."[76] Dahlem presumably attacked Schirdewan in order to "prove" his party loyalty—and to claw his way back into the inner sanctum of top SED leaders. Much later, Schirdewan stated that he was personally "disappointed" in Dahlem because of these denunciations.[77]

In their initial speeches to the Thirty-fifth Central Committee Meeting, the veteran communists under attack all denied that they had engaged in wrongdoing. Schirdewan rhetorically asked, "Is there a factional group or a factional activity? There is no such factional activity! It does not exist."[78] Oelßner insisted that "it is . . . not true . . . that I broke party discipline."[79] But just as the charges against these Old Communists escalated, so too did these functionaries' attempts at exculpatory self-criticism. In his second speech to the Central Committee, Schirdewan declared, "I was blind and got carried away vis-à-vis criticism in the Politburo . . . I was blind vis-à-vis the objective effect of my conduct." He also admitted that behind his mistakes "a platform was concealed, even though it was not written or thought out." He acknowledged that he had met (on different occasions) with both Wollweber and Ziller and had mentioned that he intended to criticize Ulbricht at this Central Committee meeting. Schirdewan now admitted that this was "factional activity."[80] Oelßner and Selbmann also self-critically reiterated the charges that had been leveled against them. Oelßner declared that "although I did not belong to [the Schirdewan group], I gave it in every way protective help." This, he stated, was his "main guilt." Oelßner also admitted that his views on "the LPG matter" had been "wrong."[81] Similarly, Selbmann told the Central Committee, "I don't belong to a faction. But perhaps I would have fallen into such a faction without wanting to and without perhaps initially knowing it." Selbmann also admitted that he had made various political mistakes and that "arrogance" and an "exaggerated self-assurance" were signs of his "weakness."[82]

Schirdewan and Oelßner now lost their Politburo functions; in addition, both men, along with Selbmann and Wollweber, lost their Central Committee positions. Schirdewan became head of the State Archival Administration in Potsdam and, as such, Herrnstadt's nominal boss. Oelßner became director of the Institute of Economics of the German Academy of Sciences; Behrens worked at that institute. Selbmann became deputy chairman of the State Planning Commission. Schirdewan,

Oelßner, and Selbmann also were forced to write self-critical statements that appeared in *Neuer Weg* in 1959. They now admitted an even more dramatic failing: that they had hindered the advance of socialist construction in the GDR. Schirdewan later wrote that Matern had threatened him with criminal prosecution if he did not write this self-criticism.[83] Selbmann evidently had difficulties formulating a self-critical statement that met with party approval. In March, he sent a five-page typewritten statement to Matern, along with a handwritten note stating: "Please read through my current statement once again. If you think that it is now sufficient, please send it on; otherwise, I would be grateful if you would once again give me your opinion." On the back of this note, Matern wrote "'Personal!': Comrade Ulbricht! It seems to me that Comrade Selbmann is seriously trying to draw the [right] conclusions."[84]

In his published self-criticism, Schirdewan claimed that he had underestimated the GDR's readiness for a faster pace of socialist construction. As a result, he had advocated "that matters take their own course," that is, that a slowing of the construction of socialism in the GDR be allowed to occur.[85] Selbmann declared that he had aided the factional activity of the "Schirdewan Group," activity that had hindered the party in the solution of important tasks, especially those "to accelerate the tempo of the construction of socialism." As Selbmann declared, "It is my honest conviction that the great successes of the party in all areas in the last year would not have been possible without the ideological and organizational liquidation of the Schirdewan Group."[86] Oelßner also claimed that his past views had been detrimental to socialist construction: "My view that the speedy development of the LPG could make more difficult supplying the population [with food stuffs] has proved to be wrong and opportunistic. In this question I underestimated the strength and superiority of the socialist form of production in agriculture. My proposal to not give state support to 'unviable LPGs' was especially wrong because it would have led to a slowing down of socialist development in rural areas."[87] Such self-criticism was intended both to prove the strength and correctness of Ulbricht's leadership and to convince party functionaries that these veteran communists really had endangered the socialist project. It also seemingly explained East German shortcomings: the GDR was not all it should be because leading communists had sabotaged the socialist project.

BETWEEN 1953 and 1958 Ulbricht and his supporters exploited the political values of veteran communists to further their political aims. Schirdewan, Oelßner, and the others were thus somewhat complicit in their own purges. In part, of course, they participated in the communist purge ritual because they feared for their well-being or even their lives. But at the same time, they remained hostage to their longtime communist values. They insisted on upholding the fiction of party unity, and so refused to publicly press their grievances. In turn, they were unable to mobilize support for themselves in the party bureaucracy. Moreover, wary of accusations of factional activity, they did not cooperate with each other. Although Ulbricht and his supporters thought, or at least claimed to think, that these longtime communists were united in one grand subversive conspiracy, this was simply not the case. Purged Old Communists also practiced self-criticism, thereby buttressing Ulbricht's claims about their alleged factional activity. In the process, they provided other longtime communist functionaries with little cause to question even the most bizarre allegations. Finally, once they fell from power, they did not renounce their party; they refused to discredit Ulbricht or the SED regime.

Archival evidence from the years 1953–1958 does not suggest that high-ranking veteran communist functionaries opposed Ulbricht because they wanted to implement far-reaching reforms. None of the allegedly "factional" pre-1933 KPD members wanted or intended to relinquish SED power in East Germany. Long invested in the Marxist-Leninist movement and convinced of the superiority of Soviet-style socialism, these Old Communists could not imagine alternative socialist scenarios. While some of these longtime communist functionaries resented Ulbricht's personal rule, for the most part, they did not even want to depose the first secretary. Instead, they wanted to rein in Ulbricht and moderate some of his more draconian policies. Curiously, the very Old Communists who were charged with factional or other nefarious activity had often played leading roles in castigating other longtime communists in the past; at one time or another, Schirdewan had vilified Herrnstadt, Zaisser had criticized Oelßner, Oelßner had attacked Behrens, and so on. Franz Dahlem denounced Schirdewan and others even *after* he himself had been purged. Such conduct on the part of longtime communists who have sometimes been characterized as "reformers" suggests that these individuals were really rather typical Marxist-Leninist functionaries. During their years in power, it is most unlikely that they advocated systemic reforms.

The political events of the 1950s challenge widespread notions about how veteran communists with particular biographical pasts acted in East Germany. They suggest, for example, that former Soviet exiles were not fearful apparatchiks, but rather the veteran communists most likely to challenge Ulbricht's rule; Ackermann, Herrnstadt, Zaisser, and Oelßner were all former émigrés to the Soviet Union. At the same time, although it appears that veteran communist intellectuals who had emigrated to Western countries were more likely to question the SED regime, this was not true of high-level veteran communist functionaries who had been West émigrés. Indeed, none of the high-level functionaries who challenged Ulbricht's rule had been in Western emigration. Moreover, Kurt Hager, who had emigrated to England, played an important role in suppressing "revisionist" views in the mid-1950s, and Albert Norden, who had been exiled in the United States, castigated Fritz Selbmann in 1958. And although Schirdewan and Selbmann opposed Ulbricht and were survivors of Nazi captivity, so too were some of those who played an important role in their purges: Erich Honecker, Heinrich Rau, and Franz Dahlem. What is most striking, however, is that virtually all veteran communists—regardless of their biographical pasts—hewed to the SED's socialist orthodoxy.

The Herrnstadt / Zaisser and Schirdewan affairs set the tone for future SED politics. Veteran communists were unable to fathom the notion of a loyal or nonsubversive opposition; for them, all opposition undermined party unity and assumed cooperation with the class enemy. This view starkly limited inner-party dialogue and undercut potential attempts by veteran communists or others to promote alternatives to stale SED policies. These affairs also served as potent reminders to veteran communist and other functionaries that it was best not to tangle with Walter Ulbricht and later, Erich Honecker. Given that Old Communists, who enjoyed revolutionary authority, were unwilling to challenge the SED leadership, it is hardly surprising that other functionaries also refused to do so. Moreover, since veteran communists held so many influential positions in the GDR, they provided a ubiquitous model of political conduct that was to be widely imitated by other East German functionaries. The remarkable (and later stagnant) stability that characterized the GDR elite throughout the East German years resulted in no small measure from veteran communists' political conduct during the 1950s.

BEFORE 1989, scholars thought that Ulbricht continued his orthodox communist politics until he was deposed in 1971. The story of Ulbricht's last decade of rule, however, has been one of the great revelations of post-1989 archival research on East Germany.[88] In the latter half of the 1960s, it is now quite clear, Ulbricht and Honecker were engaged in a power struggle in which Honecker, and not Ulbricht, generally advocated the more conservative or dogmatic policies. Ulbricht had been the quintessential Stalinist leader in the 1950s, but he took on a new role in the 1960s. Although he maintained and even heightened the cult of his personality, he now fostered an image of himself as the "wise and good father of the country."[89] Ulbricht's new persona was linked to the building of the Berlin Wall in August 1961. The Wall stanched the outflow of professionals and skilled labor. It also proved that the Soviet Union and the Western powers would, respectively, neither abandon nor stand in the way of a semi-independent socialist state on German territory. With the imminent demise of the GDR no longer a threat, Ulbricht began to entertain reform measures that might have significantly changed the character of the SED regime. This raises intriguing questions about Ulbricht. Did he, once the GDR enjoyed a certain stability, simply abandon his earlier Stalinist persona in favor of that of a wise, benevolent father of his country? Or were his reforms but a guise for yet another experiment in the Stalinist reshaping of society?

In his waning years, Ulbricht combined Stalinist bravado with a vision of socialist modernity that ranged well beyond the communist goal of increasing industrial output. Ulbricht expected his reforms to allow the GDR economy to catch up with, if not to surpass, the West German economy. Ulbricht planned to revamp the GDR through the so-called New Economic System, or NES. NES was introduced in 1963 and implemented slowly over the following years. Ironically, it drew on the ideas of veteran communist Fritz Behrens and his colleagues, who had been roundly attacked as "revisionist" in the late 1950s. NES involved a series of administrative reforms, initiated from above, that were to streamline and rationalize the GDR economy.[90] It foresaw a measure of bureaucratic decentralization and enterprise autonomy; some economic decision-making was devolved to factory managers and to the directors of some seventy industry-wide administrative associations. It also entailed individual material incentives, in the form of bonuses, for both labor and management. Finally, NES promoted industries that Ulbricht hoped would be competitive on world markets: chemicals, electronics, cybernetics, machine tools, and metallurgy. Although NES was neither an attempt to introduce markets nor a strategy to abandon central planning, it nonetheless marked the SED leadership's most important attempt at internal reform.

To many leading Old Communists, Ulbricht's reforms posed a threat to long-held political axioms. NES seemed to threaten the party's power in the all-important realm of economic affairs. The spirit of NES also threatened longtime communists' role as the revolutionary avant-garde. Whereas their antifascist credentials had assured veteran communists leading positions of power in the past, a greater emphasis on professional training could only devalue their vanguard role, and thus their stature, in the SED regime. NES also challenged the veteran communist preoccupation with struggle; it assumed that a well-managed economy would have little use for voluntaristic campaigns to raise, for example, worker productivity. In addition, NES's focus on the production of goods for world markets necessitated cooperation with, rather than hostility toward, Western capitalist countries. Finally, NES challenged another basic tenet of the Old Communist world view: that the Soviet Union was *the* socialist model. While the Soviet Union saw a brief discussion of economic reform in the early 1960s, Soviet leaders never seriously implemented economic changes. The GDR, it soon became clear, would have to chart its own economic course. Ulbricht even became explicit about abandoning the Soviet Union as a model for the GDR. When a State Planning official, Herbert Wolf, tried to explain how the Soviet Union dealt with a particular economic issue at a 1963 Politburo meeting, Ulbricht cut him off by saying, "Forget about what the Soviet Union is doing; that is its affair."[91] Ulbricht essentially overturned the notion that the Soviet Union was to be a model for all other socialist states: the GDR, and not the Soviet Union, was to be the model socialist state.

Among veteran communists in the SED leadership, only Ulbricht wholeheartedly advocated NES. Ulbricht found support for his reforms among younger, more technocratic functionaries. Within the SED leadership, there thus emerged a clear-cut, although not immutable, generational divide. Ulbricht and some younger SED leaders vied against Erich Honecker and such veteran communists as Willi Stoph, Paul Fröhlich, Albert Norden, Paul Verner, and Alfred Neumann, as well as some younger Politburo members.[92] Honecker and his supporters wished to preserve the classic Soviet model for East Germany; they did not believe that the GDR should strive for a legitimacy based on its own model of socialism.[93] They also wanted to bind the GDR economy more closely to that of the Soviet Union. They were "security fanatics" and "demarcation politicians" who wanted to preserve the stark Cold War divisions that had characterized the postwar decades.[94] As the West German magazine *Der Spiegel* (The mirror) reported in 1964, "Old Communists" were telling their Western contacts that Ulbricht was working with "opportunist young people" and threatening to "betray the old ideas of the KPD."[95]

While longtime communist Politburo members had reluctantly followed Ulbricht's lead between 1963 and 1965, their resistance to NES and other reforms crystallized by the end of 1965. Their opposition gained momentum both from the ongoing difficulties of the GDR economy and

Khrushchev's fall from power in the Soviet Union in 1964. Leonid Brezhnev, the new Soviet leader, had little interest in socialist experiments; opposition by Old Communists to NES and other reforms was now welcomed in Moscow. At a December 1965 Politburo meeting, Stoph thus proposed measures to recentralize state planning and the direction of the economy. He also harshly criticized Erich Apel, a leading NES proponent and chairman of the State Planning Commission; Apel committed suicide the next day. That same month, the Eleventh Central Committee Meeting marked the first successful, although oblique, attack by Honecker and his sympathizers on Ulbricht's reform policies. At the end of this meeting, Stoph's measures to recentralize the direction of the economy were adopted. As a result, this meeting marked the moment at which NES and other attempts to modernize GDR society were put on the defensive. In 1967, the program was scaled back and renamed the Economic System of Socialism. Because NES was never fully implemented, it is impossible to know what its results might have been. What is certain, however, is that veteran communist orthodoxy stymied this most far-reaching attempt to reform East German socialism.

Tensions between Ulbricht and Honecker escalated in the late 1960s. At a Politburo meeting in June 1970, Ulbricht even removed Honecker from his position as second secretary of the Central Committee of the SED. But the dismissal lasted all of one week. In events reminiscent of those surrounding the ouster and reinstatement of Ernst Thälmann as KPD party leader in 1928, Soviet officials insisted that Honecker retain his position. In the face of Soviet demands, Ulbricht relented.[96]

The attempt to oust Honecker stoked the rivalry between the SED's two most powerful leaders. But it was a rivalry in which Honecker was increasingly gaining the upper hand. By 1970, the state of the East German economy had made Ulbricht vulnerable. There were shortages of energy and consumer goods, incomes were outpacing available consumer products, and shortfalls in raw materials and other deliveries kept factories from meeting their production targets. At a Politburo meeting in August 1970, from which Ulbricht was absent, Honecker demanded less "modeling and more strict management" in economic affairs. Alfred Neumann criticized the economic disorganization wrought by Ulbricht's policies of promoting "structure-determining tasks," that is, of giving selected projects in the chemical, machine-building, and electronics industries special access to labor and material resources.[97] In September, the Politburo issued a decree calling for the "planned proportional development of the economy." This language signaled the scrapping of what was left of Ulbricht's program. The provision of consumer goods was now to be

The rivals clink glasses. Erich Honecker and Walter Ulbricht at a reception following an awards ceremony on the twentieth anniversary of the founding of East Germany. From left to right: Paul Verner, Erich Correns, Erich Honecker, Walter Ulbricht, Willi Stoph. Berlin, October 4, 1969. (Bundesarchiv, Koblenz, Bild 183/H 1004/01/31)

balanced with investment in future-oriented industries.[98] In December 1970, at the Fourteenth Central Committee Meeting, numerous veteran communists (and others) criticized Ulbricht's policies. In his concluding speech to the meeting, Ulbricht fought back, arguing against the "planned proportional development of the economy." He was not, however, able to force the publication of this speech in *Neues Deutschland*. In an unheard-of action, eight members and candidates of the Politburo, including the longtime communists Honecker, Hermann Axen, Hager, Horst Sindermann, Stoph, and Verner, sent him letters asking him to refrain from publishing his speech. Faced with the prospect of publicizing political differences within the Politburo, Ulbricht relented.[99]

Honecker now wrote a memorandum on "The correction of Walter Ulbricht's economic policy at the Fourteenth Central Committee Meeting of the SED." This document can be read as the manifesto of the Honecker camp. Honecker complained of Ulbricht's "disproportional" promotion of some industries at the cost of others. The one-sided favoring of certain technical industries, he claimed, had left East Germany undersupplied with consumer goods and apartments. Honecker also stated (not without good reason) that Ulbricht's hopes for GDR economic growth were wildly unrealistic and that he had "attached exaggerated expectations" to electronic data processing. In addition, he charged that Ulbricht had allegedly attempted to decouple the GDR economy from that of the Soviet Union and to promote the "capitalist sector of the economy"—the small private firms still permitted in the GDR. Honecker further complained that Ulbricht had raised the East German debt to both socialist and capitalist countries. According to Honecker, Ulbricht's economic policy "played into the hands of the FRG to gain an economic foothold in the GDR."[100] By the end of 1970, Honecker and his supporters had articulated a conservative alternative to Ulbricht's economic policies: a greater emphasis on consumer goods, less concern with the GDR's technical prowess, and more economic cooperation with the Soviet Union and other socialist countries.

It was long thought that Ulbricht was removed as first secretary in 1971 because he rejected détente and was proving an obstacle to ongoing superpower negotiations. New archival evidence, however, suggests that perhaps the opposite was true: Ulbricht was possibly *too* eager to pursue a rapprochement with West Germany.[101] For Ulbricht, better relations with West Germany were essential to improve the GDR economy. Not only would friendlier relations with the other Germany open export markets for GDR products, but they would also allow for easier East German access to Western technology and know-how. These advances would help the GDR become attractive—so attractive, Ulbricht anticipated, that it would exercise a dynamic influence on West German workers to vote for the DKP, the West German Communist Party. In time, Ulbricht hoped that this might pave the way for a united Germany under socialist rule.[102] Although it remains a matter of historical debate, Ulbricht appears to have been more willing than his veteran communist Politburo colleagues to negotiate and compromise with West Germany.

In any event, it is very clear that Ulbricht wished to maintain his own and East Germany's independence vis-à-vis Brezhnev and the Soviet Union in the late 1960s. This, more than anything else, hastened his political downfall. In matters of Soviet-Western détente, for example, Ulbricht was unwilling to simply follow Moscow's lead and to subsume East Germany's interests to those of the Soviet Union.[103] He even hoped to play an independent role in these negotiations. His attempted interventions, however, were viewed by the Soviet leadership as annoying meddling.[104] Ulbricht also made it very clear that he wanted the GDR to be an equal and independent partner in all areas of Soviet–East German relations. He wanted the GDR to have a more equal economic relationship with the Soviet Union and was eager to negotiate, rather than to have dictated, the sale price and delivery of raw materials and industrial goods to East Germany. In August 1970, Ulbricht thus toasted Soviet leaders in Moscow: "In the cooperation [between the GDR and the Soviet Union] we want to develop ourselves as a genuine German state. We are not Byelorussia, we are not a Soviet republic. So, genuine cooperation."[105]

Ultimately, Ulbricht's position as first secretary rested on Soviet support. In a sense, Ulbricht never had a chance; not only did Brezhnev personally dislike Ulbricht, but the policies of the SED's first secretary went against Soviet interests. Meanwhile, from the summer of 1970 onward, Honecker urged Brezhnev to replace Ulbricht. After the Fourteenth Central Committee Meeting, Honecker convinced many of his fellow Politburo colleagues to move against Ulbricht. In January 1971, thirteen of twenty Politburo members and candidates signed a seven-page letter, initiated by Honecker, asking Brezhnev to help them depose Ulbricht. Besides Honecker, the longtime communists Axen, Hager, Sindermann, Stoph, and Verner signed the letter; two Old Communists, Alfred Neumann and Albert Norden, did not. According to the letter, Ulbricht had brought the SED leadership into an "extraordinarily difficult situation": he had not held to Politburo or Warsaw Pact decrees and was wholly unrealistic about GDR economic developments. In keeping with veteran communist political tactics, Ulbricht was also accused of a host of personal failings. He allegedly often spoke from a "position of infallibility," liked to see himself "on par with Marx, Engels, and Lenin," and claimed that he was "unrepeatable." Furthermore, Ulbricht supposedly "transfers the exaggerated estimation of his person onto the GDR that he always wants to maneuver into the role of a 'model' and 'master.'" The letter closed by asking Brezhnev to convince Ulbricht to resign because of his age (he was seventy-eight) and the state of his health (it was not the best).[106] Ulbricht remained in power for several more months. In April, however, Brezhnev, according to Axen, had a "very difficult conversation" with Ulbricht until the latter "recognized the arguments."[107] On May 3, the SED leader "asked" the Central Committee to officially relieve him of his position.

Until Ulbricht's death in August 1973, Honecker let no opportunity pass to humiliate his predecessor. Although Ulbricht was formally chairman of the SED and the East German State Council, he was subjected to the sorts of chicanery that he had earlier heaped on other longtime communists. Shortly after his downfall, the former leader suffered a severe heart attack. Supposedly to benefit his health, Ulbricht was forbidden to attend various meetings and had to remain within a thirty-five-kilometer radius of Berlin. In October, further restrictions were added. Ulbricht was not to attend meetings for longer than two hours and was not to speak for longer than fifteen minutes. He was also subject to Stasi surveillance; his bodyguard wrote up reports for his superiors.[108] Other indignities followed. The Walter Ulbricht Stadium in East Berlin was now referred to as the Chaussee Street Stadium.[109] When Ulbricht asked for tickets to attend the Fifty-fifth Anniversary Celebration of the Bolshevik Revolution, Honecker denied his request.[110] In December 1972, Ulbricht even complained to Brezhnev about his treatment: "I want the Politburo to better use my knowledge and experiences. At the same time, I hope that the first secretary and the Secretariat of the C[entral] C[ommittee] will spare me petty harassments and that all questions concerning my party and state work will be discussed with me personally. I want the campaign 'Ulbricht is to blame for everything,' that has been going on since the Fourteenth Plenum, to be discontinued."[111] The once all-powerful Ulbricht was reduced to begging for better treatment from his party. The tactics used against Ulbricht mirrored those that he had long used against other veteran communists: nasty intrigues, ad hominem attacks, and contemptible humiliations. In East Germany, veteran communist politics was as petty as the communist vision was grand.

Ulbricht's downfall was unique in the annals of GDR history. Until October 1989, it was the only transfer of power that occurred in East Germany. It marked the only time in East German history when Old Communists vied against each other with two distinct political programs. The organized effort to keep Ulbricht from publishing his closing speech at the Fourteenth Plenum and the common letter to Brezhnev in January 1971 prove that Honecker and his co-conspirators were operating behind the first secretary's back. The communist obsession with party discipline was, in a sense, well-founded: the only true "faction" in SED history (until 1989) successfully forced a transfer of power that, in turn, had significant influence on SED policy. Under Honecker, a claque of conformist and conservative veteran KPD cadres would reassert their communist orthodoxy on SED policy.

7

LEGENDS

Veteran Communists as Antifascist Heroes

THE TWO BEST-KNOWN EAST GERMAN NOVELS THAT TREAT VETERAN communists critically share a striking plotline: both feature retired Old Communist protagonists engaged in memoir writing. In *Collin*, Stefan Heym's stinging roman à clef of the East German elite, author and long-time communist Hans Collin decides to write his autobiography. In writing his memoirs, however, Collin is caught between the fear of a "Voodoo-Death"—social ostracism among longtime communists should he honestly recount his life—and the fear of submission to "a lasting spiritual self-castration" should he remain silent on past events.[1] The dilemma is so taxing that he suffers a heart attack. Brought to a special hospital for high-ranking party functionaries, Collin encounters Comrade Urack, the long-serving minister of state security. When Urack learns that Collin is writing his memoirs, he becomes concerned about what they may reveal. The two Old Communists become engaged in a macabre psychological contest as to who will outlive the other and thus determine the fate of the memoirs. Although Collin resolves to record his past life honestly, the arduous task of writing his memoirs kills him before his autobiography is complete.

In *Stille Zeile Sechs* (Silent close no. 6), Monika Maron writes about a retired longtime communist and once-powerful functionary, Herbert Beerenbaum, who has a lame right hand and cannot put pen to paper. He hires a forty-two-year-old disenchanted East German historian, Rosalind Polkowski, to write down the memoirs that he is, on party orders, to author. The encounter between Beerenbaum and Rosalind becomes a tormented struggle between an Old Communist's conviction that his life was led in a just cause and a younger woman's hatred of all that his life symbolizes. As with Collin, the critical interrogation of Beerenbaum's past life story ultimately brings on his demise: Beerenbaum too dies from the anxiety incurred by confronting his past.[2]

It is no accident that memoir writing plays such a central role in the plots of both *Collin* and *Stille Zeile Sechs*. Beginning in the 1960s, memoir writing by veteran communists was actively encouraged by the SED regime. Indeed, it was an important feature of the larger mission assigned to longtime communists: the propagation of the past heroic antifascist struggle. Scores of Old Communists wrote and published their memoirs.[3] Fritz Selbmann, Franz Dahlem, and Erich Honecker all published full-scale autobiographies. Emmy Koenen published fragments of her memoirs. As the plots of *Collin* and *Stille Zeile Sechs* suggest, however, memoir writing was fraught with dilemmas—both for longtime communists and their regime. Although party authorities wanted to foster an official memory of communist resistance and redemption, many Old Communist memories had no place in the SED's master narrative of communist history. And although party leaders wished to pay tribute to a common communist past, veteran party members wanted to celebrate their individual pasts and often, to rehabilitate their revolutionary biographies. While many veteran communists faced Collin's dilemma, they overwhelmingly chose Beerenbaum's solution. Rather than risk excommunication from the Old Communist community by honestly confronting their past lives, veteran communists wrote clichéd narratives that obscured their past lives but conformed to SED dictate. They produced memoirs of the sort that Collin had hoped to avoid but that Beerenbaum, to Rosalind's frustration, busily dictated.

Two decades after the establishment of East Germany, the inspiration and revolutionary élan of the early postwar years had waned. The GDR had become a thoroughly routinized socialist state run by aging apparatchiks. A "Great Future" for socialism no longer seemed so certain and, rather than dwell on a future that threatened to become mundane, the SED now focused the GDR population's attention on a golden "Great Past."[4] Just as the Brezhnev leadership in the Soviet Union created a full-blown cult of World War II to reinspire an apathetic and cynical population, the SED leadership revived the myth of a glorious "antifascist" struggle during the Nazi era.[5] This official memory was endlessly rehearsed in East German *lieux de mémoire* (places of memory)—in films, museum exhibits, primary- and secondary-school textbooks, newspaper articles and eulogies and, not least, memoirs.[6] Veteran communists, who personally embodied the "antifascist" struggle, commanded renewed importance in the GDR: they took on the role of official antifascist heroes. This role, however, involved considerable tensions.

ULBRICHT'S AMBITIOUS attempts to revamp GDR society through NES and other measures had a significant influence on the lives and careers of

Karl Schirdewan, party veteran, examines old photographs. Potsdam, April 22, 1981. (Bundesarchiv, SAPMO-BArch, Bild Y 10-179/00; photo by Rolf Kißling)

veteran communists. Ulbricht had always privileged those with technical, economic, and administrative expertise at the expense of those with mere revolutionary experience. This predilection became even more pronounced in the 1960s. Although veteran communist members of the Politburo and Central Committee were often allowed to retain their positions despite advancing age, longtime communists at the middle and lower levels of the party and state bureaucracies were now retired en masse.[7] Even the Institute for Marxism-Leninism (IML), the SED's premier institute for ideological matters, saw a turnover of leading positions from veteran communists to younger comrades in the early 1960s. As Wilhelm Eildermann, an Old Communist who worked at the institute, noted in a 1962 diary entry: "[Kurt] Hager . . . announced the principle that one must take leading functions away from old comrades because they are no longer up to [these positions]. They should occupy themselves with preparing manuscripts, etc."[8] Veteran communists were now to transmit a revolutionary ethos to younger East Germans by "preparing manuscripts" and participating in other propaganda efforts.

The lives and careers of the veteran communists featured in these pages illustrate not only SED personnel policies in the 1960s, but also the link between retirement and antifascist propaganda efforts. Emmy

Koenen, for example, had already retired in 1958 to care for her husband. After Wilhelm Koenen's death in 1963, she wrote her memoirs, worked on various official histories, and gave talks to East German audiences about the antifascist struggle. Similarly, Fritz Selbmann, who lost all of his economic functions in 1964, devoted himself to writing his memoirs and a series of autobiographical novels. As he reportedly stated: "If one doesn't want me anymore in a political function then I will write books. Literature is also politics."[9] From 1969 until 1975, Selbmann served as vice president of the East German Writers' Union. In 1965, Erich Honecker took an opportunity to oust Karl Schirdewan from his position as head of the state archives in Potsdam. As Honecker claimed in a letter to Ulbricht, "considerable shortcomings" in the archives were due to Schirdewan's (mis)management.[10] Schirdewan spent the next quarter century as a retiree in Potsdam; from 1976 onward, however, he headed the local branch of the Committee of Antifascist Resistance Fighters. Fred Oelßner retired from his position as director of the Institute of Economics at the Academy of Sciences in 1969; thereafter he wrote some memoir fragments. Franz Dahlem remained deputy minister of university and technical education until 1974 and a member of the Central Committee until his death in 1981. From the mid-1960s onward, however, he focused much of his energy on writing his memoirs. Only Gerhart Eisler did little to popularize the past antifascist struggle. This may have been due to his relatively early death from a heart attack in 1968. At that time, Eisler was chairman of the State Radio Committee and a Central Committee member.

ONCE RETIRED, longtime communists and socialists became "party veterans."[11] In East Germany, former combatants of World War I or II were never granted a special status. Instead, party veterans occupied the place that war veterans enjoy in other societies. The graveyard for prominent East German socialists, for example, the Memorial for Socialists in the Friedrichsfelde district of Berlin, resembles cemeteries for fallen soldiers and war veterans found all over Europe; it is made up of hundreds of simple, identical stone graves arranged in neat rows. In addition, the perquisites generally granted war veterans—such as supplementary pensions and superior medical attention—were granted to party veterans in East Germany. In 1956, the SED Secretariat issued "Guidelines for the Care of Party Veterans." Among other measures, party veterans were to be given special medical attention and help in securing reservations for health resorts and vacation areas. Small honorary pensions were to be granted to needy "old outstanding comrades who throughout their lives have dedicated themselves to the struggle of the working class against capitalist exploitation and repression."[12] In addition, in the next years, concerted efforts were made to invite party veterans to social occasions celebrating or commemorating important historical events in the workers' movement in which they had participated. They were also awarded the GDR's various medals, banners, and awards, usually on important birthdays or significant anniversaries of East German history. These distinctions ranged from the highest honor, the Karl Marx Medal, to medals honoring particular experiences in the "antifascist" struggle. To receive these or other perquisites, however, party veterans had to have solid revolutionary biographies, be in good standing with the party, and, health permitting, to participate in the ongoing antifascist effort.

Beginning in 1957, party veterans were sent on group trips to the Soviet Union. In a later remembrance, Emmy Koenen wrote of such a veterans' trip and the meaning it had for her. In 1966, she and other party veterans traveled to Volgograd (formerly Stalingrad). The group met with former war veterans who had defended the city in the 1943 Battle of Stalingrad. Emmy was told to give a speech on behalf of the group. According to Emmy, "My heart was beating so hard that it practically burst. I was as excited as when I gave my first political speech a few decades earlier." As Emmy was speaking about the GDR's socialist development and "our indestructible friendship with the Soviet Union," one of the "Soviet friends impulsively pinned his Lenin-badge on me and hugged and kissed me. All the other Soviet and German comrades who were proven in class struggle and in the struggle against fascism also hugged . . . That Lenin-badge is very dear to me."[13]

Like so many veteran communists, Emmy had a deep sentimental attachment to the Soviet Union; this visit was no doubt one of the high points of her later years. She was one of some 5,340 party veterans who by 1966 had received the opportunity to visit the first workers' and peasants' state.[14] According to party officials, these trips were "on the one hand, an honor and distinction and, on the other, to be viewed as a party task by old comrades."[15] Like so much else in the GDR, these trips involved a quid pro quo: on their return, party veterans were to lecture audiences about their (positive) experiences in the Soviet Union. In 1966, party veterans reportedly spoke about their trips at some 2,418 events, for a total audience of 110,000, including some 38,000 youth.[16]

Besides the privileges accorded party veterans, virtually all pre-1933 KPD cadres enjoyed the perquisites given to those officially recognized as "fighters" against or "persecuted" by fascism. In the mid-1960s, these privileges were enhanced. This happened just as Ulbricht was beginning to face the Old Communist backlash against his economic reforms. Having angered longtime communists with his ambitious plans, Ulbricht may have instituted these measures to placate veteran communists. Alternatively, perhaps Honecker and his supporters, over Ulbricht's opposition, insisted on these measures. In any event, in April 1965, officially recognized "fighters against fascism" and those "persecuted by fascism" were granted higher honorary pensions. "Fighters against fascism" were to receive honorary pensions of eight hundred marks a month; those "persecuted by fascism," honorary pensions of six hundred marks a month. In addition, surviving dependents—widows, widowers, orphans, and in some cases, parents—of deceased "fighters" and the "persecuted" were eligible for modest pensions.[17] In 1966, another decree granted financial advantages to the sons and daughters of officially recognized antifascist resisters. Those who were university students or secondary-school pupils from grades nine and up were, regardless of their parents' income, granted scholarships or allowances; for secondary-school pupils, these ranged from sixty to eighty marks a month.[18] The benefits accorded family members of antifascist resisters thus created something of an East German hereditary caste—one based not on wealth or merit, but on biography.

Once Erich Honecker came to power in 1971, there was a striking increase in the benefits accorded recognized "fighters" against, and those "persecuted" by, fascism. This change underscores the importance Honecker attached to those like himself who were living symbols of the antifascist struggle. There were, for example, many more honorary medals awarded for past contributions to the working-class movement. Beginning in 1974, officially recognized antifascist resistance "fighters" and "victims" of fascism were also granted the right to free transportation on all trains, streetcars, subways, and buses in the GDR; in addition, they were allowed to take along a companion at no charge.[19] They also enjoyed increasingly lucrative pensions. By 1988, "fighters" were receiving 1,700 marks a month.[20] Other East Germans clearly resented these honorary pensions. In the late 1980s, the West German historian Lutz Niethammer visited a coffee hour organized for GDR retirees. When talk turned to pensions, one woman, who had married a mechanic who had joined the KPD in 1922, said that she received a monthly pension of 1,850 marks because her husband, now deceased, had been an officially recognized "fighter against fascism." The other retirees all but one of whom received monthly pensions of between 290 and 390 marks, found the contrast between their pensions and hers "outrageous, yes, humiliating." Furthermore, they were infuriated by the notion that "one could quasi marry into the status *(Stand)* of a resistance fighter."[21] From the summer of 1945 to the fall of 1989, the perquisites enjoyed by veteran communists did not endear these individuals to broad strata of the East German population.

SED AUTHORITIES were particularly eager for party veterans to inspire East German youth with "revolutionary tradition." Veteran communists were thus sent to schools, youth groups, and military formations to recount their experiences to new generations of socialists-in-the-making. In 1960, for example, it was suggested that "old outstanding comrades, who on account of their age have retired from the armed forces of the Ministry of the Interior," should become, health and talents allowing, honorary staff members in the political departments of the armed forces. There they would "help the younger comrades . . . with the organization of political work, especially agitation/propaganda."[22] Similarly, during the 1960s, the function of Old Communists in the Ministry of State Security changed. According to historian Jens Gieseke, veteran communists "moved ever more into the role of . . . carriers of tradition who personified the Chekist-antifascist founding myth and therefore filled important transmission functions vis-à-vis the young people streaming into [the ministry]."[23]

To popularize the antifascist struggle, the SED deployed veteran communists in many ways. Longtime communists belonged to local Commissions for the Research of the History of the Workers' Movement. In this capacity, they gathered information, planned exhibitions, lectured to audiences, and wrote small brochures and articles for the provincial press on the local "antifascist struggle."[24] They also contributed to the ubiquitous "tradition cases"—display cases featuring local memorabilia from the various phases of the antifascist struggle—found in schools, factories, and state and party office buildings. Veteran communists served as functionaries of the Committee of Antifascist Resistance Fighters in the GDR.[25] The committee established "working groups" for the major Nazi prisons and concentration camps and a "section" for the Spanish Civil War. At the sites of former concentration camps, members of these working groups led tours, helped organize exhibitions, and participated in commemorative rituals; they also coordinated the research and writing of official histories of the antifascist struggle in the camps.

In her later years, Emmy Koenen led a typical party veteran's life. According to a biographical statement that she wrote in 1969, she was participating in a commission working on the past history of the DFD and in a working group that was researching the history of the women's movement in Berlin. She was also doing "continuous work with two secondary schools, one of which fights under the name of Wilhelm Koenen"; this surely involved talking to pupils about her past antifascist activities. Emmy was also organizing Wilhelm Koenen's archival papers and was preparing to write her own memoirs.[26] In 1976, when Franz Dahlem asked Emmy to help him with his memoirs, Emmy replied that even "with the best will in the world" she was unable to do so. She was simply too busy. She was writing her memoirs of emigration in Czechoslovakia and England. She had recently given talks at three schools and one regiment that carried Wilhelm Koenen's name and would soon be doing the same at a "fighting group" of a construction company and a woman's brigade in Buna. And she felt overwhelmed by mail from school-age children questioning her about the past antifascist struggle.[27]

IN THE late 1940s and 1950s, memoir writing by Old Communists had actually been viewed with disdain. One scholar has commented that among Old Bolsheviks memoir writing was "rare, almost heretical"; it was "something out of the ordinary and regarded as unseemly immodesty to write down one's own life and thoughts."[28] Wilhelm Pieck was known to disapprove of autobiographies by veteran communists.[29] But all of this changed in the 1960s. As one Old Communist noted in 1966, "Memoirs by veterans are highly desired."[30] The regime had come to see veteran-communist memoirs as an important propaganda tool. Moreover, as historian Lutz Niethammer has suggested, "the administration of memory" was an "instrument of power for the party."[31]

The SED charged a party institution with overseeing the writing and publication of memoirs: the Memoir Section of the Central Party Archives located in the IML. This section had its roots in a collection of memoirs begun by Paul Lenzner (a social democrat before 1933) in 1951–1952. These memoirs were soon considered an important didactic tool for raising new generations of committed communists. According to 1961 guidelines, memoirs "constitute an important contribution to the political-ideological educational work of the party. The portrayal of the life and deeds of authors in the form of their memoirs gives our people, and especially our youth, an encouraging example and educates them."[32] But these memoirs were more than a mere educational tool. As a staff member of the IML later wrote, they were a "fighting instrument" in the ongoing socialist struggle. Indeed, memoirs were such potent weapons that they, like all dangerous arms, were to be stored in depots: "All memoirs that have been written or recorded on tape belong in an archive . . . If memoirs are in the desks or drawers of private individuals, there is no guarantee that they can be used in the socialist interest; these memoirs are also not protected from unauthorized use. Should such memoirs end up in the hands of persons who do not handle them with political responsibility and the necessary vigilance, they could cause great harm both to the party and to the author."[33] Although party authorities believed that memoirs could be useful propaganda weapons, they were also clearly very concerned about what these memoirs might reveal about past communist history.

The IML Memoir Section developed procedures to ensure that party veterans wrote appropriate memoirs. As guidelines on party archives noted: "Memoirs must first be created in cooperation between the author and collector (a comrade who is appropriate for such a task—historian, archivist, party propagandist, social scientist, or like [individual]). In the rarest of cases are memoirs presented to history commissions or archives that were written spontaneously. The collection of memoirs, that is, the purposeful, systematic work with those comrades who are potential authors of valuable memoirs, is therefore of utmost importance."[34] A staff member of the Memoir Section, Ilse Schiel, wrote a dissertation on memoir literature in socialist societies. She described how the IML went about collecting memoirs by longtime party members. The Memoir Section first established a list of potential memoir authors—those comrades who had held important functions, had participated in significant events, or who simply knew how to recount their pasts in "lively and interesting" ways. This list was then confirmed by the administration of the IML. Next, the section set out to establish "good and comradely contact" with potential authors. Institute staff members contacted such individuals and then met with them to discuss the matter. These conversations involved an exchange of ideas on the possible contents of an author's memoirs. Schiel claimed that these meetings often ended with the party veteran declaring himself ready to develop a prospectus of the main themes and the time period that he would cover in his memoirs. In "exceptional cases" the author agreed to write a full-scale autobiography; however, only "a relatively small circle of authors are able to manage such a demanding, extensive, and strenuous mental activity, since the authors are usually of an advanced age." A firm promise to actually publish the memoirs was never given at this stage. Schiel also outlined the various ways in which the IML could help an author complete a memoir project. The institute could supply useful books and other periodicals, provide archival documents and newspaper clippings from the period in question, and compile chronologies and lists of events that the author might cover in his life story. According to Schiel, "The purpose of these measures consists in refreshing the memory of the author, strengthening his ability to remember, and steering [that ability] in the appropriate direction of the topic."[35]

The prompting of memories was a central concern of the Memoir Section. Only certain recollections, framed in set narratives, served the SED's ideological goals. Old Communists were not asked to record what they perhaps remembered, or associated with, a particular event or set of episodes. Instead, they were told what to remember and how to structure their memories in a predetermined historical narrative. Thus when the Memoir Section planned an anthology on a given time period or set of experiences, it first drew up a list of topics and themes to be covered by authors. The section, for example, drew up a list of "Main Themes" that were to be covered in "an anthology of memoirs on the problems of the Marxist-Leninist development of the SED and the realization of the general laws of socialist revolution in the period from the 1946 Unity Party Congress until the beginning of the 1950s." The list included themes such as "the process of blending former communists and social democrats," "help from the SMAD to the working class of the Soviet occupation zone in all areas of social life," and "clashes with the reactionary forces in the bourgeois-democratic parties"—all topics that determined the memories authors were to bring to their contributions.[36] Letters sent to potential authors asking for their participation in this memoir anthology included this list of main themes. As these letters noted, "The accompanying Main Themes will facilitate an orientation over the conception [of the project] and will surely give you stimulation for the writing down of your memoirs."[37]

The control exerted by the Memoir Section helps to explain the formulaic quality of veteran-communist autobiographies. The master narrative of these memoirs began with the birth of the longtime communist into the poverty of working-class life in Imperial Germany. After a miserable childhood, he or she was politicized during adolescence—often as a soldier in World War I—and joined the KPD as a young adult. He or she then participated in the political struggles of the Weimar era, frequently becoming acquainted (or at the very least attending political events) with legendary communist heroes such as Lenin, Rosa Luxemburg and, most of all, Ernst Thälmann. Between 1933 and 1945, the veteran communist took part in the antifascist struggle and, by dint of communist solidarity and resistance, survived the hell of Nazi captivity or emigration abroad. Liberation was followed by a second period of heroic activity when, through remarkable ingenuity and improvisation, the longtime communist helped create East German socialism. Once the GDR was firmly established, a life of revolution had been redeemed. Old Communist memoirs usually petered out at an indeterminate moment in the early 1950s.

The themes and metaphors of these memoirs were also very formulaic. Veteran communists, for example, frequently referred to the fascist era as a "night" or a "long night." Communists and their solidarity, in turn, were often portrayed as stars; the title of one veteran-communist memoir of the Nazi era was even *Je dunkler die Nacht, desto heller die Sterne* (The darker the night, the brighter the stars).[38] Although communists had often faced death on a daily basis in Hitler's camps, their memoirs did not dwell on the physical sufferings that they had endured. Fritz Selbmann was typical when he wrote, "It is not my intention to report in detail the atrocities practiced in the concentration camp."[39] Themes that so characterize the camp memoirs of Jewish survivors—dehumanization, the assault on the personality, physical deprivation and pain, and the war of all against all—were rare in Old Communist memoirs. Instead, Selbmann and other veteran communists emphasized the heroic solidarity and resistance that allowed the communist (or antifascist) collective to persevere in the face of seemingly insurmountable obstacles. Longtime communists described at great length the solidaristic aid—from extra food rations to a few weeks' rest in the sick bay—that they had received from their fellow comrades. They also wrote about the organization of illegal political activity and actions undertaken on behalf of foreign communists and Soviet prisoners of war. The Old Communist narrative of life in captivity transformed the daily battle against death into a resistance struggle against fascist Germany.

SOME VETERAN communists had great difficulties matching their memories to official SED memory. Cläre Quast, a veteran communist who worked at the IML, once noted that "it is by no means always so easy to write memoirs that not only should accord with the truth, but that simultaneously should depict the situation in those days."[40] Quast meant that it was not always easy to write memoirs that accorded with the party's line on past events (the "truth"), while faithfully recording past events. Veteran communists' memories included the "white spots" of communist history, such as the Great Purges in the Soviet Union in the 1930s and the waves of East German purges in the early 1950s; conflicts within the party and rifts among top communist leaders; abrupt, seemingly inexplicable changes of communist policy, such as the Nazi-Soviet Pact of 1939; and disappointments and slights encountered in the postwar years. All of these memories were difficult, if not impossible, to integrate into the SED's official master narrative.

Longtime communists were fully aware of the liberties taken by SED ideologues in matters of party history; they even acknowledged as much in letters to each other. When Bruno Fuhrmann, a victim of the Noel Field Affair, wrote Franz Dahlem to tell him that he would, in time, answer Dahlem's questions concerning the West emigration, he added: "Franz, I will only write how it really was, without somehow emphasizing some particular comrades, as unfortunately has already been done."[41] Hans Teubner, an IML staff member, wrote another victim of the Noel Field Affair, Georg Stibi, to encourage him to write his memoirs for the benefit of future historians. He acknowledged that at present not everything could be published:

> All "the drama in your life" should be written down on paper even though it is not *yet* intended for publication *today,* but rather for the writing of history tomorrow. The discipline of history pushes more and more to a *truthful* portrayal of all events . . . "Dry-cleaned" history and "manipulated" history is useless! The truth is in accordance with party thought and benefits us, *not* the enemy, whereby I freely admit that today the *full* truth cannot yet always be published. But that which is published must be *true,* so that in the future only a rounding out is necessary. How many good comrades have taken irretrievable treasures into the grave.[42]

For Teubner, the truth of past party history would eventually be publishable; he presumably thought that the mistakes and excesses along the party's road to socialism would be overridden by future socialist accomplishments.

Veteran communists adopted several strategies to address the discrepancies between their memories and those called for by their party. One was to write just for "the archives." These memoirs were of little use in fostering official East German memory, but they nonetheless provided party historians with additional information and, at the same time, gave Old Communist authors the hope that their revolutionary deeds would not be lost to future generations. Paul Merker, for example, was asked by the IML to write memoirs of his time in Mexico. He agreed to do so, but as he noted in a letter to Franz Dahlem, "This work is written for the party archive and not for publication."[43] Emmy Koenen took it upon herself to classify one of her memoir fragments as "strictly confidential": an eight-page piece titled "Friends and Comrades Lost without a Trace."[44] This fragment described the Soviet purges of the 1930s. Other Old Communists planned to omit certain passages when their memoirs were readied for publication. Wilhelm Eildermann once recorded a chance encounter with Ernst Goldenbaum, the veteran communist chairman of the DBD: "Spoke with Goldenbaum at the snack bar. He has gotten up to 1923 in his memoirs. They are meant for the archive." Eildermann then quoted Goldenbaum's words: "Of course, for publication, I would have to leave out a great deal."[45]

Some longtime communists simply altered their memories to fit the prescribed narrative. Sepp Hahn, an inmate in Sachsenhausen concentration camp during the Nazi years, vividly recalled atrocities committed by the SS in the camp. He remembered much less clearly episodes of communist solidarity and resistance. In the late 1950s, Hahn, then vice-chairman of the Central Revision Committee, became concerned that there was no official SED history of Sachsenhausen concentration camp. He collected materials, wrote a draft, and then submitted this work to the IML. The institute praised Hahn's manuscript for its intention, but criticized its execution. According to H. Schumann in the IML's Resistance Department, Hahn had overemphasized SS barbarities while neglecting organized communist resistance in Sachsenhausen:

> But there are also severe gaps in your manuscript . . . This observation refers specifically to the still insufficient portrayal of the political work of our comrades imprisoned in Sachsenhausen C[oncentration] C[amp]. (Only first on page 14 do you report on the conscious work of the communists). We believe that the very broad depiction of examples of the barbaric terror of the SS must not push the political activity of comrades into the background. What matters most is to pay tribute to the uncompromising stance of communists, their great solidarity with foreign prisoners, and the common struggle of all antifascists against the SS.[46]

Hahn took the IML's criticism to heart. In a revised version of his manuscript, he declared that the history of Sachsenhausen "must evaluate all reports based on personal experience and documented facts. In this, the criminal methods of mass murder by the fascists matter less than the way, form, and methods of the organized resistance struggle of the antifascists and the leadership of communists in the hells of the SS gangs."[47] Hahn suppressed his own memories of camp atrocities so as to achieve greater accord with official SED memory of communist resistance in the camps.

MOST VETERAN communist memoirs were written by cultural figures—well-known writers, artists, or actors; professionals such as doctors, lawyers, or academics; or relatively low-ranking SED functionaries with a flair for storytelling. These works sometimes enjoyed considerable popularity and, despite the GDR's perennial paper shortages, were often published in print runs large even by Western book-publishing standards. The most popular Old Communist memoir ever published in East Germany was *Sonjas Rapport* (Sonya's report), by Ruth Werner. Werner, the sister of Jürgen Kuczynski, wrote a dramatic account of her twenty years as a Soviet spy in China, Poland, Switzerland, and England from 1930 to 1950.[48] Although Werner was the intermediary who passed Klaus Fuchs's atomic secrets to the Soviet Union, there is no mention of this in her autobiography.[49] Nonetheless, her electric mix of espionage tales and revealing passages about her personal life makes for a good read. Published in 1977, some 311,000 copies of the book had been produced in five printings by 1979; in 1982, *Sonjas Rapport* was in its ninth printing.[50] The book was also made into a film. While no other Old Communist autobiography soared to such popular heights of success, other memoirs by longtime communists saw high numbers of copies produced in multiple print runs. Such memoirs—by relatively "ordinary" veteran communists, as opposed to high-ranking functionaries—served to foster the general, stereotypical image of the veteran communist as a socialist hero, as one of many such living legends who had led simple, honest lives of struggle. The average reader, while unable to recreate the veteran-communist experience, could nonetheless emulate the spirit animating the lives of longtime communists: despite hardships, personal shortcomings, and professional disappointments (even Sonja of *Sonja's Rapport* was left high and dry by her Soviet handlers), devotion to the party and the socialist cause had made veteran communists' lives both meaningful and worthwhile.

By the late 1960s, it had become fashionable for high-level functionaries to write and publish their memoirs. The first full-scale autobiography by a former high-ranking Old Communist functionary was Willy Sägebrecht's *Nicht Amboß, sondern Hammer Sein* (Not anvil, but hammer); it was published in 1968.[51] This was soon followed by Selbmann's much-acclaimed *Alternative—Bilanz—Credo* in 1969; in this autobiography, Selbmann covered his life until 1945.[52] In 1971, memoirs appeared by another longtime party functionary, Karl Mewis—*Im Auftrag der Partei* (On party orders).[53] Even Walter Ulbricht planned to write his memoirs after his downfall in 1971. A well-known East German historian, Gerhard Keiderling, was to assist Ulbricht in this project and met with him several times. Keiderling later recalled that whenever he and Ulbricht touched on sensitive matters, security officials entered the room, leading him to believe that these conversations were being bugged.[54] By the time of his death, however, Ulbricht had made little headway on his memoirs project.

In April 1974 the SED Secretariat abruptly restricted the publication of memoirs by high-ranking functionaries. It decreed that its approval was necessary for the publication of all memoirs by current and past members and candidate members of the Central Committee, as well as those by comrades "who had or have a deep knowledge of the internal affairs of the party or state leadership."[55] The SED leadership apparently feared that memoirists might reveal *Interna,* details of party history that would embarrass or even delegitimate the East German regime. Top SED leaders also worried that memoirists might treat delicate subjects coarsely. In the era of détente, for example, the SED was careful not to publish nasty polemics against Herbert Wehner, the West German social democrat who had reneged on communism in the early 1940s; several veteran communist memoirs were probably squelched for this reason.[56] Personal jealousies and rivalries probably also prompted the decree. SED leaders were reluctant to allow each other opportunities to celebrate their individual biographies; highlighting one leader's past role in the antifascist struggle or the founding years of the GDR by definition undermined that of all other leaders.

Even Erich Honecker's autobiography was subject to this decree. The most official of official memoirs, Honecker's *Aus meinem Leben* (From my life) had an unusual history for an autobiography by a socialist leader. In 1979 Robert Maxwell, the British publisher, suggested that a biography of Honecker appear in his series "Leaders of the World." Honecker was doubtlessly titillated by joining this elite club, and negotiations with Maxwell soon proceeded apace. The proposed biography then became an autobiography. In fact, however, this "memoir" was designed, researched, compiled, written, and edited by teams of party functionaries. High-level functionaries, including Politburo members and candidates such as Günter Mittag, Horst Dohlus, and Inge Lange, were involved in producing Honecker's life story.[57] In February 1980, the Politburo charged a working group with evaluating the draft autobiography, and in March, Honecker received approval for the publication of his memoirs.[58] The work was initially published in August 1980 in Great Britain as *From My Life.* The general secretary of the SED chose to publish his autobiography not only in the West, but also in a foreign language. The German translation then appeared in West Germany.[59] Only after months of circulation in Western countries was the GDR population treated to its leader's autobiography, and then to an edition printed on lower-quality paper. Even the production of official memory was subject to the GDR's policy of exporting its best products to the West, while distributing second-rate goods to the East German population.

In *Aus meinem Leben,* the implicit parallel between Honecker's supposed life trajectory and official SED communist history could not be missed. Honecker devoted the bulk of his memoirs to his East German years. His memoirs thus focused on the final chapter of the antifascist myth—communist resurrection and redemption in the form of the successful achievement of a socialist East Germany. Just as Honecker had risen from his lowly beginnings in Wiebelskirchen to the heights of socialist leadership, the GDR had risen from the moral and physical ruins of 1945 to become a full-blown socialist state. From the glossy photos of Honecker's meetings with world leaders, to chapters entitled "Allied with Sports" and "The Millionth Apartment," this work reveled in East Germany's supposed achievements. In the 1980s, stacks of copies of *Aus meinem Leben* were ubiquitous in East German bookstores—a measure of the regime's attempt, if not its success, at fostering an official memory among the East German population.

THE STORY of Fritz Selbmann's postwar memoirs illustrates what happened when former high-ranking SED functionaries wished to publish memoirs that did not accord with official GDR memory.[60] In the early 1970s, Selbmann wrote a sequel to his pre-1945 memoirs titled *Acht Jahre und ein Tag* (Eight years and one day)—the eight years were 1945–1953, the one day, June 17, 1953. Much of this work was conventional Old Communist autobiographical fare in which Selbmann recounted the successes and difficulties of the Aufbau years. But Selbmann also touched on topics that had no place in the official party narrative of the postwar period. He recounted, for example, his attempts to prevent the Soviet dismantling of factories; the enormous difficulties that accompanied the founding of the EKO metallurgical complex; and the events surrounding the June 1953 Uprising.

Selbmann died in 1975, before his manuscript could be published. According to his son Erich, a longtime press functionary in the GDR, Fritz Selbmann passed away under the impression that his book would be published by Neues Leben publishing house; this knowledge made him "very happy."[61] After Selbmann's death, the head of Neues Leben, Hans Bentzien, decided "to publish the book quickly without official fuss."[62] Publication seemed imminent; galley proofs were produced and Erich Selbmann and others proofread the text. Bentzien, however, lost his position as publishing house director and his successor decided—in accordance with the 1974 Secretariat guidelines—to seek official sanction for the publication of these memoirs. Selbmann's memoirs then languished in the offices of chief ideologist Kurt Hager until Erich Selbmann raised the issue some two years later. At this time, Lucie Pflug, the head of the Publishing House Section in the Department of Culture in the Central Committee bureaucracy, reviewed the situation. She suggested that the manuscript be sent to the IML for evaluation because Erich Selbmann would otherwise "keep on and on" and "to be fair to the last literary work of Fritz Selbmann."[63]

Evaluations written by IML staff members suggest why this book failed to appear. Ernst Diehl, the deputy director of the IML, wrote Kurt Hager that "we in principle approve" of the publication of these memoirs, but that the "correction of blatant mistakes" as well as a "careful, well-considered change of a number of assessments" was "necessary." Diehl noted that some of Selbmann's historical judgements—such as that the Second Party Conference in July 1952 marked the beginning of the creation of the foundations of socialism in the GDR—"no longer . . . correspond . . . to our *present-day* assessments." Diehl then turned to Selbmann's description of June 17, 1953: "[The pages of the description] are of special importance because of the fact that they mark the first time that a leading functionary of the party offers detailed memoirs [of these events]. Comrade Selbmann provides an assessment that is fully in accord with the party line and at the same time a very vivid description . . . I consider the publication [of these passages] tenable, especially since the summary *Geschichte der SED* [History of the SED] has been published." As Diehl correctly noted, Selbmann basically analyzed the Uprising according to the official party line. Selbmann argued that the Uprising was a "profascist coup attempt," the "planned attempt to restore the old capitalist class and power relations on the territory of the German Democratic Republic."[64] But, as Diehl wrote, a number of Selbmann's passages went beyond what the SED regime had published about these events. Diehl thus argued that "the reporting of a number of details . . . about Fritz Selbmann's opposition to the decrees of March / April 1953; . . . on the party leadership's misjudgment on the eve of June 17; . . . [and] about the 'strike' movement in *July* 1953 in the Buna-factory (about which no details have been published in the GDR to date) need further consideration [before publication]."[65]

Diehl also provided Hager with the evaluation of Selbmann's memoirs written by the East German historian Günter Benser. Like Diehl, Benser thought that, on the whole, Selbmann's memoirs merited publication, but he also found some passages unsuitable. He noted that "the collectivity in the elaboration and realization of our policies as well as the dialectical relationship between the SED and the state executive bodies is not adequately expressed. Without wishing to diminish the contributions of Comrade Selbmann, it must nonetheless be said that the course of economic policy was set by the leadership of the KPD and the SED in close cooperation with the responsible comrades of the SMAD and particularly directly with the Politburo of the CPSU. It is astonishing that Fritz Selbmann barely mentions the party's process of conceptualizing economic policy and the guidance of state institutions by the party." Benser also thought that Selbmann had recorded several memories that "the enemy" might exploit. Selbmann had described how he had illegally detained an oppositional politician, Ferdinand Friedensburg, at the border of Saxony and then briefly held him captive in an apartment. Benser commented: "This passage makes clear the toughness and also the methods of the clashes of those days. But one cannot overlook that such confessions supply the enemy with ammunition that will be used against us." Similarly, Selbmann had described how the ceremonial inauguration of the first blast furnace in Eisenhüttenstadt had actually taken place before it was in working order. Here Benser noted: "One might also question whether the time is ripe for such statements that our enemies will pass off as characteristic of our planned economy in general."[66] Selbmann's memories, the IML readers' reports suggest, ranged too far afield from the official narrative of GDR history. Even after his death, Fritz Selbmann continued to have conflicts with the party for which he had sacrificed so much. His postwar memoirs were published only a decade after the fall of the SED regime, in 1999.[67]

TENSIONS BETWEEN veteran communists and their regime were especially great when longtime communists sought to publish their memoirs so as to secure public rehabilitation. In East Germany, public recognition signified political favor. Since the SED regime seldom granted formally disgraced veteran communists high political office, the publication of a full-scale autobiography, or even a short memoir fragment, came to symbolize official rehabilitation. Moreover, a published autobiography sanctified an author's revolutionary biography. Old Communists who had been charged by the SED with alleged past misdeeds were thus particularly eager to publish their memoirs. Indeed, they generally wanted to write about precisely those periods of their lives that the SED had earlier called into question. Fritz Selbmann, for example, wrote about his experiences in Nazi captivity in *Alternative—Bilanz—Credo;* his conduct in Sachsenhausen and Flossenbürg concentration camps had been the subject of repeated party investigations. Similarly, in the unpublished sequel to *Alternative,* Selbmann wrote about his work in establishing the EKO metallurgical complex in the early 1950s; this had brought him a party censure in 1952. Karl Mewis focused his *Im Auftrag der Partei* on his time in Swedish emigration; it was his actions in Swedish exile in the 1940s— he had allegedly betrayed KPD comrades to the Swedish police—that had led to career setbacks in East Germany in the 1960s.[68] Hans Teubner, a Noel Field Affair victim, published a history of the communist emigration in Switzerland, *Exilland Schweiz* (Switzerland as a country of exile), that also included some personal recollections; it was contacts between Noel Field and German communists in Switzerland that had brought him and other West émigrés disgrace in 1950.[69] Teubner expressed his pleasure to Franz Dahlem when his book finally appeared: "Now I also have some joy: my book has come out."[70] This book marked the first time that Field's name appeared, in a neutral context, in GDR print.[71] This in and of itself marked a public rehabilitation of sorts for those communists implicated in that affair.

Franz Dahlem's 1977 *Am Vorabend des zweiten Weltkrieges* was the most striking case of memoir publication as rehabilitation in East Germany.[72] The history of this autobiography demonstrates that veteran-communist memoirs were no trifling matter—they were an affair of state. Moreover, the saga of the publication of these memoirs suggests many of the tensions inherent in Old Communist memoir writing and publication. While veteran communists anxiously sought rehabilitation, the SED leadership was unwilling to acknowledge the party's past wrongs; while longtime communists wanted to honor past purge victims, the party leadership wished to ignore the darker sides of twentieth-century communism; and while longtime communists wished to write their memories, party authorities were intent on upholding official SED historiography.

After Dahlem was purged for alleged biographical infractions in 1953, he was bent on securing public rehabilitation. As he wrote Ulbricht in 1956, "For an old party functionary in my situation the highest dignity is the public restoration of his and his family's party honor."[73] At the same time, Dahlem was unique in that he sought not only his own rehabilitation, but also that of all other veteran communists unfairly purged in the 1950s. For some two decades, Dahlem waged an unprecedented letter-writing campaign concerning this matter. As Dahlem knew, however, public rehabilitations—the acknowledgment that the party had erred— would inevitably harm the SED's reputation. In a letter to Ulbricht in March 1956, Dahlem tortuously argued that public rehabilitation was nonetheless necessary because "the prerequisite for overtaking the developed capitalistic countries in the historically shortest period is that one do away with the mistakes and injuries that were committed in order to achieve the greatest development of the initiative of the working class and the whole population." Dahlem continued:

> The mistakes and injuries of the norms of party life and legality that were committed in connection with the Field matter and the Yugoslavian question must be publicly disclosed and liquidated. They arose on the foundation of a hysteria . . . In connection with the Rajk and Slansky trials this attitude led to . . . discrimination against many antifascist fighters, to years' long silence of the fact that there were heroic International Brigades in Spain and courageous German cadres among the resistance fighters in France, etc. . . . Furthermore, I consider it necessary that something be said about the discrimination brought on by the general measures against a large number of individuals who were disqualified in some manner either because of their West emigration or their Western imprisonment [in prisoner-of-war camps].[74]

Despite his pleas, Dahlem had no success in securing his own or others' public rehabilitation. In the 1960s, he thus began to focus his rehabilitation efforts on the writing of his memoirs, apparently drawing on a suggestion from Ulbricht that he "begin to write!"[75] Dahlem's correspondence of the 1960s is full of requests for memories, factual details, and additional sources that could help him reconstruct his past political activity. So long as Ulbricht remained in power, however, Dahlem received little public acknowledgment and his memoirs were given little official support; it appears that Ulbricht was dead set against bestowing recognition on his erstwhile rival.

Once Honecker became first secretary, Dahlem's fortunes improved. On the occasion of his eightieth birthday on January 14, 1972, Dahlem received a fulsome congratulatory message in *Neues Deutschland*.[76] He nonetheless continued both his memoir project and his efforts to secure the public rehabilitation of many longtime communists who had been unfairly purged during the early years of the SED regime. In a 1975 letter to Honecker, Dahlem suggested that a medal be created and awarded to "those who experienced grave injustice during the years before the Twentieth Party Congress of the CPSU and who nonetheless remained steadfast socialists; the deceased of this circle of comrades should receive the [medal] posthumously." In this way, Dahlem wrote, "one would avoid directly commenting on this unfortunate problem, but these irreproachable comrades would clearly and unambiguously be inserted into the first row of the fighters of our country."[77] Honecker, however, responded: "There is no basis for more far-reaching decisions [on the matter of rehabilitations]. I assume that after meticulous consideration you

share our [i.e., the Politburo's] opinion. Every attempt to push the party
back from the decrees of the Eighth Party Congress [in 1971] could not
help, but only harm our cause."[78] Two decades after the purges of the
1950s, the SED leadership was still reluctant to publicly acknowledge its
past mistakes.

Although Dahlem was unsuccessful in his attempts to have former
purge victims honored with an official medal, he now made considerable headway on his memoir project. He secured official support for his
memoirs: Horst Blumberg, a professor of history at Humboldt University,
was to spend two years working full-time on the autobiography. With
Blumberg's help, Dahlem completed memoirs that focused on the period
1938–1939, precisely the time when he had made controversial decisions
as head of the KPD leadership in Paris—decisions that had ostensibly
caused his downfall in 1953. In painstaking detail, this manuscript, eventually filling two densely printed volumes and numbering some 938
pages, recounted the actions of the Paris KPD Secretariat in the late
1930s.

These memoirs represented the culmination of Dahlem's decades-long
attempt to secure the public rehabilitation of former purge victims.
Dahlem, for example, devoted pages to the exemplary political and personal character traits of Paul Merker, the most important longtime communist purged in the Noel Field Affair. He also praised the political work
of many other veteran-communist victims of that affair. In addition,
Dahlem devoted two paragraphs to Walter Janka, the longtime communist who had been arrested and jailed for his participation in the Harich
Affair of 1956. And finally, Dahlem wrote many pages on Walter
Trautzsch, who had served for years, at great personal risk, as the main
courier between the KPD leadership in exile and Ernst Thälmann during Thälmann's long imprisonment by the Nazis. Trautzsch was later arrested by the Gestapo and, in the postwar years, was alleged to have
made incriminating statements during Gestapo interrogations; he thus
had a very undistinguished career in the GDR. Although Trautzsch died
in relative ignominy in 1971, Dahlem's memoirs brought him a measure
of posthumous glory.[79]

Although Dahlem sought to rehabilitate many fellow veteran communists, his memoirs were primarily intended to restore his own political
honor. He devoted over two hundred pages of volume 2 of *Am Vorabend*
to August 1939, the month in which he had carried out his alleged misdeeds. He recounted the political situation facing the communist movement at the time of the Nazi-Soviet Non-Aggression Pact, then justified
his own actions during this period. He rationalized his decision to have

German communists register with the French police by arguing that it would have been impossible for the KPD to maintain hundreds of German communists illegally; the party's infrastructure was insufficient for the task and the French Communist Party could not have been counted on to aid German comrades. Furthermore, Dahlem claimed that French communist leaders had instructed the KPD to follow the stipulations concerning foreigners, and Dahlem assumed that communists who registered would soon be allowed to return to their Paris quarters. He justified his own registration with the police by arguing that it was his duty to share the fate of his fellow comrades. Dahlem argued that with benefit of hindsight his actions had constituted a "wrong decision," but that "if I place myself back in my situation *of that time*," then "today I still uphold [it]."[80] In his memoirs, Dahlem adopted a strategy of justification combined with self-criticism; he portrayed his past actions as well considered even though, in the language of communism, they were "objectively" false. He thus sought rehabilitation while respecting official historiography.

The writing of these memoirs was psychologically difficult for Dahlem. The events that he described could not be separated from their eventual upshot, his removal from all political functions in 1953. In 1977, Dahlem wrote a fellow veteran communist, Georg Stibi, about the psychological toll that his memoir writing had taken: "During my life I have myself experienced much that was difficult and had to endure countless insults, both direct and veiled. I therefore know the [psychological] state when 'the past' again rises up and threatens to fully control me. Especially with the writing of this part of my memoirs [i.e., 1938–1939], of which the essential is and will be published, I often had to struggle hard with myself, so that the rising bitterness would not obscure my clear thoughts. But I consider all this finished, even though I can, of course, never forget what happened."[81]

If Dahlem found writing his memoirs difficult, their publication was an outright challenge. As he neared completion, Dahlem became increasingly preoccupied with their publication; after all, when he first completed a draft of his memoirs in 1974, he was eighty-two years old. Countless letters, readers' reports, and memoranda by Dahlem, IML staff members, and Politburo members Honecker, Hager, and Hermann Axen were now exchanged on the matter of these memoirs. In November 1975 the Secretariat approved the publication of *Am Vorabend,* with two provisos. The IML was to work with Dahlem to prepare the manuscript for publication so "that no insight into the internal affairs of the party leadership will be given." In addition, "The parts not designated for print are to be kept in the Central Party Archive."[82] One year earlier, IML staff members had completed a twelve-page evaluation of Dahlem's memoirs. They had praised many aspects: "Com[rade] Dahlem fits party historical events into the process of the class struggle in Germany and the international class altercations between socialism and imperialism . . . Com[rade] Dahlem brings out the bourgeois character of opportunism, unmasks the hostility to a United Front and the anti-communist policy of right-wing leaders of social democracy and . . . makes clear the disastrous consequences of this policy for the struggle against fascism." But although the authors in general recommended publication, they found fault with a number of passages in the text. For example, they thought that the many pages criticizing Ulbricht and his alleged tactical mistakes in Paris in the mid-1930s should be removed. They recommended that Dahlem's remarks on Wilhelm Pieck's reaction to the arrests of communists in Moscow during the 1930s not be printed. They also considered derogatory remarks on the character traits of Anton Ackermann (who had denounced Dahlem in Moscow in 1940 and in East Berlin in 1953) inappropriate for publication. Furthermore, they recommended that facts concerning the Gestapo arrest of Trautzsch, the Thälmann courier, be removed. Finally, they thought the chapter on August 1939 too detailed; in particular, they believed that a lengthy discussion of the German-Soviet Non-Aggression Pact should be abbreviated.[83]

The director of the IML, Günter Heyden, also evaluated Dahlem's manuscript. Outlining the difficulties that the publication of these memoirs posed, Heyden noted: "It is not a question of the factual accuracy of Comrade Dahlem's observations on party-internal problems that is to be decided, but rather the political expediency of their publication in the current situation of the ideological class altercations." On the August 1939 chapter, Heyden wrote: "Comrade Dahlem undertakes a critical and self-critical evaluation of this decree [urging KPD members to register with the police], with which one can, to a certain extent, agree. But this is combined with an unbalanced, very detailed portrayal of the prior history and the circumstances that led to this decree . . . The whole design of this chapter, despite the self-criticism already mentioned, makes the Secretariat's wrong decree seem not only understandable, but in many respects unavoidable." Heyden added:

It must be considered that the *whole* manuscript, in its design, its main points, the approach to problems, is strongly determined by the intention of personal vindication. With these memoirs the author is pursuing the goal of achieving a *full* personal rehabilitation that in his opinion has not yet resulted. Comrade Dahlem has unequivocally stated this in personal conver-

sations. In this connection there are repeated references, scattered throughout the whole manuscript, to the party decrees of 1952 / 1953 that
concerned him. To our suggestion to reduce the number of these references,
Comrade Dahlem responded that these statements were necessary in the
present form.[84]

In response to the IML evaluations, Dahlem wrote a spirited letter to
Hager in which he defended the passages he wished to keep in his memoirs. For example, Dahlem argued for retaining passages on Pieck's reac-
tions to the arrests of communists in Moscow in the 1930s. Among other
reasons, Dahlem wished to demonstrate Pieck's alleged concern for those
arrested; he had thus described a conversation with Pieck on the purges
in the late 1930s.[85] As Dahlem wrote: "I find it problematic to block this
passage. The enemy has repeatedly attacked our leading comrades, including Wilhelm Pieck, for idly looking on at [these events] . . . Such
views are also still held by the families of many of those affected. I know
for myself and for others that Wilhelm Pieck did not act in this way at all.
This also came out in my conversation with him. I therefore feel it my
duty to state this openly. The fact itself—of the arrests—we have also
published (e.g., *Biographisches Lexikon*). Why, therefore, are there such
misgivings in my case?" On the matter of Trautzsch, Dahlem wrote: "By
no means can I follow the recommendations of the comrades to remain
silent on the question of Com[rade] Trautzsch's arrest . . . There is no reason not to show the complexity of our struggle at that time that now and
again forced us to make very difficult decisions. Insofar as this affected
[Trautzsch's] fate after 1945, I have refrained from a description for the
public." Dahlem also raised the issue of his repeated references to the
1952–1953 decrees: "I have with great restraint here and there made
short mention of the events of 1952 / 53 and at the same time had to re-
fer to them in the Preface. The remarks I have made in the Preface on
[these events] are for me indispensable . . . The opposite case [i.e., not to
mention these events] . . . would have to awaken in the reader the impression that I myself, at least to a certain degree, recognize the disciplinary measures as just."[86]

Despite Dahlem's protestations, his published memoirs prove that
this Old Communist compromised on virtually every point that the IML
raised.[87] In the published version of Dahlem's memoirs there is no mention of his conversation with Pieck nor, indeed, of the Great Purges at all.
The passage on Trautzsch that found its way into Dahlem's memoirs totally obfuscated the courier's biography during the Nazi years. According
to Dahlem's memoirs, Trautzsch was arrested by French police, not the
Gestapo; Dahlem's readers could not possibly have had an inkling of why

Thälmann's courier had had so difficult a career in East Germany.[88] There is no mention of the decrees of 1952 and 1953 in the preface nor, indeed, in any of the more than nine hundred pages of text that follow. Dahlem was unable to override the IML's judgments. He was, however, unwilling to jeopardize the publication of his memoirs by insisting on the inclusion of those passages. As he wrote Honecker eight months later: "Above all in the interest of political necessities, but also in the interest of seeing the publication [of my memoirs] during my lifetime, we [i.e., Dahlem and Hager] agreed not to publish some of my statements, which was not always easy for me. But I was, am, and remain a disciplined comrade, for whom the party interest as well as the party's unity and accord was and is always a sacred cause."[89]

After more delays and compromises, Dahlem finally secured the assurance that his memoirs would be published during 1977. In gratitude, he then expressed the meaning he attached to the publication of his memoirs in a letter to Hager:

> After all, with my memoirs the stakes are the correction of the fact that my whole active work [was] in the German revolutionary workers' movement: . . . Activity almost always at the pinnacle of the KPD and SED until 1953 . . . [when] I was erased—with almost scientific thoroughness—from *written history* through the elimination of my printed books [and] photos. The stakes are my party honor, that through [these memoirs] will be fully restored, over and above the full rehabilitation that the Central Committee and the Politburo bestowed on me in the message of greeting on the occasion of my eightieth birthday.[90]

Dahlem lived to see the publication of his memoirs and, although in somewhat truncated form, they brought him great personal satisfaction. Dahlem's correspondence, however, suggests that in his last years he was writing memoirs that he knew would not be published during his lifetime. In 1977, Dahlem wrote Else Zaisser, Wilhelm Zaisser's widow, that "on account of the class enemy, the events of 1953 must still remain 'taboo'; I am writing about them, but for the time being [these pages] will go into the cellar of the IML."[91] Those pages were published only after the fall of the SED regime, in 1990.[92]

The story behind the publication of Dahlem's memoirs illustrates the dilemmas that Old Communists faced in seeking rehabilitation through memoir publication in East Germany. Dahlem, of course, wanted to have his memoirs published so that his rehabilitation would be on public record. But to secure the publication of his memoirs, his text had to fit the shackled formulas of SED dictate: he could not expose the actual workings of communism in the Nazi era, he could not avoid the hackneyed argumentation of East German history books, and he could not mention all too many taboo topics. Dahlem had to filter his memories through the SED's ideological lenses. But this Old Communist was still able to further his aims. In the peculiar style of the GDR, he rehabilitated numerous longtime communists who had been purged in the 1950s; he justified his own past actions as a KPD leader; and, most of all, he saw his biography on GDR shelves. These memoirs, the tightrope exercise of a disciplined communist, are at once intriguing and disappointing: intriguing on account of their history prior to publication, disappointing in that, on balance, they too are cut of the same stereotypical cloth as so many other memoirs by veteran communists.

WHO OWNED the lives of Old Communists? The story of memoir writing by longtime communists begs this question. From the Weimar era onward, the party determined what longtime communists were to believe, which party tasks they were to accomplish, where they were to live, and with whom they were to associate. But the KPD / SED not only decided the most basic facts of Old Communists' lives. It also, for better or worse, determined the representation of veteran communists' biographies. In the early 1950s, of course, the SED had negatively reinterpreted these biographies so as to purge longtime party members. And from the 1960s onward, party authorities popularized a whitewashed version of veteran communists' biographies for propaganda purposes. While some longtime communists relished the heroization of their past lives, others were surely less sanguine about this form of hagiography. After all, through the stereotypical presentation of their biographies, veteran communists and their past revolutionary deeds were stripped of all individuality. In any event, by following the prescriptions of party ideologues, Old Communists ceded autonomy over their biographies to SED authorities. The story of Old Communist memoir writing once again illustrates the fundamental dynamic that animated relations between longtime communists and their party: the KPD / SED ruthlessly exploited its most committed followers, who in turn willingly sacrificed their personal interests for the supposed good of the party.

Official GDR memory was hammered on a delicate anvil. It was at odds with a dominant East German popular memory that fondly recalled much of the Nazi era and shuddered at the events of 1945 and thereafter. It was also at odds with the memories of longtime communists on whose lives it was supposedly based. Official GDR memory was thus born of discrepancies between official and popular memory, and inconsistencies between official memory and veteran communists' actual remembered past. Although East Germans continued to pay lip service to the antifascist myth until 1989, the legitimating power of that myth waned over time. Endless repetition gave the idealized, interchangeable veteran communist biography a hollow ring. Moreover, the antifascist myth exercised little allure for younger East Germans who were troubled by a very different set of historical concerns.

Official GDR memory thus foundered on two fronts. Its base, memories attributed to veteran communists, was too fragile a foundation for so important a project. Its aim, revamping GDR collective memory, was too ambitious, given that popular memory rested on so different a set of memories. In his *Life of Galileo,* Bertolt Brecht has a character declaim, "Unhappy the land that has no heroes!" Galileo responds: "No. Unhappy the land where heroes are needed."[93] As events would soon prove, it was indeed an unhappy SED regime that needed to create heroes of its Old Communists.

8

OUTDATED

East German Generational Dynamics

IN HIS FAMOUS ESSAY ON GENERATIONS, THE GERMAN SOCIAL THEO-
rist Karl Mannheim declared: "One is old primarily in so far as he comes
to live within a specific, individually acquired framework of useable
past experience, so that every new experience has its form and its place
largely marked out for it in advance." Noting "that biographical factors
(such as youth and age) do not of themselves involve a definite intellectual or practical orientation (youth cannot be automatically correlated
with a progressive attitude and so on)," Mannheim suggested that being
"old" could be measured by the limited range of responses that new situations and events evoked.[1] By the mid 1970s, veteran communists were
not only "old" in terms of longtime communist commitment and advancing biological age; they were also "old" in Mannheim's sense. This
was especially true of those veteran communists who sat on the SED's
Politburo until the fateful fall of 1989—Erich Honecker, Erich Mielke,
Willi Stoph, Horst Sindermann, Kurt Hager, Hermann Axen, and Alfred
Neumann.

The longtime communists who dominated the SED leadership were
hostage to an "antifascist" worldview that they had adopted during the
Weimar era, solidified during the Nazi years, and frozen during their
long years in power in East Germany. Abroad, veteran communists saw a
world of class struggle in which antifascists were forever on the brink of
deadly confrontation with the capitalist-imperialist juggernaut. At
home, they refused to countenance a market economy or even most
market mechanisms. They believed in providing the basic necessities of
life, at heavily subsidized prices, to the East German population—but
not much else. And they were convinced that the ever-present, rarely
named "opponent" *(Gegner)* or "enemy" *(Feind)* menacingly threatened
to undermine GDR achievements. With the passing years, this worldview

seemed increasingly anachronistic to much of the East German population. But veteran communists clung tenaciously to their antifascist
agenda.

Communist leaderships never developed mechanisms to renew themselves in a timely manner. In this regard, the East German gerontocracy
was no different from other communist regimes. In the GDR, however,
a specific generational constellation allowed aging veteran communists
to hold on to the reins of power even though they proved unable to address, let alone solve, the daunting economic and other problems that
the GDR faced. Slightly younger functionaries—the so-called Hitler
Youth generation—were unwilling to challenge veteran communists; the
two generations shared a "symbiosis."[2] Generational analysis provides
compelling answers to some of the most intriguing questions of GDR history.[3] Why did the SED leadership continue its rigid economic and other
policies even as these threatened to undermine East Germany? Why
were veteran communists able to maintain their grip on GDR politics?
And why didn't younger functionaries challenge longtime communists
to stem East Germany's decline?

SCHOLARS NOW debate a host of causes to explain East Germany's dissolution. These range from the structural to the personal—from the inability of command economies to function efficiently to the actions or inac-
tions of the SED leadership. Ultimately, East Germany fell because of
forces that lay beyond its leadership's control: the structural problems of
Soviet-style command economies, the refusal of the Soviet Union to uphold its German satellite, and the fact that after forty years the GDR was
still considered part of a divided nation. But the specific character of East
German socialism and its fall was inextricably linked to the GDR's Old
Communist rulers and, after 1971, particularly to Erich Honecker.

As first secretary of the SED, Honecker was responsible "for the preparation of all questions of the Politburo of the Central Committee" as
well as for decision-making power over all "operative and ongoing questions of the activity of the Central Committee of the SED."[4] He was
also chairman of the National Defense Council and, from 1976 onward,
chairman of the State Council. But beyond accruing these formal positions, Honecker arrogated ever more actual decision-making power to
himself. Under Honecker, the Central Committee, never particularly influential, became even less so. Even more importantly, the Politburo lost
influence. Honecker often circumvented the Politburo by making decisions through more informal channels—in one-on-one meetings with
the powerful economics secretary, Günter Mittag (not a veteran commu-

nist), or with the minister of state security, Erich Mielke. Behind the vapid half-smile captured in his omnipresent official photograph, Erich Honecker came to wield near absolute power.

Before coming to power, Honecker made the upholding of communist orthodoxy the hallmark of his postwar career. As FDJ leader between 1946 and 1955, Honecker injected KJVD practice into the SED's youth organization: party discipline was privileged, while alternative viewpoints were not tolerated. In the 1960s, Honecker was Central Committee secretary of security affairs. In this capacity, he supervised the building of the Berlin Wall in 1961; he thus cemented his two-camp view of the world in stone and mortar. In the late 1960s, Honecker spearheaded the conservative communist backlash against Ulbricht's attempted economic and other reforms. Once he became first secretary in 1971, however, Honecker tried to present himself as a youthful, flexible leader. Many of his policies, particularly his economic and foreign policies, signaled a new and refreshing departure for the SED regime. But although Honecker cultivated an image of himself as a modern communist leader, his tenure as SED leader actually marked the reassertion of traditional communist orthodoxy and the attempt to fashion the GDR according to veteran communists' Weimar-era ideals.

As first secretary, Honecker revived some time-honored communist practices. Perhaps most importantly, he reestablished the primacy of the party; this was in marked contrast to Ulbricht, who had come to favor state institutions in the administration of East Germany. Honecker celebrated ideological commitment and declared ideological work the "main substance of our Marxist-Leninist party."[5] He revived the KPD's tradition of struggle; the party's encouragement of veteran-communist memoir writing was but one element of the renewed emphasis on revolutionary struggle. At the 1976 Party Congress, Honecker, in imitation of Stalin, retitled himself general secretary of the SED. And like other past and present communist leaders, Honecker was not shy to foster his own personality cult. In one infamous edition, *Neues Deutschland* carried thirty-two pictures of the SED leader meeting with each and every foreign ambassador present at the Leipzig Trade Fair.[6]

Honecker also made something of an attempt to recast SED functionaries back into traditional KPD cadres. In the 1960s and 1970s, many West German scholars observed that those with technical expertise were gaining influence in the SED hierarchy. The most important of these analysts, Peter Ludz, argued that a younger, technically trained "institutionalized counter elite" had emerged in East Germany in the early 1960s. This counter elite contrasted sharply with a "strategic clique" of veteran party members who still exercised decision-making power in the GDR. The new counter elite, Ludz contended, was managing the modernization of East German society according to rational, technocratic criteria.[7] With the benefit of hindsight and new archival evidence, however, it is clear that Ludz overestimated the influence of the counter elite. Even more importantly, he failed to recognize that its fortunes were tied to Walter Ulbricht. Whereas Ulbricht had always privileged technical expertise among East German functionaries, Honecker favored functionaries who had both strong technical *and* political skills (generally measured by completion of studies at the SED's various political schools).[8] At the highest levels of the SED hierarchy, Honecker placed those like himself who had made careers in the party bureaucracies and who had special competence in agitprop, security, and party organizational matters. In ruling the GDR, Honecker privileged voluntarism and ideological persuasion over economic or technocratic rationale.

Honecker's economic policies seemed to offer a fresh course for the GDR. Like other East Central European leaders, Honecker made a concerted attempt to buy political acquiescence with material plenty. In contrast to Ulbricht, Honecker thus had the East German economy focus more on the production of consumer goods—the bête noire of socialist command economies. He also proclaimed the so-called Main Task *(Hauptaufgabe)*, the creation of a higher standard of living through increased productivity, at the Eighth Party Congress in 1971; the "Main Task" was later formulaically known as the "Unity of Economic and Social Policy" *(Einheit von Wirtschafts- und Sozialpolitik)*. Although productivity increases never matched those planned, Honecker significantly raised wages, pensions, and other state subsidies. This, in turn, allowed GDR citizens to afford the new consumer offerings. As some scholars have argued, the early to mid-1970s was a time when the SED regime achieved at least partial acceptance among much of the GDR population.[9]

Despite their novelty, Honecker's policies in fact reflected Weimar-era communist goals and values. At the heart of the new program, for example, lay a massive apartment building and renovation program. As Erich Mielke told a Soviet official in 1989, this had been a goal of the KPD / SED ever since Thälmann had been party leader: "The centerpiece of our social-political program is to resolve the apartment question as a social problem by 1990, an old fighting goal of the German working class. Thälmann spoke about this."[10] By Western standards, the apartments built—such as those unveiled in the Ernst Thälmann Park apartment complex in East Berlin in 1986—were rather mediocre. As one perceptive

Erich Honecker (seated left on couch) visits Hermann Großkopf and his family. Just before, Honecker had given Großkopf the keys to the millionth apartment built in East Germany since the Eighth Party Congress in 1971. The Großkopf apartment is all too typical of the petite-bourgeois milieu that veteran communists created in East Germany. Berlin, July 6, 1978. (Bundesarchiv, Koblenz, Bild 183/T 0706/39)

historian, Alan Nothnagle, has written, "Cultivating the spirit of Ernst Thälmann meant using modern technology to fulfill the values and ideals of the 1920s and 1930s in the 1970s and 1980s."[11]

Honecker's policies also reflected other Weimar-era communist ideals. The SED leader insisted that the East German state subsidize the basic necessities of life for GDR citizens. Although all East Central European countries pursued similar policies, these had special resonance for veteran KPD cadres; longtime communists had lived through the German state's utter failure to provide workers even a modicum of social security during the Great Depression. In the GDR, apartment rents were thus held stable at their 1936 levels and streetcar fares continued to cost a mere twenty pfennig. Honecker and other veteran communists expected that these policies would not only satisfy East Germans, but also generate support for the regime. As Herbert Häber, a Politburo member in 1984–1985, observed of his older colleagues: "They just thought that they could get by with . . . the thought categories, standards, and patterns of values from that time [i.e., Weimar] . . . Certain developments of modern times were not at all, not at all understood. They always thought that if the streetcar cost twenty pfennig that was a great advantage, but if one had to wait fourteen years for a car, that didn't matter . . . they thought that the twenty-pfennig streetcar fare made socialism convincing, whereas the fourteen-year wait for a car did not harm socialism. There it is. In their youth, they had never been confronted with the issue of a car."[12] Similarly, Otto Reinhold, the influential rector of the Academy of Social Sciences who actually helped formulate Honecker's policies, has said of the SED leader: "Honecker always remained the Saarland Communist Youth functionary of 1932. That had a negative influence on much of his politics, especially later . . . For him . . . the highest that could be achieved was that everyone had enough to eat at cheap prices, that everyone had work, and that everyone had a good and cheap apartment. For example, many proposals were made to introduce a differentiated rent policy. And Honecker rejected even the smallest proposal because he thought that everyone was happy. Everyone had cheap bread, a cheap apartment, and work."[13] Drawing on his Weimar-era experiences, Honecker assumed that satisfactory economic conditions would insure domestic stability.

But were these conditions satisfactory? Under Honecker, East Germans enjoyed living standards as never before. According to official GDR statistics, for every 100 East German households in 1970, there were 15 cars, 69 television sets, 56 refrigerators, and 53 electric washing machines. By 1981, there were 37 cars, 90 television sets, 99 refrigerators, and 82 washing machines for every hundred households.[14] For Old Communists, the great majority of whom had grown up with very little at all, such numbers could only confirm their view of the positive effect of communism on the lives of German workers. As Rainer Eppelmann, an important dissident in the 1980s, observed: "He [i.e., Honecker] no doubt measured the reality of the GDR in 1989 with his life as a youth in Wiebelskirchen in the Saarland. At that time, there were gas lanterns in the streets, most people rode bicycles, and wooden carts were the most important means of transport. By contrast, the GDR was almost a hyper-modern industrial state with automobiles, trains, airplanes, computers, and huge factories."[15] Unlike Honecker, however, most East Germans did not measure life in the GDR with that of Imperial or Weimar Germany. Their point of comparison was not even the Soviet Union or other East Central European states (against which the GDR came out on top), but rather the postwar West German "economic miracle" (or its broadcast on West German television). As a result, for East Germans, the earlier statistics were a sign of the GDR's relative poverty; the relatively low numbers of cars and the inferior quality of other consumer goods were sources of particular frustration.

In any event, even the anachronistic expectations of the Main Task overtaxed the GDR's cumbersome economy. Like most veteran communists, Honecker was singularly unprepared to lead a complex economy; he was versed in agitprop and the rules of revolutionary conspiracy, not in statistics or the principles of complex organization. When he first came to power, Honecker had ended all economic experiments and had recentralized the planning and direction of the GDR economy. In 1972, he even nationalized the small remaining private sector of the East German economy. Once the economy proved unable to match either the regime's promises or the population's hopes (as was the case by the mid-1970s), Honecker faced the daunting dilemma of improving East German economic performance. He did not, however, even consider ways in which the economy might be restructured. Instead, he turned to another solution to solve the GDR's economic woes: borrowing on world markets. From the mid-1970s onward, East Germany, like Poland, relied heavily on Western credit to import various technologies and other necessary goods to pursue the Main Task. While this helped the East German economy in the short run, it also began a cycle of chronic indebtedness that was to plague the SED regime until its end.

In another new departure for SED politics, Honecker eagerly embraced official East-West détente. Once the GDR signed the Basic Treaty with West Germany in 1972, Honecker steered East Germany into membership in the United Nations, established diplomatic relations with some 131 states, and presided over the signing of over five hundred multilateral international treaties.[16] These foreign successes brought Honecker and his regime a measure of respect. More importantly, due to East Germany's new international status, GDR athletes could now regularly compete on the world athletic stage. Their enormous successes—particularly in winning much-prized Olympic medals—brought the small country considerable international renown. At the same time, these sporting achievements lent the regime a certain legitimacy even among East German citizens.

Honecker's pursuit of détente initially hewed to Soviet policy. But in the late 1970s, relations between the Soviet Union and the West soured. Honecker nonetheless insisted on seeking closer economic and political relations with West Germany. In contrast to his predecessor, Honecker was successful in upholding some independence in GDR relations with the FRG; he benefited from the Soviet leadership crises of the early 1980s. Other veteran communists and Soviet officials, however, viewed

Honecker's pursuit of closer ties to West Germany with unease: it was, after all, done independently of the Soviet Union, it left East Germany reliant on the "enemy," and it opened the GDR to Western influence (in return for cash and credit, the FRG demanded increased contact between East and West Germans).

Within the Politburo, Honecker faced opposition from a number of longtime communists grouped loosely around Willi Stoph, chairman of the Council of Ministers. To one degree or another, Mielke, Heinz Hoffmann, Alfred Neumann, and Kurt Hager all shared Stoph's criticisms of Honecker; so too did a number of younger functionaries. Rather like Honecker in the late 1960s, Stoph and the others were "Moscow-oriented traditionalists" who were wary of a leader who did not strictly follow the CPSU course.[17] In 1984, information sent by Stoph concerning Honecker's preparations to visit Bonn led Soviet leaders to force the general secretary to abandon his plans. In 1986, Stoph also sent Mikhael Gorbachev, the new Soviet leader, a memorandum in which he provided information on Honecker's opposition to Soviet reforms and the miserable state of the GDR economy. Gorbachev, however, did not respond—probably because he knew that Stoph, if he did mount a successful coup against Honecker, would not advocate reforms thereafter.[18] Stoph, in turn, was unwilling to act against Honecker without Soviet backing. Honecker thus persisted in his course. In September 1987, the general secretary even scaled his diplomatic ambitions: he was welcomed on an official state visit to Bonn in September 1987.

Although Honecker pursued better official German-German relations, he did not abandon his confrontational worldview. To counter those aspects of détente that he deemed threatening (particularly increased contacts between ordinary East and West Germans), Honecker pursued a policy known as *Abgrenzung*. Variously translated as "demarcation" or "delimitation," this policy sought to "mark off" East Germany from West Germany. Starting in 1975, for example, the anniversary of the founding of the GDR, October 7, was celebrated as a national holiday; this was to help foster a GDR identity distinct from—and opposed to—West Germany. Honecker also tried to separate East Germans from their brethren across the Wall. To this end, he introduced numerous measures including the raising of postal, telephone, and telegram rates to West Germany. In the following years, Honecker raised and lowered these and other rates depending on the state of official relations (particularly financial relations) between the two Germanys. Honecker's policy of Abgrenzung raised the traditionally divisive, two-camp communist ideology to a delicate art form. In the end, however, the general secretary could not master the art: the price of economic cooperation with West Germany was an influx of Western tourists, and thus Western influence, into the GDR.

Honecker did not shy away from coercion to uphold the East German order. Indeed, the GDR became what what one historian, Jürgen Kocka, has called a "pervasively ruled" society.[19] True to communist ideology, Honecker believed that class warfare was the salient characteristic of modern societies. He thus placed renewed emphasis on "political vigilance." He brought two veteran-communist security officials into the Politburo: Mielke and the minister of defense, Heinz Hoffmann. During the Honecker years, the Stasi saw an unprecedented expansion of its scope and activities. By 1989 it employed 91,015 full-time employees and worked with approximately another 180,000 unofficial informers. For every 180 East Germans (including children), the Stasi had one full-time employee and used two unofficial informers; this astonishingly high surveillance rate remains unparalleled in the history of repressive regimes.[20] Even Honecker was policed; Mielke had the SED leader's anti-fascist past investigated and kept in his personal safe potentially compromising files on Honecker's biography.[21]

Honecker, Mielke, and other veteran communists were enormously suspicious of any political opposition. They viewed dissent, whether within the party's ranks or in the country at large, as "enemy" activity, directed from abroad. Longtime Politburo member Alfred Neumann, for example, construed the opposition of Robert Havemann, a veteran communist, as part and parcel of the GDR's struggle with its worldwide imperialist enemies. Neumann has alleged that Havemann became a critic of the regime because the CIA sent a young woman, Katja, later Havemann's wife, to seduce him into dissidence.[22] Such charges are absurd. But they suggest that longtime communists could only imagine opposition as part of a grand fascist conspiracy to undermine the GDR. Moreover, they could not fathom the notion of a "loyal" opposition intent on democratizing or otherwise improving socialism in the GDR. Many of East Germany's better-known critics, including Havemann, the singer-songwriter Wolf Biermann, the writer Stefan Heym, and the great majority of dissidents who emerged in the 1980s, did not actually want to abolish socialism; they wanted to make it more viable. But to Old Communists, such individuals, as Mielke told a Soviet official in 1989, were "inspired and directed by the enemy."[23] The SED leadership resorted to tyrannical measures against regime critics—including professional demotion, Stasi harassment, arrest and imprisonment, and expulsion to West Germany.

Many scholars have noted a set of dual qualities that characterized the

East German regime: "paternalism and paranoia," "repression and beneficence," "care and coercion," or "welfare dictatorship."[24] Veteran communists combined a paternalistic impulse to improve the material lot of East Germans with a coercive bent to preserve the political status quo. The one reflected their Weimar-era dreams to create a society in which the state would provide its citizens with basic necessities, the other, traditional communist views on the salience of class warfare. Under Honecker, these two features generated a curious set of contradictions. On the one hand, the standard of living in East Germany was significantly higher than it had been under Ulbricht; GDR citizens enjoyed many more material comforts than they had in the past. But the gap between economic conditions in East and West Germany had measurably widened, and this frustrated the GDR population. On the other hand, the regime's repressive features were much less harsh than under Ulbricht; in particular, the Stalinist terror that had marked the 1940s and 1950s had no counterpart during the Honecker years. But East Germans suffered from the debilitating insidiousness of a society under constant surveillance. These dissatisfactions led to widespread grumbling and laid the groundwork for what would become the groundswell of revolutionary upheaval in 1989. Until the mid-1980s, however, they led to very little political opposition per se. In fact, the GDR was notable for the absence of political opposition.

OF ALL East Germans, it was veteran communists, sheathed in a golden antifascist aura, who had the political stature to oppose the SED leadership. Although very few longtime communists ever publicly criticized their regime, those who did proved to be sharp thorns in the regime's side. The physicist Robert Havemann was the most critical and outspoken longtime communist; indeed, he is the only longtime communist who may be truly termed a "dissident." A member of the KPD since 1932, Havemann had a dramatic antifascist past. During the Nazi years, he had worked as a scientific researcher while engaging in illegal resistance activities. Arrested and sentenced to death in 1943, the Nazis commuted his sentence on condition that he work on research projects "important to the war effort." To conduct this research, they built Havemann a laboratory in a prison cell in the Brandenburg Penitentiary—the very same jail in which Honecker was imprisoned. Rather than help the Nazis, Havemann used the laboratory to continue his resistance activities. He ordered parts that could be used to build a shortwave radio, listened to foreign broadcasts, and then used the laboratory typewriter to write out an illegal daily newspaper for his fellow prisoners. After the war,

Havemann became professor of physical chemistry and an institute director at East Berlin's Humboldt University. His scientific renown, combined with his antifascist past, lent him considerable stature in the GDR.

A self-described Stalinist in the 1940s and early 1950s, Havemann began to rethink his political views after the CPSU's Twentieth Party Congress. As early as 1956, Havemann publicly questioned the relevance of Marxist-Leninist philosophy to the natural sciences. By the early 1960s he had further developed his critique of Marxism-Leninism. During the winter semester of 1963–1964, Havemann gave a widely visited lecture series on "Scientific Aspects of Philosophical Problems." Among other themes, Havemann argued that open and engaged discussion on philosophical and scientific matters was essential for the advance of knowledge. And just as critical debate was necessary for scientific discoveries, so too, he suggested, was the democratization of the party for true socialism. Havemann thus called for an end to the rule of the party bureaucracy, free elections to party bodies, and the abolition of rigid party discipline on the expression of political opinions.[25] As long as Havemann voiced his views inside the GDR, he was criticized, but not silenced, by party authorities. In March 1964, however, Havemann publicized his political views in an interview with a West German newspaper. To the SED leadership, this smacked of cooperation with the "enemy." The party's response was as swift as it was harsh: Havemann was stripped of his professorship and soon expelled from the SED. This veteran communist nonetheless maintained a deep loyalty to East Germany and the socialist project; it was this loyalty that made his criticisms at once poignant and devastating. As Havemann told his Stasi interrogators in May 1966, "As an Old Communist this all [i.e., criticizing Stalinism in the GDR] weighs heavily upon me, particularly because I belong to those who co-founded this state and, despite all of its imperfections, . . . [I] still consider it the best German state that has ever existed."[26] Believing it more effective to criticize the regime as a citizen than as an expatriate, Havemann refused to leave East Germany. With time, he became something of a nemesis to the SED leadership: the fact that this veteran communist and antifascist resistance fighter criticized the GDR from an avowedly communist perspective proved a significant blow to the regime's reputation.

By the 1970s, Havemann had been subject to constant Stasi surveillance, house arrest, and state prosecution on trumped-up charges. He nonetheless continued to popularize his views in the West German media. His books and other writings were smuggled into the GDR, while his statements and interviews were broadcast over airwaves that knew no borders. He relentlessly criticized economic and political conditions in the GDR. For Havemann, the main source of the ills of "really existing" socialism lay in the absence of freedom and democracy. Havemann believed that "if socialism in the socialist countries is to prosper . . . freedom . . . has become a necessity as never before."[27] He thus called for numerous democratic reforms in the GDR, including the reintroduction of the right to strike, the licensing of an independent newspaper and at least one oppositional party, and multiple and independent candidates for Volkskammer elections.[28] Among well-known veteran East German communists, Havemann alone fundamentally opposed the SED regime. His fellow Old Communists spurned him and, with the exception of his lawyer, Götz Berger, did not defend him or his views. The grand old man of East German dissent, Havemann became an inspiration to those who eventually organized the grassroots demonstrations that helped topple the SED regime in 1989.

After Robert Havemann, the most outspoken Old Communist critic of the GDR was Stephan Hermlin, the renowned lyricist. Although Hermlin protested some of the party's more draconian policies, he never outrightly condemned SED rule. Hermlin was primarily concerned with ensuring the right of East German authors to publish texts critical of conditions in the GDR, provided that their criticism was "serious."[29] His best-known act of defiance was the initiation of the famed "Biermann petition" in 1976. Signed by thirteen prominent intellectuals, this statement protested the expatriation of singer-songwriter Wolf Biermann. The signers declared that "we do not agree with Biermann's every word or action," but that "we protest against his expatriation and ask for the action that has been decided upon to be reconsidered."[30] When, in private correspondence, Franz Dahlem asked Hermlin how he could stand up for a man such as Biermann who "sells his deviating opinions for good pay in the FRG," Hermlin replied: "As a person who was once expatriated, I believed and still believe that in our state one may not strip anyone of their citizenship . . . The man . . . is a talented artist and a political chatterer; he was and is not my friend . . . But in this case I had to say something in his favor. Moreover, he is the son of one put to death by the Nazis. One may not allow anyone to be wronged."[31] Hermlin suffered the party's wrath for his outspoken views: he was not permitted to publish some of his writings and was expelled from the governing body of the Writers' Union. Two other Old Communists, the sculptor Fritz Cremer and the poet Erich Arendt, were signatories of the Biermann petition; Cremer, however, withdrew his signature a few days after the petition was initially publicized.

Jürgen Kuczynski, the prolific economic historian, published *Dialog mit meinem Urenkel* (Dialogue with my great-grandson), one of the most critical texts ever published in the GDR.[32] Although completed in 1977, Kuczynski's book languished in Kurt Hager's office until it was published in a censored version in 1983. In this text, Kuczynski touched on Stalinism and other topics long taboo in East Germany. He harshly criticized the media politics of the SED, at one point even quoting Lenin: "We may not keep secret our mistakes just because the enemy might exploit them. He who fears this is no revolutionary." Kuczynski also raised topics such as "bureaucratism," the "large role of the state," and the underdeveloped "participation of individual persons" in "grassroots democracy." In Kuczynski's view, however, these shortcomings were mitigated because "we find ourselves in a world class struggle."[33] Kuczynski titled his post-1989 memoirs of the GDR decades *"Ein linientreuer Dissident"* (A dissident loyal to the party line), a rather fair estimation of his politics during the East German years—especially if one emphasizes "loyal" over "dissident."[34] He was, like many other veteran communists, painfully aware of shortcomings in the GDR. But his memoirs show that he confined his most biting criticisms to the pages of his diary; publicly, he almost always defended SED policy.

Many other veteran communists no doubt harbored dissatisfactions with the regime they had helped to found. But it is their failure to publicize their criticisms that is significant. Havemann, Hermlin, and Kuczynski were all able to attract attention—at times, considerable attention—to the shortcomings of the East German regime. What if other veteran communists had done the same? For most Old Communists, however, this was virtually unthinkable. Long committed to the party and sentimentally attached to the state they had helped establish, they always feared that the "enemy," West Germany, would exploit their criticism. Indeed, after 1989, they often justified their silence on the more oppressive conditions in East Germany with reference to the harsh realities of the Cold War. More importantly, though, veteran communists refused to criticize their regime because the experiences that had made their lives meaningful had stemmed from the KPD / SED. It was through the party that longtime communists had shared a lifetime of hopes and aspirations, events and experiences, successes and failures. It was through the party that they had struggled and survived the Nazi era. It was through the party that they had participated so fully in what they saw as the great East German socialist experiment. Their identities as Old Communists, as antifascist resistance fighters, and as veterans of the German working-class movement all rested on their continued commitment to the SED. Openly criticizing SED policies would, they feared, sever their ties to the party. For most veteran communists, this was un-fathomable.

ONE MIGHT have thought that upper-level functionaries, fully aware of and frustrated with the SED's poor leadership, might have challenged veteran communists for political power. As it turns out, however, these functionaries belonged to a generation that, for historical reasons, was little inclined to oppose Old Communists. This generation, known as the Hitler Youth generation, was born roughly between 1925 and 1935. It was socialized in the Hitler Youth, the Nazi youth organization for boys (hence the generation's name). Some, but not all, of its members fought for the Nazis during World War II. For this generation, the combination of national defeat and personal upheaval in 1945 was a defining mo-ment. At war's end, members of this generation saw the complete bank-ruptcy of the ideology in which they had grown up. They also suffered material deprivation, fire bombings, loss of family members, forced mi-gration from the eastern parts of Hitler's Reich and, last but not least, a very uncertain future.

These experiences were shared by young Germans in what would later become both East and West Germany. Some significant studies of the West German Hitler Youth generation are illuminating for its East Ger-man counterpart. In 1957, the West German sociologist Helmut Schelsky published *Die skeptische Generation* (The skeptical generation). Schelsky argued that these West Germans, in contrast to earlier generations, were reluctant to adopt overtly ideological worldviews; having seen the col-lapse of Nazism, this generation was "skeptical" of all-encompassing po-litical dogmas. At the same time, this generation had experienced enor-mous upheaval following the German defeat that "had prematurely placed" it "in the position of having to take over responsibility or co-re-sponsibility for the establishment and stabilization of its private exis-tence." This, Schelsky believed, had predisposed this generation to en-deavor "to conform in every way early to the successful forms of adult social interaction."[35] Schelsky concluded that this generation was given to "concretism," by which he meant it was pragmatic, practical, and pri-marily concerned with its own personal advancement.

In a fascinating study of the *Flakhelfer*—young Nazi soldiers who be-longed to the Hitler Youth generation and staffed the anti-aircraft auxil-iary units in the last war years (a military task thought appropriate to their age)—Heinz Bude further developed some of Schelsky's arguments. Bude argued that a threefold absence marked the Flakhelfer: they were without fathers, without speech, and without history. The fathers of the

Flakhelfer had supported the Nazi rise to power and had fought in Hitler's armies; if they came home from the war at all, they were broken men. The Flakhelfer thus did not need to define themselves against their rather pathetic fathers. This, in turn, meant that they never advanced their own political language; they simply accepted the political discourse of their grandfathers, of Konrad Adenauer or of the pre-1933 social democratic leaders. Finally, even though the Flakhelfer were too young to bear the brunt of responsibility for Nazi crimes, they had nonetheless fought for the Führer. The Flakhelfer thus found themselves in an ambivalent position in regard to their Nazi pasts. In the postwar years, Bude concluded, the Flakhelfer reacted to their historical situation by seeking personal stability and professional success through conformity to the new mores of the Federal Republic. By the 1970s, many Flakhelfer had become important figures in West German society.[36]

Like its West German counterpart, the East German Hitler Youth generation also sought personal and professional advancement through conformity to the new postwar order. Once it was clear, for example, that political commitment was the key to success, members of this generation joined the FDJ and the SED in droves. While this was an act of political conformity, it was accompanied by a genuine idealism; in this respect, members of the East German Hitler Youth generation differed from their coevals in West Germany. In the early GDR years, many members of the Hitler Youth generation found the KPD / SED's antifascism convincing; fascism, after all, had delivered them only chaos and uncertainty. Under SED influence, they came to see the barbarity of the Nazi regime and to view with shame their past participation in the Hitler Youth. In return for loyalty to the new order, the SED essentially absolved these young people of their Hitler Youth pasts. In addition, the SED offered young East Germans, particularly those of working-class origin, impressive educational and career opportunities. As one former functionary has said, "In this party I then enjoyed a dizzying career—without really even trying, it was automatic."[37] By the time they were in their thirties, members of this generation had often become professors, factory directors, or high-level party and state functionaries; by the 1970s, they had become the mainstay of the East German order. This heady social mobility ensured the Hitler Youth generation's loyalty to the SED regime.[38]

Another generational dynamic further underscored these functionaries' loyalty to the East German order. As in any revolutionary regime, veteran communists enjoyed the exalted status granted the founding generation. In the early postwar decades, many individuals of the Hitler Youth generation experienced Old Communists as forceful teachers, supervisors, and colleagues. As Konrad Naumann, later a Politburo member and the first secretary of the Berlin District SED, declared in 1965: "It was 1945. The comrades who had returned from the concentration camps, from Buchenwald, Dachau, and Maidanek, firmly seized us by the collar. We could barely breathe and, without even asking us, they pushed us in the direction they wanted and molded us into decent, serviceable persons."[39] Günter Schabowski, Naumann's successor, has written that his communist convictions "were not generated by a crash course in Marxism-Leninism. They were shaped and deepened in casual, unsystematic conversations with people such as Erx [the Old Communist Günter Erxleben], who answered and suffered for their ideas. The atrocities and the end of fascism showed that they were right."[40]

In the early years, Old Communists' charisma left an indelible impression on many then-young functionaries. Horst Grunert, a deputy foreign minister, later said of his first years in the Ministry of Foreign Affairs: "I had the luck to meet splendid people who were my examples and from whom I learned a great deal: for example, Fritz Große, whose many years in jail and in concentration camps had ruined his health, but who now, after the liberation, was convinced that his ideals could be put into action. I think of Sepp Schwab, of Georg Stibi, all distinctive personalities with great charisma. Contact with them was marvelous, and criticism was practiced without harming human dignity. Unfortunately, such individuals were later more and more replaced with soulless bureaucrats."[41] All of the individuals named by Grunert were veteran communists. For Günter Sieber, the last head of the Central Committee's Department of International Relations, Old Communists were also long-lasting role models. When asked why he continued to work so hard despite the GDR's obvious shortcomings, Sieber referred to the stalwart veteran communists whom he had encountered as a young party worker at the State Planning Commission: "Perhaps my persistence can also be traced back to the influence of the founders of the GDR, to such persons as Bruno Leuschner, Heiner Rau, Fritz Selbmann, Grete Wittkowski, who suffered totally different burdens in their lives and yet did not give up. At a very young age, I had the honor of working with [them] at the Planning Commission."[42] In the late 1940s and 1950s, Old Communists exuded moral fiber; they had suffered mightily under the Nazis and were now selflessly helping to create a socialist society. To younger functionaries in search of new role models, veteran communists offered compelling examples of personal and political conduct. As Lutz Niethammer has aptly suggested, the Hitler Youth generation of SED functionaries was a "generation of politically adopted sons."[43]

In a series of post-1989 exculpatory writings and interviews, functionaries of the Hitler Youth generation claimed to have been critical of SED
rule, yet condemned to *Ohnmacht,* powerlessness or impotence;
OhnMacht is even the title of a volume of interviews with former high-
level functionaries, many of whom belonged to the Hitler Youth generation.[44] Hans Modrow, longtime first secretary of the Dresden District SED
and minister-president of East Germany in 1989–1990, has argued: "For
party functionaries, the risk [connected with] oppositional statements or
actions was high. Any full-time functionary who came out against the
Politburo would surely have been fired immediately."[45] Gerhart Neuner,
the longtime director of the Academy of Pedagogical Sciences, has stated
that "the fate of those who nonetheless tried to make a criticism or to say
something thoughtful was always in mind."[46] Similarly, the longtime
minister of culture, Hans-Joachim Hoffmann, believed that "in order to
do more, in order to really make a statement, I would have had to leave
the GDR."[47] Many of these functionaries later claimed that because they
held on to their positions, they were able to "preserve some freedoms
and to prevent worse [from happening]."[48] To be sure, functionaries did
suffer career setbacks for voicing views critical of the GDR. But it is nonetheless striking that so little has emerged from the East German archives
that might link this generation to oppositional or reform tendencies.[49]

One high-level functionary of this generation, Gerhard Schürer, chairman of the State Planning Commission, dared to offer significant criticism of SED economic policy. In fact, however, Schürer's example suggests his generation's unwillingness to take a principled stand against the
top SED leadership. As early as 1972, and throughout the 1970s and
1980s, Schürer kept telling the Politburo that East Germany could not afford Honecker's social and economic policies. Schürer's best-known criticism came in 1988, when he once again tried to convince Honecker
and other Politburo members that the GDR, in the face of mounting
debt, could not continue its current policies. In a memorandum, the
Planning Commission chairman proposed that Honecker and Mittag
abandon some of their most cherished economic tenets. Schürer suggested, for example, raising the rents on some apartments and lifting
subsidies on consumer durables.[50] His memorandum, however, met an
unhappy fate. Honecker asked Mittag to comment on the memorandum,
and the powerful economics secretary simply denied the validity of
Schürer's criticisms. In a subsequent Politburo meeting, Honecker stated
that he supported Mittag's views. Any discussion of the matter was thus
stopped before it could even begin. At the same time, Schürer did not insist on a fuller hearing for his views. As he later admitted: "Mind you, I

myself also did not take further steps"; he never, for example, resigned his position in protest of SED policies.[51] That Schürer was not dismissed for his critical views suggests that high-level functionaries could, at times, express criticism without suffering a reprisal.

Functionaries of the Hitler Youth generation appear to have become frustrated with the close-mindedness of the SED's Old Communist leaders. In post-1989 memoirs and interviews, they have repeatedly referred to the political doggedness or, in Mannheim's sense, the "oldness" of their veteran-communist superiors. Erich Honecker has borne the brunt of such accusations. For example, Egon Krenz, Honecker's brief successor in 1989, has written: "But Honecker also failed because of his lack of perception and his inability to give in to the objective needs for a change of course. This was because of his growing need to arbitrarily intervene in developments according to his own ideas."[52] Former functionaries in the Central Committee's Department of Security have said of the GDR's internal-security policies: "An objective evaluation of the situation . . . [was] urgently necessary. But the general secretary's rigid positions on domestic security increasingly hardened."[53] Other Old Communists have also been remembered for stubbornly clinging to their political views. Speaking of Politburo member Hermann Axen, Joachim Böhm, a functionary in the Central Committee's International Department, has said, "I must say, despite all his education, he was indeed dogmatic, it was difficult to discuss new things with him." And also: "Axen, the older he became, was not very willing to involve himself in new things."[54]

Despite these frustrations, functionaries of the Hitler Youth generation did not stand up to Old Communists. In part, members of this generation did not oppose Honecker and other veteran-communist leaders because they were too invested in East Germany; they had devoted their entire working lives to the SED regime and it, in turn, had brought them great career success. But they also did not challenge the veteran-communist leadership because they respected Old Communists and their antifascist biographies. Herbert Hörz, a prominent philosopher and academic administrator, has claimed that he and like-minded friends would have been more critical of new SED leaders: "And we assumed that a new group, no longer enjoying an antifascist bonus, would soon come under criticism. For this bonus always prevented one . . . from attacking the political leadership more sharply."[55] Even as the GDR tottered on the brink of disintegration in 1989, Egon Krenz preferred to "wait for a biological solution," Honecker's death, to rid the SED of its general secretary.[56] Krenz has written that he felt that he did not have the "right" to challenge his older comrades. When he finally did oppose Honecker, Krenz has stated, "I felt as if I were about to play Brutus. The older comrades had presented their power as a natural right after what they had suffered under fascism. That was deeply instilled in our political culture. It meant that we, the younger ones, did not have the right to challenge them."[57] Günter Schabowski has argued that veteran communists refused to grant his generation political power. "There were two criteria for a place at the top," Schabowski explained after 1989, "having been in the Spanish Civil War or in prison under the Nazis. That excluded any of my generation from a decisive role as far as they were concerned."[58] Schabowski was not quite right—Mittag, a member of the Hitler Youth generation, did play a decisive role in East German economic questions. But he was an exception. While Old Communists were generally unwilling to cede their political power to the Hitler Youth generation, younger functionaries also failed to appropriate that power for themselves.

Thus the coincidence of two sets of generational dynamics—one stemming from the historical situation of postwar Germany, the other from the SED's revolutionary tradition—prevented the Hitler Youth generation of SED functionaries from challenging Honecker and the rest of the veteran-communist leadership. Longtime communists and this younger generation of SED functionaries were caught in a symbiotic relationship. While Old Communists depended on the younger generation to implement its political vision, the Hitler Youth generation, like its West German counterpart, adopted the political ideals of veteran communists. Moreover, it always remained respectful of the antifascist biographies of veteran communists. Ironically, however, although their antifascist biographies kept longtime communists in power, they also helped to undermine the SED regime. The Hitler Youth generation's deference to Honecker and other veteran-communist leaders led to a debilitating stagnation in GDR politics. Unwilling to rock the SED boat, functionaries of this generation stood by for more than a decade as the GDR slowly sailed into economic and political disaster. The veteran-communist stranglehold on GDR politics would only be broken by those outside of the SED's ranks: by East Germany's younger generation and, ultimately, by changes in the Soviet Union.

VETERAN COMMUNISTS had initially placed great hopes in those East Germans born after 1945. Unlike older East Germans, these GDR citizens, Old Communists thought, were not tainted by Nazi ideology or upbringing; since childhood, they had been raised in socialist mores. Moreover, longtime communists had spent considerable energy—speaking to audiences and writing their memoirs—to convince younger East Germans of the superiority of socialism. But the experiences of younger GDR citizens had not led them to enthusiastically embrace the GDR order. The poet Uwe Kolbe coined the term *Hineingeborene*—those born into (the GDR)—that captures the broad experiences of all those born in the GDR between 1945 and the mid-1960s.[59] The Hineingeborene were born into fixed structures of society, politics, language, and even topography. For them, little in life was left to chance, nothing to experimentation. Consumption was limited, travel restricted, and leisure activities were often very organized. Political participation was scripted and thoroughly routinized. The life trajectories of the Hineingeborene were also largely predetermined: school, studies or apprenticeship, military service (for men), a secure job, marriage, and children. Even social and professional mobility was sharply curtailed; as the Hitler Youth generation dug into influential positions, there was no place for East Germany's youngest generation to go. Like no other trope, the Wall symbolized this generation and its dilemmas. Physically bound by cement and mortar, the lives of the Hineingeborene were rigidly circumscribed by the sociopolitical order. In Kolbe's stark words, this generation found a "little green country narrow, barbed-wire landscape."[60]

The historical events experienced by the Hineingeborene, unlike those by their elders, did not lead to revolutionary upheaval. On the contrary, the Hineingeborene seemed to have been born into a historical standstill; every major historical event that they experienced reiterated the unyielding character of the "really existing socialist" order. The building of the Berlin Wall in 1961 prevented individuals from escaping westward; the Hineingeborene were now locked into the GDR. The Warsaw Pact invasion of Czechoslovakia in 1968—the crushing of "socialism with a human face"—dulled all hope that Marxist-Leninist societies could be reformed from within. The 1976 expatriation of singer-songwriter Wolf Biermann and the 1981 imposition of martial law in Poland only reminded them of the seemingly leviathan nature of Soviet-style socialism. For the Hineingeborene, it seemed impossible that History could ever sweep away the countless walls that bound their lives.

The Hineingeborene also had few links to Old Communists. Unlike the functionaries of the Hitler Youth generation, the Hineingeborene had not personally "bonded" with veteran communists; by the time they had entered the work force, longtime communists had generally retired (with the exception, of course, of the Old Communist leadership). The Hineingeborene thus never experienced veteran communists as colleagues or superiors—as the gritty characters, laced with steel, that the

Hitler Youth generation so fondly remembered. They knew veteran communists only from scripted encounters, or from the increasingly stale media image of Old Communists as antifascist heroes. With little invested in the SED regime or its longtime communist leaders, most Hineingeborene responded to their existential confinement with a studied political apathy and resignation. Their involvement in the SED's ritualistic politics became ever more perfunctory and, for them, official SED doctrine became an "eight-hour ideology": at work, they professed belief in the SED's unconvincing propaganda, yet at home they ridiculed official doctrine. In search of self and meaning, many of these Hineingeborene withdrew into private "niches," earning the GDR its epithet of the "niche society"; little did they know that even these private retreats were shadowed by Stasi informers.[61]

Some Hineingeborene refused to make their peace with the SED regime. Over the years, thousands of young East Germans tried to escape the GDR; while some were successful in often daring endeavors, others landed in prison after failed attempts. Hundreds of thousands of young GDR citizens also applied to leave the country legally. In what became a symbol of ubiquitous discontent, those who had applied to leave the GDR flew white ribbons on their car antennas. Many of these individuals lost their jobs. Others were imprisoned. The SED regime, however, allowed some of these East Germans to leave the country; between 1984 and 1988, some 114,500 individuals (some of whom were also older persons) abandoned the country legally.[62] After 1989, it was learned that the SED regime had a monetary interest in exporting discontent: West Germany had bought many East Germans' freedom and entry into the FRG. In what many termed "trafficking in human beings" (Menschenhandel), the West German government had often paid the GDR tens of thousands of marks per person; the exact sum paid depended on factors such as age, education, and training.

A few Hineingeborene chose dissidence as the answer to their existential confinement. Although these dissidents made up a negligible fraction of the GDR population, they would eventually play an important role in East Germany's demise. By the late 1980s, the Stasi estimated that roughly 2,500 individuals were involved in "resistance activities" in the GDR, six hundred of whom were considered leaders.[63] In an ironic twist to East Germany's generational dynamics, many of these Hineingeborene claimed Robert Havemann as their spiritual grandfather. Stephan Bickhardt, who was involved in church and other dissident activities in the 1980s, has stated that "[Havemann's] authority, in part based on his opposition to National Socialism, made him the spiritual mentor of the GDR opposition."[64] This role of "spiritual mentor" was based less on Havemann's ideas for democratic socialism and more on his outstanding personal example; this courageous Old Communist had, in Václav Havel's famous phrase, "lived in truth" under both the Nazi and the SED regimes. Rainer Eppelmann, for example, who together with Havemann initiated the widely publicized 1982 "Berliner Appell" (Berlin appeal), a call for nuclear disarmament in Europe, deeply respected his co-initiator, but did not share Havemann's views: "He wanted a very different Germany than I, but with his courage, his optimism, and his experience, he gave all who wanted to replace the SED regime with democratic conditions an example of steadfastness."[65]

In stark contrast to the Hitler Youth generation of SED functionaries, dissident Hineingeborene did not adopt the veteran-communist political agenda. Although most of these dissidents wished to preserve a socialist GDR until well into 1989, this was the only matter on which they and Old Communists agreed. The Hineingeborene dissidents appropriated the political discourse of the new social movements of Western countries: feminism, nuclear disarmament, environmental responsibility, the peaceful resolution of conflict, grassroots political participation, and solidarity with the Third World. For the most part, these were strikingly at odds with the 1930s issues that so preoccupied Old Communists—class struggle, the battle against fascism, the provision of basic welfare, and an unflagging belief in industrial progress. When peace activists called for nuclear and other disarmament, Old Communists felt that they were merely succumbing to Western governments' aims to undermine the military prowess of the Warsaw Pact countries. When activists condemned the compulsory military education introduced in East German schools in 1978 as a dangerous militarization of society, longtime communists countered that it was necessary to prepare younger East Germans to defend socialist achievements. When dissidents called for the fostering of mutual understanding between the GDR and other European countries, they challenged Abgrenzung policies and the regime's restrictions on travel to other Eastern European countries, both of which veteran communists hoped would prevent the spread of "pernicious" ideas to East Germany. Finally, when dissidents demanded environmental responsibility, they clashed with longtime communists' belief in the virtues of untrammeled industrial growth. Dissident Hineingeborene and Old Communists spoke two political languages that translated into clashing political visions.

By the late 1980s the political discourse of East Germany's dissidents, in part legitimated by glasnost and perestroika in the Soviet Union, had come to influence a broad segment of the Hineingeborene generation. An interesting 1989 text, planned well before the end of the East German regime, documents the extent to which glasnost views, once the purview of only a small number of dissidents, had now reached many younger East Germans. *Einmischung der Enkel* (The grandchildren intervene) is a slender volume of "letters" from younger, rather ordinary East Germans—neither dissidents nor party functionaries—to Jürgen Kuczynski in response to his 1983 *Dialog mit meinem Urenkel*. Kuczynski's book, which had gone through nine print runs, consisted of his answers to nineteen "difficult" questions—such as "Since you think socialism is so splendid, why do you constantly criticize conditions?"—posed by his imaginary great-grandson. The letter writers in *Einmischung*, however, were disappointed by Kuczynski's answers: not only was his criticism of the GDR timid, but he had also failed to address many issues of importance to them.

The fact that these younger East Germans were at such odds with Kuczynski, a relatively critical Old Communist, underscores the deep chasm between veteran communists and the Hineingeborene. Whereas Kuczynski was preoccupied with issues such as Stalinism and the ongoing struggle between capitalism and socialism, the "grandchildren" were concerned with world peace, the environment, and the absence of democracy in the GDR. As Ute Dietrich, a twenty-seven-year-old postal worker, wrote: "Has not the passing time made some of the questions in Kuczynski's book out-of-date? . . . I read Jürgen Kuczynski's answers, and they are true and honest and open. But they don't move me . . . I fear the questions of my children. They will ask why I looked on as the forests were dying. They will ask why I was so apathetic in the face of great hunger and the countless little wars of this world."[66] To Dietrich, Kuczynski's issues were anachronistic. She was concerned with the environment and with starvation in the Third World, as well as with the dangers of regional conflicts (as opposed to those posed by Cold War superpower confrontation). Other letter writers thought that Kuczynski used the ongoing class struggle to justify too many of the GDR's shortcomings. Thirty-seven-year-old Karlheinz Sydoruk, a member of the District Planning Commission in Cottbus, wrote: "Too often you excuse, for example, the insufficient development of democracy with the existence of the world class struggle."[67] A thirty-nine-year-old technician, Michael Fritzsch, questioned whether "world class struggle" was even still an issue: "Is it not so that we are simply forced to get along peacefully with our neighbors? Around us is a half-poisoned environment." He continued: "Are we really still in this world class struggle? Or only just our politicians? Do we need this world class struggle? Do we need hatred and the concept of an enemy in order to shoot other people dead?" The author then challenged Kuczynski: "What would you say to that, Mr. Kuczynski? Is this a retreat from certain established positions? Is this a betrayal of the old comrades?"[68]

Several younger letter writers suggested that since they did not share the biographies of Old Communists, they could not share their political passions. Reinhard Stöckel, a thirty-two-year-old librarian, wrote of Kuczynski's defense of the superiority of socialism: "I by no means doubt the sincerity of your professions . . . But this can only be understood emotionally by those like you who know the other side of the world from their own experience."[69] Similarly, a thirty-three-year-old metal worker, Bernd Ruscher, wrote that he could not share Kuczynski's hatred for capitalism: "Hatred is the mother of war. I believe that we, who did not have to struggle against capitalism in the illegal resistance, who did not have to show all our courage, [who did not have to] act directly in life-threatening circumstances, [that] we can no longer sympathize with your hatred."[70] Having never personally experienced capitalism, the Hineingeborene were neither convinced that capitalism was pure evil, nor confident that socialism was inevitably the better system.

These younger letter writers were also exasperated by the antifascist aura that surrounded Old Communists. A thirty-eight-year-old agricultural engineer, Lothar Aermes, for example, described his reluctance to challenge Kuczynski in a 1987 public forum about *Dialog*. After reading the book, Aermes had gone to the event feeling "rage in [my] stomach, disappointment and the will to criticize." The event began when the eighty-three-year-old Old Communist was welcomed with a bouquet of flowers. Kuczynski then began to speak and, according to Aermes, told "about how he, after returning home from long years of emigration, with all his strength began to build up the Friendship Society between the peoples of the Soviet Union and the GDR. How proud he was as its first successes became apparent. And then followed the news that he couldn't take over the chairmanship, that is, he was to give up his office—he, the Jew Kuczynski, in the Stalin era." Aermes then asked: "Who would have been able to interject a criticism of the *Dialog* book in the suspense-filled silence of the room? At any rate, something like a deep respect swallowed my voice, I remained silent, had a dedication written into the book, and later put it away on the bookshelf."[71] The exalted status of a veteran communist had brought Aermes to a frustrated silence.

In a "letter" dated November 1988, Kuczynski responded to the "grandchildren." Sadly he had noticed, he wrote, that "so many of you have a streak of angry pessimism." Kuczynski nonetheless suggested the areas in which he and the grandchildren concurred: "[Your] demand for more openness in the media, in public discussion, in the evaluation of our conditions . . . totally agrees with my remarks." Kuczynski also admitted some shortcomings in his text. He had been wrong, he wrote, not to have raised the issues of global disarmament and the environment. He nonetheless largely defended his Old Communist worldview. Insisting on the superiority of socialism, Kuczynski even suggested that the GDR media should spend a few minutes each day demonstrating the "unique achievements of socialism over capitalism." He also reiterated how the "world class struggle" negatively affected the daily lives of all East Germans.[72] The veteran communist Kuczynski and the Hineingeborene remained a world apart.

Although many Hineingeborene were not adverse to socialism per se, their views did not augur well for the future of the GDR. The political pathos of Old Communists had failed to inspire them. Unlike the Hitler Youth generation, younger East Germans lacked the life experiences that made the "anti" agenda (antifascism, anticapitalism, anti-imperialism) attractive or even tenable. The noticeable lack of enthusiasm and engagement among the Hineingeborene suggested the erosion of the regime's legitimacy. The Old Communist leadership thus faced a dilemma common to many revolutionary regimes—how to maintain revolutionary élan once the revolution has been won. In the political sociology of Max Weber, the charismatic ethos of a revolutionary order is always bureaucratized. Recast in generational terminology, the founding fathers (or grandfathers) then have difficulty convincing the children (or grandchildren) of the compelling urgency of upholding revolutionary accomplishments. Barring historical events that relegitimize the regime (such as World War II in the Soviet Union), the fathers must accommodate the aspirations of new generations. Otherwise, political transformation is all but inevitable. In the GDR, Old Communists did little to meet the needs and hopes of the Hineingeborene generation. Even if Gorbachev had not initiated reforms that would eventually bring down communism in Europe, a political transformation (albeit less dramatic than that of 1989) would probably have taken place in the GDR. After the "biological" end to veteran communist rule and a brief interlude in power by the aging Hitler Youth generation, the Hineingeborene would have come to rule the GDR. While a few Hineingeborene functionaries might have tried to continue East German state socialism, they would have faced vocal opposition from longtime dissidents and shallow support from their politically apathetic coevals. The SED regime would have been hard-pressed to march into the future.

AS IT was, though, breathtaking changes took place in the Soviet Union that would soon bring on the GDR's demise. Under Gorbachev, the Soviet Union began to break with time-honored practices of communist rule. Honecker was initially chary and later outright opposed to Gorbachev's reforms. While Gorbachev wanted to shake up Soviet society so as to spur on greater economic prosperity, Honecker believed that East Germany had long since attained the economic prosperity to which the Soviet Union aspired; he saw no need for the GDR to follow suit with an East German glasnost and perestroika. Even more importantly for the future of East Germany, Gorbachev came to believe that the Soviet Union could and should no longer uphold the satellite communist regimes in Eastern Europe. But as Honecker knew, the Soviet Union's past insistence on a divided Germany had been the main guarantee of the GDR's continued existence.

Honecker's opposition to Gorbachev also had a generational component. Honecker had known Weimar-era revolutionary politics, had participated in the antifascist struggle, and had spent a decade in prison for his convictions. By contrast, Gorbachev had never known the world of revolutionary politics; he had not even fought in World War II. For Honecker, it must have been galling to see the communist project, for which he had suffered so greatly, undermined by a young Soviet leader who seemed to ride roughshod over sacred communist truths. Günter Schabowski later characterized the relationship between the two men as "a close enmity." As Schabowski explained in his post-1989 memoirs: "It not only seems reasonable but it is also right that the Old Communist Honecker, who was consecrated to Stalinism while at the international Lenin School in Moscow in 1930 / 1931, who defied the Nazis and survived the Brandenburg Penitentiary, should have initially watched the newcomer Gorbachev with skepticism. In the following period, he judged him as ever more disastrous for the continued existence of the real socialist community, as well as for its spiritual brace, Marxist-Leninist ideology." Writing of Gorbachev, Schabowski observed further: "A younger and not by a long shot so proven a communist as the antifascist resistance fighter Honecker allowed himself, knowingly or out of ignorance, to intervene in his [Honecker's] life work. Here is where I see the real roots of [Honecker's] prejudice against and dislike of Gorbachev."[73] Gorbachev, on the other hand, was little invested in upholding anachronistic structures of communist rule; he thus had little use for aging social-ist leaders such as Honecker. As the new Soviet leader would later tell Egon Krenz: "Comrade Erich Honecker evidently thought himself the Number One in socialism, if not in the world. He no longer realistically saw what was going on."[74]

Many of the most telling incidents concerning Old Communist intran-sigence in the waning years of the GDR stem from Honecker's and other veteran communists' actions and statements concerning Gorbachev's re-form policies. In 1987, for example, Kurt Hager, the SED's chief ideolo-gist, rhetorically asked "whether one must also hang new wallpaper" when a neighbor redecorates his apartment.[75] Hager's infamous quip was widely taken to mean that the SED leadership thought perestroika un-necessary for the GDR; it also suggested that perestroika was a superficial affair. In November 1988, Honecker banned the Soviet periodical *Sputnik* from the list of newspapers distributed by the GDR postal service because it had published critical remarks about the role of the KPD and the Com-intern in the 1930s. Honecker's arbitrary decision displayed both an utter disdain for glasnost and the Old Communist allergy to confronting long-taboo communist subjects. And in January 1989, Honecker declared that if necessary, the Wall would "still be standing in 50 and also in 100 years."[76] This remark was a sober warning not only to East Germans, but also to Gorbachev, who was eager to bridge a divided Europe.

Inspired by ongoing events in the Soviet Union, a small but deter-mined opposition movement had coalesced in East Germany by the summer of 1989. The SED leadership, however, was seemingly paralyzed. In July, Honecker had gallbladder trouble and, unbeknownst to the general public, was also suffering from liver cancer. In August, he had an operation for his cancer; he then recuperated until the end of September. In Honecker's absence, the Politburo was unwilling to take any deci-sive action. This was, however, just when events that would usher in the East German revolution were taking place. In early September, Hungary, without discussing the matter with SED authorities, opened its borders to the West. This allowed GDR citizens to cross freely into Austria (from where they could go to West Germany). Thousands of East Germans also sought political asylum in the West German embassies in Prague, Buda-pest, and Warsaw. In East Germany, too, discontented citizens began to make their voices heard. In early September, a group of dissidents founded an independent political party, New Forum, that gained wide-spread attention. In Leipzig, there were ongoing Monday evening pro-tests against the regime. By October 2, these protests had swollen to twenty thousand participants.[77]

Honecker, now returned to work, appears to have been undaunted by these manifestations of discontent; he apparently believed that the situation could be contained by force. On October 7, the regime went on with its grandiose celebrations of the fortieth anniversary of the founding of the GDR. With Gorbachev in attendance, Honecker once again made his opposition to reform clear; the Soviet leader, in turn, indicated that his country would not intervene in GDR affairs. Even during Gorbachev's visit, some three thousand demonstrators were arrested; others were beaten and sprayed with a water cannon.[78] By Monday, October 9, Honecker was apparently ready to use live ammunition against protesters in Leipzig; in anticipation of the demonstration that evening, hospital beds and blood plasma were prepared.[79] The following week, Honecker briefly considered deploying a tank regiment in the streets of Leipzig.[80] In a sign of Honecker's waning authority, however, local and national authorities refrained from the use of bloody force.

In the face of the ever-growing demonstrations, Egon Krenz and other Politburo members finally decided to oust Honecker and his closest allies, Günter Mittag and Joachim Herrmann, the propaganda secretary (not an Old Communist). Krenz, a former FDJ leader and the secretary of security affairs, had long been considered Honecker's crown prince. During the first weeks of October, he carefully organized a coup against his former mentor. Krenz lined up Stoph and other Politburo functionaries who were critical of Honecker, as well as those who controlled the East German security forces.[81] On October 17, the plotters finally acted. At a routine Politburo meeting on that day, Stoph calmly interrupted Honecker's opening remarks and said that he wished to make a change in the agenda. He then proposed that the first topic of discussion be the removal of the general secretary. It is no accident that it was an Old Communist who first broached Honecker's removal in the general secretary's presence: it lent a certain legitimacy to the entire undertaking. In answer to Stoph's suggestion, one Politburo member later recalled, "Honecker responded with a stony face. He allowed the debate to proceed."[82] At the end of the debate, Honecker, after eighteen years at the SED's helm, was unceremoniously deposed. The very next day, Honecker "asked" the Central Committee to release him from the function of general secretary and several other positions. The Honecker era had come to an end.

In the next weeks, popular protests against the SED regime continued. Even some Old Communists joined in oppositional rallies. The excitement of the autumn of 1989 seems to have brought some longtime revolutionaries back into their roles as critics of the established order. Hilde Eisler, Gerhart Eisler's widow, and Steffie Spira, a well-known veteran-communist actress, both participated in a huge demonstration at East Berlin's Alexanderplatz that took place on November 4. Spira even addressed the crowd with a short speech. She began by invoking her antifascist past: "In 1933 I went alone to a foreign country. I took nothing along. But in my head I had a few lines from a poem by Bertolt Brecht." She then quoted some Brecht lines to the effect that what had once seemed unchanging, could, in fact, change this very day. After stating that she hoped that her great-grandchildren would grow up without roll calls, civics classes, and FDJ torch parades, Spira concluded: "I have one more proposal. We will make Wandlitz [the exclusive enclave where the top SED leadership lived] an old-age home. Those who are over 60 and 65 years old can continue to live there, provided that they do what I will now do: go off the stage."[83]

Behind the scenes, Egon Krenz, the new general secretary, pressured veteran communists in the Politburo to resign their positions so as to give the party a new, younger leadership. At the Central Committee meeting that began on November 8, Krenz was able to announce that all Old Communists on the Politburo (as well as several other individuals) were retiring from that body. Krenz now told the assembled Committee: "Comrades, despite all that must be said critically about the whole Politburo, I think that we must give our comrades-in-arms heartfelt thanks. Some of them placed their lives in jeopardy for their ideals and worldview under the skies of Spain, in the antifascist resistance, [and] in the fascist penitentiaries. As activists of the first hour, along with all those forces who were interested in peace and in a new society, they took the first, difficult steps toward a new beginning in the ruins of the war, when the GDR was nothing more than a vision. They helped organize the building of socialism in the GDR and helped shape its good development for many years. With heads held high, they all have good reason, comrades, to receive the thanks of our party, our Central Committee, and all our best wishes for their health." This passage soon became the subject of controversy. Later in the day, the Central Committee began to discuss the official communiqué that it would publish of its proceedings. Kurt Hager, although he claimed to find it "painfully embarrassing," asked Krenz why this passage, which he found very appropriate, seemed not to be included in the communiqué. Hager asked point-blank: "Will this now be withheld or will this be published? Is the party now capable of expressing thanks to comrades who have struggled for decades or will we only take note of this behind closed doors? That is my question." Krenz responded that the passage would indeed be published. At this point, however, a Central Committee member, Lothar Stammnitz, suggested that the passage not be published. Stammnitz argued that at that moment every sentence published by the Central Committee was being carefully scrutinized by the public. He added that some of those thanked, notably the FDGB chairman Harry Tisch (not a veteran communist), were extremely unpopular. The Central Committee then voted on the matter. Although ten members voted against it, publication of this passage won overwhelming support from Central Committee members. As an afterthought, Günter Schabowski even reiterated how important it was to publish the formulation "under Spanish skies."[84] These words once again invoked the powerful myth of antifascist resistance from which the SED, even in 1989, still hoped to draw sustenance. With these official words of thanks, Old Communists left the SED in the hands of younger comrades—one day before the Berlin Wall fell.

November 1989 marked the end of veteran communist rule in East Germany. Although they were longtime revolutionaries, Old Communists could not muster the energy to uphold their socialist order. Like so many founding generations, they had been unable to transmit the revolutionary impulse to new generations. Although the Hitler Youth generation of SED functionaries had always supported Old Communists, this was based more on conformity than conviction. In 1989, this generation was unable either to revitalize the revolution by reform, or to marshal the military to uphold a socialist GDR. Younger East Germans, however, were alienated from the veteran-communist order that promoted a hopelessly anachronistic future. In a few short months, the SED would no longer be in power and, in less than a year, the GDR would also disappear.

EPILOGUE

THE FALL OF THE BERLIN WALL IN NOVEMBER 1989 EFFECTIVELY ENDED communist rule in East Germany. In a few short months, the world that veteran communists had created all but vanished. Veteran communists, once famed and feted in East Germany, became infamous and ignominious in the new Germany. They were forced to exchange a comfortable familiarity for a trying uncertainty. Their party, once all-powerful in the GDR, was but tolerated in the united Germany. Their values, at one time the mainstay of the GDR's ruling ideology, were now scorned in the Federal Republic. And their biographies, once central to the GDR's antifascist legitimacy, commanded little respect in the new Germany. As with so much other History that they had lived, veteran communists adapted to their changed circumstances. But what happened to them in the united Germany? How did they make sense of their past and present situations? And finally, how should we interpret their long political lives in the service of the communist movement?

ALTHOUGH VETERAN communists were no longer active participants in historical events, they still retained a symbolic importance in the new Germany: they came to represent the old, fallen order. In November and December 1989, revelations about the privileged lifestyles of top party leaders shocked the SED rank and file, as well as the East German public. This led the SED / PDS (the successor to the SED) to jettison Erich Honecker, Erich Mielke, Horst Sindermann, and Willi Stoph from the party's ranks in early December 1989, and Kurt Hager and Alfred Neumann in late January 1990. By the standards of either the Western rich or twentieth-century despots, the SED's top leaders had actually led anything but lavish lifestyles. SED Politburo members lived in Wandlitz, an exclusive enclave about thirty kilometers north of central Berlin.

Sometimes dubbed "Volvograd" because of the leadership's penchant for the Swedish car, Wandlitz had been supplied by a special shop stocked almost exclusively with Western goods. Top SED leaders also enjoyed comfortable dachas and hunting lodges for weekend retreats. Party leaders had used huge tracts of forest lands for private hunting expeditions; some 20 percent of East German forest lands had apparently been reserved for this purpose. And, it was discovered, veteran communists had engaged in financial improprieties. Honecker, for example, had received a stipend of twenty thousand marks per year as an honorary member of the Construction Academy.[1] Although these trappings of luxury were relatively understated—visitors to Wandlitz were often disappointed by its decidedly petite-bourgeois quality—they nonetheless seemed outrageous. In a society of scarcity, veteran communists, who espoused an egalitarian ethos, had condoned a regime of privilege. Longtime communists were scorned not for the scale of the opulence that they had enjoyed, but for the degree of hypocrisy that they had embodied.

Some veteran communists now faced criminal proceedings for alleged crimes committed during their years in power in the GDR. In January 1990, Erich Honecker was arrested. He was, however, soon pronounced unfit to remain in prison. He then spent a few months at a pastor's home in Lobetal, and the better part of 1990 in the Soviet military hospital in Beelitz. After German reunification in October 1990, a new warrant for his arrest was issued. In March 1991, Honecker fled to Moscow. Later that year, Russian authorities refused to grant him continued refuge, but Honecker found safety in the Chilean embassy in Moscow. In July 1992, Honecker was nonetheless returned to Germany. He then spent 169 days in Moabit Prison—the very same prison in which the Nazis had imprisoned him for some eighteen months almost sixty years earlier. In an indictment that ran some eight hundred pages, Honecker was charged with manslaughter for allegedly authorizing border guards to shoot at East Germans attempting to escape the GDR. In January 1993, however, Honecker was deemed too sick to stand trial and his arrest warrant was rescinded. He then went to Chile, where he spent the remaining sixteen months of his life with his wife and daughter, who had married a Chilean leftist exiled in East Berlin in the 1970s.

After his death in May 1994, Honecker's *Moabiter Notizen* (Notes from Moabit) was published. This work included his musings in prison, as well as transcripts of conversations that Honecker had had with West German politicians during his official visit to Bonn in 1987. The juxtaposition of these two sets of documents captured the irony of Honecker's situation after 1989: just a few years earlier, the prisoner had been welcomed by those who would soon be bent on his prosecution. In *Moabiter Notizen,* Honecker nonetheless reserved his most trenchant criticism for those who succeeded him in the SED leadership. In his view, the proceedings against him and others belonged to the "crimes of the SED": "The criminalization from one's own ranks led to a far-reaching breakdown of solidarity that made it easier for the reactionary forces of the FRG to carry out their extensive campaign of revenge against communists and other leftists."[2] As he had throughout his life, Honecker interpreted his difficulties as part and parcel of the ongoing class war: just as during the Weimar, Nazi, and Cold War years, he and other veteran communists were the underdogs in a brutal antifascist struggle in which the enemy knew no bounds.

Like Honecker, other former Old Communist Politburo members also faced criminal proceedings. Intended in part as a form of *Vergangenheitsbewältigung* (mastering the past), these proceedings became, instead, judicial farce. Prosecuting authorities were hampered both by the poor health of the defendants and by the lack of indictable crimes (longtime communists had acted well within East German legal norms). Although Hermann Axen, Stoph, and Sindermann were all briefly arrested on charges of corruption and / or manslaughter, they were released for reasons of ill health and the criminal charges against them were dropped. In accordance with German law, Stoph even received compensation— about $6,000—for the time he served in jail before his release from trial.[3] In a peculiar twist of justice, Mielke, the longtime Stasi chief, was put on trial not for crimes connected with the East German regime, but for the murder of two Berlin policemen in a communist street battle in 1931. Convicted in 1993, Mielke received a six-year sentence for this crime; by 1995, though, he was a free, if sick man. Mielke was the only Old Communist tried, convicted, and held (however briefly) to a prison sentence after 1989. Finally, Hager, along with five younger Politburo members, faced manslaughter charges in a trial that began in 1995. In May 1996, however, due to his poor health, the case against him was halted and separated from that of the other defendants.

While the threat of criminal proceedings harassed a few once-powerful Old Communists, all veteran communists suffered, in one way or another, from the loss of their exalted status as past participants in the antifascist resistance to Hitler. The financial benefits and other privileges accorded longtime communists as antifascist resistance fighters were now gradually rolled back. The 1990 Unification Treaty between East and West Germany allowed for the payment of honorary pensions through 1991. In 1992, the German Parliament passed a law stipulating that these pensions would continue to be paid out. The language of the law, however, was indicative of the altered status of veteran communists in the new Germany. Whereas earlier these pensions were denoted as "honorary pensions" for "fighters" *(Kämpfer)* against fascism and those "persecuted" *(Verfolgte)* by fascism, they became "compensation pensions" *(Entschädigungsrenten)* for "victims" *(Opfer)* of National Socialism. The new, passive designation of "victim" militates against the long-held active, masculine self-image of veteran communists as "fighters." As an author partial to the East German cult of the antifascist resistance states: "Fighters have . . . become mere victims . . . Both groups [i.e., the "fighters" and the "persecuted"] are explicitly no longer *honored,* but instead reluctantly *compensated.*" In accordance with the new language, former "fighters" of fascism saw their pensions reduced to the level of those received by the former "persecuted" in East Germany—all these "victims" were to receive 1,400 marks a month (paid, of course, in DM). In fact, however, these pensions were a rather more complicated matter. The 1992 law stipulated that "compensation pensions" were not to be paid out to individuals who had violated principles of humanity or the rule of law or who had abused official positions for personal gain. Those thus found to have been "close to the system" *(systemnah),* as many veteran communists allegedly were, received pensions of only 802 DM a month in 1994; at that time the official poverty line was 1,254 DM a month.[4] Once assured a secure retirement, many surviving Old Communists faced significant financial hardship in the united Germany.

Veteran communists were not only confronted with straitened material circumstances after 1989. They also witnessed the denigration of their antifascist struggle against Hitler, the most meaningful chapter of their personal biographies. Among other measures, countless streets in the former East Germany that had honored revolutionary heroes, including veteran communists who had passed away in the GDR, were renamed. In Berlin, for example, Wilhelm Pieck Street became Tor (Gate) Street. In Dresden, Wilhelm Koenen Square became Albert Wolf Square, while Wilhelm Koenen Street became Boxberger Street. Residents of the Saxon capital also renamed other streets that had honored longtime communists mentioned in previous pages: Fritz Grosse Street became Rosen Street, Hermann Matern Street became Coventry Street, and Johannes R. Becher Square became Stresemann Square.[5] In addition, although many plaques and institutions honoring Walter Ulbricht had already been removed or renamed during the Honecker years, this trend continued after 1989. In Leipzig in the early 1990s, for example, a plaque commemorating Ulbricht on a secondary school was removed, and the memorial tablet identifying the house in which he had been born was covered with graffiti.[6] Although many schools, factories, work brigades, and other institutions once carried the names of veteran communists, today these appellations (as well as many of the institutions themselves) have all but disappeared in the former East Germany.

Since 1989, the memorial exhibitions at Buchenwald, Sachsenhausen, and Ravensbrück concentration camps have been dramatically altered. Sarah Farmer, an American historian, has written that concentration camps were sites of "national pride" in the former East Germany—they articulated the SED's legitimizing myth of the "triumph of the communist-led resistance over fascism." For West Germans, however, concentration camps are sites of "national shame"—they commemorate a barbarous German past.[7] While the old East German exhibitions or parts thereof have sometimes been preserved as historical artifacts of another era, these concentration-camp memorials are now organized according to the dominant West German interpretation. Exhibitions focus on Nazi atrocities rather than communist resistance and, to the extent that resistance is discussed, the communist resistance no longer enjoys a revered place. In a further delegitimation of the past communist regime, labor camps run by Soviet occupation forces at Buchenwald and Sachsenhausen between 1945 and 1950 are now also commemorated at these concentration-camp sites. Finally, museum exhibitions and other monuments celebrating the communist movement have been altered or dismantled in the former East Germany.[8] Old Communists, long accustomed to seeing their participation in the communist movement heroized, now find this antifascist struggle at best forgotten, at worst vilified.

Besides no longer enjoying official, public veneration, Old Communists have seen their individual biographies intensely scrutinized. The biographies of veteran communists have thus once again seen a reinterpretation for political purposes. Erich Honecker, who had commanded respect from many Western observers for the ten years he spent in Nazi prisons, saw his antifascist biography undermined by revelations about his conduct in Nazi captivity after his 1935 arrest. In 1990, the news magazine *Stern* (Star) published an article claiming that Honecker betrayed fellow comrades after his arrest.[9] In a 1991 book titled *Tatort Politbüro* (The Politburo as crime site), Peter Przybylski, a former press secretary for the GDR attorney general's office, made similar allegations.[10] In several writings, Honecker vigorously defended himself against the charges. He not only rejected the accusations outright with a detailed refutation of the charges, but also argued that the allegations were motivated by personal gain and political opportunism. According to Honecker, this "Tatort-Pryzibilski" (sic) "lies so that after twenty-five years of work in the attorney general's office he can rescue himself from the 'sinking ship' regardless of what becomes of others who remained decent. And all for dear money." Honecker also questioned whether the denigration of his biography was intended to ease West Germany's "takeover" of the GDR: "Should the slandering of the antifascist Honecker, the statements against other party and state functionaries . . . make the annexation of the GDR by the FRG easier?"[11] As Honecker bitterly concluded in *Moabiter Notizen:* "Now one wants to hurl the old antifascists from a pedestal on which they never placed themselves. They worked so that this Germany would become and remain an antifascist Germany."[12]

Like Honecker, other veteran communists, championed by their defenders, did not give up easily their haloed antifascist reputations. In 1994, Lutz Niethammer published *Der "gesäuberte" Antifaschismus* ("White-washed" antifascism), a book in which he showed that communists had taken on prisoner functions and had thus been complicit in upholding the brutal SS regime in Buchenwald concentration camp.[13] An organization called the "Camp Working Group Buchenwald-Dora and Kommandos in Germany" angrily retorted with a statement titled "Cold War against Buchenwald, Shamelessness as 'Scholarship.'" The working group questioned Niethammer's sources, methodology, and conclusions.[14] Similarly, in 1996, a literary critic, Karl Corino, created a stir by proving that the lyricist Stephan Hermlin, who had frequently criticized SED cultural policies, had embellished his antifascist past.[15] Not only in his semi-fictional autobiographical work, *Abendlicht* (Evening light), but also in interviews and official documents, Hermlin had claimed, among other details, that he had been imprisoned in Sachsenhausen concentration camp in 1934 and had participated in the Spanish Civil War; he had also repeatedly stated that his father had died in a German concentration camp. None of this, Corino discovered, was true. Hermlin had simply invented his imprisonment in Sachsenhausen, his father had died of liver cancer in England in 1946, and it could not be determined whether Hermlin had actually fought in the Spanish Civil War. Corino's findings, although not challenged on their merits, raised a storm of protest from Hermlin's defenders. Corino, they claimed, was a "liar" and suffered from "destruction rage." Hermlin himself, then eighty-one years old, argued that one had to distinguish between the good, helpful lies of communists and the evil, destructive lies of anticommunists.[16] The controversy not only hurt Hermlin's political and literary reputation, but also underscored how veteran communists' biographies, the texts of their lives, continued to be highly politicized even after 1989.[17]

In a measure of the new political situation, once-honored veteran communists were denigrated, but those once disgraced were now celebrated. Those longtime communists who had been purged by the SED regime saw a positive reinterpretation of their biographies. They came to represent "good" communists who had been wronged by a vengeful party. In November 1989 and the months thereafter, the SED / PDS rehabilitated numerous longtime communists—including Robert Havemann, Rudolf Herrnstadt, Walter Janka, and Karl Schirdewan—who had been purged in earlier decades. For those veteran communists who were still alive, these rehabilitations were very meaningful; in the appendix to his memoirs, for example, Schirdewan even published a copy of the letter from the SED / PDS informing him of his rehabilitation.[18] Moreover, Schirdewan and Janka, who was also still alive, were now celebrated in the news media and in many public forums. At a public lecture in February 1995, the present author saw how Schirdewan was greeted with thunderous and long-lasting applause; the audience clearly wished to show its respect for a man who had stood up to the SED dictatorship. Feted as failed East German communist reformers, Schirdewan and Janka now symbolized alternative socialist roads that the GDR had not taken. This was, perhaps, somewhat undeserved. Both men had long supported and practiced the Marxist-Leninist politics of their party. Furthermore, the evidence linking Schirdewan in particular to an alternative socialism at the time of his purge is skimpy at best. But there is no question that both men were treated abominably by a party to which they had given their all. For this reason alone, they deserved the respect and attention lavished on them after the end of SED rule.

A HALF decade after the fall of the Berlin Wall, I set out to interview Karl Schirdewan and other surviving Old Communists. I wanted to know how veteran communists had made sense of their long political lives, their lost illusions, and their all too ready compromises with party dictatorship. In all, I spoke with over twenty veteran communists, often for hours, occasionally with long follow-up interviews. Frequently surprised by the topic of my research, longtime communists invariably had two questions. Why would anyone in the United States study East German veteran communists? And why would anyone interest themselves in a collective biography of Old Communists that stretched into the postwar period, that is, *after* the struggle against Nazism, the heroic age of German communism?

With a few exceptions, all of the interviews took place in veteran communists' homes in or around Berlin. Only two of those I interviewed, Kurt Hager and Alfred Neumann, had moved since 1989; both of these longtime Politburo members used to live in Wandlitz. Hager now lived in a smallish apartment near Potsdamer Platz, while Neumann occupied a fifty-seven-square-meter (or so he told me) apartment in Friedrichshain. Anxious to keep his living costs down, Neumann had no telephone and turned on the lights only when we were in semi-darkness. Many other longtime communists lived in residential Pankow, near the Hohenschönhausen Palace, the first seat of the East German government, or on the former Stalin Avenue, now Karl Marx Avenue, in the grand apartment complexes built by workers who were among the initiators of the June 1953 Uprising.

Typically, veteran communists lived in drab apartment buildings with dingy entrance hallways and stairwells that, surprisingly, opened up into roomy, comfortable apartments. Overstuffed with 1950s furniture, books, and knickknacks, their living rooms reflected the stolid socialist taste for wooly-brown and pale-green upholstery as well as their inhabitants' penchant for never throwing anything away. Fred Müller, a jack-of-all-trades functionary, took me into a room that he called his study. It might better, however, be described as his private museum of communist trophies. The bookshelves were lined with photo albums of informal snapshots of himself with Wilhelm Pieck, Walter Ulbricht and Erich Honecker; medals awarded for long service in the German workers' movement; and countless souvenirs from trips with GDR delegations to socialist or Third World countries. The petite-bourgeois furnishings of their homes reiterated the fundamental transformation that veteran communists had undergone during their lifetimes: these once proletarian revolutionaries had become established members of a Soviet-style socialist elite.

Longtime communists were brilliant evaders of questions. In some cases, seeming non sequiturs or rambling on unrelated topics may have been attributed to old age (by definition Old Communists had to be at least seventy-eight in 1994). All too often, however, longtime communists deliberately avoided what they considered to be taboo subjects. Accustomed to propagandizing the "antifascist struggle" against Hitler, many switched into storytelling mode and once again retold their favorite anecdotes of the pre-1945 period. Only an abrupt change of subject could return the interviewee to the postwar era. Harking back to their days of illegality, longtime communists frequently adopted an air of conspiratorial silence, suggesting a deeper knowledge of an issue, yet adamant in refusing to share information. Questions concerning the purges of the 1950s or political contestation in the highest party echelons inevitably clashed with their longtime commitment to maintaining secrecy on internal party matters. When pressed for particulars, they would respond "no names"; communist taboos persisted well after the denouement of the Cold War.

I visited Karl Schirdewan in December 1994. By this time, Schirdewan was getting old. He told numerous anecdotes that he had just published in his memoirs. It was also virtually impossible to pin him down on the particulars of his reform plans in 1956–1958. Schirdewan interpreted East German history through the lens of a deep chasm between former Soviet émigrés and former concentration-camp inmates. According to Schirdewan, the SED had been led astray by the "left sectarianism" of Ulbricht and other former Soviet émigrés. Had those like himself with concentration-camp pasts been in power, Schirdewan implied, things would have been very different in the GDR. Schirdewan had neither a feeling of guilt nor a sense of responsibility for what had taken place in the state that he had helped found and, for a time, rule. He had done his best, even though he had not been successful; he repeatedly emphasized the "honesty" *(Ehrlichkeit)* of the life that he had lived. Although Schirdewan was clearly critical of the SED regime, he nonetheless defended the GDR. Indeed, he was much more exercised by the modalities of German unification than the shortcomings of the East German regime. There had been, he reminded me, much that was good about the GDR—particularly its social welfare policies. Schirdewan was both personally engaging and historically unconvincing.[19]

Although Gerhart Eisler had died in 1968, Hilde Eisler, his widow, was still alive in 1995. Hilde herself had joined the KPD in 1931. In the GDR, she spent twenty-five years as editor in chief of *Das Magazin*. Widely viewed as one of the most popular and liberal GDR periodicals, *Das Magazin* was particularly known for its nude photographs of women. Eisler, a petite woman, greeted me in her Karl Marx Avenue apartment in an orange sweater and blue slacks. She immediately let me know that I was about the one hundred fiftieth person to come speak with her, and insisted that she could not possibly understand what was interesting about my topic. But she then turned to what interested her: her newfound Jewish identity. Eisler's parents and sister were murdered in the Holocaust and Eisler, as she now noted, had been a Jew before she was a communist. After 1989, Eisler had become active in the Jewish Cultural Association. As she said, after the *Wende* ("turn around," as the 1989 revolution was frequently called), a number of longtime party members had come to the Jewish Cultural Association; this was true even though most had not thought about their Jewish roots for decades. In Eisler's words, the Jewish Cultural Association was "also a community." Like Eisler, some veteran communists now found solace in a secular form of the religion they had once rejected. This was, perhaps, one way to address the disappointment of a lifetime spent in the service of a now shattered ideal.

Although Eisler voiced criticism of the GDR regime, she was scathing in her views on the united Germany. She was dismayed by the poverty, homelessness, and other social problems that now plagued the former East Germany. When asked what had been best about the GDR, Eisler replied that it was the ban on expressing "racist and anti-Semitic ideas." She was clearly horrified by the outbreaks of neo-Nazi violence that occurred after 1989. For Eisler, the *"verordneter Antifaschismus"* (decreed antifascism) of the GDR was infinitely "better than the anti-antifascism" of the united Germany.[20] Eisler remained a member of the PDS until her death, at the age of eighty-eight, in October 2000; she chose to be buried, however, not with Gerhart Eisler in the Memorial Cemetery for Socialists in Berlin-Friedrichsfelde, but in the Jewish Cemetery in Berlin-Weißensee.

Virtually all of the Old Communists whom I interviewed—including Schirdewan and Eisler—continued to maintain the official SED line, although somewhat tempered, on the major events of East German history. Most argued that although GDR workers had legitimate reasons for going on strike in June 1953, the West was nonetheless deeply involved in the Uprising. As Müller said, June 17 was not directed by "the enemies," but "the enemies were on the ball, they don't sleep."[21] Most Old Communists also agreed on the necessity of building the Berlin Wall in 1961. The majority would have agreed with Paul Wandel, Central Committee secretary of culture and pedagogy in the 1950s, that "I was for it" because it was a "necessity," although some, like Hager, claimed that "I [merely] accepted it."[22] Veteran communist opinion, however, diverged on the Prague Spring of 1968. Jakob Segal, a biophysicist, argued that this "was the first attempt to destroy socialism in [Czechoslovakia]," and Ernst Hoffmann, a former historian at the Humboldt University, labeled the Prague Spring "simply counterrevolution" directed by West Germany.[23] Other Old Communists viewed the Prague Spring more positively. Karl Schirdewan described how he "sat and trembled" and, a nonsmoker, even began smoking because he was so excited by the ongoing events. He believed that "if it had been successful, everything would have turned out very differently."[24] Max Kahane, a journalist, expressed surprise when told that not all longtime communists shared his view that the Prague Spring offered a beacon of hope for sclerotic socialism.[25]

For longtime communists, socialism as an ideology and political practice was not to blame for the defects of the East German system. Instead, the Cold War headed the list of Old Communist bogeymen. As though convinced younger individuals could not fathom the intensity of this drawn-out struggle, Neumann asked me straight out: "Do you remember the Cold War?"[26] According to veteran communists, the Cold War compelled the socialist countries to invest their resources in an unproductive arms race and forced the GDR to adopt harsh measures against its domestic enemies. Some Old Communists, such as the author Jan Koplowitz, also argued that the Cold War kept them from oppositional activities; such activity, they reasoned, would have been exploited by the West German "enemy."[27] Blaming the Cold War squared well with veteran communists' siege mentality. Surrounded by bitter enemies, beleaguered communist states, rather like longtime communists during the Nazi era, battled for survival in a hostile world. At the same time, veteran communists blamed the Soviet Union for the deformities found in East German socialism. This was particularly true for the purges of the early 1950s; many longtime communists, still adhering to the official SED line, attributed these purges solely to the machinations of Lavrenti Beria, Stalin's security man. The Soviet Union was also charged with creating the economic pitfalls that had plagued the East German economy, whether by forcing the GDR into the Comecon division of labor or by controlling the flow of raw materials into the GDR. Although the communist tenet that the Soviet Union could do no wrong had persisted for decades, Old Communists seemed to have had little difficulty in jettisoning this dogma. Indeed, a subtle pride that the GDR could "do" socialism better than the Soviet Union shined through the wizened features of these German communists.

According to Old Communists, the SED leadership, and particularly Erich Honecker, helped undermine East Germany. In this context, Walter Ulbricht had enjoyed a striking rehabilitation. Although many veteran communists personally suffered under Ulbricht's rule, they now grudgingly admired his political tenacity and often argued that he was the best leader the SED could muster given communist losses during the Nazi period. Not so with Erich Honecker. Neumann characterized Honecker as "a cowardly dog," Max Kahane described him as "a very limited man," and Hilde Eisler suggested that his position as general secretary was "five shoe sizes too big for him."[28] Old Communists shared the commonly held view that Honecker had lost touch with reality and was uninterested in the true state of the GDR economy. They did not care, however, to broach the subject of just how it was that an individual such as Honecker came to be SED leader. Nor did they care to entertain the contradiction between Marxist-Leninist theory and the historical role they ascribed to individuals such as Honecker and, in explaining 1989, Gorbachev.

Quick to point out their own upstanding conduct during the GDR years, Old Communists displayed little sense of personal blame or responsibility for the political system they served so long. They insisted that all talk of privileges was hopelessly overblown; Alfred Neumann even quipped, "We had the privilege of long working hours."[29] Speaking of veteran communists in general, Walter Kresse, a former lord mayor of Leipzig, insisted several times during an interview: "We did our duty, we didn't go easy on ourselves."[30] In response to questions about how they acted when they perceived injustices or disagreed with SED policy, Old Communists claimed that they spoke up at SED party meetings; discussed the matter with the responsible SED officials; or wrote letters, that generally went unanswered, to the SED leadership. They often related anecdotes about how they intervened on this or that issue, for this or that individual. Kurt Goldstein, an Auschwitz survivor and radio journalist, claimed to practice "thinking aloud," that is, voicing doubts and raising objections at official meetings.[31] At the same time, some now felt that they could, or perhaps should, have spoken out more forcefully on certain issues. In some cases, they suggested that as veteran communists they were in a position to criticize SED policies without fear of reprisal, particularly in the last decades of SED rule. In most cases, however, longtime communists pointed out that had they voiced criticism, they would have been expelled from the party or, at the very least, found themselves alone in their critical views.

Veteran communists frequently claimed that they simply had not known what was going on in East Germany. Over and over again, they insisted that they had not known about the widescale arrests of old comrades, former SPD members, or other individuals. Several said they had been unaware of the extent of Stasi surveillance of GDR society. Both those who had, and those who had not, been in Soviet emigration said that they had not known the breadth of Stalin's crimes before 1956. Many also claimed unfamiliarity with the dissident ideas of Robert Havemann. Old Communists suggested that their professional work had left them little time to learn about the down sides of GDR life; they had, they claimed, "worked day and night."

When asked what they had found disappointing in the GDR, some longtime communists hemmed and hawed. More often, however, they mentioned empty store shelves, the lack of travel freedom, the aging leadership, GDR dependence on the Soviet Union, and frequently, the fact that Ulbricht had privileged former Nazis who had been reeducated in Soviet prisoner-of-war camps. *"Mangel an Demokratie"* (lack of democracy) was occasionally cited, as was the lack of "spiritual freedom." Although Old Communists generally stated that East Germany had not been the society that they had struggled for during the Nazi period, it had nonetheless been a worthwhile "experiment that unfortunately went astray." They remained proud of East German achievements, particularly the widely cast social-welfare net. Indeed, when asked what had been best about the GDR, they always pointed to the educational system, free health care, universal day care, right-to-work legislation, and low prices for basic necessities. Mention of low East German rents was invariably coupled with a statement about skyrocketing rents since 1990: Neumann's rent had jumped from 49 East German marks to 490 DM, that of Arthur Mannbar, a journalist, from 105 marks to 600 DM, and so on.[32]

Most veteran communists admitted that they had been surprised by the fall of the GDR. When I inadvertently called 1989 a "revolution," Neumann bellowed "Girl, Girl, that was no revolution—that was a counterrevolutionary uprising."[33] Unlike Neumann, however, most veteran communists recognized that the East German population had had legitimate grievances by the fall of 1989. But in explaining the collapse of the GDR, they tended toward conspiracy theory, influenced perhaps by their decades-long preoccupation with Nazi or Western agents infiltrating the world communist movement. Most chalked up the GDR's demise to Gorbachev's "dropping" of East Germany. Hager believed that Gorbachev had carried out an intentional project of destroying the Soviet Union, a project whose beginnings lay in Khrushchev's denigration of Stalin in 1956.[34] Müller argued that Gorbachev acted as he did because he "wanted to create a new world order" in which he would become "vice-president of the world."[35] Neumann believed that Honecker betrayed the GDR because he had been susceptible to Western blackmail; the West, he claimed, knew of Honecker's compromising statements to the Gestapo during his time in Nazi prison.[36] Kresse suggested that 1989 had been "organized," although when asked who or what had "organized" the collapse of the GDR, Kresse could only answer: "I'd like to know exactly that."[37] He nonetheless intimated that the West had somehow been involved in the organization of the now-famous Monday demonstrations in Leipzig. Most veteran communists believed that the SED's fatal mistake was the opening of the Berlin Wall, after which events could no longer be controlled. They also thought that the GDR was "sold under price" in 1990; negotiators should have been able to command better terms for East Germans in the unified Germany.

Old Communists perceived a grim future for Germany and the world. They voiced concern about Germany's emergence as the strong man of Europe, often pointing to its role in the Yugoslav debacle. They spoke apocalyptically about the need to improve the environment and to redistribute wealth between rich and poor nations. Although outraged by the poor economic situation of many East Germans after 1989, most veteran communists, like Hager, said "I grew up in capitalism . . . I know what it's like" to explain why they were unsurprised by the negative consequences of capitalism in the former GDR.[38] In this connection, they argued that the GDR had forced West Germany to maintain and expand its welfare services; with East Germany gone, Germany now had free rein to dismantle its social welfare system.

My interviews always concluded on a warm and friendly tone, often fostered by the bourgeois German tradition of mid-afternoon *Kaffee und Kuchen* (coffee and cake) and its accompanying small talk. Occasionally, I was presented with little gifts as a memento of my visit. Neumann whipped out a miniature, red-leather-bound copy of the *Communist Manifesto;* with the perennial paper shortage in the GDR, such tiny books were popular East German souvenirs. Other Old Communists gave me copies of books or articles in which they were discussed, or recent speeches or articles so that I could immerse myself more deeply in their current views. The interviews frequently ended on a personal note when my subjects questioned me about family and plans for the future. They always wished me well and "much success" in my project. Once militantly aggressive in socialist triumph, Old Communists were warmly gracious in political defeat.

THE LIVES of those veteran communists featured in this book—Emmy Koenen, Gerhart Eisler, Karl Schirdewan, Fritz Selbmann, Fred Oelßner, Franz Dahlem, Walter Ulbricht, and Erich Honecker—are broadly representative of the twentieth-century German communist experience. But each biography also illustrates particular aspects of that experience. Emmy Koenen, for example, led a life that was typical for longtime women communists. In an overwhelmingly masculine party culture, female KPD members were marginalized from the Weimar era onward. Emmy was relegated to "women's work" in Weimar Germany and in postwar East Germany. In addition, Emmy was typical of longtime communists who emigrated abroad during the Nazi era. Her experiences in the Soviet Union during the Great Purges did not lead her to question communism. And her emigration to England did not temper her militantly negative views on capitalism and bourgeois democracy. In the postwar period, her career was linked to that of her husband, Wilhelm Koenen. Although Emmy briefly headed the DFD, she and Wilhelm both lost influence once West émigrés came under attack in 1949. Thereafter, she held unimportant posts. She died in 1987. More than anything else, Emmy's life suggests the marginal position that women occupied in the German communist movement. Despite a lifetime of sacrifice for the cause, Emmy Koenen was never more than a foot soldier in the army of German communism.

Gerhart Eisler's position in the German communist movement was hampered from the start by three shortcomings: he was intellectual, bourgeois, and of Jewish descent. He soon added several more: he was Ruth Fischer's brother, he belonged to the "reconciler" faction in the late 1920s, and he eventually emigrated to the United States. Eisler's trajectory, although uncommonly dramatic, was also typical of KPD cadres with his background. Like so many communists of Jewish origin, Eisler neither practiced Judaism nor otherwise identified with the religion of his ancestors. But his life was nonetheless fundamentally marked by his Jewish descent. Forced to flee Nazi-occupied Europe in 1941, Eisler found refuge in the United States. There, in the opening act of the Cold War, he was accused of Soviet espionage; he just barely—and only by sheer wit—avoided a multiyear term in American prisons. Once in East Germany, Eisler, like so many other former West émigrés, was no more "liberal," "tolerant," or "reform-minded" than veteran communists with other biographical backgrounds. But as a West émigré of Jewish origin, he was nonetheless purged in the early 1950s. Eisler's trajectory also illustrates the predicament of intellectuals in communist parties. Always viewed with some suspicion, intellectuals bent over backward to profess their loyalty to the communist cause. In the process, however, they compromised their calling. As party intellectuals, they might have raised the conscience of their movement; as party hacks, they merely earned some deserved scorn. Although Gerhart Eisler set out to better the world, the movement he chose got the better of him. This charismatic veteran revolutionary nonetheless added sparkle to the often lackluster annals of German communism.

Karl Schirdewan and Fritz Selbmann, old comrades in arms from Sachsenhausen and Flossenbürg concentration camps, lived the quintessential German communist experience. Arrested and imprisoned by Nazi authorities, these longtime communists survived Hitler's camps by dint of KPD solidarity. Rather than undermining their communist faith and Stalinist proclivities, the experience of Nazi persecution deepened these cadres' party loyalty and broadened their practice of Stalinist politics. In the first postwar decade, both men worked hard to implement Soviet-style communism in East Germany; there is little indication that these survivors of Nazi captivity advocated anything but the party line imported from Moscow. In the 1950s, however, both men ran afoul of Walter Ulbricht.

Although Karl Schirdewan was courageous in his opposition to Ulbricht, he did not realize that Ulbricht's style of rule was a product not only of the man, but more importantly, of the communist system. Based on the available documentary evidence, had Schirdewan successfully ousted Ulbricht, he might have relaxed some of the first secretary's hard-line policies, but he hardly would have introduced a more "democratic" or "human" socialism; at the time, this was beyond his political imagination. Despite the wrongs visited upon him in 1958, Schirdewan refused to abandon the SED regime. Some thirty-two years later, after the fall of the Berlin Wall, he saw his communist career vindicated: he not only enjoyed an official rehabilitation, but also received much attention as an erstwhile rival to Ulbricht. Three decades on the margins of the SED dictatorship had led Schirdewan to reconsider the politics of the party for which he had once sacrificed so much. In December 1989, he heard an SED / PDS politician, Michael Schumann, declare at an extraordinary Party Congress: "We will irrevocably break with Stalinism as a system." This, Schirdewan later wrote in his memoirs, "accorded with a conviction that I had held for decades."[39] In July 1998, this veteran communist passed away at age ninety-one. As he aptly titled his last set of memoirs, Karl Schirdewan had truly lived "A Century-Long Life" *(Ein Jahrhundert Leben)*.

Fritz Selbmann's party career suggests the hard knocks that the communist movement delivered to its most loyal cadres. During the postwar years, Selbmann was investigated for past biographical infractions in 1945, censured for shortcomings in his work with EKO in 1952, purged for all matter of personal and professional failings in 1958, and refused posthumous publication of his postwar memoirs in the 1970s. A gruff man, Selbmann was known to both work and play hard; he was unable to control his pride and arrogance; and he had a penchant for speaking out and making himself heard. Selbmann did have a softer side, though; with considerable literary talent, he was able to sensitively convey his past experiences in autobiographical and other writings. Selbmann was

always something of an odd man out in a party that valued personal ab-
negation and individual subordination. He could not, however, imagine
a life without the party. In his altercations with the KPD / SED, Selbmann
always swallowed his pride and persevered in his party loyalty. This
could not have been easy. According to his son, Erich, Selbmann and
Franz Dahlem exchanged letters in which they wrote of disappointments
with their socialist regime. Selbmann was often "angry" and "sad" that
things were not better with GDR socialism. But as Erich Selbmann suggested, for his father, the GDR was his state and the "best of the possible."[40] Fritz Selbmann died of lung cancer in 1975. Like all the other veteran communists featured in these pages who passed away before 1989,
he was buried in the cemetery at the Memorial for Socialists.

Fred Oelßner belies the stereotypical notion that former émigrés to the
Soviet Union were cowed apparatchiks who never challenged their communist leaders. His career also suggests that some former Soviet émigrés
had difficult trajectories in the GDR; they, too, suffered their share of career and other setbacks. Anton Ackermann and Rudolf Herrnstadt, both
former Soviet émigrés, also defied Ulbricht and had difficult careers in
East Germany. In the late 1960s, too, Ulbricht himself challenged his Soviet superiors—and found himself ousted from his position. Precisely because they had survived the Great Purges, these former émigrés to the
Soviet Union may have felt more confident than other party members in
voicing their views or otherwise challenging their superiors; after all, at
a time when longtime KPD members were carefully scrutinized, these
communists had passed muster with Soviet authorities. But as with all
veteran communists, there were limits to how far these longtime communists would go in defying their regime. Oelßner left a remarkable paper trail (in the form of notes taken during Politburo meetings) indicating his opposition to both Ulbricht's policies and dictatorial ways. But
although he vehemently criticized Ulbricht in Politburo meetings in the
1950s, Oelßner refused to do so in public or semipublic forums. Like so
many other veteran communists, Oelßner sacrificed principled opposition to political opportunism. Anxious to preserve his career, Oelßner
turned on other critics of Ulbricht in 1953. And once under political attack in 1958, he, like virtually all veteran communists, bowed to his
party's judgment and practiced self-criticism. After a long career as a
party ideologist, Fred Oelßner died in 1977.

Franz Dahlem was a communist survivor. From the late 1920s until
1953, he was at the pinnacle of KPD / SED power. Dahlem saw it all: factional battles in the Weimar-era KPD, émigré political squabbling, the
Spanish Civil War, internment in French camps, and imprisonment in

Nazi jails and concentration camps. Until he was purged in 1953, Dahlem, as one of the SED's top leaders, imposed Soviet-style communism in East Germany. To survive both Nazism and Stalinism, Dahlem was often hardbitten, harddriven, and hardhearted. But survive he did. By the end of his life, as he frequently reminded others, he was the sole remaining member of Thälmann's Politburo. Although Dahlem knew all too well the injustices perpetrated by his party, he nonetheless maintained his loyalty to the SED and even participated in the regime's further wrongs. After his downfall, for example, he denounced Karl Schirdewan at a Central Committee meeting in 1958. He also had little sympathy for those who criticized East Germany from a socialist perspective; in 1976, he was scathing in his opinion of Wolf Biermann, the singer-songwriter expatriated from the GDR. But Dahlem always maintained a degree of decency. Virtually alone among veteran communists, he tried to intervene on behalf of other purged comrades. He also kept up with those in political disgrace; his correspondence contains numerous letters to and from persona non grata. And through his memoir project, he helped to publicly rehabilitate many former purge victims. Franz Dahlem died in December 1981—just shy of his ninetieth birthday. He and his life capture the tragedy of the German communist experience: although veteran German communists suffered enormous injustices and personal deprivation, they nonetheless created and upheld a regime that itself proved repressive and profoundly unjust.

Walter Ulbricht and Erich Honecker represent the face of Old Communist rule in East Germany. Both men drew on their experiences in the pre-1945 KPD during their long years in power in East Germany. Ulbricht brought a hard-edged Stalinism to the GDR. During the late 1940s and 1950s he deployed a regime of terror against the East German population—as well as against veteran communists. He zealously transformed the GDR into a Soviet satellite state: industry was nationalized, agriculture collectivized, political opposition muted, security organs expanded, educational institutions brought into line. All of this resulted in many East Germans voting "with their feet"; between 1945 and 1961, East Germany saw almost three and a half million inhabitants depart to West Germany.[41] In 1961, Ulbricht had the Berlin Wall built, an act that allowed the SED to consolidate its rule. Thereafter, drawing on a veteran communist tradition of avant-gardism, he attempted to make the GDR *the* model socialist society. In the process, however, he rode roughshod over some Old Communist political tenets. In response, Erich Honecker spearheaded a successful veteran-communist coup against Ulbricht. Under Honecker, the GDR saw a reassertion of more traditional practices of communist rule as well as a renewed emphasis on the past antifascist struggle. Harking back to some old KPD goals, Honecker also made a concerted effort to raise the living standard of all East Germans. But his vision of the good society remained rooted in Weimar-era expectations, the modalities of his antifascist struggle grounded in Nazi-era battles. By the 1980s, this worldview had become positively anachronistic. In East Germany, 1989 was a revolution not only against Soviet-style socialism, but also against Old Communist rule.

VETERAN GERMAN communists have a historical significance that ranges well beyond their individual lives. They are crucial for an understanding of East German history. The GDR was, in fact, an Old Communist regime. From 1945 until October 1989 veteran communists ruled East Germany according to their political vision. They infused the SED with a political culture that they had learned as young communists enamored by Soviet-style communism. Many of the most salient values of the regime were veteran-communist values: paternalism, antifascism, class struggle, and even a pronounced masculinity. Longtime communists also introduced to East German politics Soviet political practices that they had followed since joining the KPD: the purges of real or alleged opponents, the enforcement of an unswerving party discipline, the secrecy of political decision-making, and an uncompromising rigidity in adhering to set policies. Their political agenda was and remained rooted in their experiences as longtime KPD cadres. The obsession with providing basic needs at very low prices, for example, was a response to the communist experience of the Depression in the early 1930s. And the SED's insistence on maintaining sharp Cold War divisions—between East and West Germany, between the socialist and capitalist worlds—reflected the protracted war that veteran communists had waged since their Weimar days against what they saw as fascist oppression.

Although this political vision had often served persecuted communists in Weimar and Nazi Germany well, this was not true in the postwar GDR. The vision was strikingly inappropriate for a regime that wished to create a prosperous socialist society in what was fast becoming the information age. Moreover, by education and temperament, most longtime communists were singularly unsuited to manage a complex modern society. All of their efforts notwithstanding, they were often not up to the task of running institutes, factories, or party or state bureaucracies. The SED gradually retired many Old Communists and replaced them with younger, better-educated cadres. But veteran communists remained at the center of SED power—and proved very mediocre rulers. Even Walter

Ulbricht did not belong to the most impressive ranks of twentieth-century communist leaders; as Jürgen Kuczynski once noted, Ulbricht was a "first rate second class man."[42] And although even the wisest leader probably could not have salvaged East German socialism, Erich Honecker was directly responsible for the GDR's fiscal irresponsibility and many of its other shortcomings.

Veteran German communists believed in a creed of liberation, but implemented a regime of oppression. In the hierarchy of twentieth-century criminal regimes, the GDR occupies a rather low rung; it did not engage in war, genocide, or colonial or other forms of foreign exploitation. But it was nonetheless fundamentally repressive. In the immediate postwar period, longtime communists condoned Soviet military rule in Eastern Germany; at the very least, the Soviet military government imprisoned some 122,671 Germans in the first postwar years—42,889 of whom died.[43] The SED regime itself was far less brutal. Over the decades, however, veteran communists countenanced the arrest and imprisonment of hundreds of thousands of alleged political opponents, as well as the politically motivated murder of some hundreds of East Germans.

Beyond these obvious crimes, longtime communists condoned numerous other wrongs in the GDR. They accepted the most bizarre of Stalinist practices, the claiming of truth in impossible fictions. They assented to the absence of democracy, the silencing of regime critics, severe travel restrictions, and widespread surveillance of the GDR population. At East Germany's various border installations, they countenanced the shooting of those eager to flee the GDR. And they accepted the Wall's heart-wrenching division of families—parents from children, brothers from sisters, grandparents from grandchildren. Finally, they upheld a regime that sharply curtailed the life trajectories of its subjects. Perhaps more than anything else, the East German population represented countless life opportunities that had been lost: careers not pursued, studies not undertaken, books not written, travels not taken. Even though the GDR was "only" a rather old-fashioned police state (authoritarian it was, murderous it was not), it nonetheless caused great suffering for millions of East Germans.

Despite the repressive conditions that veteran communists implemented, East Germany was a remarkably stable regime: there were no outbursts of popular unrest after the June Uprising in 1953, and no inner party conflicts after the ouster of the "Schirdewan Group" in 1958. Coercion—or the threat thereof—certainly played a role in this stability. As the Berlin Wall suggested, veteran communists were willing to resort to force to uphold their regime. But the stability of East Germany was also rooted in other factors. For one, veteran communists practiced a staunch party discipline. They did what their party demanded—with few questions asked. As Fritz Selbmann told the Central Committee in 1958: "You can believe me . . . if it were demanded, I would hack myself to pieces for the party."[44] This party discipline was widely imitated by younger SED functionaries. At the same time, East German generational dynamics fostered the regime's stability. Since functionaries of the Hitler Youth generation held a genuine regard for the past antifascist exploits of veteran communists, they did not challenge their older comrades.

In one of the many ironies of history, the very dynamics that helped stabilize the SED regime also undermined it. Veteran communists and their antifascist agenda were never replaced by younger leaders with new ideas to reinvigorate GDR socialism. Many younger East Germans thus found the GDR and its veteran-communist agenda at best unappealing— and at worst appalling. By 1989, even many SED functionaries had lost whatever revolutionary enthusiasm they might once have had. As the end of the regime was fast approaching, Mielke mused: "In our day, in the avant-garde of the KPD, we worked day and night, Saturday, Sunday. That's what's needed today. Now people have cars, go their own way. They can't be bothered with us, they tell us they just want their peace and quiet. But the enemy is always active."[45] In the Stasi chief's view, the party avant-garde had gone soft; functionaries were unwilling to sacrifice their creature comforts for the socialist struggle. Veteran communists had failed to transmit both their revolutionary ardor and the importance of the antifascist effort to younger East Germans. Mielke and other veteran communists had good reason to mourn the loss of revolutionary zeal. Once veteran communist authority had fallen away in the autumn of 1989, there was no one left to uphold the unpopular SED regime. In a matter of months, the GDR crumbled.

ALTHOUGH VETERAN communists are pivotal for understanding East German history, their lives are also paradigmatic of the twentieth-century communist experience. Indeed, their collective biography actually mirrors the trajectory of European communism: a youth of charismatic resistance and revolution, a midlife of authoritarian bureaucracy, and an old age of decay and loss. The stages of this trajectory are, of course, inextricably linked. In the German case, pre-1933 KPD cadres made sacrifices and deployed survival strategies in the Weimar and Nazi periods that toughened these fervent revolutionaries. When they finally came to power in East Germany, they brought an inflexible mind-set that found reflection in an authoritarian, bureaucratic form of rule. This kind of rule, however, was unable to respond to the changing demands of the times. It thus brought on a long twilight of communist decay, eventually followed by the loss of power.

All national communist movements that came to power saw a similar trajectory, but the German case is unusual in that it was a single generation of cadres that accompanied the rise and fall of the movement. Pre-1933 KPD cadres rode all the waves and crests of German communism: the formation of the party, the Stalinization of the KPD, the underground struggle in Hitler's Germany, survival abroad or in Nazi concentration camps, victory on the coattails of Soviet armies, the institutionalization and routinization of communist rule in the GDR, the spiral of East German decline, and finally, the fall of the SED regime. And it did not end there: veteran German communists also lived through the progressive delegitimation of the GDR and its rulers in the years after German unification.

The historian Charles Maier has written that "human life in the first half of the twentieth century has been repeatedly hammered on the anvil of politics."[46] This is perhaps especially true of veteran German communists. Longtime communists came of political age during the interwar years, when political ideologies not only gave meaning to the upheavals of the times, but also fundamentally dictated life choices. For Old Communists, their politics of choice had a profound influence on their fortunes—in both the first and second halves of this century. Communism proved a "Via Dolorosa," but it was a path of sorrows paved with paradox.[47] No twentieth-century political movement demanded more of its members, yet treated its own so cruelly. No movement was more difficult to belong to, yet incurred such loyalty among its own. By the time longtime KPD members had reached East Germany, they had, as communists, spent years as pariahs of the German nation. Yet while they had suffered mightily for their political convictions during the Weimar and Nazi eras, their reward was all too often suspicion and mistrust in the new socialist state. In the GDR, they saw their past antifascist lives mercilessly distorted. They were arrested as foreign agents or enemies of the people when nothing was further from the truth. They were accused of factional activity when none had existed. And their dearest memories were distorted to serve not their own ends, but their regime's.

Despite the wrongs that their movement visited upon them, veteran KPD members retained an almost unshakable faith in communism. This is, perhaps, the most peculiar aspect of the veteran-communist experience. In the postwar era, remarkably few longtime communists left the SED. Although some came to think somewhat critically about the GDR—

particularly those like Karl Schirdewan who had been purged in the 1950s—they neither disavowed communism nor rejected the SED regime. For longtime communists, the party was the priesthood of their secular faith; it was all-knowing, all-consuming, and all-giving. To harm, challenge, or leave that body was beyond the ken of the vast majority of veteran communists. Communism was their raison d'être; to break with their faith would have dissolved the master narrative of their lives into countless meaningless episodes. Moreover, even when they had suffered setbacks in the GDR, veteran communists felt comfortable in the provincial, petite-bourgeois milieu they had created. Martin Hellberg, a longtime communist actor and director who suffered his share of career disappointments in the GDR, was once asked if he wished to visit Frankfurt am Main, the city of his birth. Quoting Goethe, Hellberg reportedly replied: "Where I fare well, that is my homeland."[48] For Hellberg and other longtime communists, the GDR was indeed their homeland. In contrast to their position in Weimar Germany, not to speak of in Nazi Germany, East German Old Communists commanded public awe and admiration, respect and reverence. For communists who had long been viewed as outcasts of the German nation, this suggested that History, however imperfect, was still on their side.

Veteran communists belonged to an era in which political ideologies could inspire a lifetime of political commitment. They became true believers in communism at a time when Marxism provided seemingly compelling answers to the great questions of the day. Their Marxist belief sustained them through the better part of a century of political turmoil. The pathos of their lives suggests the sacrifices that they were willing to make for a political faith that they believed would solve the ills of the world. As it turned out, however, veteran communists found not an egalitarian utopia, but "really existing socialism" in East Germany. Resting on their revolutionary laurels, they succumbed to the twin forces of complacency and party discipline. In the end, veteran German communists embodied the contradictory legacy of their movement. They served a political ideology that promised liberation, but that ultimately delivered disappointment and suffering—not least of all to its veteran revolutionaries.

NOTES / ACKNOWLEDGMENTS / INDEX

NOTES

ABBREVIATIONS

The following abbreviations for archives are used in the notes.

AdK   Stiftung Archiv der Akademie der Künste (Archive of the
               Academy of Arts)
BA   Bundesarchiv, Berlin
BStU MfSZ   Bundesbeauftragte für die Unterlagen des
               Staatssicherheitsdienstes der ehemaligen Deutschen
               Demokratischen Republik, Ministerium für Staatssicherheit
               Zentralarchiv (Central Archives of the Ministry of State
               Security)
HIA   Hoover Institution Archives
SAPMO-BArch   Stiftung Archiv der Parteien und Massenorganisationen der
               Deutschen Demokratischen Republik im Bundesarchiv
               (Foundation for the Archives of the GDR's Parties and Mass
               Organizations in the Bundesarchiv)

INTRODUCTION

1. Karl Schirdewan, interview by author, Potsdam, December 14, 1994.
2. Anne McElvoy, *The Saddled Cow: East Germany's Life and Legacy* (London: Faber & Faber, 1992), p. 25.
3. Horst Duhnke, *Die KPD von 1933 bis 1945* (Cologne: Kiepenheuer & Witsch, 1972), p. 455.
4. Among the small number of veteran communists who left the GDR were Leo Bauer, Karola Bloch, Heinz Brandt, Alfred Kantorowicz, Joseph Scholmer, and Leo Zuckermann.
5. Arnd Bauerkämper, Jürgen Danyel, and Peter Hübner, "'Funktionäre des schaffenden Volkes'?" in Arnd Bauerkämper, Jürgen Danyel, Peter Hübner, and Sabine Roß, eds., *Gesellschaft ohne Eliten? Führungsgruppen in der DDR* (Berlin: Metropol, 1997), p. 15.

6. Lutz Niethammer, "Erfahrungen und Strukturen: Prolegomena zu einer Geschichte der Gesellschaft der DDR," in Hartmut Kaelble, Jürgen Kocka, and Hartmut Zwahr, eds., *Sozialgeschichte der DDR* (Stuttgart: Klett Cotta, 1994), p. 107.

7. Dorothee Wierling, "The Hitler Youth Generation in the GDR: Insecurities, Ambitions and Dilemmas," in Konrad H. Jarausch, ed., *Dictatorship as Experience: Towards a Socio-Cultural History of the GDR* (New York: Berghahn, 1999), p. 321.

8. See, for example, Jaff Schatz, *The Generation: The Rise and Fall of the Jewish Communists of Poland* (Berkeley: University of California Press, 1991), pp. 218, 271.

9. Bauerkämper, Danyel, and Hübner, "Funktionäre," p. 45.

10. The most important works on German communism during the Weimar period are Werner T. Angress, *Stillborn Revolution: The Communist Bid for Power in Germany, 1921–1923* (Princeton, N.J.: Princeton University Press, 1963); Ossip K. Flechtheim, *Die KPD in der Weimarer Republik* (Frankfurt am Main: Europäische Verlagsanstalt, 1969); Klaus-Michael Mallmann, *Kommunisten in der Weimarer Republik: Sozialgeschichte einer revolutionären Bewegung* (Darmstadt: Wissenschaftliche Buchgesellschaft, 1996); Hermann Weber, *Die Wandlung des deutschen Kommunismus: Die Stalinisierung der KPD in der Weimarer Republik,* 2 vols. (Frankfurt am Main: Europäische Verlagsanstalt, 1969); and Eric D. Weitz, *Creating German Communism, 1890–1990: From Popular Protests to Socialist State* (Princeton, N.J.: Princeton University Press, 1997). The most important study of the KPD during the Nazi era remains Duhnke, *Die KPD.*

11. As does Mallmann, *Kommunisten.*

12. Although Weitz's excellent study spans the century, it nonetheless concentrates heavily on the Weimar period. See Weitz, *Creating.*

13. On conflict within the highest leadership bodies, see Peter Grieder, *The East German Leadership, 1946–73: Conflict and Crisis* (Manchester, Eng.: Manchester University Press, 1999); on conflict within the SED rank and file, see, for example, Gareth Pritchard, *The Making of the GDR, 1945–53: From Antifascism to Stalinism* (Manchester, Eng.: Manchester University Press, 2000); and on grassroots conflict, see, for example, Mark Allinson, *Politics and Popular Opinion in East Germany, 1945–68* (Manchester, Eng.: Manchester University Press, 2000); Armin Mitter and Stefan Wolle, *Untergang auf Raten: Unbekannte Kapitel der DDR-Geschichte* (Munich: Bertelsmann, 1993); and Corey Ross, *Constructing Socialism at the Grass-Roots: The Transformation of East Germany, 1945–65* (New York: St. Martin's Press, 2000).

14. See Grieder, *East German Leadership.*

15. For an extended discussion of this theme, see Catherine Epstein, "The Politics of Biography: The Case of East German Old Communists," *Daedalus* 128, no. 2 (1999): 1–30.

16. For a general treatment of Old Communists based on a sample of 907 veteran communists, see Catherine Epstein, "The Last Revolutionaries: The

Old Communists of East Germany, 1945–1989," Ph.D. diss., Harvard University, 1998.

17. Since 1989, a number of important works on Ulbricht have appeared. See Mario Frank, *Walter Ulbricht: Eine deutsche Biografie* (Berlin: Siedler, 2001); Monika Kaiser, *Machtwechsel von Ulbricht zu Honecker: Funktionsmechanismen der SED-Diktatur in Konfliktsituationen 1962 bis 1972* (Berlin: Akademie, 1997); and Norbert Podewin, *Walter Ulbricht: Eine neue Biographie* (Berlin: Dietz, 1995). To date, Honecker has not received similar scholarly attention. Although there is one post-1989 biography of Honecker, it does not draw on new archival sources. See Jan N. Lorenzen, *Erich Honecker: Eine Biographie* (Reinbek: Rowohlt, 2001).

18. On the KPD in postwar West Germany, see Patrick Major, *The Death of the KPD: Communism and Anti-Communism in West Germany* (Oxford, Eng.: Oxford University Press, 1997).

19. For two important exceptions, see Schatz, *Generation;* and Robert Levy, *Ana Pauker: The Rise and Fall of a Jewish Communist* (Berkeley: University of California Press, 2001).

1. OUTCASTS

1. Franz Dahlem, *Jugendjahre: Vom katholischen Arbeiterjungen zum proletarischen Revolutionär* (Berlin: Dietz, 1982), pp. 45–48, 71–72.

2. Ibid., p. 198.

3. Guenther Roth, *The Social Democrats in Imperial Germany: A Study in Working-Class Isolation and National Integration* (Totowa, N.J.: Bedminster Press, 1963), pp. 8–9.

4. Dahlem, *Jugendjahre*, p. 261.

5. Ibid., pp. 379–380.

6. Ibid., p. 558.

7. Ibid., p. 560.

8. Ibid., p. 793.

9. Norbert Podewin, *Walter Ulbricht: Eine neue Biographie* (Berlin: Dietz, 1995), p. 38.

10. Ibid., p. 38.

11. Mario Frank, *Walter Ulbricht: Eine deutsche Biografie* (Berlin: Siedler, 2001), p. 58.

12. Hermann Duncker to Käte Duncker, December 18, 1919, SAPMO-BArch, NY 4445/143, p. 208.

13. Hermann Duncker to Käte Duncker, May 2, 1919, SAPMO-BArch, NY 4445/142, p. 69.

14. Hermann Duncker to Käte Duncker, May 14, 1921, SAPMO-BArch, NY 4445/145, p. 127.

15. Hermann Weber, *Die Wandlung des deutschen Kommunismus: Die Stalinisierung der KPD in der Weimarer Republik* (Frankfurt am Main: Europäische Verlagsanstalt, 1969), vol. 1, p. 320. These prison sentences reached a combined total of more than four thousand years.

16. Podewin, *Walter Ulbricht,* p. 60.
17. Ossip Flechtheim, *Die KPD in der Weimarer Republik* (Frankfurt am Main: Europäische Verlagsanstalt, 1969), p. 347.
18. Klaus-Michael Mallmann, *Kommunisten in der Weimarer Republik: Sozialgeschichte einer revolutionären Bewegung* (Darmstadt: Wissenschaftliche Buchgesellschaft, 1996), p. 87.
19. Dahlem's words are quoted in Carola Stern, *Ulbricht: A Political Biography* (London: Pall Mall Press, 1965), p. 29, fn.
20. Gerhart Eisler, "Biografie des Genossen Eisler," July 13, 1951, SAPMO-BArch, DY30/IV 2/11/v 749, p. 104.
21. Ibid., p. 104.
22. Mallmann, *Kommunisten,* p. 101.
23. Weber, *Wandlung,* vol. 2, p. 51.
24. Edmund Silberner, *Kommunisten zur Judenfrage: Zur Geschichte von Theorie und Praxis des Kommunismus* (Opladen: Westdeutscher Verlag, 1983), pp. 265–274.
25. This number represents less than 8 percent of the 907 longtime East German communists documented in Catherine Epstein, "The Last Revolutionaries: The Old Communists of East Germany, 1945–1989," Ph.D. diss., Harvard University, 1998.
26. Gerhart Eisler, "Kurzbiographie," January 17, 1960, SAPMO-BArch, DY30/IV 2/11/v 749, p. 49.
27. Hede Massing, *This Deception* (New York: Duell, Sloan, and Pearce, 1951), p. 57.
28. Ruth Fischer and Arkadij Maslow, *Abtrünnig wider Willen: Aus Briefen und Manuskripten des Exils,* ed. Peter Lübbe (Munich: Oldenbourg, 1990), p. 32.
29. Hermann Weber, ed., *Der deutsche Kommunismus: Dokumente* (Cologne: Kiepenheuer & Witsch, 1966), p. 185.
30. Podewin, *Walter Ulbricht,* p. 95.
31. Eric D. Weitz, *Creating German Communism, 1890–1990: From Popular Protests to Socialist State* (Princeton, N.J.: Princeton University Press, 1997), p. 233.
32. Massing, *This Deception,* p. 52.
33. Weitz, *Creating,* p. 267.
34. Mallmann, *Kommunisten,* pp. 18–19.
35. Manfred Engelhardt, ed., *Deutsche Lebensläufe: Gespräche* (Berlin: Aufbau, 1991), p. 45.
36. Ruth Werner, *Sonjas Rapport* (Berlin: Neues Leben, 1977). Translated by Renate Simpson as *Sonya's Report* (London: Chatto & Windus, 1991).
37. See Bernd Kaufmann, Eckhard Reisener, Dieter Schwips, and Henri Walther, *Der Nachrichtendienst der KPD, 1919–1937* (Berlin: Dietz, 1993).
38. F. W. Deakin and G. R. Storry, *The Case of Richard Sorge* (New York: Harper & Row, 1966), p. 89.
39. Ralph de Toledano, *Spies, Dupes, and Diplomats* (New York: Duell, Sloan, and Pearce, 1952), p. 43.

40. "Eisler's Sister Tells of Split in Political Views," SAPMO-BArch, NY 4117/8.

41. Hearing of the House Un-American Activities Committee, 80th Cong., February 6, 1947, 80 H1127–2, p. 47.

42. Arthur Koestler, *The Invisible Writing: An Autobiography* (New York: Macmillan, 1954), p. 40.

43. Fritz Selbmann, *Alternative—Bilanz—Credo: Versuch einer Selbstdarstellung* (Halle: Mitteldeutscher Verlag, 1969).

44. Ibid., p. 40.

45. Ibid., p. 55.

46. Ibid., p. 86.

47. Ibid., p. 110.

48. Ibid., p. 137.

49. Weitz, *Creating*, p. 196.

50. Arnd Bauerkämper, Jürgen Danyel, and Peter Hübner, "'Funktionäre des schaffenden Volkes'?" in Arnd Bauerkämper, Jürgen Danyel, Peter Hübner, and Sabine Roß, eds., *Gesellschaft ohne Eliten? Führungsgruppen in der DDR* (Berlin: Metropol, 1997), p. 72.

51. Selbmann, *Alternative*, p. 163.

52. Ibid., p. 152.

53. Ibid., p. 195.

54. Dahlem, *Jugendjahre*, p. 756.

55. Ibid., p. 798.

56. Massing, *This Deception*, p. 31.

57. Mallmann, *Kommunisten*, pp. 131–133.

58. Michael Rohrwasser, *Saubere Mädel, Starke Genossen: Proletarische Massenliteratur?* (Frankfurt am Main: Roter Stern, 1975), p. 9.

59. Weitz, *Creating*, p. 205.

60. Ibid., p. 211.

61. See Babette Gross, *Willi Münzenberg: Eine politische Biographie* (Stuttgart: Deutsche Verlags-Anstalt, 1967), p. 44.

62. Weber, *Wandlung*, vol. 2, p. 26.

63. Emmy Koenen, "Lebenslauf," January 17, 1969, SAPMO-BArch, SgY30 1308/1, pp. 1–6.

64. Emmy Koenen, "Erinnerungen an die Reichsparteischule 'Rosa Luxemburg' der KPD 1932/1933," SAPMO-BArch, ZPA, NY 4074/300, p. 93.

65. Fred Oelßner, "Fahrt nach Moskau," *AZ* (Aachen), April 28, 1926, SAPMO-BArch, NY 4125/14.

66. Fred Oelßner, "Das Zentralhaus der Bauern in Moskau," *AZ* (Aachen), May 22, 1926, SAPMO-BArch, NY 4125/14.

67. Fred Oelßner, "Schuhfabrik Sturmvogel," *AZ* (Aachen), June 2, 1926, SAPMO-BArch, NY 4125/14.

68. Fred Oelßner, "Mit Budjonnie bei der Roten Kavallerie," *AZ* (Aachen), July 8, 1926, SAPMO-BArch, NY 4125/14.

69. Selbmann, *Alternative*, p. 177.

70. Frank, *Walter Ulbricht*, p. 80.

71. Peter Erler, Horst Laude, and Manfred Wilke, eds., *"Nach Hitler kommen wir":*

Dokumente zur Programmatik der Moskauer KPD-Führung 1944/45 für Nachkriegsdeutschland (Berlin: Akademie, 1994), p. 411.

72. Franz Dahlem, "Politische Orientierung im Gestapo-Gefängnis, Prinz Albrechtstraße Berlin und Parteiarbeit im Konzentrationslager Mauthausen," SAPMO-BArch, DY30/IV 2/4/373, p. 84.

73. Götz Aly, "Der Jahrhundertprozeß: Erich Mielke, die Morde auf dem Berliner Bülowplatz und die deutsche Strafjustiz," in Christian Jansen, Lutz Niethammer, and Bernd Weisbrod, eds., *Von der Aufgabe der Freiheit: Politische Verantwortung und bürgerliche Gesellschaft im 19. und 20. Jahrhundert; Festschrift für Hans Mommsen zum 5. November 1995* (Berlin: Akademie, 1995), pp. 559–560.

74. Remarks by Emmy Koenen, SAPMO-BArch, NY 4074/300, p. 112.

75. Karl Schirdewan, *Ein Jahrhundert Leben: Erinnerungen und Visionen* (Berlin: edition ost, 1998), p. 31.

76. For a discussion of generational cohorts in the Weimar-era KPD, see Mallmann, *Kommunisten,* pp. 106–118. On the "Lost" Generation, see Detlev Peukert, "The Lost Generation: Youth Unemployment at the End of the Weimar Republic," in Richard J. Evans and Dick Geary, eds., *The German Unemployed: Experiences and Consequences of Mass Unemployment from the Weimar Republic to the Third Reich* (London: Croom Helm, 1987), pp. 172–192. In my sample of 907 longtime East German communists, 24.4 percent belonged to the Front Generation born between 1890 and 1899 and 62.3 percent to the Lost Generation born between 1900 and 1914. Of the sample, 5.3 percent were born before 1890, 2.5 percent in 1915 and 1916. See Epstein, "Last Revolutionaries," p. 43, fn. 15.

77. Schirdewan, *Ein Jahrhundert Leben,* p. 35.

78. Mallmann, *Kommunisten,* p. 189.

79. Dietrich Orlow, *A History of Modern Germany: 1871 to Present* (Upper Saddle River, N.J.: Prentice Hall, 1999), p. 150.

80. Mallmann, *Kommunisten,* p. 87.

81. The 1927 statistic is from Eva Cornelia Schöck, *Arbeitslosigkeit und Rationalisierung: Die Lage der Arbeiter und die kommunistische Gewerkschaftspolitik, 1920–28* (Frankfurt am Main: Campus, 1977), p. 108; the 1930 data are found in Conan Fischer, *The German Communists and the Rise of Nazism* (Houndsmills, Eng.: Macmillan, 1991), p. 132.

82. Ruth Fischer, *Stalin and German Communism: A Study in the Origins of the State Party* (New Brunswick, N.J.: Transaction Books, 1982), p. 504; and Weber, *Wandlung,* vol. 1, pp. 191, 350, and vol. 2, p. 6.

83. Mallmann, *Kommunisten,* p. 147.

84. For an extended discussion of this process see Weitz, *Creating,* pp. 160–187.

85. Schirdewan, *Ein Jahrhundert Leben,* p. 82.

86. Erich Honecker, *Aus meinem Leben* (Berlin: Dietz, 1981), p. 12.

87. Ibid., p. 24.

88. Ibid., p. 36.

89. Ibid., p. 41.

90. Ibid., p. 58.

91. Benedict Anderson, *Imagined Communities: Reflections on the Origin and Spread of Nationalism*, rev. ed. (London: Verso, 1991), p. 6.
92. Mallmann, *Kommunisten*, p. 89.
93. Mallmann estimates that "significantly under 100,000" communists made up the loyal core of the KPD during the Weimar era. Ibid., p. 93.

2. PERSECUTED

1. Emmy Koenen-Damerius, "Erinnerungen an die Reichsparteischule 'Rosa-Luxemburg' der KPD 1932/1933," August 1, 1976, SAPMO-BArch, NY 4074/300, p. 96.
2. Fred Oelßner, "Erinnerungen an die Rosa-Luxemburg-Schule," February 14, 1977, SAPMO-BArch, SgY30 1333, pp. 80–81.
3. Koenen-Damerius, "Erinnerungen," p. 96.
4. Fritz Selbmann, *Alternative—Bilanz—Credo: Versuch einer Selbstdarstellung* (Halle: Mitteldeutscher Verlag, 1969), pp. 218–219.
5. Precise figures for the number of communists arrested in 1933 are unavailable. In any event, many of those arrested were released by year's end. Horst Duhnke, *Die KPD von 1933 bis 1945* (Cologne: Kiepenheuer & Witsch, 1972), p. 101, n. 1.
6. Karl Schirdewan, *Ein Jahrhundert Leben: Erinnerungen und Visionen* (Berlin: edition ost, 1998), pp. 85–86.
7. Ibid., p. 98.
8. Ibid., p. 87.
9. Ibid., p. 100.
10. Dieter Borkowski, *Erich Honecker: Statthalter Moskaus oder deutscher Patriot? Eine Biographie* (Munich: Bertelsmann, 1987), p. 84.
11. Erich Honecker, *Aus meinem Leben* (Berlin: Dietz, 1981), p. 80.
12. Ibid., p. 85.
13. Selbmann, *Alternative*, p. 225.
14. Schirdewan, *Ein Jahrhundert Leben*, p. 119.
15. Honecker, *Aus meinem Leben*, pp. 91–92.
16. See Peter Przybylski, *Tatort Politbüro*, vol. 1: *Die Akte Honecker* (Berlin: Rowohlt, 1991), pp. 48–50. For a contrasting view, see Jan N. Lorenzen, *Erich Honecker: Eine Biographie* (Reinbek: Rowohlt, 2001), pp. 32–35. For Honecker's own account, see Reinhold Andert and Wolfgang Herzberg, *Der Sturz: Erich Honecker im Kreuzverhör* (Berlin: Aufbau, 1990), pp. 163–171; Honecker, *Aus meinem Leben*, pp. 91–107; Erich Honecker, *Erich Honecker zu dramatischen Ereignissen* (Hamburg: Runge, 1992), pp. 65–71; and Erich Honecker, *Moabiter Notizen: Letztes schriftliches Zeugnis und Gesprächsprotokolle vom BRD-Besuch 1987 aus dem persönlichen Besitz Erich Honeckers* (Berlin: edition ost, 1994), pp. 99–100.
17. Fritz Selbmann, "Politische Arbeit von 1933–1945," SAPMO-BArch, DY30/IV 2/11/v 1984, p. 182.
18. Fritz Selbmann to Käte M., January 1, 1934, SAPMO-BArch, NY 4113/1, pp. 98–100.

19. Selbmann, *Alternative,* p. 227.
20. Emmy Koenen, "Illegale Frauenarbeit der KPD in Berlin im Jahre 1933," February 1969, SAPMO-BArch, NY 4074/300, pp. 1–10.
21. Emmy Koenen, "Lebenslauf," January 17, 1969, SAPMO-BArch, SgY30 1308/1, pp. 8–9.
22. Koenen, "Illegale Frauenarbeit," pp. 5–6.
23. Letters from Käte Duncker to Hermann Duncker, March through October 1933, SAPMO-BArch, NY 4445/150.
24. Schirdewan, *Ein Jahrhundert Leben,* p. 26.
25. More precise figures are unavailable. Tischler estimates that there were 4,000 to 5,000 German communists in the Soviet Union in the mid-1930s. See Carola Tischler, *Flucht in die Verfolgung: Deutsche Emigranten im sowjetischen Exil 1933 bis 1945* (Münster: Lit, 1996), pp. 108, 227. Of my sample of 907 longtime communists in East Germany, 121 veteran KPD members had spent the better part of the Nazi era in Soviet emigration. See Catherine Epstein, "The Last Revolutionaries: The Old Communists of East Germany, 1945–1989," Ph.D. diss., Harvard University, 1998, p. 102.
26. Precise figures for the numbers of KPD members murdered in Stalin's purges are unavailable. Tischler states that over 70 percent of KPD members in the Soviet Union were under arrest in April 1938 and suggests that this would have involved "just under 3,000 persons." Tischler, *Flucht,* p. 108. Some of those arrested, however, survived the purges.
27. See Fridrich I. Firsow, "Die 'Säuberungen' im Apparat der Komintern," in Hermann Weber and Dietrich Staritz, eds., *Kommunisten verfolgen Kommunisten: Stalinistischer Terror und "Säuberungen" in den kommunistischen Parteien Europas seit den dreißiger Jahren* (Berlin: Akademie, 1993), p. 45; and Georg Lukács, Johannes R. Becher, Friedrich Wolf, et al., *Die Säuberung: Moskau 1936; Stenogramm einer geschlossenen Parteiversammlung,* ed. Reinhard Müller (Reinbek: Rowohlt, 1991).
28. Emmy Koenen, "Die wahre neue Welt der Arbeiter," in Institut für Marxismus-Leninismus beim ZK der SED, ed., *Im Zeichen des roten Sterns: Erinnerungen an die Traditionen der deutsch-sowjetischen Freundschaft* (Berlin: Dietz, 1974), p. 251.
29. Emmy Koenen, "Erinnerungen II: Freunde und Genossen, die verschollen sind," 1970–1971, SAPMO-BArch, SgY30 1308/1, pp. 187–188.
30. Ibid., pp. 184–187.
31. Fred Oelßner to the SED, Kreisleitung Treptow, January 30, 1965, SAPMO-BArch, NY 4215/11, pp. 67–68.
32. Fred Oelßner, "Lebenslauf," January 15, 1950, SAPMO-BArch, DY30/IV 2/11/v 2562.
33. Norbert Podewin, *Walter Ulbricht: Eine neue Biographie* (Berlin: Dietz, 1995), p. 134.
34. Helmut Damerius, *Unter falscher Anschuldigung: 18 Jahre in Taiga und Steppe* (Berlin: Aufbau, 1990), p. 40.
35. Ibid., p. 113.
36. Ibid., pp. 214–216.

37. Ibid., pp. 243–244.

38. Helmut Damerius to Arthur Pieck, March 19, 1956, SAPMO-BArch, DY30/IV 2/11/v 4225.

39. Gustav Sobottka to Dimitov, Manuilsky, and Pieck, December 22, 1939, SAPMO-BArch, NY 4008/13.

40. Gustav Sobottka to Molotov, February 14, 1940, SAPMO-BArch, NY 4008/13.

41. Emmy Koenen, "Erinnerungen I: Studium und Arbeit in Moskau 1934–1936," 1970–1971, SAPMO-BArch, SgY30 1308/1, pp. 177–178.

42. Koenen, "Lebenslauf," p. 10.

43. Duhnke, *KPD*, p. 251.

44. On the Comintern investigation of Ulbricht, see Mario Frank, *Walter Ulbricht: Eine deutsche Biografie* (Berlin: Siedler, 2001), pp. 133–144.

45. Patrik v. zur Mühlen, *Spanien war ihre Hoffnung: Die deutsche Linke im Spanischen Bürgerkrieg, 1936 bis 1939* (Berlin: Verlag Neue Gesellschaft, 1983), pp. 13, 228.

46. In my sample of 907 longtime communists in East Germany, some 121 (or 13 percent) had participated somehow in the Spanish Civil War. See Epstein, "Last Revolutionaries," p. 65.

47. Walter Janka, *Spuren eines Lebens* (Berlin: Rowohlt, 1991), p. 88.

48. Franz Dahlem to "Liebe Freunde," August 24, 1937, SAPMO-BArch, NY 4072/207, pp. 54–55.

49. V. zur Mühlen, *Spanien*, pp. 155–156.

50. Duhnke, *KPD*, p. 279.

51. Franz Dahlem, "Aus der Entwicklung der internationalen Brigaden," Report to the Comintern, March 28, 1938, SAPMO-BArch, NY 4072/207, p. 97.

52. Heinrich Rau to Ruth Rewald, November 25, 1937, BA, N 2235/5, p. 5.

53. Dahlem, "Aus der Entwicklung," pp. 96, 83.

54. Gerhart Eisler, "Bericht von Gerhart Eisler," SAPMO-BArch, DY30/IV 2/4/ 155, pp. 26–28.

55. Heinrich Rau to Ruth Rewald, April 15, 1937, BA, N 2235/5, p. 20.

56. Heinz Roth (the pseudonym of Heinz Hoffmann) to Käthe Dahlem, November 17, 1937, SAPMO-BArch, NY 4072/155, p. 15.

57. Franz Dahlem, *Am Vorabend des zweiten Weltkrieges: 1938 bis August 1939; Erinnerungen,* 2 vols. (Berlin: Dietz, 1977).

58. Franz Dahlem, "Nachgelassenes: Ausgelassenes; Über einen Prozeß und die Schwierigkeiten seiner richtigen Beurteilung," *Beiträge zur Geschichte der Arbeiterbewegung* 32, no. 1 (1990): 18–21.

59. Dahlem, *Am Vorabend,* vol. 1, p. 139.

60. Eisler, "Bericht," pp. 28–29.

61. Hilde Eisler, "Nachwort," to Gerhart Eisler, *Auf der Hauptstraße der Weltgeschichte: Artikel, Reden und Kommentare 1956–1968* (Berlin: Dietz, 1981), p. 384.

62. Dahlem, *Am Vorabend,* vol. 1, p. 362.

63. Grete Keilson, "Wiedergabe der mündlich von ihr gegebenen Informationen," October 11, 1972, SAPMO-BArch, NY 4072/146, p. 45.

64. Dahlem, *Am Vorabend,* vol. 2, p. 357.

65. Heinrich Rau to Helene Rau, August 23, 1939, SAPMO-BArch, NY 4062/146, p. 23.
66. Hermann Duncker to Käte Duncker, August 24, 1939, SAPMO-BArch, NY 4445/151, p. 152.
67. Hermann Duncker to Käte Duncker, September 29, 1939, SAPMO-BArch, NY 4445/151, p. 173.
68. Dahlem, *Am Vorabend,* vol. 2, pp. 396, 414–415.
69. Wilhelm Pieck, "Stellungnahme des ZK der KPD," August 12, 1940, SAPMO-BArch, DY30/J IV 2/202/4.

3. SURVIVORS

1. Horst Duhnke, *Die KPD von 1933 bis 1945* (Cologne: Kiepenheuer & Witsch, 1972), p. 525.
2. Karl Schirdewan, *Aufstand gegen Ulbricht: Im Kampf um politische Kurskorrektur, gegen stalinistische, dogmatische Politik* (Berlin: Aufbau, 1994), p. 27; and Heinz Brandt, *Ein Traum, der nicht entführbar ist: Mein Weg zwischen Ost und West* (Frankfurt am Main: Fischer, 1985), pp. 184–185.
3. Scholars who argue that Western emigration influenced German communists to adopt less Stalinist viewpoints include Duhnke, *Die KPD,* p. 455; Wolfgang Kießling, *Partner im "Narrenparadies": Der Freundeskreis um Noel Field und Paul Merker* (Berlin: Dietz, 1994), p. 211; Judith Marschall, *Aufrechter Gang im DDR-Sozialismus: Walter Janka und der Aufbau-Verlag* (Münster: Westfälisches Dampfboot, 1994), pp. 30–31; and Eric D. Weitz, *Creating German Communism, 1890–1990: From Popular Protests to Socialist State* (Princeton, N.J.: Princeton University Press, 1997), pp. 306–307. In his autobiography, Janka also made this argument. See Walter Janka, *Spuren eines Lebens* (Berlin: Rowohlt, 1991), pp. 191, 198–201.
4. Karl Schirdewan, *Ein Jahrhundert Leben: Erinnerungen und Visionen* (Berlin: edition ost, 1998), pp. 145–146.
5. Fritz Selbmann, *Alternative—Bilanz—Credo: Versuch einer Selbstdarstellung* (Halle: Mitteldeutscher Verlag, 1969), p. 308.
6. Schirdewan, *Ein Jahrhundert Leben,* pp. 146.
7. Quoted from Hermann Langbein, *Against All Hope: Resistance in the Nazi Concentration Camps* (New York: Paragon House, 1994), p. 112.
8. Selbmann, *Alternative,* pp. 331–338.
9. Karl Schirdewan, "Zur Sache des Genossen Selbmann," August 28, 1945, SAPMO-BArch, DY30/IV 2/11/v 1984, p. 207.
10. Fritz Selbmann, "Politische Arbeit von 1933–1945," SAPMO-BArch, DY30/IV 2/11/v 1984, p. 183.
11. Selbmann, *Alternative,* p. 359.
12. On communist Kapos in Buchenwald, see Lutz Niethammer, ed., *Der "gesäuberte" Antifaschismus: Die SED und die roten Kapos von Buchenwald* (Berlin: Akademie, 1994).
13. Schirdewan, *Ein Jahrhundert Leben,* p. 166.
14. Selbmann, *Alternative,* p. 311.

15. Schirdewan, *Ein Jahrhundert Leben,* p. 153.
16. Niethammer notes the "exceptional success of the KPD as a survival community." Niethammer, *Der "gesäuberte" Antifaschismus,* p. 45.
17. Schirdewan, *Ein Jahrhundert Leben,* p. 175.
18. Ibid., p. 177.
19. Selbmann, "Politische Arbeit," p. 183.
20. Schirdewan, *Ein Jahrhundert Leben,* p. 181. See also Selbmann, *Alternative,* p. 367.
21. Selbmann, *Alternative,* p. 368.
22. Franz Dahlem, "Politische Orientierung im Gestapo-Gefängnis, Prinz Albrechtstraße Berlin und Parteiarbeit im Konzentrationslager Mauthausen," June 11, 1945, SAPMO-BArch, DY30/IV 2/4/373, p. 91.
23. Ibid., pp. 97–99.
24. Ibid., pp. 102–103.
25. Ibid., p. 105.
26. Ibid., pp. 113–116.
27. Erich Honecker, *Aus meinem Leben* (Berlin: Dietz, 1981), pp. 95–96.
28. Ibid., p. 96.
29. Heinz Lippmann, *Honecker: Porträt eines Nachfolgers* (Cologne: Verlag Wissenschaft und Politik, 1971), p. 40; and Dieter Borkowski, *Erich Honecker: Statthalter Moskaus oder deutscher Patriot? Eine Biographie* (Munich: Bertelsmann, 1987), pp. 106–107.
30. See Honecker, *Aus meinem Leben,* p. 106; and Borkowski, *Erich Honecker,* p. 129.
31. Alan L. Nothnagle, *Building the East German Myth: Historical Mythology and Youth Propaganda in the German Democratic Republic, 1945–1989* (Ann Arbor: University of Michigan Press, 1999), p. 125.
32. For similar arguments, see Arnd Bauerkämper, Jürgen Danyel, and Peter Hübner, "'Funktionäre des schaffenden Volkes'?" in Arnd Bauerkämper, Jürgen Danyel, Peter Hübner, and Sabine Roß, eds., *Gesellschaft ohne Eliten? Führungsgruppen in der DDR* (Berlin: Metropol, 1997), p. 74; and Niethammer, *Der "gesäuberte" Antifaschismus,* p. 145.
33. Hermann Weber, "Im Dschungel der Wolfsgesellschaft," *Die Zeit* (Hamburg), November 4, 1994, p. 19; and Niethammer, *Der "gesäuberte" Antifaschismus,* p. 30.
34. Hannah Arendt, *The Origins of Totalitarianism* (1951; reprint, New York: Harcourt Brace Jovanovich, 1973), p. 450.
35. Jean Améry, *Jenseits von Schuld und Sühne: Bewältigungsversuche eines Überwältigten* (Munich: Szczesny, 1966), pp. 27–28.
36. Bruno Bettelheim, *Surviving and Other Essays* (London: Thames & Hudson, 1979), pp. 56, 74–75.
37. Jeffrey Herf, *Divided Memory: The Nazi Past in the Two Germanys* (Cambridge, Mass.: Harvard University Press, 1997), p. 80.
38. Duhnke, *KPD,* pp. 370–373.
39. Ibid., p. 376.
40. Ibid., p. 392.

41. Peter Erler, Horst Laude, and Manfred Wilke, eds., *"Nach Hitler kommen wir":* *Dokumente zur Programmatik der Moskauer KPD-Führung 1944/45 für* *Nachkriegsdeutschland* (Berlin: Akademie, 1994), pp. 411, 133.

42. Mario Frank, *Walter Ulbricht: Eine deutsche Biografie* (Berlin: Siedler, 2001), p. 174.

43. Erler, Laude, and Wilke, *"Nach Hitler,"* pp. 82–83.

44. See ibid.

45. Norbert Podewin, *Walter Ulbricht: Eine neue Biographie* (Berlin: Dietz, 1995), p. 155.

46. In my sample of 907 longtime East German communists, 182 found themselves in Western emigration (synonymous with *not* being in the Soviet Union or Nazi Germany). Of these, 46 found refuge in Great Britain, 23 in Mexico, 20 in Switzerland, 18 in the United States, 17 in Sweden, and 5 in China, including Shanghai. And 34 longtime German communists spent these years in France—either in internment camps or in illegal resistance activity in southern France. The remaining communists were scattered all across the globe. German communists found their way back to East Germany from Algeria (1 individual), Argentina (1), Bolivia (1), Brazil (1), Colombia (1), Cuba (1), Denmark (3), India (1), Italy (1), Palestine (2), Spain (1), and Turkey (1). It should be noted that this sample represents only a fraction of all longtime German communists who emigrated to Western countries; it is, however, representative of influential longtime German communists in East Germany. See Catherine Epstein, "The Last Revolutionaries: The Old Communists of East Germany, 1945–1989," Ph.D. diss., Harvard University, 1998, pp. 67–68.

47. As Alexander Stephan has documented, government agencies engaged in massive surveillance operations against left-wing German-speaking writers in exile in the United States during the Nazi era. See Alexander Stephan, *"Communazis:" FBI Surveillance of German Emigré Writers* (New Haven: Yale University Press, 2000).

48. See Duhnke, *KPD,* p. 455; Kießling, *Partner,* p. 211; Marshall, *Aufrechter Gang,* pp. 30–31; Weitz, *Creating,* pp. 306–307; and Janka, *Spuren,* pp. 191, 198–201.

49. Emmy Koenen, "Zum antifaschistischen Kampf der KPD in der CSR," SAPMO-BArch, SgY30 1308/2, p. 5.

50. Ibid., pp. 5, 23.

51. Ibid., p. 19.

52. Ibid., p. 25.

53. Emmy Koenen, "Lebenslauf: Emmy Koenen," SAPMO-BArch, SgY30 1308/1, p. 12.

54. Emmy Koenen, "Exil in England," *Beiträge zur Geschichte der Arbeiterbewegung* 20, no. 4 (1978): 540.

55. Koenen, "Lebenslauf," p. 11.

56. Koenen, "Exil in England," p. 550.

57. Anthony Glees, "The German Political Exile in London, 1939–1945," in

Gerhard Hirschfeld, ed., *Exile in Great Britain: Refugees from Hitler's Germany* (Leamington Spa: Berg, 1984), p. 92.

58. At least 94 individuals—about half of all "West émigrés" in my sample of 907 longtime East German communists—were interned in Western countries between 1940 and 1945. See Epstein, "Last Revolutionaries," p. 68.

59. Koenen, "Exil in England," p. 552.

60. Emmy Koenen, "Exil in England: Leben und Kampf im Frauenlager," *Beiträge zur Geschichte der Arbeiterbewegung* 20, no. 6 (1978): 884.

61. Ibid., p. 891.

62. Koenen, "Exil in England," p. 561.

63. Koenen, "Exil in England: Leben und Kampf," pp. 893, 895.

64. Lieselotte Maas, "Paul Merker und die Exildiskussion um Deutschlands Schuld, Verantwortung und Zukunft," *Beiträge zur Geschichte der Arbeiterbewegung* 32, no. 2 (1990): 155.

65. On Merker's politics in Mexico, see Herf, *Divided Memory,* pp. 40–68.

66. Marschall, *Aufrechter Gang,* p. 27.

67. Alexander Abusch, "Ergänzungen zu meinem Bericht über die innerparteilichen Gruppierungen in Mexiko," March 25, 1953, SAPMO-BArch, DY30/IV 2/11/v 5250, p. 179.

68. Steffie Spira, *Trab der Schaukelpferde: Autobiographie* (Berlin: Aufbau, 1984; reprint, Freiburg im Breisgau: Kore, 1991), pp. 229–231 (page citations are to reprint edition).

69. Hearing of the House Un-American Activities Committee (HUAC), 80th Cong., 1st sess., February 6, 1947, 80 H1127–2, pp. 4–10.

70. Gerhart Eisler, Albert Norden, and Albert Schreiner, *The Lesson of Germany: A Guide to Her History* (New York: International Publishers, 1945).

71. Gerhart Eisler, "Bericht von Gerhart Eisler," April 16, 1953, SAPMO-BArch, DY30/IV 2/4/155, pp. 38–40.

72. Ellen Schrecker, *Many Are the Crimes: McCarthyism in America* (Boston: Little, Brown, 1998), pp. 125, 127.

73. "Communists," *Time,* October 28, 1946, p. 29.

74. Hilde Eisler, "Leben mit dem FBI," 1946, SAPMO-BArch, NY 4072/176, pp. 243–244.

75. Carol King to the Federal Bureau of Investigation, October 29, 1946, SAPMO-BArch, NY 4117/7, pp. 23–24.

76. HUAC, p. 42.

77. Ibid., pp. 42, 45.

78. Ruth Fischer and Arkadij Maslow, *Abtrünnig wider Willen: Aus Briefen und Manuskripten des Exils,* ed. Peter Lübbe (Munich: Oldenbourg, 1990), pp. 160, 31.

79. F. K. Kaul to Verlag Librairie Droz, November 15, 1966; and memorandum signed by H. Wieland, October 19, 1966, SAPMO-BArch, DY30/IV 2/11/v 749, pp. 31–33.

80. HUAC, pp. 31, 54, 48.

81. Ibid., p. 35.

82. Roger Morris, *Richard Milhous Nixon: The Rise of an American Politician* (New York: Henry Holt, 1990), pp. 344–345.
83. Schrecker, *Many Are the Crimes,* p. 127.
84. "Mr. Eisler on Bail," *New York Times,* April 28, 1947, p. 22.
85. Schrecker, *Many Are the Crimes,* p. 128.
86. Statement before Judge Morris, undated, SAPMO-BArch, NY 4117/7, p. 129.
87. Schrecker, *Many Are the Crimes,* p. 129.
88. Gerhart Eisler to Hanns and Lou Eisler, February 22, 1949, AdK, Hanns-Eisler-Archiv, folder 67.
89. Gerhart Eisler to Paul Merker, December 26, 1947, SAPMO-BArch, NY 4036/662, p. 244.
90. Vorschlag für die Einleitung einer Kampagne zur Befreiung des Gen. Gerhart Eisler, February 23, 1947, SAPMO-BArch, NY 4036/662, pp. 241–242.
91. Wilhelm Pieck to Vladimir Semenov, February 24, 1947, SAPMO-BArch, NY 4036/662, p. 243.
92. Rudi Feistmann to Walter Bartel, November 18, 1948, SAPMO-BArch, NY 4036/662, p. 248.
93. Wilhelm Pieck to Paul Wandel, November 20, 1948, SAPMO-BArch, NY 4036/662, p. 250.
94. Wilhelm Pieck to Gerhart Eisler, November 29, 1948, SAPMO-BArch, NY 4036/662, p. 251.
95. Eisler, "Bericht," p. 24.
96. Hubert Kay, "The Career of Gerhart Eisler as a Comintern Agent," *Life,* February 17, 1947, p. 99.
97. Schrecker, *Many Are the Crimes,* p. 122.
98. "Communists," *Time,* October 28, 1946, p. 29.
99. Schirdewan, *Aufstand,* pp. 22–23.
100. Erich W. Gniffke, *Jahre mit Ulbricht* (Cologne: Verlag Wissenschaft & Politik, 1966), p. 98.

4. VICTORS

1. Heinrich Rau to Helene Rau, May 23, 1945, SAPMO-BArch, NY 4062/146, p. 30.
2. Karl Schirdewan, *Ein Jahrhundert Leben: Erinnerungen und Visionen* (Berlin: edition ost, 1998), p. 205.
3. Willi Bredel to Maj, May 10, 1945, Willi-Bredel-Archiv, AdK, folder 3110.
4. Franz Dahlem, "Mit Wilhelm Pieck im Flugzeug zurück nach Deutschland," in *Vereint sind wir alles: Erinnerungen an die Gründung der SED* (Berlin: Dietz, 1966), p. 24.
5. Schirdewan, *Ein Jahrhundert Leben,* p. 199.
6. Fred Oelßner, "Die Anfänge unserer Parteischulung," in *Vereint,* p. 155.
7. "Aufruf der Kommunistischen Partei Deutschlands," in Hermann Weber, ed., *Der deutsche Kommunismus: Dokumente* (Cologne: Kiepenheuer & Witsch, 1963), pp. 431–438.

8. Wolfgang Leonhard, *Child of the Revolution* (Chicago: Henry Regnery, 1958), p. 381.

9. Peter Erler, Horst Laude, and Manfred Wilke, eds., *"Nach Hitler kommen wir":
Dokumente zur Programmatik der Moskauer KPD-Führung 1944/45 für
Nachkriegsdeutschland* (Berlin: Akademie, 1994), pp. 107–108.

10. Gerhard Keiderling, ed., *"Gruppe Ulbricht" in Berlin April bis Juni 1945: Von
den Vorbereitungen im Sommer 1944 bis zur Wiedergründung der KPD im Juni
1945; Eine Dokumentation* (Berlin: Arno Spitz, 1993), pp. 427, 474, 542.

11. Norman M. Naimark, *The Russians in Germany: A History of the Soviet Zone of
Occupation, 1945–1949* (Cambridge, Mass.: Harvard University Press, 1995),
pp. 254–257, 265–269; and Gareth Pritchard, *The Making of the GDR, 1945–
53: From Antifascism to Stalinism* (Manchester, Eng.: Manchester University
Press, 2000), pp. 63–65.

12. Gustav Sobottka to Wilhelm Pieck, May 30, 1945, SAPMO-BArch, NY 4036/
629, p. 85.

13. Pritchard, *Making*, p. 67.

14. In my sample of 907 veteran communists, for example, 77 of 121 longtime
communists returned from Soviet exile to the SBZ in 1945. By contrast, only
48 of 182 veteran communists exiled in Western countries—mostly those in
France and Switzerland—returned to the SBZ in 1945. See Catherine Epstein,
"The Last Revolutionaries: The Old Communists of East Germany, 1945–
1989," Ph.D. diss., Harvard University, 1998, p. 102.

15. Emmy Koenen, "Erinnerungen von Emmy Koenen-Damerius," January 15,
1969, SAPMO-BArch, SgY30 1308/1, p. 54.

16. Emmy Koenen, "Lebenslauf," January 17, 1969, SAPMO-BArch, SgY30 1308/
1, p. 13.

17. Heinz Schmidt to Franz Dahlem, May 20, 1946, SAPMO-BArch, DY30/IV 2/
11/189, p. 43.

18. Memorandum, signed Ja/cr. (Walter Janka), August 28, 1947, SAPMO-BArch,
DY30/IV 2/2.022/37, p. 138.

19. Günter Benser, "Die SED zwischen Massenpartei und Kaderpartei neuen
Typs (1946–1948)," in Dietmar Kelleret, Hans Modrow, and Herbert Wolf,
eds., *Ansichten zur Geschichte der DDR* (Bonn: PDS/Linke Liste im Deutschen
Bundestag, 1993), vol. 1, p. 87.

20. Günter Benser, "Zur sozialen und politischen Struktur der KPD und ihres
Kaders (1945/1946)," *Beiträge zur Geschichte der Arbeiterbewegung* 39, no. 4
(1997): 20.

21. The former KPD members were Anton Ackermann, Dahlem, Hermann
Matern, Paul Merker, Pieck, Elli Schmidt, and Ulbricht.

22. The longtime communists who were full members of this Politburo were
Pieck, Ulbricht, Dahlem, Matern, Oelßner, Rau, and Wilhelm Zaisser. The
Old Communists who were candidate members were Ackermann, Rudolf
Herrnstadt, Honecker, Hans Jendretzky, and Schmidt.

23. These figures do not include candidate members of the Politburo. See Peter
C. Ludz, *The Changing Party Elite in East Germany* (Cambridge, Mass.: MIT
Press, 1972), pp. 444, 446, 449.

24. Jens Gieseke, *Die hauptamtlichen Mitarbeiter der Staatssicherheit: Personalstruktur und Lebenswelt, 1950–1989/90* (Berlin: Links, 2000), pp. 94–96.

25. Anita Dasbach Mallinckrodt, *Wer macht die Außenpolitik der DDR? Apparat, Methoden, Ziele* (Düsseldorf: Droste, 1972), p. 188.

26. Ralf Kessler and Hartmut Rüdiger Peter, *Wiedergutmachung im Osten Deutschlands, 1945–1953: Grundsätzliche Diskussionen und die Praxis in Sachsen-Anhalt* (Frankfurt am Main: Peter Lang, 1996), p. 11.

27. Olaf Groehler, "Integration und Ausgrenzung von NS-Opfern," in Jürgen Kocka, ed., *Historische DDR-Forschung: Aufsätze und Studien* (Berlin: Akademie, 1993), p. 106.

28. Margarete Wittkowski, unpublished memoirs, SAPMO-BArch, SgY30 160/1, p. 8.

29. Kessler and Peter, *Wiedergutmachung*, pp. 277–279, 282–287.

30. Herta Geffke, unpublished memoirs, SAPMO-BArch, SgY30 257/1, p. 410.

31. Naimark, *Russians*, p. 302.

32. Oelßner, "Die Anfänge," p. 156.

33. Fritz Selbmann, "Erinnerungen des Genossen Fritz Selbmann," SAPMO-BArch, SgY30 1098, pp. 39–40.

34. Dahlem, "Mit Wilhelm Pieck," p. 25.

35. "Protokoll Nr. 7 der Sekretariatssitzung am 26.7.1945," in Günter Benser and Hans-Joachim Krusch, eds., *Dokumente zur Geschichte der kommunistischen Bewegung in Deutschland: Reihe 1945/1946* (Munich: K. G. Saur, 1993), vol. 1, p. 45.

36. Emmy Koenen, "Die antifaschistische Frauenarbeit in Sachsen (1946–1949)," SAPMO-BArch, SgY30 1308/1, pp. 92–93.

37. Fritz Selbmann, *Acht Jahre und ein Tag: Bilder aus den Gründerjahren der DDR* (Berlin: Neues Leben, 1999), p. 38.

38. Maria Rentmeister, unpublished memoirs, SAPMO-BArch, SgY30 1213/1, p. 108.

39. Mario Frank, *Walter Ulbricht: Eine deutsche Biografie* (Berlin: Siedler, 2001), pp. 410–412.

40. Schirdewan, *Ein Jahrhundert Leben,* pp. 213–214.

41. For the text of the memorandum, see Rainer Karlsch, "Das 'Selbmann-Memorandum' vom Mai 1947," *Beiträge zur Geschichte der Arbeiterbewegung* 35, no. 2 (1993): 107–121.

42. Selbmann, *Acht Jahre,* p. 193.

43. Ibid., p. 249.

44. FDGB-Landesvorstand Sachsen-Organisation to Colleagues Baumann, Thal, and Bauer, September 1, 1950, BStU MfSZ, Allg. P 1895/65, p. 9.

45. Müller to the Verwaltung Sachsen, Abt. III, March 3, 1952, BStU MfSZ, Allg. P 1895/65, p. 134.

46. Magnus, "Bericht," January 31, 1952, BStU MfSZ, Allg. P 1895/65, p. 82.

47. Transcript of interrogation of Fritz Selbmann, July 20, 1951, SAPMO-BArch, DY30/IV 2/11/v 1984.

48. Selbmann, *Acht Jahre,* pp. 249–253.

49. "Maßnahmen zur Verbesserung," Politburo decree, February 5, 1952, SAPMO-BArch, DY30/IV 2/2/191, pp. 13, 18.

50. See Fritz Selbmann to Walter Ulbricht, April 24, 1956, SAPMO-BArch, DY30/ J IV 2/202/4/1.

51. Walter Ulbricht to Editorial Board of *Einheit,* July 2, 1951, SAPMO-BArch, NY 4125/110, p. 2.

52. Fred Oelßner, "Erklärung zu der an meiner Arbeit auf der II. Parteikonferenz geübten Kritik," August 1, 1952, SAPMO-BArch, NY 4125/110, pp. 4–6.

53. Minutes of Politburo Meeting, August 5, 1952, SAPMO-BArch, DY30/IV 2/2/ 224, p. 4.

54. The text of Emmy's letter is found in Helmut Damerius, *Unter falscher Anschuldigung: 18 Jahre in Taiga und Steppe* (Berlin: Aufbau, 1990), pp. 286– 289.

55. The various letters and memoranda concerning Emmy Koenen's removal as chairman of the DFD are found in SAPMO-BArch, DY30/IV 2/11/v 4408.

56. Emmy Koenen, "Lebenslauf," January 17, 1969, SAPMO-BArch, SgY30 1308/ 1, pp. 14–15.

57. Gabriele Gast, *Die politische Rolle der Frau in der DDR* (Düsseldorf: Bertelsmann, 1973), p. 123.

58. Emmy Koenen to Franz Dahlem, undated note, SAPMO-BArch, NY 4072/ 178, p. 47.

59. Frank, *Walter Ulbricht,* p. 277.

60. Henry Krisch, *German Politics under Soviet Occupation* (New York: Columbia University Press, 1974), p. 54; and Hans-Joachim Krusch, "Neuansatz und widersprüchliches Erbe," *Beiträge zur Geschichte der Arbeiterbewegung* 33, no. 5 (1991): 616.

61. See endnotes to Chapter 3.

62. Siegfried Suckut, "Die Entscheidung zur Gründung der DDR: Die Protokolle der Beratungen des SED-Parteivorstandes am 4. und 9. Oktober 1949," *Vierteljahrshefte für Zeitgeschichte* 39 (1991): 161.

63. Eisler was quoted by his widow, Hilde Eisler, in a public lecture at the Institut für politische Bildung, Berlin, April 25, 1995.

64. Victor Klemperer, *"So sitze ich denn zwischen allen Stühlen,"* vol. 1: *Tagebücher, 1945–1949* (Berlin: Aufbau, 1999), p. 689.

65. Selbmann, *Acht Jahre,* pp. 170, 182–183.

66. Fritz Selbmann to Wilhelm Zaisser, January 27, 1951, BStU MfSZ, Allg. P 1895/65, p. 16.

67. Karlsch, "Das 'Selbmann-Memorandum,'" p. 96.

68. See Ulrich Mählert, "'Im Interesse unserer Sache würde ich empfehlen . . . :' Fritz Große über die Lage der SED in Sachsen, Sommer 1946," *Jahrbuch für Historische Kommunismusforschung* (1996): 215–245.

69. Ibid., p. 239.

70. Hans Lauter, interview by author, Chemnitz, July 10, 1995.

71. See Heinz Brandt, *Ein Traum, der nicht entführbar ist: Mein Weg zwischen Ost und West* (Frankfurt am Main: Fischer, 1985), p. 202; Horst Duhnke, *Stalinismus in Deutschland: Die Geschichte der sowjetischen Besatzungszone* (Cologne: Verlag für Politik und Wirtschaft, 1955), p. 215; Ernst Richert, *Das zweite Deutschland: Ein Staat, der nicht sein darf* (Frankfurt am Main: Fischer,

1966), p. 43; and Carola Stern, *Ulbricht: Eine politische Biographie* (Cologne: Kiepenheuer & Witsch, 1964), pp. 146–147.

72. Stern, *Ulbricht*, p. 125.

73. Fred Oldenburg, *Konflikt und Konfliktregelung in der Parteiführung der SED, 1945/46–1972*, Berichte des Bundesinstituts für ostwissenschaftliche und internationale Studien, no. 48 (Cologne, 1972), p. 31.

74. Carola Stern, *Porträt einer bolschewistischen Partei: Entwicklung, Funktion und Situation der SED* (Cologne: Verlag für Politik & Wirtschaft, 1957), p. 130.

75. Karl Schirdewan, *Aufstand gegen Ulbricht: Im Kampf um politische Kurskorrektur, gegen stalinistische, dogmatische Politik* (Berlin: Aufbau, 1994), p. 40.

76. Peter Grieder, *The East German Leadership, 1946–73: Conflict and Crisis* (Manchester, Eng.: Manchester University Press, 1999), pp. 32–36.

77. Wolfgang Kießling, *Partner im "Narrenparadies": Der Freundeskreis um Noel Field and Paul Merker* (Berlin: Dietz, 1994), pp. 208–212.

78. Speech by Paul Merker to the Eighteenth Party Executive Meeting, May 4–5, 1949, SAPMO-BArch, DY30/IV 2/1/63, p. 13.

79. Grieder, *East German Leadership*, pp. 25–28.

80. For an extended discussion of Merker's views in the early postwar years, see Jeffrey Herf, *Divided Memory: The Nazi Past in the Two Germanys* (Cambridge, Mass.: Harvard University Press, 1997), pp. 85–105.

81. Kessler and Peter, *Wiedergutmachung*, pp. 154–171, 264–265.

82. Anton Ackermann, "Gibt es einen besonderen deutschen Weg zum Sozialismus?" *Einheit* 1 (1946): 23–42.

83. Speeches by Anton Ackermann and Wilhelm Pieck to the Ninth Party Executive Meeting, February 14, 1947, SAPMO-BArch, DY30/IV 2/1/16, pp. 84–86.

84. "Protokoll Nr. 75 der 9. Tagung des Parteivorstandes am 14.2.1947," SAPMO-BArch, DY30/IV 2/1/17, p. 2.

85. Speech by Anton Ackermann to the Thirteenth Party Executive Meeting, September 15–16, 1948, SAPMO-BArch, DY30/IV 2/1/52, pp. 187–199.

86. Schirdewan, *Ein Jahrhundert Leben*, p. 239.

5. PURGED

1. Wolfgang Kießling, *Der Fall Baender: Ein Politkrimi aus den 50er Jahren der DDR* (Berlin: Dietz, 1991), p. 180.

2. Peter Erler, Horst Laude, and Manfred Wilke, eds., *"Nach Hitler kommen wir": Dokumente zur Programmatik der Moskauer KPD Führung 1944/45 für Nachkriegsdeutschland* (Berlin: Akademie, 1994), p. 104.

3. Franz Dahlem, speech, May 1945, SAPMO-BArch, DY30/IV 2/4/373, p. 118.

4. Fritz Selbmann, *Acht Jahre und ein Tag: Bilder aus den Gründerjahren der DDR* (Berlin: Neues Leben, 1999), pp. 76, 78.

5. See, for example, Bruno Baum, "Wir funken aus der Hölle," *Deutsche Volkszeitung* (Berlin), July 31, 1945, p. 3.

6. Alexander Abusch, *Der Irrweg der Nation: Ein Beitrag zum Verständnis deutscher Geschichte* (Berlin: Aufbau, 1946), pp. 262–263.

7. Rundschreiben Landesverband Gross-Berlin, Abteilung Personalpolitik to Kreisleitung der SED, Abteilung Personalpolitik, September 28, 1948, SAPMO-BArch, DY30/I 2/3/116, p. 1.

8. Michel Foucault, *Discipline and Punish: The Birth of the Prison* (New York: Vintage, 1979), pp. 191–192.

9. "Richtlinien zur Arbeit der Parteikontrollkommissionen und zur Verhängung von Parteistrafen," *Beilage zu "Neuer Weg"* 17, no. 33 (1952): 5.

10. In 1954, for example, Kurt Wagner, a veteran-communist police official, received a party censure for incorrectly stating in a biographical questionnaire the year in which he joined the KPD. Minutes of ZPKK Meeting, July 26, 1954, SAPMO-BArch, DY30/IV 2/4/451, p. 78; and Minutes of Secretariat Meeting, August 11, 1954, DY30/J IV 2/3/437, p. 15.

11. Foucault, *Discipline*, p. 227.

12. Klaus-Georg Riegel, "Kaderbiographien in marxistisch-leninistischen Virtuosengemeinschaften," *Leviathan* 22, no. 1 (1994): 27–29.

13. "Protokoll Nr. 2 der Sekretariatssitzung am 8.7.1945," in Günter Benser and Hans-Joachim Krusch, eds., *Dokumente zur Geschichte der kommunistischen Bewegung in Deutschland: Reihe 1945/1946* (Munich: K. G. Saur, 1993), vol. 1, p. 34.

14. Wilhelm Burkhardt, Report, May 30, 1945, SAPMO-BArch, DY30/IV 2/11/v 1984, p. 180.

15. Walter Vosseler, Report, July 20, 1945, SAPMO-BArch, DY30/IV 2/11/v 1984, p. 195.

16. "Abschrift aus einem Bericht des Gen-Fugger vom 23.7.45 über KZ Flossenbürg," SAPMO-BArch, DY30/IV 2/11/v 1984, p. 196.

17. Karl Schirdewan, "Zur Sache des Genossen Selbmann," August 28, 1945, SAPMO-BArch, DY30/IV 2/11/v 1984, pp. 207–208.

18. Fritz Selbmann, "Erklärung," undated, SAPMO-BArch, DY30/IV 2/11/v 1984, p. 186.

19. Fritz Selbmann, *Alternative—Bilanz—Credo: Versuch einer Selbstdarstellung* (Halle: Mitteldeutscher Verlag, 1969), p. 380.

20. Fritz Selbmann, "Politische Arbeit von 1933–1945," SAPMO-BArch, DY30/IV 2/11/v 1984, p. 184.

21. Walter Vosseler, "Die Stellung der Parteiorganisation des K. L. Floßenbürg zur Lagerpolizei," August 12, 1945, SAPMO-BArch, DY30/IV 2/11/v 1984, pp. 198–199.

22. See, for example, Benser and Krusch, *Dokumente,* vol. 1, p. 26.

23. Heinz Lippmann, *Honecker: Porträt eines Nachfolgers* (Cologne: Verlag Wissenschaft & Politik, 1971), pp. 42–43.

24. Memorandum from the personnel department, initialled Br., to Franz Dahlem and Erich Gniffke, April 19, 1947, SAPMO-BArch, DY30/I 2/3/111, p. 7.

25. Karl Schirdewan, *Ein Jahrhundert Leben: Erinnerungen und Visionen* (Berlin: edition ost, 1998), p. 217.

26. Karl Schirdewan, *Aufstand gegen Ulbricht: Im Kampf um politische Kurskorrektur, gegen stalinistische, dogmatische Politik* (Berlin: Aufbau, 1994), p. 30.

27. Lutz Niethammer, ed., *Der "gesäuberte" Antifaschismus: Die SED und die roten Kapos von Buchenwald* (Berlin: Akademie, 1994), p. 355.

28. Carola Stern, *Porträt einer bolschewistischen Partei: Entwicklung, Funktion und Situation der SED* (Cologne: Verlag für Politik & Geschichte, 1957), p. 118.

29. Minutes of Secretariat Meeting, Anlage No. 3, October 28, 1949, SAPMO-BArch, DY30/J IV 2/3/60, pp. 10–11.

30. Jochen von Lang, *Erich Mielke: Eine deutsche Karriere* (Berlin: Rowohlt, 1991), p. 74.

31. "Erklärung des Zentralkomitees und der Zentralen Parteikontroll-kommission zu den Verbindungen ehemaliger deutscher politischer Emigranten zu dem Leiter des Unitarian Service Committee Noel H. Field," in *Dokumente der Sozialistischen Einheitspartei Deutschlands* (Berlin: Dietz, 1952), vol. 3, pp. 202–205.

32. Lex Ende and Maria Weiterer were also expelled from the SED. Walter Beling, Bruno Fuhrmann, Wolfgang Langhoff, and Hans Teubner lost their positions.

33. For more on ZPKK investigations of the Noel Field and OSS Affairs, see Catherine Epstein, "The Last Revolutionaries: The Old Communists of East Germany, 1945–1989," Ph.D. diss., Harvard University, 1998, pp. 181–185.

34. Rudi Feistmann to Paul [Merker], June 3, 1950, SAPMO-BArch, NY 4036/662, p. 333. Paul Bertz also committed suicide.

35. Franz Dahlem, *Am Vorabend des zweiten Weltkrieges: 1938 bis August 1939; Erinnerungen* (Berlin: Dietz, 1977), vol. 2, p. 289.

36. For an extended discussion of the SED's anticosmopolitan campaign, see Jeffrey Herf, *Divided Memory: The Nazi Past in the Two Germanys* (Cambridge, Mass.: Harvard University Press, 1997), pp. 106–161.

37. "Lehren aus dem Prozeß gegen das Verschwörerzentrum Slansky," in *Dokumente der sozialistischen Einheitspartei Deutschlands* (Berlin: Dietz, 1954), vol. 4, pp. 199–219.

38. Hermann Weber, "Schauprozeß-Vorbereitungen in der DDR," in Hermann Weber and Dietrich Staritz, eds., *Kommunisten verfolgen Kommunisten: Stalinistischer Terror und "Säuberungen" in den kommunistischen Parteien Europas seit den dreißiger Jahren* (Berlin: Akademie, 1993), p. 437.

39. Franz Dahlem to Hilde Eisler, February 10, 1978, and Hilde Eisler to Franz Dahlem, February 15, 1978, SAPMO-BArch, NY 4072/176, pp. 211–212.

40. Transcript of ZPKK interrogation of Gerhart Eisler, July 23, 1951, SAPMO-BArch, DY30/IV 2/11/v 749, pp. 93–95.

41. Rudolf Herrnstadt, *Das Herrnstadt-Dokument: Das Politbüro der SED und die Geschichte des 17. Juni 1953*, ed. Nadja Stulz-Herrnstadt (Hamburg: Rowohlt, 1990), p. 273.

42. Minutes of Politburo Meeting, February 10, 1953, SAPMO-BArch, DY30/J IV 2/2/261, p. 8.

43. Weber, "Schauprozeß-Vorbereitungen," pp. 445–446.

44. Gerhart Eisler to Walter Ulbricht and Hermann Matern, September 27, 1955, SAPMO-BArch, DY30/IV 2/11/v 749, p. 85.

45. Gerhart Eisler, "Kurzbiographie," January 17, 1960, SAPMO-BArch, DY30/IV 2/11/v 749, p. 49.
46. Manfred Engelhardt, ed., *Deutsche Lebensläufe: Gespräche* (Berlin: Aufbau, 1991), pp. 45–46.
47. Paul Baender, Leo Bauer, Bruno Goldhammer, Ernst Jungmann, and Hans Schrecker, all of whom were of Jewish origin, were held captive by SED or Soviet authorities during these years.
48. Hans Schrecker to the Central Committee of the SED, September 1, 1956, SAPMO-BArch, DY30/IV 2/4/131, pp. 324–340.
49. "Lehren aus dem Prozeß," pp. 211–212.
50. Weber, "Schauprozeß-Vorbereitungen," p. 445.
51. Speech by Hermann Matern to the Thirteenth Central Committee Meeting, May 13–14, 1953, SAPMO-BArch, DY30/IV 2/1/115, pp. 235–246.
52. Speech by Anton Ackermann to the Thirteenth Central Committee Meeting, May 13–14, 1953, SAPMO-BArch, DY30/IV 2/1/115, pp. 258–263.
53. "Über die Auswertung des Beschlusses des Zentralkomitees zu den 'Lehren aus dem Prozeß gegen das Verschwörerzentrum Slansky,'" in *Dokumente der Sozialistischen Einheitspartei Deutschlands* (Berlin: Dietz, 1954), vol. 4, pp. 405–407.
54. Speech by Otto Grotewohl to the Fifteenth Central Committee Meeting, July 24–26, 1953, SAPMO-BArch, DY30/IV 2/1/120, pp. 215–219.
55. ZPKK interrogation of Karl Mewis, December 3, 1953, SAPMO-BArch, DY30/IV 2/4/391, p. 386.
56. Weber, "Schauprozeß-Vorbereitungen," p. 445.
57. Franz Dahlem, "Nachgelassenes: Ausgelassenes; Über einen Prozeß und die Schwierigkeiten seiner richtigen Beurteilung," *Beiträge zur Geschichte der Arbeiterbewegung* 32, no. 1 (1990): 22–23.
58. Transcript of ZPKK Meeting, May 20, 1953, SAPMO-BArch, DY30/IV 2/4/446, p. 123.
59. For many examples of such charges and the resulting career demotions of veteran communists, see Epstein, "The Last Revolutionaries," pp. 161–253.
60. On Ziller and the various investigations against him, see SAPMO-BArch, DY30/IV 2/11/v 520; and Epstein, "The Last Revolutionaries," pp. 200–202.
61. Horst Sindermann to the ZPKK, July 6, 1950, SAPMO-BArch, NY 4036/664, pp. 84–89.
62. Niethammer, *Der "gesäuberte" Antifaschismus,* pp. 85–88, 90–91.
63. Report signed by Magnus to Department III, January 31, 1952, BStU MfSZ, Allg. P 1895/65, pp. 82–83.
64. The veteran communist in question was Arthur Dorf. Minutes of ZPKK Meeting, January 5, 1951, SAPMO-BArch, DY30/IV 2/4/440.
65. Nathan Leites and Elsa Bernaut, *Ritual of Liquidation: The Case of the Moscow Trials* (Glencoe, Ill.: Free Press, 1954), p. 359.
66. Ludwig Renn to Hermann Duncker, May 8, 1952, SAPMO-BArch, NY 4445/191, p. 133.
67. Emmy Koenen-Damerius to Hermann Matern, February 28, 1953, SAPMO-BArch, DY30/IV 2/11/189, p. 126.

68. Hans Schrecker to the Central Committee of the SED, September 1, 1956, SAPMO-BArch, DY30/IV 2/4/131, p. 329.

69. Ibid., p. 337.

70. Paul Merker to Wilhelm Pieck, April 14, 1956, SAPMO-BArch, NY 4102/27, p. 85.

71. Dahlem, "Nachgelassenes," p. 24.

72. Gareth Pritchard, *The Making of the GDR, 1945–53: From Antifascism to Stalinism* (Manchester, Eng.: Manchester University Press, 2000), pp. 186–187.

73. Leo Bauer in an untitled contribution in Horst Krüger, ed., *Das Ende einer Utopie* (Olten: Walter-Verlag, 1963), p. 82. Leo Zuckermann was the other purge victim to leave the GDR.

74. Alfred Kantorowicz in an untitled contribution in Krüger, *Das Ende*, p. 171.

75. See Horst Duhnke, *Die KPD von 1933 bis 1945* (Cologne: Kiepenheuer & Witsch, 1972), p. 454; and Herf, *Divided Memory*, p. 106. This line of interpretation also informs Grieder's meticulous study of political differences within the SED leadership. See Peter Grieder, *The East German Leadership, 1946–73: Conflict and Crisis* (Manchester, Eng.: Manchester University Press, 1999), pp. 25–36.

76. See, for example, George H. Hodos, *Show Trials: Stalinist Purges in Eastern Europe, 1948–1954* (New York: Praeger, 1987), p. 1.

77. Alan L. Nothnagle, *Building the East German Myth: Historical Mythology and Youth Propaganda in the German Democratic Republic, 1945–1989* (Ann Arbor: University of Michigan Press, 1999), pp. 104–105.

78. Manfred Overesch, *Buchenwald und die DDR oder Die Suche nach Selbstlegitimation* (Göttingen: Vandenhoeck & Ruprecht, 1995), pp. 281, 275.

6. RULERS

1. Rolf Stöckigt, "Ein Dokument von großer historischer Bedeutung vom Mai 1953," *Beiträge zur Geschichte der Arbeiterbewegung* 32, no. 5 (1990): 651–654.

2. Peter Grieder, *The East German Leadership, 1946–73: Conflict and Crisis* (Manchester, Eng.: Manchester University Press, 1999), pp. 56–60.

3. Elke Scherstjanoi, "'Wollen wir den Sozialismus?' Dokumente aus der Sitzung des Politbüros des ZK der SED am 6. Juni 1953," *Beiträge zur Geschichte der Arbeiterbewegung* 33 (1991): 662.

4. Ibid., pp. 665–666, 669.

5. Ernst Wollweber, "Aus Erinnerungen: Ein Porträt Walter Ulbrichts," *Beiträge zur Geschichte der Arbeiterbewegung* 32, no. 3 (1990): 361.

6. Charles S. Maier, *Dissolution: The Crisis of Communism and the End of East Germany* (Princeton, N.J.: Princeton University Press, 1997), p. 153.

7. Mario Frank, *Walter Ulbricht: Eine deutsche Biografie* (Berlin: Siedler, 2001), p. 241.

8. For accounts of the Herrnstadt/Zaisser Affair, see Grieder, *East German Leadership*, pp. 53–107; Rudolf Herrnstadt, *Das Herrnstadt-Dokument: Das Politbüro der SED und die Geschichte des 17. Juni 1953*, ed. Nadja Stulz-Herrnstadt (Hamburg: Rowohlt, 1990); Helmut Müller-Enbergs, *Der Fall*

Rudolf Herrnstadt: Tauwetterpolitik vor dem 17. Juni (Berlin: LinksDruck, 1991), pp. 171–348; and Frank Stern, *Dogma und Widerspruch: SED und Stalinismus in den Jahren 1946 bis 1958* (Munich: Tuduv, 1992), pp. 130–144.

9. Speech by Fred Oelßner to the Fourteenth Central Committee Meeting, June 21, 1953, SAPMO-BArch, DY30/IV 2/1/117, p. 44.

10. Wilfriede Otto, ed., "Dokumente zur Auseinandersetzung in der SED 1953," *Beiträge zur Geschichte der Arbeiterbewegung* 32, no. 5 (1990): 659–667.

11. Speech by Walter Ulbricht to the Fifteenth Central Committee Meeting, July 24–26, 1953, SAPMO-BArch, DY30/IV 2/1/119, pp. 106–111.

12. Speech by Fred Oelßner to the Fifteenth Central Committee Meeting, July 24–26, 1953, SAPMO-BArch, DY30/IV 2/1/119, pp. 241–251.

13. Herrnstadt, *Das Herrnstadt-Dokument,* p. 115.

14. Ibid., p. 158.

15. Speech by Wilhelm Zaisser to the Fifteenth Central Committee Meeting, July 24–26, 1953, SAPMO-BArch, DY30/IV 2/1/120, p. 66.

16. Speech by Rudolf Herrnstadt to the Fifteenth Central Committee Meeting, July 24–26, 1953, SAPMO-BArch, DY30/IV 2/1/120, pp. 118–119.

17. For "reformer," see James Richter, "Re-Examining Soviet Policy towards Germany in 1953," *Europe-Asia Studies* 45 (1993): 678; for "historic chance," see Otto, "Dokumente," p. 658.

18. Herrnstadt, *Das Herrnstadt-Dokument,* pp. 190–191, 218.

19. Stern, *Dogma,* p. 143.

20. Speech by Johannes R. Becher to the Fifteenth Central Committee Meeting, July 24–26, 1953, SAPMO-BArch, DY30/IV 2/1/120, p. 132.

21. Jürgen Kuczynski, "Parteilichkeit und Objektivität in Geschichte und Geschichtsschreibung," *Zeitschrift für Geschichtswissenschaft* 4 (1956): 873–888.

22. Alfred Kantorowicz, *Deutsches Tagebuch* (Berlin: Bibliothek Anpassung & Widerstand, 1979), vol. 2, pp. 664–665.

23. Robert Havemann, *Fragen Antworten Fragen: Aus der Biographie eines deutschen Marxisten* (1970; reprint, Munich: Piper, 1990), pp. 104–105.

24. Fritz Behrens and Arne Benary, *Zur ökonomischen Theorie und ökonomischen Politik in der Übergangsperiode* (Berlin: Verlag Die Wirtschaft, 1956).

25. Michael F. Scholz, *Bauernopfer der deutschen Frage: Der Kommunist Kurt Vieweg im Dschungel der Geheimdienste* (Berlin: Aufbau, 1997), pp. 235–242.

26. Wolfgang Harich, *Keine Schwierigkeiten mit der Wahrheit* (Berlin: Dietz, 1993), pp. 111–160.

27. Walter Janka, *Spuren eines Lebens* (Berlin: Rowohlt, 1991), pp. 254, 284, 432.

28. "Analyse der Feindtätigkeit innerhalb der wissenschaftlichen und künstlerischen Intelligenz," SAPMO-BArch, DY30/IV 2/1/182, p. 76.

29. Janka, *Spuren,* p. 345.

30. Grieder, *East German Leadership,* pp. 109–111.

31. Harich, *Keine Schwierigkeiten,* p. 52.

32. "Analyse der Feindtätigkeit innerhalb der wissenschaftlichen und künstlerischen Intelligenz," SAPMO-BArch, DY30/J IV 2/202/16, p. 31.

33. "Analyse," SAPMO-BArch, DY30/IV 2/1/182, pp. 147–148.

34. Hilde Eisler, interview by author, Berlin, February 9, 1995.

35. Janka, *Spuren,* p. 374.

36. Ibid., pp. 385–386.

37. Anna Seghers, "Der gerechte Richter," *Sinn und Form* 42 (1990): 479–501.

38. Robert Havemann is the major exception.

39. These were Erich Arendt, Johannes R. Becher, Fritz Behrens, Karola Bloch, Willi Bredel, Ernst Busch, Gerhart and Hilde Eisler, Rudi Engel, Johannes Gerats, Bruno Haid, Harold Hauser, Robert Havemann, Stephan Hermlin, Wieland Herzfelde, Rudolf Hirsch, Walter Janka, Siegbert Kahn, Alfred Kantorowicz, Georg Klaus, Jürgen Kuczynski, Herbert Sandberg, Heinz Schmidt, Anna Seghers, Wolfgang Steinitz, Kurt Stern, Kurt Vieweg, Paul Wengels, and Rudolf Wetzel. For information about these individuals, see Catherine Epstein, "The Last Revolutionaries: The Old Communists of East Germany, 1945–1989," Ph.D. diss., Harvard University, 1998, pp. 278–295.

40. "Analyse," SAPMO-BArch, DY30/J IV 2/202/16, p. 2+.

41. Fritz Behrens, "Die Planung und Leitung der Wirtschaft—Eine Stellungnahme," June 1957, SAPMO-BArch, DY30/IV 2/1/183, pp. 104–116.

42. Fritz Behrens, "Meine Konzeption war revisionistisch," *Neues Deutschland* (Berlin), March 4, 1958.

43. "Erklärung des Genossen Prof. Dr. Fritz Behrens," *Neuer Weg* 15 (1960): 650–651.

44. Norbert Podewin, *Walter Ulbricht: Eine neue Biographie* (Berlin: Dietz, 1995), p. 285.

45. Karl Schirdewan, *Aufstand gegen Ulbricht: Im Kampf um politische Kurskorrektur, gegen stalinistische, dogmatische Politik* (Berlin: Aufbau, 1994), p. 91.

46. Ibid., p. 103.

47. Karl Schirdewan, interview by author, Potsdam, December 14, 1994.

48. Schirdewan, *Aufstand,* pp. 184–210.

49. Wollweber, "Aus Erinnerungen," p. 373.

50. Grieder, *East German Leadership,* pp. 115–132.

51. Grieder often tempers his argument by using terms such as "Schirdewan claims" or "Schirdewan allegedly."

52. Schirdewan, *Aufstand,* pp. 184–210.

53. Schirdewan, interview.

54. Karl Schirdwan, *Ein Jahrhundert Leben: Erinnerungen und Visionen* (Berlin: edition ost, 1998), pp. 317–320.

55. Grieder, *East German Leadership,* p. 128; and Carola Stern, *Ulbricht: Eine politische Biographie* (Cologne: Kiepenheuer & Witsch, 1964), p. 125.

56. "Fred Oelßner: Erklärung im Politbüro," found in Schirdewan, *Aufstand,* pp. 181–183.

57. Fred Oelßner, "Vermerk 1956," SAPMO-BArch, NY 4215/112, p. 64.

58. Fred Oelßner, Notes from Politburo Meeting, December 4, 1956, SAPMO-BArch, NY 4215/112, pp. 86–87. Oelßner's emphasis.

59. Fred Oelßner, Notes from Politburo Meeting, December 29, 1956, SAPMO-BArch, NY 4215/112, p. 90.

60. Speech by Fred Oelßner to the Twenty-ninth Central Committee Meeting, November 12–13, 1956, SAPMO-BArch, DY30/IV 2/1/166, pp. 171–172.

61. Speech by Fred Oelßner to the Thirtieth Central Committee Meeting, January 30–February 1, 1957, SAPMO-BArch, DY30/IV 2/1/170, pp. 285–291.

62. Fred Oelßner, "Erklärung an das Politbüro des Zentralkomitees der SED," January 5, 1958, SAPMO-BArch, NY 4215/112, pp. 150–154.

63. Speech by Erich Honecker to the Thirty-fifth Central Committee Meeting, February 3–6, 1958, SAPMO-BArch, DY30/IV 2/1/191, p. 68.

64. Schirdewan, *Aufstand,* p. 99.

65. Frank, *Walter Ulbricht,* p. 413.

66. Schirdewan, *Aufstand,* p. 99.

67. Speech by Walter Ulbricht to the Thirty-fifth Central Committee Meeting, February 3–6, 1958, SAPMO-BArch, DY30/IV 2/1/193, p. 193.

68. Grieder, *East German Leadership,* p. 116.

69. Schirdewan, *Aufstand,* pp. 211–218.

70. Speech by Erich Honecker to the Thirty-fifth Central Committee Meeting, February 3–6, 1958, SAPMO-BArch, DY30/IV 2/1/191, pp. 68–84. Wilhelm Girnus had been one of the "Blue Points" in Flossenbürg concentration camp; in 1958, he was state secretary of higher and technical education.

71. Speech by Hermann Matern to the Thirty-fifth Central Committee Meeting, February 3–6, 1958, SAPMO-BArch, DY30/IV 2/1/191, p. 159.

72. Speech by Albert Norden to the Thirty-fifth Central Committee Meeting, February 3–6, 1958, SAPMO-BArch, DY30/IV 2/1/192, pp. 73–74.

73. Speech by Kurt Hager to the Thirty-fifth Central Committee Meeting, February 3–6, 1958, SAPMO-BArch, DY30/IV 2/1/192, p. 144.

74. Speech by Walter Ulbricht to the Thirty-fifth Central Committee Meeting, February 3–6, 1958, SAPMO-BArch, DY30/IV 2/1/193, p. 204.

75. Report of Comrade "Erwin," August 6, 1958, BStU MfSZ, AOP 317/59, p. 287.

76. Speech by Franz Dahlem to the Thirty-fifth Central Committee Meeting, February 3–6, 1958, SAPMO-BArch, DY30/IV 2/1/193, p. 123.

77. Schirdewan, interview.

78. Speech by Karl Schirdewan to the Thirty-fifth Central Committee Meeting, February 3–6, 1958, SAPMO-BArch, DY30/IV 2/1/191, p. 134.

79. Speech by Fred Oelßner to the Thirty-fifth Central Committee Meeting, February 3–6, 1958, SAPMO-BArch, DY30/IV 2/1/192, p. 8.

80. Speech by Karl Schirdewan to the Thirty-fifth Central Committee Meeting, February 3–6, 1958, SAPMO-BArch, DY30/IV 2/1/193, pp. 60–66.

81. Speech by Fred Oelßner to the Thirty-fifth Central Committee Meeting, February 3–6, 1958, SAPMO-BArch, DY30/IV 2/1/193, pp. 78–82.

82. Speech by Fritz Selbmann to the Thirty-fifth Central Committee Meeting, February 3–6, 1958, SAPMO-BArch, DY30/IV 2/1/193, pp. 74–77.

83. Schirdewan, *Aufstand,* p. 152.

84. Fritz Selbmann to Hermann Matern, March 9, 1959, SAPMO-BArch, DY30/J IV 2/202/4/1.

85. "Erklärung des Genossen Karl Schirdewan," *Neuer Weg* 14 (1959): 1237–1238.
86. "Erklärung des Genossen Fritz Selbmann," *Neuer Weg* 14 (1959): 1238–1240.
87. "Erklärung des Genossen Fred Oelßner," *Neuer Weg* 14 (1959): 1407–1408.
88. For new archival findings on Ulbricht in the 1960s, see Frank, *Walter Ulbricht*, pp. 373–427; Grieder, *East German Leadership*, pp. 160–211; Monika Kaiser, *Machtwechsel von Ulbricht zu Honecker: Funktionsmechanismen der SED-Diktatur in Konfliktsituationen 1962 bis 1972* (Berlin: Akademie, 1997); Podewin, *Walter Ulbricht*, pp. 368–457; Jochen Staadt, "Walter Ulbrichts letzter Machtkampf," *Deutschland Archiv* 29 (1996): 686–700; and Jochen Stelkens, "Machtwechsel in Ost-Berlin: Der Sturz Walter Ulbrichts 1971," *Vierteljahrshefte für Zeitgeschichte* 45 (1997): 503–533.
89. Frank, *Walter Ulbricht*, p. 322.
90. There are numerous descriptions of NES. See, for example, Thomas A. Baylis, *The Technical Intelligentsia and the East German Elite: Legitimacy and Social Change in Mature Communism* (Berkeley: University of California Press, 1974), pp. 238–239; and Jeffrey Kopstein, *The Politics of Economic Decline in East Germany, 1945–1989* (Chapel Hill: University of North Carolina Press, 1997), pp. 47–51.
91. Kaiser, *Machtwechsel*, p. 70.
92. Grieder, *East German Leadership*, p. 163.
93. Rainer Weinert, "Wirtschaftsführung unter dem Primat der Parteipolitik," in Theo Pirker, M. Rainer Lepsius, Rainer Weinert, and Hans-Hermann Hertle, eds., *Der Plan als Befehl und Fiktion: Wirtschaftsführung in der DDR; Gespräche und Analysen* (Opladen: Westdeutscher Verlag, 1995), pp. 290–293.
94. Kaiser, *Machtwechsel*, p. 22.
95. Grieder, *East German Leadership*, p. 162.
96. Frank, *Walter Ulbricht*, pp. 415–416.
97. Kopstein, *Politics*, p. 70.
98. Gerhard Naumann and Eckhard Trümpler, *Von Ulbricht zu Honecker: 1970–ein Krisenjahr der DDR* (Berlin: Dietz, 1990), p. 96.
99. Staadt, "Walter Ulbrichts letzter Machtkampf," pp. 695–696.
100. Weinert, "Wirtschaftsführung," p. 295.
101. Grieder, *East German Leadership*, pp. 170–183; and Stelkens, "Machtwechsel," pp. 521–529. For a contrasting view, see Staadt, "Walter Ulbrichts letzter Machtkampf."
102. Kopstein, *Politics*, p. 67; Stelkens, "Machtwechsel," p. 522.
103. M. E. Sarotte, *Dealing with the Devil: East Germany, Détente, and Ostpolitik* (Chapel Hill: North Carolina Press, 2001), p. 110.
104. Frank, *Walter Ulbricht*, pp. 405–407.
105. Staadt, "Walter Ulbrichts letzter Machtkampf," p. 697.
106. The text of the letter is found in Peter Przybylski, *Tatort Politbüro*, vol. 1: *Die Akte Honecker* (Berlin: Rowohlt, 1991), pp. 297–303.
107. Stelkens, "Machtwechsel," pp. 511–512.
108. Staadt, "Walter Ulbrichts letzter Machtkampf," pp. 698–700.
109. Stelkens, "Machtwechsel," p. 514.

110. Podewin, *Walter Ulbricht,* p. 485.
111. Ibid., p. 486.

7. LEGENDS

1. Stefan Heym, *Collin* (Frankfurt am Main: Fischer, 1981), pp. 128, 130.
2. Monika Maron, *Stille Zeile Sechs* (Frankfurt am Main: Fischer, 1993). Maron is the step-daughter of Karl Maron, the veteran communist East German minister of the interior between 1955 and 1963.
3. For a complete list of memoirs by veteran communists, see Catherine Epstein, "The Last Revolutionaries: The Old Communists of East Germany, 1945–1989," Ph.D. diss., Harvard University, 1998, pp. 593–599.
4. Geoffrey A. Hosking, "Memory in a Totalitarian Society: The Case of the Soviet Union," in Thomas Butler, ed., *Memory: History, Culture and the Mind* (Oxford, Eng.: Basil Blackwell, 1989), p. 117.
5. On the Brezhnev leadership's strategy, see Nina Tumarkin, *The Living and the Dead: The Rise and Fall of the Cult of World War II in Russia* (New York: Basic Books, 1994), p. 132.
6. Pierre Nora, "Between Memory and History: *Les Lieux de Mémoire,*" *Representations* 26 (1989): 7–25.
7. See, for example, Jens Gieseke, *Die hauptamtlichen Mitarbeiter der Staatssicherheit: Personalstruktur und Lebenswelt, 1950–1989/90* (Berlin: Links, 2000), p. 264; and Jürgen Radde, *Die außenpolitische Führungselite der DDR: Veränderungen der sozialen Struktur außenpolitischer Führungsgruppen* (Cologne: Verlag Wissenschaft & Politik, 1976), p. 15.
8. Wilhelm Eildermann, diary entry, May 15, 1962, SAPMO-BArch, NY 4251/9, notebook 5, p. 21.
9. Erich Selbmann, "Nachwort: Diese Art zu leben; der Weg des Fritz Selbmann," in Fritz Selbmann, *Acht Jahre und ein Tag: Bilder aus den Gründerjahren der DDR* (Berlin: Verlag Neues Leben, 1999), pp. 311–312.
10. Erich Honecker to Walter Ulbricht, April 29, 1965, SAPMO-BArch, DY30/3292, p. 136.
11. In 1963, approximately 140,000 individuals were "party veterans." In addition to longtime communists, individuals who had joined the USPD, the Spartakusbund, and the SPD before 1933 were considered part of this group. "Information über die Arbeit mit den Parteiveteranen und ihre Betreuung im Jahre 1963," SAPMO-BArch, DY30/IV A 3/65, Zentrale Revisionskommission.
12. "Richtlinien für die Betreuung der Parteiveteranen," Minutes of Secretariat Meeting, August 1, 1956, SAPMO-BArch, DY30/J IV 2/3/522, Anlage No. 2, pp. 17–22.
13. Emmy Koenen, "Erinnerungen von Emmy Koenen-Damerius," SAPMO-BArch, SgY30 1308/1, pp. 252–253.
14. "Beratung mit den Bezirkskommissionen zur Betreuung alter verdienter Mitglieder der Partei am 17 November 1966," SAPMO-BArch, DY30/IV A 3/66, Zentrale Revisionskommission.

15. Minutes of the Kommission zur Betreuung der Parteiveteranen bei der ZRK mit den Vorsitzenden der Kommissionen zur Betreuung der Parteiveteranen aus den Bezirken, November 11, 1960, SAPMO-BArch, DY30/IV 3/2, Zentrale Revisionskommission.

16. "Beratung mit den Bezirkskommissionen . . . am 17 November 1966."

17. "Verordnung über Ehrenpensionen für Kämpfer gegen den Faschismus und für Verfolgte des Faschismus sowie für deren Hinterbliebene," *Gesetzblatt der Deutschen Demokratischen Republik,* pt. 2, no. 41, April 9, 1965, pp. 293–294.

18. "Beschluß über die Verbesserung von Leistungen für Kämpfer gegen den Faschismus und Verfolgte des Faschismus," Minutes of Secretariat Meeting, November 9, 1966, SAPMO-BArch, DY30/J IV 2/3/1236, p. 17.

19. "Erweiterung des Tätigkeitsbereiches und Veränderung der Struktur des 'Komitees der Antifaschistischen Widerstandskämpfer der DDR,'" Minutes of Secretariat Meeting, January 30, 1974, SAPMO-BArch, DY30/J IV 2/3/2115, p. 50.

20. Minutes of Secretariat Meeting, December 22, 1988, SAPMO-BArch, DY30/J IV 2/3/4342, Anlage No. 1.

21. Lutz Niethammer, Alexander von Plato, and Dorothee Wierling, *Die volkseigene Erfahrung: Eine Archäologie des Lebens in der Industrieprovinz der DDR* (Berlin: Rowohlt, 1991), pp. 533–535.

22. Deputy chairman of the Central Revision Commission, "An alle Bezirksveteranenkommissionen," July 12, 1960, SAPMO-BArch, DY30/IV 3/71, Zentrale Revisionskommission.

23. Gieseke, *Die hauptamtlichen Mitarbeiter,* p. 263.

24. "Richtlinien für die Tätigkeit der Kommissionen zur Erforschung der Geschichte der örtlichen Arbeiterbewegung bei den Bezirks- und Kreisleitungen der SED," Minutes of Secretariat Meeting, June 19, 1973, SAPMO-BArch, DY30/J IV 2/3/2022, Anlage No. 1, pp. 11–13.

25. On this committee, see Rüdiger Henkel, *Im Dienste der Staatspartei: Über Parteien und Organisationen der DDR* (Baden-Baden: Nomos, 1994), pp. 395–407; and the entry "Komitee der Antifaschistischen Widerstandskämpfer in der DDR," in Andreas Herbst, Winfried Ranke, and Jürgen Winkler, *So funktionierte die DDR* (Reinbek: Rowohlt, 1994), vol. 1, pp. 513–521.

26. Emmy Koenen, "Lebenslauf Emmy Koenen," January 17, 1969, SAPMO-BArch, SgY30 1308/1, p. 15.

27. Emmy Koenen to Franz Dahlem, May 11, 1976, SAPMO-BArch, NY 4072/178, pp. 45–46.

28. Janos Bak, "Political Biography and Memoir in Totalitarian Eastern Europe," in George Egerton, ed., *Political Memoir: Essays on the Politics of Memory* (London: Frank Cass, 1994), p. 292.

29. As the veteran communist Frida Rubiner wrote Pieck: "I know that you are against all forms of autobiography." Frida Rubiner to Wilhelm Pieck, December 3, 1951, SAPMO-BArch, NY 4036/664, p. 71.

30. Karl Bittel to Jacob Walcher, February 9, 1966, SAPMO-BArch, NY 4127/68, p. 268.

31. Lutz Niethammer, ed., *Der "gesäuberte" Antifaschismus: Die SED und die roten Kapos von Buchenwald* (Berlin: Akademie, 1994), p. 17.

32. "Richtlinien über die Arbeit der Gruppe Erinnerungen," May 31, 1961, SAPMO-BArch, DY30/IV A 2/9.07/281, pp. 5–6.

33. Ilse Schiel, "Zum Platz und Wesen der Erinnerungen bei der Verbreitung des marxistisch-leninistischen Geschichtsbildes: Erfahrungen und Probleme des Sammelns, Gestaltens, Wertens, Ph.D. diss., Institut für Marxismus-Leninismus beim Zentralkomitee der Sozialistischen Einheitspartei Deutschlands, 1981, p. 131.

34. Büro des Politbüros, ed., *Arbeitsrichtlinien für die Parteiarchive der SED* (January 1987), p. 86.

35. Schiel, "Zum Platz," pp. 298–302.

36. "Schwerpunkte für den Sammelband mit Erinnerungen zu Problemen der marxistisch-leninistischen Entwicklung der SED und der Verwirklichung der allgemeingültigen Gesetzmäßigkeiten der sozialistischen Revolution in der Zeit vom Vereinigungsparteitag 1946 bis Anfang der 50er Jahre," SAPMO-BArch, NY 4160/1.

37. Günter Heyden to Margarete Wittkowski, May 29, 1972, SAPMO-BArch, NY 4160/1.

38. Friedrich Schlotterbeck, *Je dunkler die Nacht, desto heller die Sterne: Erinnerungen eines deutschen Arbeiters, 1933–1945* (Halle: Mitteldeutscher Verlag, 1969).

39. Fritz Selbmann, *Alternative—Bilanz—Credo: Versuch einer Selbstdarstellung* (Halle: Mitteldeutscher Verlag, 1969), p. 318.

40. Cläre Quast to a friend named Emmi, June 17, 1970, SAPMO-BArch, SgY30 740/2, p. 162.

41. Bruno Fuhrmann to Franz Dahlem, February 19, 1969, SAPMO-BArch, NY 4072/192, p. 51.

42. Hans Teubner to Georg Stibi, December 20, 1976, SAPMO-BArch, NY 4246/65, p. 8. Teubner's emphasis.

43. Paul Merker to Franz Dahlem, March 25, 1966, SAPMO-BArch, NY 4102/53, p. 33.

44. Koenen, "Erinnerungen," p. 181.

45. Wilhelm Eildermann, diary entry, December 29, 1978, SAPMO-BArch, NY 4251/15, notebook 29, p. 94.

46. H. Schumann to Josef (Sepp) Hahn, December 24, 1958, SAPMO-BArch, NY 4098/5, p. 178.

47. Josef (Sepp) Hahn, untitled manuscript, SAPMO-BArch, NY 4098/5, p. 7.

48. Ruth Werner, *Sonjas Rapport* (Berlin: Neues Leben, 1977). Translated by Renate Simpson as *Sonya's Report* (London: Chatto & Windus, 1991).

49. Anne McElvoy, *The Saddled Cow: East Germany's Life and Legacy* (London: Faber & Faber, 1992), p. 29.

50. According to Marianne Lange, as far as copies printed, *Sonjas Rapport* "was beyond all competition." See Lange, "Es hat sich gelohnt zu leben: Gedanken zur Memoirenliteratur in der DDR," *Weimarer Beiträge* 25, no. 9 (1979): 87, n. 7.

51. Willy Sägebrecht, *Nicht Amboß, sondern Hammer Sein: Erinnerungen* (Berlin: Dietz, 1968).
52. Selbmann, *Alternative*.
53. Karl Mewis, *Im Auftrag der Partei: Erlebnisse im Kampf gegen die faschistische Diktatur* (Berlin: Dietz, 1971).
54. Norbert Podewin, *Walter Ulbricht: Eine neue Biographie* (Berlin: Dietz, 1995), pp. 489–490, n. 6.
55. Minutes of Secretariat Meeting, April 24, 1974, SAPMO-BArch, DY30/J IV 2/3/2146, Anlage No. 14, p. 150.
56. See Catherine Epstein, "The Production of 'Official Memory' in East Germany: Old Communists and the Dilemmas of Memoir-Writing," *Central European History* 32 (1999): 192–194.
57. See SAPMO-BArch, vorl. SED 32839.
58. Decisions made at Politburo meetings on February 26, 1980 and March 18, 1980, SAPMO-BArch, DY 30/J IV 2/2/1826, p. 5 and 2/2/1829, pp. 5+, 200.
59. Erich Honecker, *Aus meinem Leben* (Frankfurt am Main: Pergamon; Berlin: Dietz, 1981). Translated as *From My Life* (Oxford: Pergamon, 1980).
60. For further examples of veteran communists and their difficulties with publishing memoirs in East Germany, see Epstein, "Production," pp. 181–201.
61. Erich Selbmann, interview by author, Berlin, March 13, 1995.
62. Lucie Pflug, "Gutachten: Zum Manuskript von Fritz Selbmann 'Acht Jahre und ein Tag,'" July 30, 1978, SAPMO-BArch, Dienstakte Bundesarchiv Fritz Selbmann.
63. Ibid.
64. Selbmann, *Acht Jahre*, p. 263.
65. Ernst Diehl to Kurt Hager, July 21, 1978, SAPMO-BArch, Dienstakte Bundesarchiv Fritz Selbmann. Diehl's emphasis.
66. Günter Benser, "Durchsicht des Umbruchs Fritz Selbmann: Acht Jahre und Ein Tag," May 1978, SAPMO-BArch, Dienstakte Bundesarchiv Fritz Selbmann.
67. Selbmann, *Acht Jahre*.
68. Bernd-Rainer Barth, Christoph Links, Helmut Müller-Enbergs, and Jan Wielgohs, eds., *Wer war wer in der DDR: Ein biographisches Handbuch* (Frankfurt am Main: Fischer, 1995), p. 500; and Michael Scholz, *Herbert Wehner in Schweden, 1941–1946* (Munich: Oldenbourg, 1995), pp. 185–186.
69. Hans Teubner, *Exilland Schweiz: Dokumentarischer Bericht über den Kampf emigrierter deutscher Kommunisten, 1933–1945* (Berlin: Dietz, 1975).
70. Hans Teubner to Franz Dahlem, July 7, 1975, SAPMO-BArch, NY 4072/193, p. 113.
71. Ernst Diehl to Kurt Hager, June 27, 1974, SAPMO-BArch, DY30/IV B2/2.024/119.
72. Franz Dahlem, *Am Vorabend des zweiten Weltkrieges: 1938 bis August 1939; Erinnerungen*, 2 vols. (Berlin: Dietz, 1977).
73. Franz Dahlem to Walter Ulbricht, February 27, 1956, SAPMO-BArch, DY30/IV 2/11/v 5280/2, p. 83.
74. Franz Dahlem to Walter Ulbricht, March 18, 1956, SAPMO-BArch, DY30/IV 2/11/v 5280/2, p. 87.

75. Franz Dahlem to Walter Ulbricht, May 15, 1963, SAPMO-BArch, DY30/IV 2/ 11/v 5280/2, pp. 69–70.

76. "Zentralkomitee gratuliert Genossen Franz Dahlem," *Neues Deutschland* (Berlin), January 14, 1972, pp. 1–2.

77. Franz Dahlem to Erich Honecker, January 17, 1975, SAPMO-BArch, DY30/J IV 2/2/1544, Anlage No. 12.

78. Erich Honecker to Franz Dahlem, January 28, 1975, SAPMO-BArch, ME-Nr. 11.528.

79. Dahlem, *Am Vorabend,* vol. 1, pp. 179, 260, 447–448, 274, 430–437.

80. Ibid., vol. 2, p. 437. Dahlem's justifications for this decision are found in vol. 2, pp. 394–396, 424–426, and 435–438. Dahlem's emphasis.

81. Franz Dahlem to Georg Stibi, July 21, 1977, SAPMO-BArch, NY 4246/58, p. 19.

82. Minutes of Secretariat Meeting, November 18, 1975, SAPMO-BArch, DY30/J IV 2/3/238, p. 2.

83. "Gutachten zum Manuskript von Franz Dahlem: Am Vorabend des Zweiten Weltkrieges (1938 bis August 1939)," November 5, 1974, SAPMO-BArch, ME-Nr. 11.528.

84. Günter Heyden to Kurt Hager, November 11, 1974, SAPMO-BArch, ME-Nr. 11.528. Heyden's emphasis.

85. A version of this passage was published in Franz Dahlem, "Nachgelassenes: Ausgelassenes; Über einen Prozeß und die Schwierigkeiten seiner richtigen Beurteilung," *Beiträge zur Geschichte der Arbeiterbewegung* 32, no. 1 (1990): 21.

86. Franz Dahlem to Kurt Hager, November 8, 1975, SAPMO-BArch, ME-Nr. 11.528.

87. See also Karin Hartewig, "Das 'Gedächtnis' der Partei: Biographische und andere Bestände im zentralen Parteiarchiv der SED in der 'Stiftung Archiv der Parteien und Massenorganisationen der DDR im Bundesarchiv,'" *Jahrbuch für Historische Kommunismusforschung* (1993): 312–323.

88. Dahlem, *Am Vorabend,* vol. 1, pp. 435–437.

89. Franz Dahlem to Erich Honecker, July 1, 1975, SAPMO-BArch, ME-Nr. 11.528.

90. Franz Dahlem to Kurt Hager, December 20, 1976, SAPMO-BArch, ME-Nr. 11.528. Dahlem's emphasis.

91. Franz Dahlem to Else Zaisser, November 15, 1977, SAPMO-BArch, NY 4072/ 181, p. 176.

92. Dahlem, "Nachgelassenes."

93. Bertolt Brecht, *Life of Galileo,* in John Willett and Ralph Manheim, eds., *Brecht's Plays, Poetry and Prose* (London: Eyre Methuen, 1980), vol. 5, pt. 1, p. 98.

8. OUTDATED

1. Karl Mannheim, "The Problem of Generations," in his *Essays on the Sociology of Knowledge* (London: Routledge & Kegan Paul, 1952), pp. 296, 297, n. 1.

2. Lutz Niethammer, "Erfahrungen und Strukturen: Prolegomena zu einer

Geschichte der Gesellschaft der DDR," in Hartmut Kaelbe, Jürgen Kocka, and Hartmut Zwahr, eds., *Sozialgeschichte der DDR* (Stuttgart: Klett-Cotta, 1994), p. 108.

3. While many scholars have briefly commented on East German generational dynamics, these still remain substantially unexplored. The most influential discussion remains ibid., pp. 104–108.

4. Hans-Hermann Hertle and Gerd-Rüdiger Stephan, eds., *Das Ende der SED: Die letzten Tage des Zentralkomitees* (Berlin: Links, 1997), pp. 28–29.

5. Hermann Weber, *DDR: Grundriß der Geschichte, 1945–1990* (Hannover: Fackelträger, 1991), p. 133.

6. Reinholt Andert and Wolfgang Herzberg, *Der Sturz: Erich Honecker im Kreuzverhör* (Berlin: Aufbau, 1990), p. 360.

7. Peter C. Ludz, *The Changing Party Elite in East Germany* (Cambridge, Mass.: MIT Press, 1972).

8. Gert-Joachim Glaeßner, *Herrschaft durch Kader: Leitung der Gesellschaft und Kaderpolitik in der DDR am Beispiel des Staatsapparates* (Opladen: Westdeutscher Verlag, 1977), pp. 228–230.

9. See, for example, Mary Fulbrook, *Anatomy of a Dictatorship: Inside the GDR, 1949–1989* (Oxford, Eng.: Oxford University Press, 1995), pp. 14–15.

10. Walter Süß, ed., "Erich Mielke (MfS) und Leonid Schebarschin (KGB) über den drohenden Untergang des Sozialistischen Lagers: Protokoll eines Streitgesprächs vom 7. April 1989," *Deutschland Archiv* 26 (1993): 1024.

11. Alan Nothnagle, *Building the East German Myth: Historical Mythology and Youth Propaganda in the German Democratic Republic, 1945–1989* (Ann Arbor: University of Michigan Press, 1999), pp. 126–127.

12. Herbert Häber, interview by A. J. McAdams, March 19, 1990, A. J. McAdams Collection, HIA.

13. Otto Reinhold, interview by Heinrich Bortfeldt, January 29, 1991, A. J. McAdams Collection, HIA.

14. Weber, *DDR*, pp. 144, 164.

15. Rainer Eppelmann, *Fremd im eigenen Haus: Mein Leben im anderen Deutschland* (Cologne: Kiepenheuer & Witsch, 1993), p. 376.

16. Weber, *DDR*, p. 171.

17. Hans-Hermann Hertle, *Der Fall der Mauer: Die unbeabsichtigte Selbstauflösung des SED-Staates* (Opladen: Westdeutscher Verlag, 1996), p. 125.

18. Iwan Kusmin, "Die Verschwörung gegen Honecker," *Deutschland Archiv* 28 (1995): 286–290.

19. Jürgen Kocka, "Eine durchherrschte Gesellschaft," in Kaelbe, Kocka, and Zwahr, *Sozialgeschichte*, p. 547.

20. Jens Gieseke, *Die hauptamtlichen Mitarbeiter der Staatssicherheit: Personalstruktur und Lebenswelt, 1950–1989/90* (Berlin: Links, 2000), p. 397.

21. Ibid., p. 299, fn. 22.

22. Alfred Neumann, interview by author, Berlin, December 8, 1994.

23. Süß, "Erich Mielke," p. 1028.

24. Fulbrook, *Anatomy*, p. 277; Eric D. Weitz, *Creating German Communism, 1890–1990: From Popular Protests to Socialist State* (Princeton, N.J.: Princeton

University Press, 1997), p. 362; and Konrad H. Jarausch, "Care and Coercion: The GDR as Welfare Dictatorship," in Konrad H. Jarausch, ed., *Dictatorship as Experience: Towards a Socio-Cultural History of the GDR* (New York: Berghahn, 1999), p. 47.

25. For a succinct summary of Havemann's reform ideas, see Dieter Knötzsch, *Innerkommunistische Opposition: Das Beispiel Robert Havemann* (Opladen: Leske, 1968), pp. 17–22.

26. Robert Havemann, *Fragen, Antworten, Fragen: Aus der Biographie eines deutschen Marxisten* (Munich: Piper, 1990), p. 14.

27. Robert Havemann, *Berliner Schriften* (Munich: Deutscher Taschenbuch Verlag, 1977), p. 76.

28. Ibid., pp. 161–163.

29. Stephan Hermlin, *In den Kämpfen dieser Zeit* (Berlin: Wagenbach, 1995), p. 58.

30. Roger Woods, *Opposition in the GDR under Honecker, 1971–85: An Introduction and Documentation* (New York: St. Martin's Press, 1986), p. 139.

31. Franz Dahlem to Stephan Hermlin, January 19, 1978, and Stephan Hermlin to Franz Dahlem, January 30, 1978, SAPMO-BArch, NY 4072/192, pp. 178–180.

32. Jürgen Kuczynski, *Dialog mit meinem Urenkel: Neunzehn Briefe und ein Tagebuch* (Berlin: Aufbau, 1983). In 1996, Kuczynski published the uncensored original text along with Hager's marks indicating passages that were not to be included in the East German edition. See *Dialog mit meinem Urenkel: Neunzehn Briefe und ein Tagebuch; Erstveröffentlichung der ungekürzten und unzensierten Originalfassung* (Berlin: Schwarzkopf & Schwarzkopf, 1996). All page citations are to the 1983 edition.

33. Kuczynski, *Dialog*, pp. 22, 15.

34. Jürgen Kuczynski, *"Ein linientreuer Dissident": Memoiren, 1945–1989* (Berlin: Aufbau, 1992).

35. Helmut Schelsky, *Die skeptische Generation: Eine Soziologie der deutschen Jugend* (Düsseldorf: Eugen Diederichs Verlag, 1957), pp. 86, 93.

36. Heinz Bude, *Deutsche Karrieren: Lebenskonstruktionen sozialer Aufsteiger aus der Flakhelfer-Generation* (Frankfurt am Main: Suhrkamp, 1987).

37. Gustav Just, interview by John Torpey, July 14, 1991, A. J. McAdams Collection, HIA.

38. Lutz Niethammer, Alexander von Plato, and Dorothee Wierling, *Die volkseigene Erfahrung: Eine Archäologie des Lebens in der Industrieprovinz der DDR* (Berlin: Rowohlt, 1991), p. 45.

39. Dorothee Wierling, "Die Jugend als innerer Feind: Konflikte in der Erziehungsdiktatur der sechziger Jahren," in Kaelbe, Kocka, and Zwahr, *Sozialgeschichte*, p. 421.

40. Günter Schabowski, *Der Absturz* (Berlin: Rowohlt, 1991), p. 81. Günter Erxleben was an editor (later editor in chief) of the FDGB newspaper *Tribüne;* Schabowski worked there from 1949 to 1967.

41. Horst Grunert, "Überwintern in einer Nische," in Brigitte Zimmermann and Hans-Dieter Schütt, eds., *OhnMacht: DDR-Funktionäre sagen aus* (Berlin: Neues Leben, 1992), pp. 69–70.

42. Günter Sieber, "Ustinow tobte, Gorbatschow schwieg," in Zimmermann and Schütt, *OhnMacht*, p. 229.

43. Lutz Niethammer, "Das Volk der DDR und die Revolution," in Charles Schüddekopf, ed., *"Wir sind das Volk!" Flugschriften, Aufrufe und Texte einer deutschen Revolution* (Reinbek: Rowohlt, 1990), p. 259.

44. Zimmermann and Schütt, *OhnMacht*.

45. Otfrid Arnold and Hans Modrow, "Das Große Haus: Struktur und Funktionswesen des ZK der SED," in Hans Modrow, ed., *Das Große Haus: Insider berichten aus dem ZK der SED* (Berlin: edition ost, 1994), p. 67.

46. Gerhart Neuner, "'Unsere' Menschen spielten nicht mit," in Zimmermann and Schütt, *OhnMacht*, p. 168.

47. Hans-Joachim Hoffmann, "Haupttätigkeit–Schlimmes verhüten," in Zimmerman and Schütt, *OhnMacht*, p. 123.

48. Arno Donda, "Zahlen lügen nicht," in Zimmerman and Schütt, *OhnMacht*, p. 40.

49. The Hitler Youth generation of functionaries did, however, produce one of East Germany's most famous dissidents, Rudolf Bahro. He wrote *Die Alternative: Zur Kritik des real existierenden Sozialismus* (Cologne: Europäische Verlagsanstalt, 1977).

50. Schürer's document is found in Hans-Hermann Hertle, *Vor dem Bankrott der DDR: Dokumente des Politbüros des ZK der SED aus dem Jahre 1988 zum Scheitern der "Einheit von Wirtschafts- und Sozialpolitik,"* Berliner Arbeitshefte und Berichte zur sozialwissenschaftlichen Forschung, no. 63 (Berlin, 1991).

51. Gerhard Schürer, "Die weit verschüttete Demokratie," in Zimmermann and Schütt, *OhnMacht*, p. 186.

52. Egon Krenz, *Wenn Mauern Fallen: Die friedliche Revolution; Vorgeschichte—Ablauf—Auswirkungen* (Vienna: Paul Neff, 1990), p. 41.

53. Wolfgang Herger, Werner Hübner, and Günter Frenzel, "Eigenverantwortung und Selbstbestimmung: Zur Militär- und Sicherheitspolitik der SED," in Modrow, *Das Große Haus*, p. 192.

54. Joachim Böhm, interview by A. J. McAdams, December 5, 1990, A. J. McAdams Collection, HIA.

55. Herbert Hörz, "Monopolisierung der Meinungen," in Zimmermann and Schütt, *OhnMacht*, p. 108.

56. Hertle, *Fall*, p. 127.

57. Anne McElvoy, *The Saddled Cow: East Germany's Life and Legacy* (London: Faber & Faber, 1992), p. 76.

58. Ibid., p. 27.

59. Kolbe's term actually referred to an East German literary generation born in the late 1950s. See Karen Leeder, *Breaking Boundaries: A New Generation of Poets in the GDR* (Oxford, Eng.: Clarendon, 1996), p. 4.

60. "Kleines grünes Land enges, Stacheldrahtlandschaft." The full text of the poem "Hineingeboren" is found in ibid., p. 46.

61. The term was popularized by Günter Gaus in his *Wo Deutschland liegt: Eine Ortsbestimmung* (Hamburg: Hoffmann & Campe, 1983), pp. 156–233.

62. Weber, *DDR*, p. 193.

63. Stephan Bickhardt, "Die Entwicklung der DDR-Opposition in den achtziger Jahren," in *Die Enquete-Kommission "Aufarbeitung von Geschichte und Folgen der SED-Diktatur in Deutschland" im Deutschen Bundestag*, vol. 7: *Widerstand, Opposition, Revolution* (Baden-Baden: Nomos, 1995), pt. 1, p. 477.

64. Ibid., p. 466.

65. Eppelmann, *Fremd*, p. 227.

66. Marianne Schmidt, ed., *Einmischung der Enkel in Jürgen Kuczynskis "Dialog mit meinem Urenkel"* (Berlin: Aufbau, 1989), p. 22.

67. Ibid., p. 13.

68. Ibid., pp. 81–82.

69. Ibid., p. 28.

70. Ibid., p. 91.

71. Ibid., p. 21. In 1950, Kuczynski was removed as president of the Society for the Study of the Culture of the Soviet Union because of his Jewish origin.

72. Ibid., pp. 95–114.

73. Schabowski, *Absturz*, pp. 197–198, 217.

74. "Niederschrift des Gesprächs des Genossen Egon Krenz . . . mit Genossen Michael Gorbatschow . . . am 1.11.1989 in Moskau," November 1, 1989, SAPMO-BArch, DY30/IV 2/1/704, p. 106.

75. Weber, *DDR*, p. 185.

76. Hertle and Stephan, *Ende*, p. 42.

77. Konrad H. Jarausch, *The Rush to German Unity* (Oxford, Eng.: Oxford University Press, 1994), p. 47.

78. Hertle and Stephan, *Ende*, p. 49.

79. Charles S. Maier, *Dissolution: The Crisis of Communism and the End of East Germany* (Princeton, N.J.: Princeton University Press, 1997), p. 142.

80. Hertle, *Fall*, p. 130.

81. Ibid., pp. 127–132.

82. Günter Schabowski, *Das Politbüro: Ende eines Mythos* (Reinbek: Rowohlt, 1990), p. 105.

83. Steffie Spira, *Rote Fahne mit Trauerflor: Tagebuch—Notizen* (Freiburg im Breisgau: Kore, 1990), p. 107.

84. Transcript of the Tenth Central Committee Meeting, November 8, 1989, SAPMO-BArch, DY30/IV 2/1/705, pp. 117, 138, 149, 151–154.

EPILOGUE

1. Heinrich Bortfeldt, *Von der SED zur PDS: Wandlung zur Demokratie* (Bonn: Bouvier, 1992), p. 123.

2. Erich Honecker, *Moabiter Notizen: Letztes schriftliches Zeugnis und Gesprächsprotokolle vom BRD-Besuch 1987 aus dem persönlichen Besitz Erich Honeckers* (Berlin: edition ost, 1994), p. 36.

3. Tina Rosenberg, *The Haunted Land: Facing Europe's Ghosts after Communism* (New York: Random House, 1995), p. 332.

4. Monika Zorn, ed., *Hitlers zweimal getötete Opfer: Westdeutsche Endlösung des*

Antifaschismus auf dem Gebiet der DDR (Freiburg im Breisgau: Ahriman, 1994), pp. 296–298.

5. Ibid., pp. 212–219.

6. Ibid., p. 270.

7. Sarah Farmer, "Symbols That Face Two Ways: Commemorating the Victims of Nazism and Stalinism at Buchenwald and Sachsenhausen," *Representations* 49 (1995): 97, 104.

8. For a broad, if partisan, overview of the dismantling of monuments celebrating the antifascist struggle in the former East Germany, see Zorn, *Hitlers zweimal getötete Opfer.*

9. "Die Lebenslüge des Erich Honecker," *Stern* (Hamburg), November 22, 1990, pp. 28–34.

10. Peter Przybylski, *Tatort Politbüro*, vol. 1: *Die Akte Honecker* (Berlin: Rowohlt, 1991), pp. 47–50.

11. Erich Honecker, *Erich Honecker zu dramatischen Ereignissen* (Hamburg: Runge, 1992), p. 66.

12. Honecker, *Moabiter Notizen*, pp. 99–100.

13. Lutz Niethammer, ed., *Der "gesäuberte" Antifaschismus: Die SED und die roten Kapos von Buchenwald* (Berlin: Akademie, 1994).

14. Lager-Arbeitsgemeinschaft Buchenwald-Dora und Kommandos in Deutschland, *Kalter Krieg gegen Buchenwald: Schamlosigkeiten als 'Wissenschaft'* (n.p., [1994]).

15. Karl Corino, *Aussen Marmor, innen Gips: Die Legenden des Stephan Hermlin* (Düsseldorf: Econ, 1996); and Karl Corino, "Dichtung in eigener Sache," *Die Zeit* (Hamburg), October 4, 1996, pp. 9–11.

16. Manfred Jäger, "Nachbesserungen: Zum Streit um Stephan Hermlins Biographie," *Deutschland Archiv* 29 (1996): 844–848.

17. Fritz J. Raddatz, "Der Mann ohne Goldhelm," *Die Zeit* (Hamburg), October 25, 1996, foreign ed., p. 14.

18. Karl Schirdewan, *Aufstand gegen Ulbricht: Im Kampf um politische Kurskorrektur, gegen stalinistische, dogmatische Politik* (Berlin: Aufbau, 1994), p. 171.

19. Karl Schirdewan, interview by author, Potsdam, December 14, 1994.

20. Hilde Eisler, interview by author, Berlin, February 9, 1995.

21. Fred Müller, interview by author, Berlin, June 7, 1995.

22. Paul Wandel, interview by author, Berlin, December 22, 1994; and Kurt Hager, interview by author, Berlin, August 6, 1993.

23. Jakob Segal, interview by author, Berlin, April 30, 1995; and Ernst Hoffmann, interview by author, Berlin, August 11, 1995.

24. Schirdewan, interview.

25. Max Kahane, interview by author, Berlin, May 31, 1995.

26. Alfred Neumann, interview by author, Berlin, November 30, 1994.

27. Jan Koplowitz, interview by author, Berlin, June 27, 1995.

28. Neumann, interview; Kahane, interview; and Eisler, interview.

29. Alfred Neumann, interview by author, Berlin, December 8, 1994.

30. Walter Kresse, interview by author, Leipzig, July 27, 1995.

31. Kurt Goldstein, interview by author, Berlin, December 5, 1994.

32. Neumann, interview, November 30, 1994; and Arthur Mannbar, interview by author, Berlin, May 3, 1995.

33. Neumann, interview, December 8, 1994.

34. Hager, interview.

35. Müller, interview.

36. Neumann, interview, November 30, 1994.

37. Kresse, interview.

38. Hager, interview.

39. Karl Schirdewan, *Ein Jahrhundert Leben: Erinnerungen und Visionen* (Berlin: edition ost, 1998), p. 298.

40. Erich Selbmann, interview by author, Berlin, March 13, 1995. Erich Selbmann has not made the Selbmann-Dahlem correspondence available to researchers.

41. Konrad H. Jarausch, *The Rush to German Unity* (Oxford, Eng.: Oxford University Press, 1994), p. 8.

42. Jürgen Kuczynski, *"Ein linientreuer Dissident": Memoiren, 1945–1989* (Berlin: Aufbau, 1992), p. 226.

43. Farmer, "Symbols," p. 97.

44. Speech by Fritz Selbmann to the Thirty-fifth Central Committee Meeting, February 3–6, 1958, SAPMO-BArch, DY30/IV 2/1/193, p. 75.

45. Anne McElvoy, *The Saddled Cow: East Germany's Life and Legacy* (London: Faber & Faber, 1992), p. 100.

46. Charles S. Maier, *The Unmasterable Past: History, Holocaust, and German National Identity* (Cambridge, Mass.: Harvard University Press, 1988), p. 31.

47. Jaff Schatz, *The Generation: The Rise and Fall of the Jewish Communists of Poland* (Berkeley: University of California Press, 1991), p. 129.

48. Josef Schwarz, *Bis zum bitteren Ende: 35 Jahre im Dienste des Ministeriums für Staatssicherheit; Eine DDR-Biographie* (Schkeuditz: GNN, 1994), p. 24.

ACKNOWLEDGMENTS

WHILE WRITING THIS BOOK, I HAVE ENJOYED MANY KINDS OF GENER-
ous support. As a recipient of the Chancellor's Fellowship of the Alexander von Humboldt Foundation, I spent a remarkable year in Berlin in
1994–1995. The foundation not only provided financial support for archival research, but also organized a year-long program of stimulating
seminars and, in the spirit of Alexander von Humboldt, educational
trips. In addition, the foundation subsidized a summer of research in
Berlin in 1999. As a graduate student at Harvard University, my research
and writing was funded by a Whiting Fellowship, a Frederick Sheldon
Grant, and several grants from the Program for the Study of Germany
and Europe at the Minda de Gunzburg Center for European Studies. For
the 1995–1996 academic year, I received a dissertation grant from the
American Council of Learned Societies / Joint Committee on Eastern Europe. In the later stages of this project, I was privileged to spend a year
each in the congenial environments of the history departments at Stan-
ford University and Mount Holyoke College. Most recently, I have enjoyed the collegiality of my fellow historians and other faculty members
at Amherst College. The college provided generous faculty research funds
for the completion of this book.

In the course of my research, I was able to interview a number of my
historical subjects, including Karl Schirdewan and Hilde Eisler. I grate-
fully thank these and all of the other veteran communists who discussed with me—often at great length—their lives in the German communist movement. In addition, I benefited from conversations with
Erich Selbmann and other family members of longtime communists. At
the Stiftung Archiv der Parteien und Massenorganisationen der DDR im
Bundesarchiv, where I did the bulk of my archival research, I had
the unflagging help of Carola Aehlich, Volker Lange, Anneliese Müller,

Solweig Nestler, and Grit Ulrich. The same is true of Elena Danielson at the Hoover Institution Archives.

I have been very fortunate in that thoughtful scholars have read and commented at length on my work. Charles Maier, my dissertation advisor, encouraged me to pursue interests very different from his own; he also offered many valuable comments and criticisms on the original thesis. David Blackbourn, John Connelly, Jeffrey Kopstein, and Jonathan Zatlin all read the thesis and offered excellent suggestions that I have incorporated into this book. Jeffrey Herf carefully commented on the argumentation of the manuscript; his judicious remarks convinced me that I should modify some of my more controversial statements. Norman Naimark did much more than can be expected from a manuscript reader; his insights and suggestions proved especially invaluable as I revised the manuscript for publication. Over the years, a number of friends and colleagues also read various chapters in progress. Audrey Budding, Keith Crudgington, Katharina Gerstenberger, Jeremy King, and Mary Sarotte all made useful comments to strengthen the prose and content of my work. Stephen Graubard kindly asked me to publish an article on my research in *Daedalus;* my essay on the politics of biography appeared in 1999. At *Central European History,* Kenneth Barkin sped along the publication of an article on veteran-communist memoir writing. He also invited me to share my ideas with his colleagues at the University of California, Riverside. At Harvard University Press, I could not have hoped for a more helpful editor than Joyce Seltzer. Her editorial vision decisively shaped the presentation of this work.

My husband, Daniel Gordon, has seen this project grow from an idea for a dissertation to publication as a book. Throughout this time, he has offered support and encouragement, as well as criticism and disagreement. In these and countless other ways, he has made the writing of this book a challenging, rewarding, and ultimately enjoyable experience. In recent years, our young children, Nathan and Dora, have been a source of great delight; their smiles and hugs are always an inspiration. My parents, Carl and Elizabeth Krumpe, have given me more help and backing than they know. All too often, they have kept our household up and running in Amherst and even Berlin. But most importantly, they have provided me with continuous moral support. Indeed, more than anyone else, my mother has always believed in me and my work. With great love and appreciation, I dedicate this book to her.

INDEX